M

Shakespeare Reread

Shakespeare Reread

The Texts in New Contexts

Edited by Russ McDonald

CORNELL UNIVERSITY PRESS

ITHACA AND LONDON

First published 1994 by Cornell University Press.

Printed in the United States of America

⊛ The paper in this book meets the minimum requirements of the
American National Standard for Information Sciences—Permanence of
Paper for Printed Library Materials, ANSI Z39.48-1984.

Library of Congress Cataloging-in-Publication Data

Shakespeare reread : the texts in new contexts / edited by Russ
  McDonald.
      p.   cm.
  Includes bibliographical references and index.
  ISBN 0-8014-2917-X. — ISBN 0-8014-8144-9
  1. Shakespeare, William, 1564–1616—Criticism and interpretation.
  I. McDonald, Russ, 1949–
  PR2976.S3383   1994
822.3′3—dc20   93-40492

For Gail and Jack

Contents

Acknowledgments

This volume has two godparents, one individual and one corporate. Conversations with my friend and former colleague James Longenbach about the past and future of literary criticism—I recall one exchange in a car on the New York State Thruway in February 1989 and an animated walk on upper Broadway in March 1988—led me to believe that a collection such as this one might be useful. I am grateful to him for that intellectual stimulus, although I'm grateful to him for so many things that to identify only one seems absurd. The trustees of the Shakespeare Association of America charged me with organizing the plenary session for the annual meeting in Austin in 1989, a panel titled "Close Reading Revisited." Their endorsement of my idea and their suggestions for implementing and improving it contributed much to the present book. I especially thank Alan Dessen, the head of the program committee for that year, and Nancy Hodge, Executive Director of the Association, who helped with the ideas and the mechanics of the panel and was pleasant while she did so.

The annual meeting of the Shakespeare Association is an excellent forum for testing ideas and stealing good ones from other people, and I am grateful to the membership for continued stimulation.

Conversations with Thomas Berger, Albert Braunmuller, Cyrus Hoy, Dia Lawrence, Catherine Loomis, Margaret Maurer, Barbara Mowat, Gail Paster, Jeanne Roberts, Meredith Skura, Bruce Smith, Robert Y. Turner, George Walton Williams, and many of the contributors have helped make this book better than it would otherwise have been. Patricia Parker gave sound practical advice on several occasions.

My undergraduate and graduate students at the University of Rochester and the University of North Carolina at Greensboro have helped me to think contextually about texts and textually about contexts. Members of my 1989 seminar in sixteenth- and seventeeth-century tragedy and my 1991 seminar in late Shakespeare, both at Rochester, deserve particular mention. Regular participation as Resident Scholar in the NEH–Folger Library Summer Institute, "Teaching Shakespeare," has taught me about the need for clarity and care in teaching great texts and the contexts that produced them. In thanking Peggy O'Brien, I direct my gratitude through her to all the participants, scholars, actors, master teachers, and interns who have been involved over the past decade.

I am grateful to Massimo Bacigalupo for permission to reprint the illustration from his *Ezra Pound: Una poeta a Rapallo* (Genoa: San Marco, 1982); to Routledge for permission to quote from the relevant texts in the New Arden Shakespeare series; and to Houghton Mifflin for permission to quote from *The Riverside Shakespeare*.

Bernhard Kendler demonstrated to me, as he has to many others, that he deserves his reputation as a fine editor. I wish to thank him formally, as well as the staff at Cornell University Press. Most of the readers he engaged offered helpful suggestions, but more than that they understood immediately the motives of the project, and I appreciate their assistance and encouragement.

My debt to Gail McDonald, who has repeatedly put aside the demands of her own excellent work to help with mine, is too great to be discharged in brief acknowledgments such as these.

R. McD.

Shakespeare Reread

Introduction

RUSS McDONALD

"The dominion of Exegesis is great: she is our Whore of Babylon, sitting robed in Academic black on the great dragon of Criticism, and dispensing a repetitive and soporific balm from her pedantic cup."[1] So wrote Geoffrey Hartman in a relatively early exposition of the failures of both New Criticism and some of the attempts to displace it, in this case the aggressive antiformalism of Georges Poulet. Hartman was writing at a point—the mid-sixties—when the ideals and practices of the original New Critics had contracted into a deplorably narrow interpretive range, so that concentration on minute formal detail, usually imagery and its contribution to theme, excluded virtually all other topics of inquiry. The practical effect of this restricted approach was that formulaic essays of a severely limited scope tended to tyrannize academic journals—many readers may supply from their own memories several (usually alliterative) titles—and in no corner of the discipline was this circumscription more apparent than in the study of Shakespeare.

It is difficult to date precisely the metamorphosis that produced the critical era we now inhabit. Hartman himself, as the title of his book, *Beyond Formalism*, suggests, was one of the leaders, along with several

1. Geoffrey Hartman, *Beyond Formalism: Literary Essays, 1958–1970* (New Haven: Yale University Press, 1970), p. 57.

of his colleagues at Yale, in the attempt to move beyond the dead end
of formalist criticism, but the newer methodologies had relatively little direct impact on Shakespeare studies in the 1970s. Arguably the
crucial event was the publication of Stephen Greenblatt's *Renaissance
Self-Fashioning* (1980), a book that represents a milestone not just in
Shakespeare and early modern studies but in postwar criticism as a
whole. Shaped by the more general literary, anthropological, and cultural criticism of Raymond Williams, Clifford Geertz, and Michel
Foucault, and accompanied, or followed closely, by the similar work
of Stephen Orgel, Jonathan Goldberg, and the British cultural materi-
alists, Greenblatt's approach was a self-conscious rejoinder to the circumscribed and self-referring practices of New Criticism or autotelic
formalism. Generally speaking, his promotion of a "New Historicism" or a "cultural poetics" established the terms and set the direction
for a phase in which context supplanted text and history dominated
poetry. The clarity of Greenblatt's critical voice also made it easier to
identify and to note the resemblances among other efforts to escape
the limits of formalist analysis, notably deconstruction and the various
strains of feminist criticism, movements that suddenly seemed to
dominate the scene but had been quietly gaining adherents for at least
a decade.

Owing to the acceleration of critical cycles characteristic of the
academy in the second half of the twentieth century, the poststructuralist critique of exegesis has already fostered its own excesses and instances of blindness, as a number of commentators by the end of the
1980s had begun to observe. The mechanical readings of an exhausted
New Criticism have been supplanted by another formula discernible
especially in New Historicism, contextual essays that begin with the
jar of the anecdote and then locate the text in a social or political frame
so as to expose "the half-hidden cultural transactions through which
great works of art are empowered."[2] Many New Historicists (I use
the term loosely and with the confidence that the reader will take it
synecdochically) are brilliant readers of culture and of the circulatory
role of Shakespeare's texts in early modern England, but the capacious
angle of vision from which they approach those texts has had major
critical and pedagogical consequences. The most notable result is that
the wide viewpoint has perforce diminished the details of the textual

2. Stephen Greenblatt, *Shakespearean Negotiations: The Circulation of Social Energy
in Renaissance England* (Berkeley: University of California Press, 1988), p. 4.

object. A return to the Shakespearean passage after a sojourn in the realm of Elizabethan women's diaries or medical writing or records of court conversation ought to afford an enriched understanding of the nuances of that passage, but in recent years this recursion to the text has often been perfunctory, and sometimes omitted altogether. In the essay that introduces *Shakespearean Negotiations,* Greenblatt confesses to an occasional urge "to recover the close-grained formalism of [his] own literary training" and declares his conviction "that sustained, scrupulous attention to formal and linguistic design will remain at the center of literary teaching and study."[3] The book proper, however, constitutes a suppression of such an impulse, for Greenblatt himself declines to pay much notice to formal properties. The concomitant to this diminution of the textual artifact, as Anne Barton has argued in one of the most pointed critiques of the New Historicist project, is that the triumph of context or social text tends to obscure the cultural reader's awareness that "works of art have internal as well as external 'resonances.'"[4] The practice of reading culture requires a perspective that produces a virtual disappearance of the particular and a devaluation of the "artistic." The empire of Context is now as vast as the dominion of Exegesis ever was.

We are in need of some means of reconciling the distant and recent pasts. This volume represents an attempt at a rapprochement between the intrinsic and the external, the micro- and the macrotextual, the celebratory and the suspicious. Its motive is not to deplore the new methodologies which have done so much to alter the critical landscape. Rather, it is to examine the ways in which the transformation of that scene has affected attention to the formal properties of literary texts. The contributors here seek new and potentially illuminating ways of reading closely. Although it is true that most critics no longer do "readings" of plays—the kind of totalizing interpretations to which I referred earlier—it is equally true that all of us still do "reading" in some form, whether the legible object is a play or a prince, and whether we use the term "cultural poetics" or "poststructuralist critique" or some other sophisticated label. We read Shakespeare differently these days, and it is imperative that scholars devote some thought to how and what we are reading. Patricia Parker, near the end of her chapter on Shakespeare and rhetoric in *Literary Fat Ladies,*

3. Ibid., pp. 3 and 4.
4. Anne Barton, "The Perils of Historicism," *New York Review of Books,* March 28, 1991, p. 53.

provides a thoughtful assessment of the relation between styles or subjects of reading: "To focus exclusively on questions of social and political context—as one form of reaction to decades of formalism now
proposes to do—or to foreground the 'political Shakespeare' without
also taking seriously the linguistic one, is, for all its recontextualizing
value, not just to work to the detriment of the kind of formal analysis
that still so much needs to be done but unnecessarily to short-circuit
or foreclose the process of moving from literary text to social text."[5]

   The first step in reconceiving the possibilities of close reading is
to survey, if only briefly, some of the hostility to which it has been
subjected. A convenient source for such a review is Joel Fineman's
virtuoso sketch of critical tensions in the 1980s:

> We can add that the term "New Historicism" initially carried with it a
> somewhat polemical air, for the literary criticism and literary histories
> that pronounced themselves New Historicist, and that thereby under-
> stood their own critical practices to amount to actions performed, qui-
> etly enough, in the name of history, presented themselves as overdue
> corrections of, or as morally and politically motivated reactions against,
> the formalism—more precisely and more pejoratively, the "mere for-
> malism" (which, as such, as something merely or purely formal, was
> thought to be apolitical, sexist, hermetic, elitist, etc.)—that, for one
> good or bad reason or another, had come to be associated with every-
> thing from the kind of close, immanent textual readings said to be en-
> demic to the New Criticism, to the scientistic, agentless, essentialist,
> cross-cultural typologizations said to be characteristic of what was
> called Structuralism, to the kinds of deconstructive, but still mandarin
> and still strictly textual, and therefore still formalist, and therefore
> still objectionable, formulations—mere formulations—identified with
> either the phenomenologically or the rhetorically conceived versions of
> what came to be called Post-Structuralism: Jacques Derrida, for exam-
> ple, on the one hand, Paul de Man, for example, on the other, not that
> these two hands did not let each other know what they were up to.[6]

Rarely does poststructuralism declare outright antipathy to formal

   5. Patricia Parker, *Literary Fat Ladies: Rhetoric, Gender, Property* (London: Methuen, 1987), p. 94.
   6. Joel Fineman, "The History of the Anecdote," in *The New Historicism*, ed. Aram
Veeser (London: Routledge, 1989), p. 51.

analysis, for critics of every political stripe recognize its value and utility. Jonathan Dollimore, for example, disclaims hostility to close textual study *per se,* insisting that, as a materialist critic, he rejects only
"the ahistorical and indeed antihistorical tendency of this analysis as it
has sometimes been practised."[7] But Fineman is especially acute at
identifying the need of some contextual critics to demonize or caricature the practice of formal study and to associate it with the least acceptable features of a discredited ideology. Such an Oedipal assault on
the recent past is part of a familiar pattern in the history of literary
criticism; the New Critics twitted their historicist predecessors, after
all. But the implications of this tendency to distort or disallow certain
critical practices, whether predictable or not, should not go unre-
marked. .

The flavor of politically inspired objections to close reading is captured in Paul Bové's *Intellectuals in Power,* where I. A. Richards's program of practical criticism is vilified as "conservative, even
reactionary."[8] This suspicion of the microtextual became a staple of
critical discourse in the 1980s, and those properties that make formal
study especially liable to political complaint include its tendency to
favor individuation and discrimination; its interest in exclusion, promotion, and evaluation; its concern for effects such as beauty or pleasure or complexity; and its centralization of authority in either the
passage under scrutiny or the critic performing the act.[9] John Barrell,
while apologizing for the crudeness and partiality of his summary of
British practical criticism, skewers the practice (he will not allow it
to be a methodology because it is "self-consciously untheoretical and
antitheoretical") as "middle-class." Assailing the New Critics' attachment to the correspondence between form and content, Barrell insists that

> the balance and resolution which literary texts seek to achieve bear a
> close resemblance to the political balance which, in England especially,
> was both cause and effect of the increasing power of the middle class,
> and which has made the notion of balance itself a term of value with

7. Jonathan Dollimore, "Critical Developments: Cultural Materialism, Feminism
and Gender Critique, and New Historicism," in *Shakespeare: A Bibliographical Guide,*
new edition, ed. Stanley Wells (Oxford: Oxford University Press, 1990), p. 420.
8. Paul Bové, *Intellectuals in Power: A Genealogy of Critical Humanism* (New York:
Columbia University Press, 1986), p. 53.
9. For a polemical discussion of these issues, see ibid., pp. 52–66.

a crucial function in middle-class ideology, underwriting the political authority of "consensus," or the "middle ground," by representing as irrational extremism whatever cannot, or whatever refuses to be, gathered into the middle ground.[10]

"Balance" has become a term of opprobrium in the ideology of conflict promoted by cultural materialism. Here one of its proponents finds it convenient to permit a single principle of an attenuated version of American New Criticism to stand for the entire enterprise of close textual study, and to draw grand and dire conclusions from that move. Much the same has been done with terms such as "ambiguity" and "paradox." But even in its potentially subversive poststructuralist or deconstructive forms, exegesis has frequently been written off as irrelevant or politically dubious.[11]

The close study of formal details, it is felt, is attended by philosophical risks: specifically, to focus the critical powers on textual minutiae is to expose the mind to the false security of a hermetic enterprise and, what is worse, to encourage an illusion of freedom invidious to the consciousness of social and discursive constraints, a state of mind deemed necessary for social change. Fredric Jameson makes explicit the perceived connection between close textual scrutiny and political blindness: "To imagine that, sheltered from the omnipresence of history and the implacable influence of the social, there already exists a realm of freedom—whether it be that of the microscopic experience of words in a text or the ecstasies and intensities of the various private religions—is only to strengthen the grip of Necessity over all such blind zones in which the individual seeks refuge."[12] It is hardly adventitious that formal pleasure should find itself linked with religious mystery: the association takes notice of and exploits a historically demonstrable connection among the conservative politics, Christian faith, and critical methodology of certain practitioners of American New Criticism.

Some of the most successful close readers of texts, however—figures such as R. P. Blackmur, Kenneth Burke, and William Empson—

10. John Barrell, *Poetry, Language, and Politics* (Manchester: Manchester University Press, 1988), pp. 5–6.
11. Howard Felperin, writing from the standpoint of one sympathetic to deconstruction, complains about the tendency of political criticism to dismiss exegesis, in his preface to *The Uses of the Canon: Elizabethan Literature and Contemporary Theory* (Oxford: Clarendon Press, 1990), pp. v–xiii.
12. Fredric Jameson, *The Political Unconscious* (London: Methuen, 1981), p. 20.

had no such ideological affiliations, and their work demonstrates, as does that of more recent readers, that close textual study is by no means limited to, and ought not to be identified exclusively with, a reactionary political agenda or philosophical reticulum. Catherine Belsey, for instance, appropriating close reading to the aims of feminist argument, advocates textual analysis as a way to "generate a more radical challenge to patriarchal values by disrupting sexual difference itself."[13] And in Malcolm Evans's *Signifying Nothing,* "a deconstruction which may tend towards formalism is turned against the metaphysical assumptions of traditional Shakespeare criticism."[14] Despite the recognition by some critics that the instruments of close reading are available for a multiplicity of political and critical ends, too many still allow it to stand for the political and social iniquities of the past. The farther we move from the period in which attention to form occupied a central place in the critical enterprise, the easier it becomes to promulgate a blunt and generalized construction of the nature and contribution of formal study. Finer distinctions are needed. We must discriminate as rigorously as we can between the method of exegesis and the several interested critical attitudes with which, rightly or wrongly, it has been identified: aestheticism, ahistoricism, formalism, essentialism, humanist idealism, philosophical positivism, deconstruction, and—the bathwater with which the baby has been discarded—New Criticism.[15]

A second step in restoring the utility of close reading is to historicize, and thus possibly to relieve, the conflict between critical generations. Jameson's condescension to the imaginary comforts of "the microscopic experience of words in a text" indicates the tendency of every critical school to impeach the practices of the movement that immediately preceded it; the slaughter of the critical parent is a prerequisite for growth, for the invention and development of fresh ways of

13. Catherine Belsey, "Disrupting Sexual Difference: Gender and Meaning in the Comedies," in *Alternative Shakespeares,* ed. John Drakakis (London: Methuen, 1985), p. 180.

14. Malcolm Evans, *Signifying Nothing: Truth's True Contents in Shakespeare's Texts,* 2d ed. with foreword by Terry Eagleton (London: Harvester Wheatsheaf, 1989), pp. 10–11. For a similar appropriation of textual analysis for leftist political purposes, see Eagleton's *William Shakespeare* (Oxford: Basil Blackwell, 1986).

15. See Hugh Grady, *The Modernist Shakespeare: Critical Texts in a Material World* (Oxford: Clarendon Press, 1991), esp. chap. 3.

regarding the literary text.[16] At the same time, however, most critical innovators find themselves reviving and depending on certain necessary practices associated with the previous era, although there is no admission of such dependence, and the names of the practices are invariably modified.[17] In *The Historical Renaissance: New Essays on Tudor and Stuart Literature and Culture,* Heather Dubrow and Richard Strier introduce a group of papers that participate in the effort to discern affiliations between the literary and the social texts of early modern England; in so doing, the editors are leery of the temptation to distort previous modes of criticism:

> Concerned to distinguish their stance from that of their predecessors, contemporary critics often oversimplify the work they are rejecting, much as contemporary architects are prone to oversimplify the achievements and the limitations of the International Style. It is much easier to supplant or suppress the fathers if they can be parodied as bogeymen or reduced to straw men. Despite the theoretical dogmas of New Criticism, some of its proponents did in fact comment acutely on social, historical, and political issues; and many "new critics" resolutely refused to distinguish between "internal" and "external" approaches.[18]

Such self-awareness is uncharacteristic of critical revisionism in any period and thus of much recent historical and political criticism. Most opposition to textual analysis, although grounded in a truth, depends on a distortion of the critical positions of some very subtle thinkers or a homogenization of the differences among some extremely independent critics. In the central chapters of *Professing Literature,* Gerald Graff repeatedly demonstrates that those people originally referred to as New Critics regarded their work as politically engaged and historically anchored, that they thought of their devotion to the intrinsic operations of poetic texts not as retro- but as progressive. As he puts it:

> First-generation New Critics were neither aesthetes nor pure explicators but culture critics with a considerable "axe to grind" against the

16. Gerald Graff amply demonstrates the history of this pattern in the central chapters of *Professing Literature: An Institutional History* (Chicago: University of Chicago Press, 1987); see esp. pp. 121–94.

17. See the essay by Howard Felperin, "'Cultural Poetics' versus 'Cultural Materialism': The Two New Historicisms in Renaissance Studies," in *The Uses of the Canon,* pp. 142–69.

18. Heather Dubrow and Richard Strier, eds., "Introduction," in *The Historical Renaissance* (Chicago: University of Chicago Press, 1988), p. 2.

technocratic tendencies of modern mass civilization. . . . [E]ven at its most "formalistic" (or especially then), the New Critical view of poetry made a social and cultural point, rejecting the allegedly vitiated language of "a dehumanized society," as Allen Tate put it, in which men may "communicate, but they cannot live in full communion." As Tate saw it, "the battle is now between the dehumanized society of secularism, which imitates Descartes' mechanized nature, and the eternal society of the communion of the human spirit." Again, whatever one may think of such a view, to label it formalist, aesthetic, or apolitical is misleading.[19]

A striking feature of this excerpt is, paradoxically, the resemblance of Tate's language to Jamesonian rhetoric. Later, in the 1950s and 1960s, the institutionalization of what came to be known as New Criticism brought with it a narrowing of critical vision and an increasingly formulaic application of a few principles of literary analysis; moreover, that process coincided with a general retreat among intellectuals and humanist academicians from the perilous landscape of postwar politics. Thus it is easy to appreciate the historical reasons for the identification of a critical method with a political stance; it is less easy to sympathize with the trivialization of the method and the caricaturing of its political ramifications. Most of us have come to believe that all literary criticism is to some degree political, and it is now axiomatic that critical practice is tied to the conditions of the historical moment. But there is no necessary connection between formal analysis of a text and any particular political valence.

The third precondition for renewing the process of critical explication is that we approach it with an unprecedented self-consciousness, an awareness of the limitations of the practice and the abuses that can arise from it. One of the most important lessons deriving from changes in critical thinking has to do with the historical specificity of reading. Much more than their predecessors, most recent students of the Shakespearean text are sensitive to the historicity of all reading, and the perspective afforded by this recognition alters the way they read. John Drakakis concludes the introduction to his *Alternative Shakespeares* by seeking to modify the traditional definition:

Inevitably, all of these essays address themselves to questions of "reading," but they all reject the notion that reading is itself an exclusive

19. Graff, *Professing Literature*, p. 149.

effect of the text. Rather, what is proposed in a number of very different ways is a series of explorations of the ways in which historically specific readings are generated, and which acknowledge the existence of structures within the text as devices for exclusion and repression, while at the same time insisting that the process of "making sense" of a Shakespearean text is itself determined by a multiplicity of forces.[20]

The consequence of such a redefinition is that the actual reading of texts is subordinated to discussion of the larger processes of interpretation. Most contributors to the present volume would readily concede Drakakis's challenge to "the notion that reading is itself an exclusive effect of the text," agreeing that the quest for universal effects of an unchanging form is erroneous and naive. And yet it is possible to acknowledge the partiality of one's historically conditioned reading without automatically privileging historical process over the act of reading and the insights it might produce. Whereas many recent critics, prompted in part by the exhaustion of New Critical explications of texts, have focused on "the ways in which historically specific readings are generated," we may now be in danger of wearing out, or at least overestimating the productivity of, such reflexive and theoretical investigations. What seems desirable at present is a dual goal of performing textual study while at the same time commenting on the theoretical implications of such a performance.

Greater self-consciousness about the process of close reading entails not only an awareness of the abuse it has sustained but also an appreciation that recent critical thought has created new possibilities for reading. Modifications in our understanding of the Shakespearean text, an augmented field of collateral texts available for reading, a subtler sense of the author and textual authority, the return of rhetorical study in a new and more sophisticated guise, the increased importance of politics in virtually all discussion of literature, the prominence of newly considered topics such as race and gender—all these shifts in the critical atmosphere make it necessary to reconsider how the close reading of Shakespeare ought to be done and what results it might produce. The readers represented in this volume examine the altered conditions under which we now read while offering to retrain our critical vision to include and account for our revised sense of both context and text.

20. John Drakakis, "Introduction," in *Alternative Shakespeares* (London: Methuen, 1985), pp. 23–24.

To start with, which Shakespearean text are we reading? One area in which poststructuralist innovation has had relatively little effect on Shakespeare studies is in the selection of texts to be read: these are scarcely neglected works. And yet the canon has to some small degree been enlarged by the editorial work of Michael Warren, Steven Urkowitz, Leah Marcus, Gary Taylor, and Stanley Wells, who have given us significantly different texts of *King Lear* and, potentially, alternative versions of *Hamlet, The Merry Wives of Windsor,* and several other plays. It may also be true that their work has correspondingly reduced the canon, given the designation of Thomas Middleton as joint author of *Timon of Athens* and possibly *Macbeth*.

What is more important is the way what might be called poststructuralist editing has altered our definition of the Shakespearean text.[21] Critics have come to admit more readily the collaborative nature of the Renaissance theater and to take into account the contingent and unfixed status of the printed texts we read. Scrutiny of the limits of the traditional canon has given access to a few works not hitherto considered, such as Elizabeth Carey's *Tragedie of Mariam,* and critics have turned more willingly and frequently to dramatists who, if not previously ignored, had long been relegated to secondary status as contemporaries of Shakespeare, writers such as Dekker and Greene and Heywood and Massinger. And, as I have indicated, the New Historicist redefinition of "text" and the assault on the category of the "literary" have substantially amplified the field of intertextual possibilities. Despite such new opportunities for cultural and (to a lesser degree) literary recontextualization, we return ultimately to what is more or less the same version of the same Shakespearean artifact. In confronting it anew, however, we find that we are different readers, that our relation to that artifact has been reconstituted by the intellectual modifications generated in the changed critical climate. Thus, we are faced with the problem of how to read familiar texts in ways that do more than merely reproduce the approved insights and comfortable interpretations derived from earlier modes of reading.

Studies of discourse and the range of cultural voices that go into the making of Shakespeare's texts have augmented our sense of the ends

21. For an especially illuminating example, see Paul Werstine, "The Textual Mystery of *Hamlet*," *Shakespeare Quarterly* 39 (1988): 1–26. A useful summary of postmodern thinking about textual instability is found in Margreta de Grazia and Peter Stallybrass, "The Materiality of the Shakespearean Text," *Shakespeare Quarterly* 44 (Fall 1993): 255–83.

and strategies of close reading, specifically as a result of their having modified received notions of creative agency and theatrical authority. Perhaps more than any other feature of poststructuralist thought, this attention to the cultural generation of the play has complicated the critical scene by refiguring the role of the reader as well as the identity of the author. When earlier practitioners sought to identify patterns of imagery or to isolate prosodic structures in the work of an individual dramatist and then to establish the contribution of such phenomena to the creation of meaning, their endeavors were grounded in the assumption of a certain degree of authorial control, conscious or not. Present readers, by contrast, are coming to subscribe to a broader conception of creative influence. As David Quint puts it, "The text no longer seems to speak with a single voice of its own, the voice of an individual author with whom the reader might seek a common human understanding."[22] The familiar image of the speaking writer has been supplanted by an understanding of authorship which tends to obscure the historical person, to emphasize limits on the discursive freedom exercised by the individual artist, and to disperse responsibility for aesthetic and significational effects among a broad range of cultural, social, political, and literary forces and pressures. The main result of this modified conception has been to expand awareness of the work's external affiliations, an awakening that has tilted us toward *langue* and away from *parole* and that has given priority, for a time at least, to what J. G. A. Pocock describes as *mentalité* over "individual move."[23] Moreover, textual study has come to emphasize the significant degree to which early modern theatrical texts represent the collaborative efforts of playwrights, actors, reporters, scribes, compositors, and editors from the sixteenth to the twentieth centuries. All these changes have particular relevance to that author of authors who is the subject of the present collection.

This revisionist sense of textual genetics, however, has not canceled the need for close attention to the Shakespearean play and its component parts. How the text got the way it is—how the numerous cultural and intertextual voices intermingle—poses a new challenge to readers

22. David Quint, "Introduction," in *Literary Theory / Renaissance Texts,* ed. Patricia Parker and David Quint (Baltimore: Johns Hopkins University Press, 1986), p. 7.

23. J. G. A. Pocock, "The Concept of a Language and the *Métier d'historien:* Some Considerations on Practice," in *The Language of Political Thought in Early Modern Europe,* ed. Anthony Pagden (Cambridge: Cambridge University Press, 1984), pp. 29–30.

who need to be encouraged to inspect the text both closely and from a distance. The new concern with semiotic signals, textual codes, and the interpenetration of competing or cooperating discourses instead of an individual author's choices and tastes should refresh our enthusiasm for the particulars of the text; expanding vocabularies and a variegated sense of textual identity provide new opportunities for reading. Quint describes one of these openings when he asserts that "the task of the reader or critic is to separate out the various cultural discourses that intersect in the literary text,"[24] a recommendation that bespeaks an admirable perspective on criticism past and present. Many of the contributors to this volume are especially alert to the unstable state of current critical discourse and practice and aware of the limitations to which past readings have been subject, while they seek to adapt the terms of the past to the requirements of the present.

The essays that follow, only one of which has been previously published, fall into three groups. The first is titled "Reflective Readers": it presents the work of three celebrated critics who describe how they came to do what they do and how they seek to do it now. The second section, "Reading Reflexively," contains essays that attempt both to theorize and to practice close reading in a changed critical atmosphere. The third group, "Reflexive Readings," is made up of essays that, while they offer some commentary on the practices they employ, are notable for the clarity and force with which they exemplify new strategies of reading.

Helen Vendler, Stephen Booth, and George T. Wright begin the volume by describing autobiographically the intellectual conditions and pedagogical attitudes that have shaped their views of textuality and modes of reading, and they proceed to develop these confessional remarks into critical justifications for those views. The three resulting essays are further linked by their devotion to the intellectual and material pleasures of the text, a consideration that contextual criticism has tended to scant. This is hardly the place to attempt a resurrection of Roland Barthes or to rehearse at length his endorsement of textual pleasure, but Barthes's complex and finally affirmative conception of textual erotics is worth reasserting. The recent turn away from pleasure is partly a function of a teleological shift, as the authors of a 1990 essay put it: "Critics now working on Renaissance literature are far

24. Quint, "Introduction," p. 7.

more likely than their predecessors to interpret their task as demysti-
fication rather than celebration, maintaining a skeptical distance from
the belief structures of the writers they discuss."[25] And a corollary to
this suspicion of "belief structures" is that the materiality of dramatic
language is also subjected to "skeptical distance." Wordplay, poetic
pattern, musical properties, and other pleasurable effects are too often
treated as if they were seductive or frivolous or dangerous, as if the
vitality of the word were potentially threatening to the serious business of the critical project. Harry Berger notes this tendency in describing "the principle and injunction that mark one aspect of the
change from modernism to postmodernism: *'Only de-estheticize.'*"[26]
And Robert Weimann has cautioned against the omission of *Spass*—
fun, pleasure—from current work, urging that we "begin again to talk
about the enjoyment of Shakespeare's text."[27]

Helen Vendler, in "Reading, Stage by Stage: Shakespeare's *Sonnets*," begins Part One by reflecting on a lifetime of thinking about
Shakespeare's sonnets. Dissatisfied with the term *reading*—to her it
suggests "a one-time effort" and misrepresents the necessary repetition involved in studying complex texts—Vendler watches herself experiencing the sonnets over time; in the process she comments on the
need to read "for difference," on reading texts in light of "adjunct
disciplines," and on the value of "an intellectual method that represents the nonce quality of each aesthetic experience." Her sensitive
commentary, reemphasizing as it does the centrality of artistic concerns to the enterprise of literary criticism, particularly the study of
Shakespeare, reminds us of what we may lose when we de-aesthet-
icize.

Stephen Booth cocks his famous ear for nuance at a passage in *Macbeth*. Ever an opponent of the limiting and reductive analysis to which
the less talented New Critical exegete was prone, he promotes "Close
Reading without Readings." His method connects the topic of verbal
design with the problem of value: the existence of "overlapping net-

25. Katharine Eisaman Maus and Elizabeth D. Harvey, "Introduction," in *Solicit-
ing Interpretation: Literary Theory and Seventeenth-Century English Poetry* (Chicago: University of Chicago Press, 1990), p. xi.

26. Harry Berger, Jr., "'Kidnapped Romance': Discourse in *The Faerie Queene*," in
Unfolded Tales: Essays on Renaissance Romance, ed. George M. Logan and Gordon
Teskey (Ithaca: Cornell University Press, 1989), p. 208.

27. Robert Weimann, "Towards a Literary Theory of Ideology: Mimesis, Representation, Authority," in *Shakespeare Reproduced: The Text in History and Ideology*, ed.
Jean E. Howard and Marion F. O'Connor (London: Methuen, 1987), pp. 271–72.

works of casual, substantively inconsequential relationship . . . explains why we like *Twelfth Night* and *Antony and Cleopatra* and *Much Ado About Nothing* and *Pride and Prejudice* and Shaw's *Saint Joan* and the Gettysburg Address and all the other things we like." His approach will be familiar to many readers, and Booth wittily plays on that familiarity while, at the same time, he manages to defamiliarize a major speech in a well-known play.

George Wright has taught us, in *Shakespeare's Metrical Art,* how to appreciate the effects of prosody and how to talk about those pleasures. More to the point, he has revealed that metrical analysis can involve us directly in the political struggles at the heart of a play such as *Coriolanus* or *As You Like It.* Power relations are inscribed in iambic pentameter, which is constructed on the interdependence of syllables, an ordered struggle between stressed and unstressed units of sound.[28] In short, the dynamics of the verse provide us with another means of access to that problem which, more than any other, has been the focus of much recent critical inquiry, the question of difference. In "Troubles of a Professional Meter Reader," Wright considers the marginality of metrical study, remarking on its unstable location between linguistic science and music, and deploring the efforts of critics, editors, actors, readers, and others who would neglect or depreciate the contribution of sound to the experience of the Shakespearean dramatic text. Prosody is one of those textual particulars that can sometimes be considered outmoded or mystificatory or merely aesthetic, and yet our enlarging sense of the implications of rhetorical forms should permit reevaluation of such a constant and fundamental poetic instrument.

Part Two consists of four essays that seek theoretically and practically to renovate the method of close reading and to liberate it from its formalist associations. In the dialogue between new and old, Harry Berger, Jr.'s, is a welcome and pertinent voice, especially given his description of himself as one of the "reconstructed old New Critics [who] don't find it all that hard to negotiate the leap from, say, the Intentional Fallacy to the Author Function, from the work to the text, from genre to intertextuality, from the virtual speaker or persona to the virtual reader (a very small leap), or from ambiguity to undecidability."[29] Here, in "Hydra and Rhizome," his piece on the two Henry plays in the second tetralogy, Berger develops a thesis about "emplot-

28. George T. Wright, *Shakespeare's Metrical Art* (Berkeley: University of California Press, 1988), pp. 257–58.
29. Berger, "Kidnapped Romance," p. 208.

ment": he sees Shakespeare's historical narrative of civil war as shaped
by the personal struggle between king and prince, which "is itself a
covert displacement of the private war, the conflict of discourses,
within each." The two nouns of his title serve as figures for the complex relation between text and dramatic action: "rhizome" stands for
the discursive latencies of text, while "hydra" suggests the anamorphic narrative manifestations of those concealed textual possibilities.
The value of Berger's contribution lies in his talent for complicating
our sense of "text" and for explaining the sources and results of textual
complexity in a perspicuous and convincing fashion.

Patricia Parker has been a prime mover in the revival of rhetoric
from which Shakespeare criticism is beginning to benefit, and here
she aligns text with context as she microscopically studies patterns of
Shakespearean wordplay. "*Othello* and *Hamlet:* Dilation, Spying, and
the 'Secret Place' of Woman" is a brilliant effort at "reading Shakespeare's plays closely with an eye to the historical resonance of their
terms, not just for formal interpretation of the plays but as a way of
perceiving their links with much larger contemporary discursive networks." The networks examined are the language of Elizabethan espionage and "the quasi-pornographic discourse of anatomy and an
early modern gynecology." In showing how the verbal texture of
these two tragedies is permeated by such discourse, she demonstrates
fascinating links among the epistemological, judicial, sexual, and rhetorical senses of "knowledge," "discovery," "opening" and "closing,"
"matter," "show," and "thing." Attitudes toward homonymy have
frequently served as touchstones for larger critical views—neoclassical
complaints about the fatal Cleopatra are the most obvious example—
and Parker's work demonstrates the value of studying forms after formalism as she moves back and forth between literary and social text.

The identification of multiple voices within texts has been accompanied by attention to the theatrical text as a voice in the larger cultural
conversation. Susanne L. Wofford's essay, "'To You I Give Myself,
For I Am Yours': Erotic Performance and Theatrical Performatives in
As You Like It," takes advantage of this expanded sense of voice in the
dramatic text, exploiting speech act theory in ways that J. L. Austin
himself seemed to proscribe. She manages thereby to use the play's
interest in the language of proxies to complicate our sense of theatrical
performance, suggesting that *As You Like It* "may in fact be participating in a complex way in a cultural debate about the power of fathers
and of the state to control the language that gives such actions a social

reality—in other words, that makes the language truly performative." Her reading clarifies for us Shakespeare's concerns about who is doing what with words, and how it matters.

David Willbern concludes the middle section with what may be the most self-conscious and theoretical of these essays, "Pushing the Envelope: Supersonic Criticism," where he theorizes the process of close reading in an attempt "to draw provisional lines around licit and illicit uses of Shakespeare's language." Surveying a range of passages from *Troilus and Cressida, The Merchant of Venice, The Winter's Tale, Measure for Measure,* and *Twelfth Night,* he explores how certain readers, from Samuel Johnson to an unnamed naysayer at a scholarly conference, have responded to some crucial instances of Shakespearean wordplay. In Willbern's view, Malvolio's misconstruction of the forged letter becomes a figure for the perils of willful reading. Two features of the essay make it especially appropriate here. First, Willbern's attempt to develop a model for productive reading leads him to engage directly with Stephen Booth's essay in this volume, "Close Reading without Readings," challenging Booth's refusal to assert a theoretical basis for his style of reading. Next, in place of what he calls Booth's "motiveless criticism," Willbern argues for the role of the unconscious in motivating the "play of language" that Shakespeare initiates, and in so doing he consciously seeks to push the discussion beyond the New Critical principles in which he was trained.

The final three essays represent "Reflexive Readings": they emphasize practice, illustrating new uses for close reading and providing a range of possible interpretive, textual, and political approaches. Historically informed critics, despite professions of interest in the political possibilities of close reading, have rarely been able to treat literary texts as sensitively as Lynda E. Boose does in "*The Taming of the Shrew, Good Husbandry, and Enclosure.*" She reads the narrative of Kate and Petruchio with an eye for the issues of class and gender suggested by the fictive frame and also in the context of historical episodes having to do with the manipulation of the economically disenfranchised and the enforcement of hierarchical gender relations. As she describes her method, "The issues of gender and hierarchy are pushed outside the fictive frame of the Kate and Petruchio story in order to be searched out again among a variety of historicized construction sites, including, most prominently, an overdue consideration of the ways in which the material conditions of early modern England may be implicated in this text." Boose is attentive to the play's exploitation of the discourses of social and economic class, particularly in the early wooing scenes where others have confined themselves to conflicts of gendered language; moreover, she is especially adept at maintaining a balance between her theatrical and historical texts as she argues that "this play is every bit as much a dramatization of English history as are the *Henry VI* plays, which were written at very nearly the same time."

The principal actor on the historical stage of early modern England was Elizabeth Tudor, whose words may serve as a test case for an expanded sense of text. According to Stephen Greenblatt, "If there is any value to what has become known as the 'new historicism,' it must be . . . in an intensified willingness to read all of the textual traces of the past with the attention traditionally conferred only on literary texts."[30] James R. Siemon, in "'Word Itself against the Word': Close Reading after Voloshinov," undertakes to read *Richard II* against other kinds of utterances: the supposedly familiar report of the conversation between Elizabeth I and William Lambarde, John Hayward's *History of Henry IIII,* and documents having to do with the Essex uprising. In doing so, he shows how the practice of close reading "considered according to certain underdeveloped implications of Bakhtinian sociolinguistics . . . may yet prove useful to various forms of social analysis while, simultaneously and paradoxically, suggesting a possible alternative to current interpretive modes." Siemon might be said, in reading beyond conventional boundaries, to set the New Historicist Word against itself as he delicately and surprisingly unpacks the queen's famous identification of herself with Shakespeare's Richard.

If an expanded sense of what constitutes a legible text is one of the most evident signs of the move beyond New Criticism, another is attention to Shakespearean performance, and Barbara Hodgdon is one of the liveliest readers of this new kind of text. In "The Critic, the Poor Player, Prince Hamlet, and the Lady in the Dark," she takes up the instruments traditionally associated with close reading and deploys them nontraditionally to examine the work of three notable readers of Shakespeare, F. R. Leavis, Ian McKellen, and Mel Gibson. Proposing "to examine how close reading constructs and accommodates the performing and performed body," she begins by scrutinizing a lecture Leavis delivered in Belfast in 1972, disclosing through a subtle deconstruction the antitheatricalism on which his view of the text was

---

30. Stephen Greenblatt, *Learning to Curse: Essays in Early Modern Culture* (London: Routledge, 1990), p. 14.

founded. She then teases out the critical and cultural implications of McKellen's analysis and performance of Macbeth's "Tomorrow and tomorrow and tomorrow," noticing particularly his efforts at "incorporating" the dramatic text into the acting body. This concentration on the body leads easily to Mel Gibson and a reading of Franco Zeffirelli's *Hamlet,* beginning with the design of the videocassette and its location in her local video store and advancing quickly to the latest research in film theory. As its range of reference suggests, this piece is a tour de force.

There is something in this book to offend almost everyone, and yet the corollary is that there is something to please almost everyone. Unlike some collections, this one promotes no consistent ideological or thematic stance; its unity derives instead from a focus on the Shakespearean text and the relation of very different kinds of readers to that text. Such an extraordinary critical range is beneficial in demonstrating that close reading need not be narrow or homogeneous. The multiple approaches, viewpoints, and conclusions combine to offer a faithful and coherent representation of the unsettled and eclectic nature of Shakespeare studies at the end of the twentieth century. Moreover, despite their differences, they all help to validate the principle articulated by Geoffrey Hartman in urging a move beyond the confines of the text itself: "There are many ways to transcend formalism, but the worst is not to study forms."[31]

31. Hartman, *Beyond Formalism,* p. 56.

Part One

Reflective Readers

I

Reading, Stage by Stage:
Shakespeare's *Sonnets*

HELEN VENDLER

Age: fifteen. Infatuation in search of its objective correlative finds the *Sonnets,* first some, then all. A revelation, not so much of emotional reality (of which I had enough and to spare) as of the sequence's power to include and organize every scrap of the world: the sun, poison, boats; infidelities, absences, griefs; tombs, trophies, worms.

Age: fifteen and a half. A marathon of memorizing, forty or so sonnets learned by heart, their rhythms what I walked to. Passion was what they had to teach, and I never doubted their lessons. They had the lift of apostrophe and the glamour of metaphysics, excruciating plainness and a gorgeous fanciness. I couldn't have cared less to whom, of which sex, they were addressed. They were words scored for reciting. Each sonnet had a different stock in trade. Not one was dispensable. Each "added up" to a different tone color.

Age: sixteen. The long-internalized Shakespearean rhythms force an exit for themselves. Five sonnets, some Italian and some Shakespearean, surprisingly write themselves at the tip of my pencil. (For the next eleven years I write poems, and think I might be a poet. After the first ambush, none of the poems is a sonnet.) I go on learning sonnets by heart—Ronsard, Du Bellay, Petrarch, Hopkins, Meredith (I know French and Italian and Spanish from my father, and my mother has always read poetry).

Age: seventeen to twenty-two. Hiatus. Free verse bursts upon me from the pages of Oscar Williams. *The Waste Land* drives out sonnets.

I don't even notice that Auden and Yeats and Frost write sonnets. Besides, I am busy in labs doing science.

Age: twenty-two to twenty-seven. At Boston University, a course in Renaissance nondramatic literature makes me realize that Shakespeare's sonnets are much better than anyone else's. (I still think so.) As I read Sidney, Daniel, Drayton, Spenser, I begin to wonder why Shakespeare is better, and how he made his poems better than other people's. Later, at Harvard, I look at the *Rime Sparse* to find out how it all started.

Age: twenty-seven to forty-five. Teaching and writing, but not about Shakespeare. I wring my hands and say, "I wish I could teach Shakespeare," to which my colleagues reply, "You know you can teach Shakspeare whenever you please"—but I am not ready.

Age: forty-six. I offer an undergraduate seminar at Boston University on the *Sonnets,* and begin a methodical reading of the editions, the scholarship, the criticism. I realize, with trepidation, that the *Sonnets* are a lightning rod for nuttiness. There is even a man in the *Variorum* who thinks the Dark Lady was a wine bottle, and that the later sonnets record Shakespeare's struggle with alcoholism. My seminar members and I see feelingly our way through the *Sonnets.* I type all the sonnets triple-spaced and interline them with queries. There is not enough space for the queries.

Age: fifty. At Harvard I give my first graduate seminar in the *Sonnets,* and decide to try to write on them. I write two chapters. Each treats three sonnets. At this rate, I realize, I will write either a book on thirty sonnets or a book with fifty chapters. Faced with these unacceptable alternatives, I suspend decision and begin taking lengthy and systematic notes on each sonnet. I buy three hardbound ledgers and paste into them, on facing pages, the Quarto version and a modern version of each sonnet. I decide to memorize each poem. When I cannot remember a word, it means I have not understood its function in the poem. As soon as I grasp its function, the word does not leave me. This is instructive.

Age: fifty-four. I finish annotating, but not memorizing (that is still going on). I decide to write a commentary rather than a book. The *Sonnets* have had editions and annotations, but never a systematic commentary giving each sonnet its due. I have been interested by how rarely Shakespeare repeats himself; since each sonnet strikes me as a little aesthetic program worked out to Shakespeare's satisfaction, I want to give each of his experiments its moment of attention.

Age: fifty-six. I have finished rough drafts of commentaries on the first hundred sonnets. More than ever, I feel like someone who has come upon an extraterrestrial playing one strange game after another; the task is to figure out the rules from watching the moves. Shakespeare's games are delightful, but his rules are obscure and full of cunning.

Now. I am asked to look at myself reading the *Sonnets* and give a report on what I find my procedures to be. A theory of reading might begin: Know your texts for forty years. Recite many of them to yourself so often that they seem your own speech. Type them out, teach them, annotate them. A critical "reading" is the end product of an internalization so complete that the word "reading" is not the right one for what happens when a text is on your mind. The text is part of what has made you who you are.

What I can say something about, perhaps, is my dissatisfaction with current accounts of the *Sonnets,* and the procedures which have generated my (different) accounts of them. In my two abandoned chapters I had wanted to take anthology pieces (Sonnets 73, 116, 129) and to see why available critical accounts of them seemed to me so feeble, flat, and unsatisfactory, so foreign to Shakespeare's performance. I had realized that I processed the *Sonnets* differently from most other people. It seemed to me that others tended to read along a static axis of similarity (generally a thematic axis, but sometimes a rhetorical or linguistic one). They wanted to make each sonnet hang together as a statement or a performance of an attitude. I too wanted to make the sonnet hang together, but along a dynamic curve of emotional evolution, so that if it began at point A, it ended, say, at point M. Others, in searching for logical or rhetorical resemblances among the four parts of a sonnet, produced an account of a sonnet that said (although in more exalted terminology), "Shakespeare says lust is bad. Shakespeare shows how bad lust is. Shakespeare says lust always ends badly. And it is bad for everyone always." Those were the thematic readings. A slightly more sophisticated criticism collected all of Shakespeare's examples of hyperbole, or polyptoton, in order to assimilate some pieces of some sonnets to other pieces of other sonnets. These readings made generalizations about Shakespeare's tropes. A yet more sophisticated criticism denied that one could do a reading of the *Sonnets* at all, given the polysemy of the language, and so produced atoms of interpretation but refused to connect the pieces.

None of these, I realized, represented my way of reading. I did believe one could come to a satisfactory reading of these poems, since Shakespeare, for all his love of puns and wordplay, knew very well how to put contextual constraints on his lexicon. I am not of the school that believes we read word by word; by the time we arrive at the period, we know what we've read, and what Shakespeare means. "Meaning" is not the problem in the *Sonnets* (nor indeed in lyric poetry in general). The problem is why poems with such very banal apparent meanings ("I love you; do you love me?"; "Lust is bad"; "The world is evil") should seem so ravishing.

My way of reading the *Sonnets* (and other poems) is to read for difference. Not, "How does quatrain 2 resemble quatrain 1?" but "How does quatrain 2 *differ* from quatrain 1?" What would make someone who has just said he is a *ruined choir* say he is a *twilight* and then say he is a *glowing*?[1] These betoken powerful changes of attitude. Why would soemone define lust by nouns *(expense, spirit, waste, shame, lust, action, action, lust)* while talking about the *act* of lust, and then switch to adjectives *(perjured, murd'rous, bloody, full of blame, savage, extreme, rude, cruel, not to trust)* when talking about the *pursuit* of lust? This seemed to me a linguistic token of an implied mental change. And so on.

The intent to assimilate—to gather information along an axis of static similarity—is the proper intent in reading expository material. This is how we are trained to read at school. This is also a "good enough" technique for reading the subliterary and dispossessed narrative prose ("Spot runs. Dick sees Spot run.") on which children are (disgracefully) trained in their increasingly sociological "literary" indoctrination during the elementary years. But this technique will not do for genuinely literary narrative, where all the interest lies in *how* one of the pitifully few archetypal plots (the marriage plot, the status plot, the quest plot, the tragic plot) is being retold. And it certainly will not do for lyric poems, where all the interest lies in how some recognizable emotion—love, grief, perplexity, rebellion—is being analytically re-presented in means accessible to its culture.

It is, in fact, the analytic function of lyric which is forgotten when

1. Quotations from the *Sonnets* are taken from *Shakespeare's Sonnets,* ed. Stephen Booth (New Haven: Yale University Press, 1977); subsequent references appear in the text.

one reads along an axis of thematic or rhetorical similarity. A Shake-spearean sonnet is an ideal analytic vehicle, with its four movable parts (twice as many as the Italian octave-sestet sonnet). Though the rhyme scheme of the Shakespearean sonnet suggests one distribution of parts (4-4-4-2), and its Petrarchan inheritance another (8-6 or 8-4-2), in fact Shakespeare adapted it to any number of structural and logical sche-mata, such as the 1-11-2 scheme of "Tired with all these" or the 4-6-4 scheme of "So are you to my thoughts." These structures function as ways to embody several responses to the issue at hand, responses that cry out to be distinguished from one another.

I realize now that it was because I had possessed the *Sonnets* themati-cally for so many years that I tended naturally, as an adult, to read them aesthetically, that is, for difference. Because I had so long known everything they "said," I was ready to ask, "What is Shakespeare do-ing now? And now what? What is diverting him in the way of inven-tion in this line? in this couplet? in this quatrain?" I was writing about what had become my own speech and thoughts, and I could ask, "Why am I talking this way?" "What does it mean that *these* thoughts, and not the sort I was uttering five lines back, are coming out of my mouth?"

This oral model of discourse opens up useful questions of rhetoric, speech acts, semantic and aural repetition, and so on (to which I will return), but by itself it can't suffice. It tacitly agrees to forget that the *Sonnets* are a printed book (whatever their dramatic, oral, and aural dimensions). I found, as I read the poems on the page, that I was seeing things that uttering the sonnets as my own speech had not revealed. What I noticed on the page, especially in reading the Quarto version, were the many meaningful repetitions of words, syllables, and even letters. These last included symmetries lost in modern printing. In "Is it for fear to wet a widow's eye," for instance, a modern printing loses the bilateral symmetry of "widdow" and the slightly less symmetrical "issuelesse"; it loses, too, the visual proliferation of *v* (for *u*) and *vv* in the poem, till that symbol becomes the arbitrary token of widow-hood: *vv*et, *vv*iddo*vv*es, *vv*orld, *vv*ill, *vv*aile, *vv*ife, *vv*orld, *vv*ilbe, *vv*iddo*vv*, *vv*eepe, *vv*iddo*vv*, *vv*ell, *v*nthrift, *vv*orld, *vv*orld, *vv*aste, *vv*orld, *v*n*vs*de, *vs*er, to*vv*ard.

On a larger scale, one perceives that many of the sonnets are orga-nized by arbitrary rules that Shakespeare seems to have relished setting for himself. One such rule (apparent, by my count, in more than twenty sonnets) is that each of the four parts of a sonnet had to exhibit one use of the same word. In Sonnet 7, for instance, the word is *look:* quatrain 1 has "looks," 2 "looks," 3 "look," and the couplet "unlooked on"; in Sonnet 26 it is *show.* Shakespeare can enjoy playing games with his key word: in Sonnet 55 the key word is *live,* palpably there in quatrain 1's "outlive," 2's "living," and the couplet's "live," but apparently "missing" in quatrain 3 until one's eye lights on "ob-*liv*-ious," and one is delighted by the secret play. Other kinds of secret play appear in the sequence. To mention only one example, Sonnet 87 secretes *a king* in "mist*aking*," "m*aking*," and "w*aking*," thereby rendering true the closing couplet,

> Thus have I had thee as a dream doth flatter,
> In sleep a king, but waking no such matter.

Often, the reason for Shakespeare's use of particular words (here, the *-aking* words) is not evident from sound alone; one must have grasped his scheme of written play. The *Sonnets,* then, need to be read as written documents as well as oral ones.

I discovered, too, that the *Sonnets* need to be read as speech acts. This is slightly different from reading them, as we are often enjoined to do, "dramatically." That injunction has been applied chiefly to those poems which appear to be directly addressed to another person, such as "Then hate me when thou wilt, if ever, now." It has not been applied to sonnets that seem to be philosophical meditations, such as 116 ("Let me not to the marriage of true minds") or 129 ("Th' expense of spirit"). Nor has it been applied to sonnets of apparently self-directed discourse, such as "Why is my verse so barren of new pride?" But error lies precisely in the prejudging of these sonnets (because they do not immediately exhibit a direct address to another) *as* philosophical meditations or soliloquies. The queries, "Why would someone be talking like this?" "What sort of speech act is this: a rebuttal? an apology? a homily? a boast?" lead to a closer generic definition of a sonnet, and to the revelation (in some cases) of an embedded anterior discourse to which the given sonnet is addressed. When the young man says, "Why do you always use the same old-fashioned form over and over; why don't you ever vary it?" Shakespeare replies by echoing the question: "Why, you ask, is my verse so barren?" and then replies, with a gentleness painful to read, "O know, sweet love, I only write of you. . . ."

One is driven to the sort of speech act query I have instanced by peculiarities in the surface of the poem. For instance, Sonnet 116 exhibits a strange proliferation of negatives; this is the normal sign of a rebuttal. Also, Shakespeare's iambic measure suggests that a normal reading of the opening line of 116 would emphasize the second word: "Let *me* not to the marriage of true minds / Admit impediments." "*You* may; but *I* won't." If we read Sonnet 116 not as a serene definition of love but rather as the rebuttal of the embedded anterior discourse of another—the same way we necessarily read the sonnet that follows it—we hear the anterior discourse that is being rebutted. The faithless young man, we might deduce, has said something like: "You would like the marriage of minds to have the same permanence as the marriage of bodies; but even the church admits impediments which are invoked to annul the marriage of bodies, and there are impediments to a lifelong marriage of minds, too. After all, things alter; and when love finds alteration, it alters in consequence; and things are removed; and love removes itself when it sees the remover. I did love you once, but now that's ended." Shakespeare counters: "Let *me not* to the marriage of true minds / Admit impediments. Love is *not* love / Which alters etc. / Oh, *no*. . . / [It] is *never* shaken. / Love's *not* Time's fool; / Love alters *not*. / I *never* writ, *nor no* man ever loved." Any short poem with four *nots*, two *nevers*, two *nos*, and one *nor* is refuting *something*. Readers intent on what the sonnet seems to mean ("Love is eternal and immutable") have for almost three hundred years missed the anger and scorn in the utterance, and the implication of its chosen form, the rebuttal. (A rebuttal is neither serene nor unthreatened). Such astonishing critical blindness is to be found everywhere in existing criticism of the *Sonnets*.

It is perhaps a modern impatience with rhetoric that leads to an inability to read the *Sonnets*. In the highly diverting, if appalling, history of the reception of the *Sonnets*, one of the most shocking episodes is provided by Ezra Pound. Wanting to wring the neck of rhetoric, he instructed Basil Bunting, one of his students at the "Ezuversity," to go through Shakespeare's *Sonnets* deleting all the "superfluous words." Massimo Bacigalupo, in his monograph *Ezra Pound: Un poeta a Rapallo*,[2] has reproduced a page from the edition "cleaned up" by Bunting under Pound's direction (see figure). Now, what was produced by this process, however barbarous, certainly appears at first glance

2. Massimo Bacigalupo, *Ezra Pound: Un poeta a Rapallo* (Genoa: Edizioni San Marco dei Giustiniani, 1985), p. 75.

103

A~~LACK~~, what poverty my Muse brings forth,
That having such a scope, ~~to show her pride,~~
The argument, all bare, is ~~of~~ more worth
Than when it hath my ~~added~~ praise beside!
O, blame me not, if I no more can write!
Look in your glass, and there appears a face
That overgoes my blunt invention ~~quite,~~
~~Dulling my lines, and doing me disgrace.~~
Were it not sinful, ~~then,~~ striving to mend,
To mar the subject that ~~before~~ was well?
~~For to no other pass my verses tend~~
~~Than of your graces and your gifts to tell;~~
  ~~And~~ more, much more, than ~~in~~ my verse ~~can sit,~~
  Your ~~own~~ glass shows you, ~~when you look in it.~~

104

TO ME, ~~fair friend,~~ you never can be old,
  For as you were when first your eye I ey'd,
Such seems your beauty still. Three winters ~~cold~~
Have from the forests shook three summers' pride,
Three ~~beauteous~~ springs to ~~yellow~~ autumn turn'd
~~In process of the seasons have I seen,~~
~~Three April perfumes in three hot Junes burn'd,~~
Since first I saw you fresh, which yet are green.
Ah, yet doth beauty, like a dial-hand,
Steal from his figure, and no pace perceiv'd;
So your ~~sweet~~ hue, ~~which methinks still doth stand,~~
Hath motion, and mine eye may be deceiv'd:
  ~~For fear of which, hear this, thou age unbred,~~
  ~~Ere you were born was beauty's summer dead.~~

105

LET not my love be call'd idolatry,
　Nor my beloved as an idol show,
Since all alike my songs and praises be
~~To one, of one, still such, and ever so.~~
Kind is my love to-day, to-morrow kind,
~~Still~~ constant in ~~a wondrous~~ excellence;
Therefore ~~my verse to constancy confin'd,~~
~~One thing expressing, leaves out difference.~~
"Fair, kind, and true," is all my argument,
"Fair, kind, and true," varying to other words;
~~And in this change is my invention spent,~~
Three themes in one, ~~which wondrous scope affords.~~
　"Fair, kind, and true," ~~have often liv'd alone,~~
　Which three till now never kept seat in one.

106

WHEN ~~in the chronicle of wasted time~~
　I see ~~descriptions of the fairest wights,~~
~~And~~ beauty making beautiful old rime,
In praise of ladies dead and lovely knights,
~~Then,~~ in the blazon of ~~sweet beauty's best,~~
Of hand, of foot, of lip, of eye, of brow,
I see their antique pen would have express'd
Even such a beauty as you ~~master now,~~
~~So all~~ their praises are ~~but~~ prophecies
~~Of this our time,~~ all you prefiguring;
And, for they look'd but with divining eyes,
They had not ~~still~~ enough your worth to sing:
　~~For~~ we, which now behold ~~these present days,~~
　Have eyes to wonder, but lack tongues to praise.

to preserve the theme or statement of any given sonnet. Are the deleted words then "superfluous?" Is their function thematic, or other than thematic? Let us take Sonnet 105 as our test case.

John Kerrigan, editor of the *Sonnets* for the New Penguin Shakespeare, finds 105 a boring sonnet. Like Bunting, and presumably Pound, he regards it as "tautologous," as his commentary on it reveals:

> A poem like 105 is scrupulously and Shakespearianly dull, but it is dull nonetheless. . . . The text is stripped of metaphor; . . . the result is a poem which, for all its charm [which Kerrigan does not specify] (and integrity) [the absence in it of what Kerrigan calls "false comparisons"], lacks the compelling excitement of a metaphoric sonnet such as 60, "Like as the waves make towards the pebbled shore." In so far as Shakespeare . . . shun[s] "variation" for the sake of tautologous recurrence, his verse palls.[3]

Of course, if one is "excited" only by metaphor, and can perceive no other figure at work, one might find 105 "dull," its repetitions "superfluous" or "tautologous." I believe such verdicts arise from considering aesthetically desirable one thing only—unadorned statement in Pound's case, metaphor in Kerrigan's case.

Now, 105 is a poem that says, in mock refutation of an accusation, "You, a Christian worshipping one God in three persons, have called me an idolator for worshipping my beloved. But don't you see that I worship exactly as you do? My object of worship is also a Trinity; like yours, it combines one-ness and three-ness in a unique way." The playful self-defense of the sonnet is framed in trinitarian imitation: the octave is devoted to oneness, the next quatrain to threeness, and the couplet to three-in-oneness. The Platonic triad (the beautiful, the good, the true) is here translated into colloquial English: "fair," "kind," and "true." Besides enacting the one, the three, and the three-in-one (an enactment entirely destroyed by Bunting's deletion of "superfluities"), this sonnet plays in another way with one-ness, repeating *one* in various literal and phonetic forms, two in each member of the sonnet: in quatrain 1 "one" "one"; 2 "won-," "one"; 3 "one," "won-"; couplet "al*one*," "one." The joking ubiquity of *two* "one's" in each member of a poem about a unique relation of one and three is one of

3. William Shakespeare, *"Sonnets" and "A Lover's Complaint,"* ed. John Kerrigan (Harmondsworth: Penguin, 1986), p. 29.

Shakespeare's private divertissements. So is the joke with reference to the young man's earlier accusation, in Sonnet 76, that Shakespeare's verse "one thing expressing, leaves out difference"; this highly ingenious sonnet, playing with one, two, and three, is full of "difference."

It perplexes me that putatively competent readers have not seen what Shakespeare is up to in this very accomplished jeu d'esprit, which responds (as does sonnet 76) to an implicit accusation (here, one of erotic "idolatry" made by a Christian objector). By pairing the formula of trinitarian theology (three in one) with the Platonic formula for the Absolute (with the good ["kind"] placed foremost in the octave, the beautiful ["fair"] placed significantly foremost in the subsequent quatrain), Shakespeare detaches the trinitarian structure from its Christian significance (Father, Son, Holy Spirit) and wittily makes a rejoinder to the Christian, using his own triune formula while detaching it from its divine dramatis personae. The Christian objector has, of course, wanted Shakespeare to worship the "true" Trinity, but the perfect structural similarity of the two objects of worship—Christian and erotic—is what Shakespeare alleges to defend his choice. It is outrageous, indeed blasphemous, of course, but it is a defense so clever that "even the ranks of Tuscany could scarce forbear to cheer." Or so it seems to me, if not to Pound or Bunting or Kerrigan.

In the history of the sonnet, the trinitarian allusion of the couplet has of course been remarked (Booth, 1977), and some have noted, as a separate phenomenon, the presence of the Platonic triad (with the good, the true, and the beautiful replaced by "kind," "true," and "fair") in the poem. But these separate facts have not been connected to the structural relation of the octave's dedication to oneness, the third quatrain's to threeness, and the couplet's to three-in-oneness. Nor has anyone noticed the double presence of *one* (when one includes the aural pun in "*won*drous" and the orthographical pun in "al*one*") in each member of the sonnet. Even the most careful examination in print of Sonnet 105, by Peter Szondi (who is concerned with Celan's translation of the poem), does not mention any of these things, nor show how they are lost in translation.[4] Can we say that Bunting or Booth or Kerrigan or Szondi—or for that matter Celan—has "read" the poem Shakespeare wrote? Can we still "read" Shakespeare's rhetoric? I wonder. But it seems to me that at the very least our working

4. Peter Szondi, "The Poetry of Constancy," in *"On Textual Understanding" and Other Essays,* trans. Harvey Mendelsohn (Minneapolis: University of Minnesota Press, 1986), pp. 161–78.

assumption should be that there are no "superfluous words" in the *Sonnets,* that Shakespeare is the least likely of our poets to be "dull" or "tautologous," and that it is our own "estrangèd faces" rather than his dullness that we reveal when we disparage his invention.

I have known most of the poets I have written at length on since my teens. The one exception is Stevens, whom I first read at twenty-three. The long subterranean process that goes on between one's first reading of a poet and the decision to write a book on that poet has many stages, which are different for each book. Sometimes (as with my wish to write a book on Whitman) I have not been able to carry out the desire to write at length because there is a gap in understanding which, for all my efforts, will not close. When I first began with Shakespeare the intensive process of study that can lead to a book (memorizing, annotating, typing out the poems, reading editions and criticism), I had hoped, as I have said, to write a critical book on the *Sonnets.* But as I read the poems with close attention, I realized that anything I wrote about Shakespeare's compositional processes in, for example, "Let not my love be called idolatry," had, strictly speaking, nothing to do with the sort of work he was up to in, say, "That time of year thou mayst in me behold." Remarks about one Shakespearean sonnet are, on the whole, not transferable to another unless they are of a level of generality that is totally banal. (This is the problem of "theory" as applied to complex art objects: of course, one can sand down the Discus Thrower until it resembles the Venus de Milo, but any remark thereby made applicable to both statues is so broad that it illuminates neither.)

Shakespeare, it is clear, must have been the most easily bored poet in the history of English lyric (closely followed by George Herbert). Herbert avoided boredom by (almost) never repeating himself prosodically; he invented a new stanza form for almost every poem he wrote, and his genius for stanzaic invention—matched,needless to say, by corresponding rhythmic invention—has never been equaled in English. Shakespeare, confined by choice (if we except a couple of anomalies in the sequence) to a single prosodic form—the iambic pentameter "Shakespearean" sonnet—decided to restrict his invention to things he could do *within* his "walls of glass":

Then, were not summer's distillation left
A liquid pris'ner pent in walls of glass,
Beauty's effect with beauty were bereft,
Nor it nor no remembrance what it was.
(Sonnet 5, 9–12)

The "walls of glass" were one of the many voluntary constraints he accepted for the sake of delight in inventing against the pressure of form. The "liquid prisoner" inside each sonnet demands individual description because, so far as I can see, Shakespeare has a horror of repeating himself. Even when he "rewrites" a sonnet—as, for instance, in 68 he seems to rewrite 67—the refinement of the donnée necessitates new invention. In 67 and 68 the donnée is the presence of a person from the Golden Age in our decayed society. But whereas 67 foregrounds the decayed present, 68 portrays an effort, doubly aborted, to dwell on praise of this Golden Age form, to turn back the clock. The repeated attempts to return to Golden Age nature ("before" X, "e'er" Y, "e'er" Z) collapse in successive returns to the ghastly present and its "false art," represented by, of all things, wigs. This is, so far as I now know, the only sonnet to attempt a rhetorical representation of a common artistic blockage—the failure to be able to sustain contemplation of an imaginary past ideal. Shakespeare's figure of invention here—successive rhetorical collapses into the debased now—does not appear elsewhere, and so in a commentary it has to be inventoried here. The inventory of rhetorical figuration made for Sonnet 105 or 73 has no relevance for 68.

An inventory of the very numerous means of literary representation—grammatical, syntactic, logical, metaphorical, rhetorical, poetic—which Shakespeare employed to do justice to human observation, perception, thought, feeling, speech, and imagination is I think the next critical step in gaining an accurate sense of his aesthetic work in the *Sonnets*. But these means of representation are literally meaningless, even if inventoried, unless they are perceived and described as part of a functioning aesthetic dynamic generating the sonnet (as we have seen with respect to 105). The failure to view Shakespeare's devices of language as functioning within such a dynamic accounts for the relative uselessness of such inventories as exist. The imagery in Shakespeare's plays has generally, from Spurgeon on, been inserted into some such dynamic (the plays being obviously evolving entities).

But imagery in poetry likewise cannot be investigated by itself; it is just one member of a complex functioning poetic system.

In deciding to write what I can only describe as a functional commentary on each sonnet, I hope to show the meaningful and evolving relation of parts within each sonnet. I am assuming a reader who has passed beyond the need for the usual semantic or syntactic editorial annotation, a reader who is ready to ask not, "What does this sonnet say?" but rather, "What is Shakespeare the inventor-in-language up to here?" Reading in this sense asks not what *the poem is saying* but what *the poet is doing*. "What is the problem of representation here?" "How does the poet solve it?" One must allow each sonnet to provoke the questions that, when answered, will show how it generates itself, by what laws of inner form. This version of the hermeneutic circle is aimed not at *interpretation*—a mistaken aim when predicated, as it usually is, on the paraphrasable cultural content of a poem—but rather at the probable *function* of observable and significant linguistic activity.

It is true that linguistic activity is theoretically infinite. The problem in "reading" is choosing which linguistic activities manifest in the poem are significant ones. The objections voiced by me and by others to Roman Jakobson's discussion of Sonnet 129 are grounded on the randomness of his choice of things to compare.[5] Jakobson chose (among other things) to compare line 1 of the sonnet with line 14, then line 2 with line 13, and so on, down to a comparison of line 6 with line 7. Such a procedure violates the "instructions for reading" encoded in the Shakespearean sonnet, which suggests by its structural form that we make comparisons among its four parts, to start with. It also suggests that we compare portions of the poem that repeat the same word, vary a common figure, or reiterate a syntactic pattern. It suggests that we compare the couplet (which often performs the function of summarizing, epitomizing, or epigrammatizing) with the body of the poem. There are many other "instructions" suggested in a given sonnet: that we should compare (contrastively as well as analogously) words that alliterate with one another, or words that pun together, or groups of words (such as "never," "not," "nor," and "no" in Sonnet 116) that enact the same sort of refusal, or parts of speech

5. See Roman Jakobson and Laurence Jones, *Shakespeare's Verbal Art in "Th' Expense of Spirit"* (The Hague: Mouton, 1970), and Helen Vendler, "Jakobson, Richards, and Shakespeare's Sonnet CXXIX," in *I. A. Richards: Essays in His Honour,* ed. Reuben Brower, Helen Vendler, and John Hollander (New York: Oxford University Press, 1973), pp. 179–98.

(nouns versus adjectives in Sonnet 129) that describe different phases of "the same thing" (in 129, sexual appetite).

These axioms of reading, however familiar, are often forgotten in practice. One of the clichés of critical discourse on the *Sonnets,* for instance, is the apparent superfluity of the couplet. This criticism is sometimes phrased as the problem of the couplet's detachment from the body of the poem, or its inconsistency with the body of the poem. I decided to see in how many cases the couplet included an explicit repetition, from the body of the poem, of a significant word or words (I excluded words such as *and* or *thee* or *I,* unless punned on with *eye* and thereby foregrounded). I called this repeated word or words the couplet tie. It meant to me, when it was present, that Shakespeare was making a distinct effort to create a visible verbal connection between the body and the "tail" of his form. I discovered that only ten of the 154 sonnets (3, 34, 37, 65, 67, 126, 141, 142, 147, and 150) lacked such a couplet tie; and even if one or two cases might be debatable, such a statistic means that in over 90 percent of his efforts, Shakespeare made an identifiable verbal connection of the body with the couplet. To explain why the articulation of the couplet has seemed unsuccessful to some readers requires a hypothesis other than that of verbal irrelevance, especially since the couplet tie is usually a word or group of words with striking thematic significance within the given sonnet. Perhaps dissatisfied readers are reading not for "words" (by which I mean linguistic play of all kinds) but for statement, and are unhappy when they find reiteration "varying to other words": there are differences in perspective, in expectation, and in satisfaction consequent upon one's method of reading.

We contributors have been asked by our editor not only to describe our own methods of reading but to compare them with past and current methods. Although one is always tempted to quote Eliot on the necessity of intelligence, the intelligence of a good reader is not only talented but trained. The discipline of "English" goes through oscillations of intra- and extralinguistic concerns: from *vie-et-oeuvre* to the New Criticism, from the New Criticism to the New Historicism. Equally it goes through a set of master narratives (currently Marx, Freud, Wittgenstein, Nietzsche, Foucault, Lacan) from which it derives the individual and social psychology and philosophy it employs to discuss experiential events and responses to them, whether in life or in art. It also veers to and fro between metaphysical notions of the literary object as unified (a view deriving ultimately from Aristotle) or as ecstatically ungovernable (a view deriving ultimately from Plato, visible most recently in deconstruction's attachment to theories of uncontrollable linguistic events). Each of these strategies is only as good as the results it produces with respect to a given work.

Because I believe Shakespeare's aesthetic in the composition of each individual sonnet was an "Aristotelian" one of coherence along a dynamic curve, I have not usually been concerned, in individual commentaries, with forces of dispersal. The forces of dispersal that Shakespeare acknowledges here are rather to be found (and the deconstructive certainty that they lurk everywhere has certainly helped to reveal them) in the troubling noncoherence of the psychological and linguistic galaxies that go to make up the universe of the sequence. The persistent wish to reorder the *Sonnets* testifies to their resistance to any conclusive ordering (the reorderings having failed to convince anyone but their originators). No reader of the *Sonnets* has been able to establish a consistent psychology of the Young Man, the Poet, or the Dark Lady; no one has been able to trace a coherent narrative; no one has explained the presence of the anomalous mythological sonnets, nor those that are formally anomalous. Once one has memorized many of the sonnets, even the quatrains begin to behave in a strangely autonomous fashion, linking themselves into new sonnets that never were on land or sea:

> That thou hast her, it is not all my grief,
> And yet it may be said I loved her dearly;
> That she hath thee is of my wailing chief,
> A loss in love that touches me more nearly.
> Gentle thou art, and therefore to be won,
> Beauteous thou art, therefore to be assailed;
> And when a woman woos, what woman's son
> Will sourly leave her till he have prevailed?
> Then if for my love thou my love receivest,
> I cannot blame thee for my love thou usest;
> But yet be blamed, if thou this self deceivest
> By wilful taste of what thyself refusest.
> Ah, but those tears are pearl which thy love sheeds,
> And they are rich, and ransom all ill deeds.[6]

6. I here restore the Quarto reading in line 11, "if thou this self deceivest." Booth accepts the traditional emendation of "thyself" for "this self."

This hybrid, composed of parts of Sonnets 42, 41, 40, and 34, is the sort of new agglutination that arises in the mind when pieces of many sonnets are floating around there. The sequence contains such a number of concerns breeding such a number of reponses that what one finally possesses, in possessing the sequence by memory, is an artifically constructed total mind full of self-generating "thoughts," "feelings," "reactions," "generalizations," "reversals," and so on. The dispersive forces of the sequence come fully into play only when one has internalized the sequence as a whole.

Earlier methods of reading the *Sonnets,* on display in the *Variorum* and elsewhere, of course teach us a philosophical humility before our own. Biographical, allegorical, historical, and thematic methods of reading return in perpetual recrudescence, no matter the dubiousness of their results, and one can only conclude that something in literary response as it has evolved among us ensures that in every century some group of people will try to reidentify the *Sonnets'* dramatis personae, will allegorize (morally, historically, or dramatically) the import of the series, and will debate the psychology and sexuality of the intrigue.

It is not so much individual methods of "reading" that we should be attacking or defending, I think. Rather, we should be accounting for, and accepting, the phenomenon of the eternal return of habitual types of reading. The personal-interest type of reading (women reading women, blacks reading blacks, Roman Catholics reading Roman Catholics) has always been with us, as have methods of reading founded on adjunct disciplines (history, philosophy, religion). In fact, the simplest way to characterize "methods of reading" is to ask each reader, "In the light of what other discipline do you read literary texts?" The answers—religion, history, linguistics, philosophy, women's studies, philology, aesthetics, sociology, Marxism, psychology—are in fact our "methods." People rarely combine more than two of these in any serious way. And they tend to choose the genre they write about by its "fit" with their favorite auxiliary discipline(s).

If one begins from a single genre (and stays with it, as I have done, being incompetent in other genres), one turns to the auxiliary disciplines most relevant to that genre. For poetry—the genre most concerned with formal experiments in language—the disciplines that seem to me most obviously useful are philology, linguistics, rhetoric, psychology, and aesthetics. (There are, of course, critics of poetry whose interest is, for example, religion-based or woman-based; but

criticism springing from such bases tends to be centrifugal with respect to the genre, centripetal with respect to the auxiliary discipline,
which becomes no longer auxiliary but dominant.)

I am not confident that any set of common grids can be applied to
secure "good" (or, if you prefer, "stimulating") readings. So often I
have sat before an opaque poetic text (the simplest often being aesthetically the most opaque) as it resisted my intelligence "almost successfully," as Stevens said it should. I waited and waited to have it tell me
what questions it would abide. Many questions were put; none fit.
After a year of doing that with Whitman, I gave up. I later discovered,
from an excellent book on Whitman by Wynn Thomas, that my questions were not sufficiently historically informed.[7] I am not enough of
a historian to write on Whitman, as I am perhaps not enough of a
philosopher to write on Shelley. My mind is so impatient with linearity that I am unable to write on narrative, in poetry as in prose. I
am too attached to meditative elaboration to enjoy the stripped-down
intensities of drama.

With each new lyric poet, I have had to learn to ask new questions.
My usual response is to be struck by recurrent features of style peculiar
to the author at hand—ways of arranging language that are not found
(at least not in such profusion) in other texts. In that sense, I am always
reading for "difference." It is understandable that cultural historians
assimilate many works of art into something that could be called "the
(normative) greater Romantic lyric" or "the representation of Venus
in art." But this, to an aesthetic critic, is rather like describing to a
parent a "normative child" or to an artist a "normative product." Who
could be interested in such a thing? One wants rather to look at the
angle where one's child differs from her cohort, or where Michelan-
gelo's *Pietà* differs from others. Whether or not the individual self is a
fiction (it hardly matters since, if so, the fiction is a necessary and
indestructible one), the individual work of art certainly is not. Not
one of the *Sonnets* is superimposable without excess or defect on any
other. Any category large enough to contain even two of these poems
is already too broad and too banal to catch the unique aesthetic vector
resultant of either one.

Others are bound to continue grouping the *Sonnets* in theoretical or
generic or thematic clumps, if only because of that inveterate taxo-

7. M. Wynn Thomas, *The Lunar Light of Whitman's Poetry* (Cambridge: Harvard
University Press, 1987).

nomizing tendency, so inimical to aesthetic experience, in human mentality. Intellectually, we read the universe for similarity, and come up with Mendelian groups and the periodic table of elements. There is room, though, for an intellectual method that represents the nonce quality of each aesthetic experience, and that stubbornly claims a value in reading for difference. It urges that one remain serenely within the differences once one has found them—"without any irritable reaching-out" for generalization about a number of grouped experiences.

Finally, some word should be found for this process instead of "reading," since "reading" implies a one-time effort. Such a word obscures the "long foreground" preceding any formal written "reading"—the forty years with the poems, the many incidental noticings, the efforts to learn by heart, the inner responses to others' books, the philological and historical acquaintance with "English" that comes only from continued exposure to the historically evolving language, the cultural possession not only of information but of poetic form (in the ear as well as in the eye). The word "reading" does not represent the love of the objects of study, the necessary leisure of many aesthetic experiences with the same object. Perhaps a better phrase would be "my history with this text." Good reading never lacks a long and taxing history. Our authors are cleverer than we are, and improve on acquaintance. And tears water the soil of understanding.

Close Reading without Readings

STEPHEN BOOTH

As many of you have noticed, and too many of you have noticed in print, I am a self-indulgent critic.[1] No one, then, should be much surprised to hear that what I plan for my share of the present program is an exercise in self-endorsement.

Today's is a session on close reading, and close reading is what I do.

I am, however, prompted to self-endorsement by more than temperament and coincidence. I have been saying the same kinds of things for all the twenty years I've been publishing criticism.

That too, alas, is regularly pointed out.

What bothers me, and primarily accounts for this display of self-absorption, is that, Costard-like (Costard confesses "much of the hearing" of Navarre's proclamation in scene 1 of *Love's Labor's Lost* "but little of the marking of it"), you people have become used to

---

1. This essay is adapted from a paper I wrote for a session at the 1989 meeting of the Shakespeare Association of America, a session called "Close Reading Revisited." Although I have altered the paper considerably for print (deleting references to handouts, for instance), I have decided against removing abundant evidence that it was intended for oral presentation to a room full of Shakespeareans, a room full of people very like the ones the essay will now speak to in print. The essay variously—and, I hope, valuably—exploits its audience's responses, and, when I set about revising it, I found no economical way to substitute for the effects I got easily and efficiently in my brash original. What is more, aside from increased bulk, formality of manner added nothing to the paper but formality. The essay, thus, is superficially as well as essentially the paper I began with.

hearing me do what I do without ever noticing at all what that is, without ever noticing that both what I do and what I pretend to do are radically different from what other close readers customarily do and pretend to be doing.

I discount the not altogether improbable possibility that you have all always seen what I was up to and were too tactful to mention it to me.

I shouldn't complain, I guess. Aside from a couple of blatantly silly exceptions, I've had years of generally adulatory reviews, and my salary has risen steadily. Besides, if people paid attention, I wouldn't need to go on trying to get them to. I would have to find something else to tell them—or even leave the academy for honest work.

But, although it may be neither reasonable nor prudent to do so, I obviously *am* complaining. And I *do* want you just this once to see that, as I keep insisting in print, what I am after is close reading that tries to avoid resulting in "readings"—in interpretations.

With that statement I approach treacherous and familiar ground. Note, however, that I said "tries to avoid," not "avoids." That was, first, to allow for simple aberrations in my apprehensions of the surfaces of texts and, more fashionably, to acknowledge that interpretation is inevitable to reading. When one reads a stop sign and takes it as a command to stop, one is interpreting (and, since one takes it as a command for vehicular traffic only, interpreting as a result of cultural staining). That is obvious and, in context of the general sense the term "critical interpretation" evokes, nowhere near so interesting as Stanley Fish has pretended to suppose. To put the matter more graciously, I grant that no one can speak about or think about or even look at anything at all in the world without limiting it and otherwise distorting it, but I insist, too, that that truth is at best peripheral to a distinction between me and critics who purposefully come between what is read and readers who think they comprehend it and tell those readers what a text "really" means.

A key distinction for the present discussion is between delivered and undelivered meanings. Like all close readers I deal in meanings of words that those words are unlikely to have delivered to my readers. Unlike most close readers, I do not suggest that, say, a meaning for a word that a context invites, but that syntax does not, should or could—once I've advertised it—be included in a paraphrase of the sentence in which it appears. I am constantly concerned with, and concerned to celebrate, the raw materials in Shakespearean texts for farfetched readings, but I try to avoid fetching them.

Close readers who want their prospective clients to accept readings that derive from some previously unobserved potential in a line are always at risk of being laughed at for wanton ingenuity. They are unlikely, for instance, to give serious attention to the pairing of the word "nature" and the word "art" when Edmund juxtaposes them in the first line of scene 2 of *King Lear,* where he says, "Thou, *Nature, art* my goddess." They cannot safely talk about the undelivered—the situationally undeliverable—noun meaning of "art" in "Thou, Nature, art my goddess." Unfortunately—as your laughter tellingly witnessed a moment ago when I used my voice to "italicize" the words "Nature" and "art"—I can't safely talk about the juxtaposition either. I can't because just about nobody sees that when I fuss over things like the substantively accidental "Nature"/"art" pair in Edmund's speech, I am not en route to a new reading of the line, the speech, or *King Lear.*

If people had paid attention twenty years ago, you would by now have begun to be almost familiar with the idea that locally unharnessed, locally unharnessable senses for words and phrases can function in the sentences that contain them—can function valuably without being delivered (or even noticed by anyone but the critic who points them out).

As your laughter just demonstrated, the presumption is overwhelming that any critic talking about the *raw materials* for a double meaning or the *raw materials* for an overt play on two meanings of a sound is suggesting that that double meaning or overt wordplay is, once was, or should henceforth be active in people's understanding of the *sense* of the passage the critic is discussing.

The source of the presumption is more than habit. And, to speak more generally, the critical habit of always validating one's study of a text in terms of *meaning* usually (but not always—consider the people who spent the 1980s trying to drive Mrs. Thatcher from office by reading Shakespeare—meaning imputed to the examined text) reflects more than literary criticism's roots in the interpretation of divine revelation in Scripture or from oracles. Literature differs radically from the other arts in that it is the only one that is made out of signifiers— *words*—things that came into being only as vehicles for communicating.

Only the most naive of music critics would read all compositions as program music ("Now he's running through the marketplace";

"That's the duck quacking from inside the wolf"). And, though he or she may give a lot of attention to ideological content in a great painting, no commentator on that painting is likely to say that ideological content is what we value in the painting or that we should henceforth abandon our frivolously aesthetic reasons for caring so much about the painting as to study it.

What I do—and encourage everybody else to start doing, too—is think about casual, unobtrusive, substantively irrelevant relationships among *meanings*—relationships like the one between the meaning the word "Nature" has in "Thou, Nature, art my goddess" and the one the word "art" does not have there—and to think about such relationships in a way analogous to the way one might think about the relationship among notes of music that present a melody and those that do not.

A good fraction of any but the most sophisticated audiences usually derails on the musical analogy. They hear an echo of familiar notions and nostrums of popular criticism; they are used to hearing about the "music" of verse, and they assume that I am recommending a Swinburnean wallow in the sound of verse and recommending that they ignore what it says.

No. What I'm talking about is a music of ideas.

"Music of ideas" usually throws some more people off track. They hear something substantively grand in it, something in the neighborhood of philosophic synthesis.

No, again. The ideas I refer to are simple ones: just the ideas that adhere to individual words and locutions, ideas that establish substantively irrelevant, ordinarily unobserved affinities among words in sentences and speeches in which the meanings that bond them may be inactive.

All right, if it is now clear what I do and don't do, it is still *not* clear why I do it. If I read closely for reasons that have nothing to do with any attempt to augment, narrow, clarify, improve, or otherwise distort perception of what is read—which is to say, if I espouse an academic criticism that is, and admits to being, academic—what do I hope to achieve by considering senses of words and phrases that are nonsensical in the particular sentences in question? I talk about undelivered meanings because I think they operate in Shakespeare and most of the rest of great literature the way things like rhythm, rhyme, and alliteration do. I talk about undelivered meanings because, instead of "What does this Shakespearean word (speech, play) *mean*?" my question as a Shakespeare critic is always, "Why do people care so much about these plays? What's all the fuss actually about?"

It may now be possible for us to return with straight faces to "Thou, Nature, art my goddess"—an assertion in which the word "art," the appropriate form of the verb "to be," says what it seems to say and nothing else. You may by now see why I think it worth saying that that assertion begins a twenty-two-line speech that later develops a common denominator in various contrasts between what is natural and what is artificial. When that theme emerges, it emerges both as an idea new to the speech *and* onto ground where it has already appeared. Both of the opposed ideas, both nature *and* art, have already sounded in an audience's ears. They have already been set out side by side for ears that have heard the pairing in "Thou, Nature, art my goddess"— although, of course, not marked it.[2]

I don't want to discuss Edmund's soliloquy in detail. I want only to note that the "Thou, Nature, art" phenomenon is not alone of its kind in the speech. Consider, for instance, the weak but steady pressure in the lines that immediately follow "Thou, Nature, art my goddess" toward reference to *place*—pressure from the materials for the standard construction "to be bound *to* some place"—pressure from the "where" in "wherefore," from the simplest, nonmetaphoric sense of "to stand in," and from the word "lag" in "lag of a brother":

> Thou, Nature, art my goddess; to thy law
> My services are bound. Wherefore should I
> Stand in the plague of custom, and permit
> The curiosity of nations to deprive me,
> For that I am some twelve or fourteen moonshines
> Lag of a brother? Why bastard?
>   (*King Lear* 1.2.1–6)

The affinity of the word "nations"—in essence a "birth" word—to the topic of legitimate and illegitimate birth also contributes a substan-

---

2. Although the issue is irrelevant to my point, it is probable that—had Shakespeare been audience to Edmund's "Nature"/"art" line rather than its author—he, supreme among mortals in his ear for opportunities to jerk words out of one context and into another, might have noticed the opening the line presents for a totally inappropriate punning response. Remember *Romeo and Juliet* 2.4.84–85: "Now art thou sociable, now art thou Romeo; now art thou what thou art, by art as well as by nature." All Shakespeare citations are from the revised Pelican text, ed. Alfred Harbage et al. (Baltimore: Penguin, 1969).

tively gratuitous, extra "rightness" to the lines—such rightness that it takes an effort of will to note that Edmund's complaints pertain to primogeniture and not legitimacy.

When I talk about extra rightness added to a sentence or a speech or a scene or a play, I'm talking about contributions that make the artificial construct feel less arbitrary, more like a thing in nature. With some notable exceptions—bougainvillea plants, for instance, and most parrots—things in nature look—well—natural. They have distinct parts, but the parts relate to one another in so many systems of coherence that they are so completely things that one never thinks of them at all as conglomerates of their perceptible parts.

Consider a hardwood tree in summer. The greens in one leaf are nearly infinite and are almost infinitely fewer than the greens of the tree as a whole. Under most conditions, light strikes the tree from a single angle, but only for a single second before that angle changes. And, though the light may strike the tree from the same angle, the angle at which it strikes each leaf differs from the angle at which it strikes every other. Moreover, all the leaves and the observer are likely to be in some degree of motion.

Each fleeting mix of greens and browns and yellows in a given leaf echoes those that preceded it. Each successive identity quietly and solemnly puns on its predecessors, just as each of the leaves puns on all the others and—in most species—on the overall shape of the whole tree.

As objects presented to the human mind, the tree's elements are in an incomprehensible number of incidental, casual, often fleeting relationships. Each of those relationships makes weak gestures for conscious recognition from the beholding mind. As a result, I submit, the tree—precisely *because* of the overwhelming number of relationships among its perceptually separable elements—has no mentally probable identity but the one it has as a whole, a *thing,* not the sum of its parts but a *tree.*

The kind of effect I pointed to in Edmund's soliloquy, and in the course of establishing myself as the Joyce Kilmer of criticism, occurs regularly in the appearance of old buildings and brings them beauty. A barn—a barn standing in a field, frankly admitting its identity as a thing put together from pieces of wood—will, once it has stood for several years and its foundations have shifted and sunk a little, take on lines that coexist with reminiscences of the builder's straight, artificial ones, lines in which the building materials have more identity as the barn than as artificially unified bits. A similar, auxiliary effect usually occurs concurrently as the distinguishable elements in the barn's facades acquire a look of natural affinity as a result of sharing the same weather and the same accidents.

In fact, a good metaphor for describing this first of three kinds of effect I attribute to the action of casual, incidental relationships among words and ideas in Shakespeare is *patina*. Networks of nonsensical relationship act upon speeches and plays the way a patina does upon artwork in metal. They smooth across seams and deny them without obliterating them. Grosser examples of the effect have been noted in literature ever since people started analyzing double plots and noticing echoing situations and spotting thematic common denominators and sustained patterns of imagery.

A second effect—one more vital and vitalizing—that I attribute to the presence of such unostentatious relationships as the ones in Edmund's "Nature" soliloquy is excitement. Minds moving matter-of-factly across plays that are mine fields of potential for punlike explosions, explosions that do not occur but that would—like the contrived puns of clowns like Grumio and Speed in the early comedies—bring chaos to the discourses in which they lie dormant, are minds in a constant state of quiet excitement.

Shakespeare's plays surround us with potentially disruptive relationships whose terms are alien to those of the straightforward discourse to which our consciousnesses attend. And, I suggest, we feel their disruptive potential and thrill at our capacity to march—godlike—through them. As we move along, the lines come repeatedly and variously close to attracting our conscious attention to the relevant or irrelevant extra identities among their elements—close, but rarely close enough to invite even momentary consideration to reading them into our sense of the sense the lines make.

I mean to use most of the rest of my time on Lady Macbeth's "raven" speech ("The raven himself is hoarse"). First, however, I want to test you by looking at eight lines from *Hamlet*, lines that, like "Thou, Nature, art," present an example of relationship nobody could take seriously if still ensnared by the assumption that all critical concern for meanings of words in literary texts is concern to modify people's understanding of what those texts are telling us.

The eight lines are lines 125 through 132 of act 1, scene 2. They are the last four lines of Claudius's exit speech and the first four of Hamlet's first soliloquy. They overlay a distinct break between two sections of the scene. The king concludes his exit speech:

> No jocund health that Denmark drinks to-day
> But the great cannon to the clouds shall tell,
> And the king's rouse the heaven shall bruit again,
> Respeaking earthly thunder. Come away.
>   *Flourish. Exeunt all but Hamlet.*
> *Hamlet.* O that this too, too sullied flesh would melt,
>   Thaw, and resolve itself into a dew,
>   Or that the Everlasting had not fixed
>   His canon 'gainst self-slaughter.

As by now you will expect, my concern is for the twin cannons. The echo of artillery from line 126 in the word "canon," meaning "law," six lines later is enough by itself to deny the completeness of the division between the soliloquy and the public conversation that precedes it.

As it is, however, before the term "self-slaughter" reduces what comes before it to a straightforward assertion about divine law, the verb "to fix against" and the sound of "canon" in "fixed his canon 'gainst" have gone a good way toward introducing the idea of gun emplacement into the speech. Moreover, by virtue of its reference to slaughter, the term "self-slaughter"—the very term that removes artillery as a topic of the speech—*also* tucks the idea of carnage back into the sentence from which it simultaneously removes it. Indeed, when the phrase "fixed his canon 'gainst self-slaughter" comes to rest, "canon"—the most warlike sounding word in its clause—is, aside from the incidental pronoun "his," the only one that has no ideational affinity left for weaponry and violent death.[3]

---

3. The "cannon"/"canon" pair has a contrasting complement in these lines. In line 131 "the Everlasting" (a euphemism for "God") does and does not echo "heaven" (the commonest of all such euphemisms) in line 127, where "heaven" in "the heaven shall bruit" makes no reference to God and just says "the sky"—but where it is personified and thus, by offering vague suggestions of pagan deities manipulating thunderbolts, presents a real, though pale, analogue to the process by which the phrase with "canon" in it does and does not echo the earlier reference to artillery. The kind of pull toward union that the "cannon"/"canon" lines effect occurs over a greater gulf when scene 4, the scene in which Hamlet and Horatio hear the king taking his rouse, echoes scene 2. If the Second Quarto stage direction—"*A flourish of trumpets and two pieces goes of[f]*—is to be trusted, and if, as is probable, the "pieces" specified are cannon, then we hear at about line 6 of scene 4 what the king promised in scene 2. Shortly afterward, in

The third of the three benefits I promised to attribute to events in the ideational underworlds of great works like *Hamlet* and *Macbeth* is that of making us temporarily but genuinely superior to the limitations of reason. Such weaves of incidental relationship as I will shortly exhibit in act 1 of *Macbeth* let us take sense from nonsense. Consider the word "himself" in "The raven himself is hoarse / That croaks the fatal entrance" (*Macbeth* 1.5.36). The idiom—which says "even the raven"—implies that there is such a thing as a raven that *isn't* hoarse. We achieve a comparable victory over probability when, in the syntactic thicket of 1.5.44–45, we both hear and fail to hear Lady Macbeth posit antipathy between her purpose and its effect (she wants nothing to shake her "fell purpose nor keep peace between / Th' effect and it"). It is similarly remarkable that context makes "letting 'I dare not' wait upon 'I would'" (1.7.44) sound as if it makes sense long before a footnote wrests "wait upon" out of its usual domestic service and into a synonym for "associate with."

We also approach superiority to the sense that one might expect would be palpable in what we hear when we matter-of-factly accept godlike capacity to understand the metaphysical double physics of the assertion that the witches "made themselves air, into which they vanished" (1.5.4–5).

An alternative, perhaps better way to deal with our apprehension of the assertion in which the witches are what they enter is to focus on its ease: we behold potentially dazzling flights of poetic fancy as if they were hourly shuttles from La Guardia Airport. The poet's grace is not noticed to be *his*. We accept our casual displays of mental aerobatics as natural to *us*.

We take similar flights in 1.4.33–35 ("My plenteous joys, / Wanton in fullness, seek to hide themselves / In drops of sorrow"—just think about the two *in*s there and the casually suppressed glitz of "seek to hide"), and in 1.5.40 ("And fill me, from the crown to the toe top-full," a line that at once presents double, superficially contradictory physics—the filling is from top to bottom *and* from bottom to top— and simultaneously follows the perceived fall of liquid into the bottom of a container and the apparent ascent it makes as its volume increases).

Now I want to continue examination of *Macbeth* 1.5.35–56, an insistently discontinuous speech in which Lady Macbeth instructs her

---

line 47, in context of ideas of bursting and of projectiles, Hamlet refers to his father's "canonized bones."

servant, the so-called messenger (the servant who reports the news the actual messenger is too winded to deliver in person), then, again alone onstage, soliloquizes, and finally greets Macbeth when—on the injunction "Hold, hold!"—he interrupts her solitude:

> Give him tending;
> He brings great news.   *Exit Messenger.*
>   The raven himself is hoarse
> That croaks the fatal entrance of Duncan
> Under my battlements. Come, you spirits
> That tend on mortal thoughts, unsex me here,
> And fill me from the crown to the toe top-full
> Of direst cruelty. Make thick my blood;
> Stop up th' access and passage to remorse,
> That no compunctious visitings of nature
> Shake my fell purpose, nor keep peace between
> Th' effect and it. Come to my woman's breasts
> And take my milk for gall, you murd'ring ministers,
> Wherever in your sightless substances
> You wait on nature's mischief. Come, thick night,
> And pall thee in the dunnest smoke of hell,
> That my keen knife see not the wound it makes,
> Nor heaven peep through the blanket of the dark
> To cry, "Hold, hold!"
>   *Enter Macbeth.*   Great Glamis! worthy Cawdor!
> Greater than both, by the all-hail hereafter!
> Thy letters have transported me beyond
> This ignorant present, and I feel now
> The future in the instant.

The speech is indeed disjointed, but its parts are also—are at the same time—variously and multitudinously linked to one another, as it is with its phonetic and ideological environment, linked by echoing incidentals of sound, sense, and undelivered sense. Such pattern-made links, unobserved by the minds to which a play delivers its substance, are, I submit, not *a* but *the* principal source of the greatness we find in Shakespeare's work.

The things I will now say will not panic you if you remember that, although I will be concerned with contextually impossible potential meanings for some of the words and syllables I list, I am not concerned

with what the speech means or with what any of its sentences mean.
I take the meanings to be neither in need of modification nor capable
of it. We all know what these lines are saying, and no amount of ink
is going to make them deliver anything else or anything more than
they do for any reader or audience familiar with the diction and syntax
of Shakespeare's contemporaries.

I will talk first about substantively inconsiderable patterns of substantively incidental relationship in the second of the speech's three
sections, 1.5.35–52, the soliloquy that begins with "The raven himself
is hoarse" and ends with "cry 'Hold, hold!'" Then I will talk about the
interaction of some of them with similarly patterned elements that
overlay the speeches and scenes that immediately precede and follow.

A good instance of an incidental, enriching relationship within the
soliloquy is the phonetic and ideational likeness and difference of "fatal" in "fatal entrance" in line 37 and "mortal" two lines later. Each is
the fourth and fifth syllable of its line, and the two words have nearly
identical second syllables.

Just as the sounds of "fatal" and "mortal" insist equally on their
likeness and their difference, so do their senses. The reference to fate
that the ominous raven brings with it pushes past the death-related
suggestions inherent in "fatal" (suggestions that syntactic difficulty
holds back from being more). And the presence in "spirits that tend
on mortal thoughts" of "spirits"—one half of a contrast between mortals and *im*mortals—weakens the capacity of the word "mortal" to
make "thoughts of murder" dominant in our understanding. But the
common meaning largely suppressed in the two words pulls them
together and counters the frantic disjunction of the two sentences—
does so, moreover, without in any way denying that disjunction.

A simpler, but similar, instance derives from the reappearances—
widely separated and in reverse order—of "make" and "thick" from
"make thick my blood" (41), in "Come, thick night" (48), and "see
not the wound it makes" (50) at the end of the soliloquy.

And, for a mind-boggling example, look at the relationships in
which line 47—"Wherever in your sightless substances"—participates. The logic of the passage dictates that "sightless" be heard to
say "unseen," "invisible." But that meaning, the meaning "sightless"
ultimately delivers, is at first less probable contextually than two
others. The first of those derives from a momentary focus on place
that "wherever" signals: unsituated, "siteless" (as awkward and unlikely a nonce meaning as the otherwise validated "invisible"). The

second is the locally insupportable meaning that "sightless" most commonly carries: blind. Within seconds after we bow to context and dispel the idea of blindness from our consciousnesses, the sense contextually denied to "sightless" in "sightless substances" receives an ideational rhyme in "see not" and, complexly, "keen" when Lady Macbeth asks that her "keen knife see not the wound it makes" (50).

That line is a good occasion to move from incidental relationships that do not reach outside the soliloquy—do not reach outside the middle section of the speech—to ones that do.

The fatal entrance to which the line about the knife and the wound refers both echoes and does not echo the one at the beginning of the passage (37), where "fatal entrance of Duncan" made no reference at all to the kind of entrance a knife makes when it pierces flesh. Between the phrase "fatal entrance" in line 37 and the knife wound in line 50 are "access and passage" in line 42—both entrance-related words that, since they occur in a sentence about blood, help prepare the ground for the knife and wound reference and give it additional extrasubstantive propriety.

The idea of entrance in "fatal entrance" in line 37 is immediately repeated in the first of the three imperative uses of "come" that stud the speech—a speech, remember, that has as its occasion news of the king's visit, news that "the king comes here tonight" (29).

The six syllables of "compunctious" and "visitings" in line 43 sum up, and are an emblem for, all that I have so far said, both in general about the activities of inert meanings and about the incidental pattern in sounds and senses in the soliloquy that relate to fatal entrances. The relevance of "visitings"—here strained to deliver what its context demands—is obvious: it justifies its presence by presenting a scarcely heard echo of the speech's occasion and as one in an alliterationlike progression of other variously muffled references to visitation. The first syllable of "compunctious" is presumably unnoticed to echo the sound "come" and the idea of entrance, but it does. And, because the rest of the syllables of "compunctious" derive from Latin -*pungere* and reverberate with their peers in English (*puncture*, for instance), "compunctious" contributes to establishing an environment already friendly to the knife and wound we will hear about in line 50. In short, "compunctious" relates not only to entrance but to "fatal entrance of Duncan" in a sense that phrase does not itself deliver, the sense in which it describes a stabbing.

Ideas of coming—and of its opposites, going and remaining—fall thick on the ear in the scenes that precede the speech I have focused on. They occur in words merely capable of reference to those ideas (like "stay" in "we stay upon your leisure" [1.3.151], and the two uses of "leave" in "Leave all the rest to me" and "By your leave, hostess"— the exit lines that conclude scenes 5 and 6, where the sense each delivers is entirely foreign to the sense delivered by the other, and where neither relates at all to departure, even though each line is, as I said, an exit line). The idea of coming occurs in the sound "cum." And that idea and its relatives occur in relatives of the verb *to come* (for instance, "Nothing in his life be*came* him like the leaving of it" [1.4.8]). As to overt reference to coming, going, and remaining, consider "New honors come upon him" (1.3.147); "Come what come may, / Time and the hour runs through the roughest day" (1.3.149–50); "Come, friends" (1.3.156); "Come back" (1.4.3); "set forth" (1.4.6); the doubly pertinent "Welcome hither" (1.4.27); and so on.

The most interesting elements that both do and do not relate to coming—elements that, of course, attract no conscious attention—are the "cum" sounds in 1.4.38–39: "Our eldest, Mal*com,* whom we name hereafter / The Prince of *Cum*berland." In addition, "Cumberland," a name that means something like "Welsh people's place" and has nothing to do with encumbrances, is immediately described as such: "The Prince of Cumberland—that is a step / On which I must fall down or else o'erleap, / For in my way it lies" (1.4.48–50).

In those lines, the pattern in "come"-related language intersects with a pattern of references to miraculous speed across space that includes the horseman who brought the message, Lady Macbeth's transportation beyond the ignorant present, and Duncan's lines in scene 6 about the spur of love that helped home Macbeth (1.6.21–24). The series culminates at the end of the soliloquy that opens scene 7: "I have no spur / To prick the sides of my intent" (listen to the inaudible spur-like pricking in the potential of "in" and "to tent"—to probe with a lancet), "but only / Vaulting ambition, which o'erleaps itself."

To come back to "come," in scene 6—the scene in which Duncan and his party actually do come to Inverness—the obviously pertinent idea of visitation is *also* introduced as an incidental. Banquo talks about "this guest of summer, / The temple-haunting martlet" (1.6.3–4). "Guest" and "haunting" echo, unmarked, two acts later—first in 3.1, the only scene besides this one in which the actual word "guest" occurs, when Macbeth refers to Banquo, the speaker of the archly phrased chatter about birds, as "our chief guest" at the evening's dinner, and then in 3.4 when that chief guest comes to dinner as a ghost.

There are lots and lots more of these patterns. For instance, the substantively unconnected raven that croaks Duncan's entrance and the "morrow" Lady Macbeth says the sun will never see (1.5.59–60) have a link in the popular medieval notion that ravens say *cras*—say the Latin word for "tomorrow." In line 53, between Lady Macbeth's reference to the croaking raven in lines 36 and 37 and the "tomorrow" exchange in lines 58 and 59, is an incidental echo of the traditional *English*-language transcription of a raven's cry: the first syllable of *Caw*dor.[4] And the "raven"/"tomorrow" pair cooperates in a succession of references to ravens, rooks, and crows in *Macbeth* and a succession of gratuitously prominent references to tomorrow.

Moreover, the speech that contains the raven soliloquy is full of words and ideas of service and servanthood that are as thick in the surrounding lines as the elements of the "come"/"stay"/"go" group. The same is true of sounds and ideas that relate to sounds and ideas that do or could pertain to the verb *to do,* the most notable components of the group being the first syllable of Duncan's name—"dunnest smoke of hell" in line 49 here, "high Dunsinane hill" (4.1.93), and the "If it were done" soliloquy (1.7.1–28).

I could go on and on. Unfortunately for all of us, I have already gone on and on.

Suffice it to say that overlapping networks of casual, substantively inconsequential relationship are the reason we value Lady Macbeth's raven speech. Those and other networks explain why we like the play at large. And the presence of comparable networks explains why we like *Twelfth Night* and *Antony and Cleopatra* and *Much Ado about Nothing* and *Pride and Prejudice* and Shaw's *Saint Joan* and the Gettysburg Address and all the other things we like.

I wanted to explain the creation of the earth and what man is that God is mindful of him, but there isn't time. Besides, it could have seemed presumptuous.

---

4. My guess—a pure one that can never be verified—is that it was the accident of the first syllable of "Cawdor" that led the ravens, rooks, and crows in *Macbeth* to nest in Shakespeare's imagination when he read the name in Holinshed. I also suspect that the first syllable of "Duncan"—assisted, perhaps, by "Dunsinane" in Holinshed— might have engendered the play's fixations on darkness and on being done with things.

3

Troubles of a Professional Meter Reader

GEORGE T. WRIGHT

In *Measure for Measure,* when Isabella first enters Angelo's presence her initial timidity is conveyed by the obliqueness of her approach, the politeness of her rhetoric, and the correctness with which her phrases sit down in the pews of her meter:

> There is a vice which most I do abhor,
> And most desire should meet the blow of justice;
> For which I would not plead, but that I must;
> For which I must not plead, but that I am
> At war 'twixt will and will not.
>
> $(2.2.29-33)$[1]

Despite the wordplay, which carries the promise of a more engaging mind than yet appears, the language has little spirit. Angelo is understandably impatient, and at his first sharp rebuff Isabella is ready to give up. Lucio, however, charging her with coldness, keeps her at her task, and gradually her language warms and reveals her intellectual power and subtlety:

> Why, all the souls that *were* were forfeit *once,*
> And He that might the vantage *best* have took

---

1. Unless otherwise noted, all Shakespeare quotations are from *The Riverside Shakespeare,* ed. G. Blakemore Evans et al. (Boston: Houghton Mifflin, 1974).

Found out the *remedy*. How would *you* be
If He, which is the *top* of judgment, should
But judge you as you *are*? O, think on *that*,
And mercy then will *breathe* within your *lips*,
Like *man new made*.

(73–79)

The meter here is not much less regular than before, but Isabella's speeches now pour emphasis on key words in her argument (the ones printed in italics). An actress might prefer to highlight other or additional words, but it seems clear that this speech moves more rapidly than the earlier one; the sentences unfold with greater freedom and suppleness; and the rhetoric, focusing on certain syllables dramatically placed at various points in the lines and in the clauses, conveys Isabella's growing engagement with the turns of her argument. By the time she is ready to indict the arrogance of "man, / Dress'd in a little brief authority" (2.2.116–17), her syntactical and metrical style has been transformed. One might argue that what succeeds in seducing Isabella (and Angelo) is her own sophisticated rhetoric, which signals her deep involvement in a worldly cause. But it is probably enough to claim only that in the course of the scene her manner has changed radically, and that the meter plays an important stylistic role in registering this change.

Shakespeare's prevailing method in the later plays is not to provide a deviant metrical style for his distinctive characters, but to write a standard verse speech for each play and let the characters' utterances vary from it according to their degree of distress, anger, or agitation. Furious as Leontes and his meter become, other characters in *The Winter's Tale* have recourse on occasion to a meter almost as disturbed as his, and when he recovers his sanity, his meter returns to what is normal for the play.

Excitement, too, may be of different sorts. It is not only anger or pleading that inspires metrical variation in a character. Wonder can bring out the trochees in a speechless king:[2]

Pericles. Gíve me | a gash, | pút me | to present pain,
Lest this | great séa | of joys | rushing | upon me
O'er béar | the shores of my mortal | ity,

2. In this passage and some others that follow, only variant feet are marked—those that seem clearly pyrrhic, spondaic, or trochaic. Secondary stresses are marked '.

And drown | me with their sweetness. O, | come hĭthĕr,
Thóu thăt | beget'st | hĭm thăt | did thee beget;
Thóu thăt | wast born at sea, | bŭriĕd | at Tharsus,
And found | at sea again!

(Pericles 5.1.191–97)

Madness may break up the verse alarmingly:

> *Lear.* I pardon that man's life. What was thy cause?
>   Adultery?
>   Thou shalt not die. Die for adultery? No,
>   The wren goes to't, and the small gilded fly
>   Does lecher in my sight.
>   Let copulation thrive; for Gloucester's bastard son
>   Was kinder to his father than my daughters
>   Got 'tween the lawful sheets.
>   To't, luxury, pell-mell, for I lack soldiers.

(King Lear 4.6.109–17)

Characters take their metrical style from the play, but gusts of feeling blow through them, testing and tempering their measures. Of course, Machiavellian personages, early and late, such as Richard III or Iago or Lear's elder daughters, can change their tune according to who it is they want to manipulate. They can wear or doff their masks of friendliness or loyalty. Some earlier characters, too, speak at several levels of emotional intensity, which are reflected in their syntax and verse. But the middle plays go much further in permitting characters to alter their speaking styles radically under the stress of strong feeling or madness. Ophelia gives up pentameter verse altogether, but Hamlet, Lear, and Timon, in moments of distress and crisis, adopt a more turbulent verse style. The increasingly subtle language produces the illusion that the anger or anxiety characters feel is mirrored in their troubled meters, that altering measures are signs of altering feeling. All the main characters in *Hamlet* use different styles at different moments, in keeping with their emotional arousal or darker purposes. Hamlet's notably ambiguous character is the result, not the cause, of his speaking so differently on different occasions.

This is one respect in which Shakespeare must have altered his verse in response to something he noticed going on in life—in this case, the surprisingly various ways of talking that any articulate person may develop under the pressure of circumstances. Other changes in his dramatic verse may have come about in response to other observations. Despite our sense of Shakespeare's language as typically elevated, despite the conviction of millions of undergraduates that it is hopelessly unlike normal speech, this is a playwright unusually alert to the way people talk. They use more or less the same English (in life or in a play); their social position may limit or fix their range of idiom, but within each class there is available to talented speakers a wide range of expressive options, to be exercised on a great variety of speaking occasions. As I have suggested elsewhere, the short scenes in *Antony and Cleopatra* that begin and end in midconversation imply a Shakespeare who has noticed how much we hear of the fragmentary conversation of others—as we move beside them in the streets, in pubs, or in the passages of great houses, as they pass in and out of our hearing.[3] We still have much to learn about other ways in which the verse reflects this playwright's alert observation of how people speak—and change their speech as circumstances, occasions, and settings keep changing.

But how marginal this subject is, in the double sense that most scholars, actors, readers, and critics pay little attention to it, and that it occupies a contested territory between various overlapping disputants: between linguistic and literary metrists, between literary analysis and theatrical performance, between those who read poetry mainly as measured speech and those who read it principally as spoken music, between the impulse to emphasize a poet's metrical debts to earlier texts and the impulse to read poems and their meters as largely autonomous achievements of proud, freestanding authors. In studying the motions of verse, is one studying language or art, text or voice, author or era? Is metrics a "human science" or a rhetorical and dramatic resource of the artist?

Such oppositions, seldom so cantankerously plotted, are still to be sniffed in the air that metrists breathe, but they do not exactly check off against those that are strongly present in the larger world of contemporary literary study. There is nothing that could be called feminist metrics; deconstructive metrical analysis is at best a mischievous offshoot of formalist poetics; and metrical theory that has a Marxist tinge—that reads iambic pentameter as bourgeois-capitalist in origin and recommends accentual poetry or free verse as ideologically prefer-

---

3. George T. Wright, *Shakespeare's Metrical Art* (Berkeley: University of California Press, 1988), pp. 137–38; hereinafter referred to as *SMA*.

able—seems hardly serious. Metrics is too technical a subject to respond with enthusiasm to political or otherwise fashionable critical creeds, though a metrist's choice of conceptual frameworks may indeed reflect a preference that is ultimately ideological and political. Or it may derive from training in a mixture of artistic or academic traditions that help to compose Western thought and art.

The personal backgrounds of metrists are probably as confusing and miscellaneous as their intellectual positions. Besides being British or American, Russian or French, they start from different pleasures and dispositions: from an interest in language or linguistics, from love of the theater, from knowledge of music, from writing or reading poetry (or even editing Shakespeare) and being puzzled or awed by a poet's skill in managing rhythms.

My own metrical interest has its source in many of these first affections: early singing and word games in a musical and verbal family, high school recitations and "oratorical" contests, boys' choirs and summer camp Gilbert and Sullivan productions, my own verse writing, and Renaissance and baroque religious music which I sang for years in Columbia University's St. Paul's Chapel choir.

In my time the choir at Columbia sang at services five weekdays at noon and on Sunday morning, a tour of duty that required three lengthy rehearsals each week. In addition, our intense enjoyment of the music we sang (Vittoria, Josquin Desprez, Palestrina, Byrd, Bach, and other expressive composers) led many of us not only to go caroling at Christmas but all through the year to sing a cappella on street corners up and down Broadway, on Riverside Drive, on subway platforms, and at parties in our homes, where we often essayed less familiar music from madrigals to oratorios. Such forays, in which feelings of love mixed uncertainly with diffuse religious (or antireligious) fervor helped train me in the double art of hearing and helping to charge with my own voice those musical works in which Renaissance artists registered the sensuous and evocative powers of words embedded in tones.

But our beginnings never know our ends. Years later, furnished with a literature Ph.D., I began to offer a course in English prosody. My "field" was modern poetry, and the puzzle most on my mind was free verse. But "free" from what? Where had it come from? Had it somehow grown out of earlier metrical verse? Why had our poets abandoned that rich old system of poetic sound for what seemed to me then (probably to the detriment of the poetry I was trying to write myself) an inferior, less emphatic, less enchanting verse? But what exactly *was* that older system? How had it worked? Why had it weakened? These questions, worried in and out of class, kept leading me back to Renaissance verse, to that decasyllabic line that had taken root so vigorously in the sixteenth century and shown such strength and resilience that poets for centuries continued to hear it (and fear it) as the great central meter of the language. What had transpired in that earlier English age between the language and the verse line (for in that interplay surely lay the secret) to produce such a wondrous technical instrument just in time for the powerful writers who came along then? And could even they have written so well without it?

Over time I worked out theories of my own and found few critics approaching the subject from a viewpoint much like mine. The metrical theory receiving most attention in the late 1960s was the dubious one (so it seemed to me from the beginning) of generative metrics, a system developed mainly by MIT linguists who showed little sensitivity to English verse but were trying to formulate sets of rules for writing it which they derived (by false analogical procedures, I suspected) from Noam Chomsky's ideas about the acquisition of language by children.[4] One book—John Thompson's *Founding of English Metre*[5]—talked sensibly about how poets from Wyatt to Sidney had married verse and speech. But Thompson stopped short of the culminating achievements of Shakespeare, Donne, Jonson, and Herbert, and he also relied on linguistic theories which, in my view, were still saddling metrics with assumptions, terms, and emphases that impeded analysis more than they facilitated it.

From Thompson I roved back to earlier studies of English meter and saw what he was up against in venturing into this territory at all. Scholars had treated meter as language, as music, as theater, as poetry, and even as literary history. When systematic metrical study of Shakespeare's plays began more than a century ago, it was undertaken largely to assist in resolving questions of chronology and authorship. The appreciation of rhythmic effects in lines or speeches, by canny critics such as George Saintsbury, was more enthusiastic or impressionistic than analytical. New Critics who studied poetic technique

---

4. See, for example, Morris Halle and Samuel J. Keyser, "Chaucer and the Study of Prosody," *College English* 28 (1966): 187–219; and Paul Kiparsky, "Stress, Syntax, and Meter," *Language* 51 (1975): 576–616.

5. John Thompson, *The Founding of English Metre* (New York: Columbia University Press, 1961).

challenged both impressionistic vagueness and aesthetically neutral scholarly exhaustiveness, but they usually concentrated on single lines or short passages, preferring to cite exemplary prosodic models rather than explore an author or a text with heroic thoroughness. Still, Yvor Winters produced some sensitive, if cranky, essays on metrical verse; Arnold Stein opened up some of Donne's accentual mysteries; Milton's rigidities and licenses were explored by Robert Bridges, S. Ernest Sprott, Edward Weismiller, and others; and W. K. Wimsatt wrote with unfailing intelligence about metrical principles.[6] But Shakespeare's work enjoyed no extended metrical analysis by modern scholars until recently, and the interest of strong researchers such as Marina Tarlinskaja and Henri Suhamy has been more linguistic than literary.[7]

From the beginning of the twentieth century, linguists have developed their own methods for analyzing the data, some of them very tellingly (see especially Otto Jespersen and Roman Jakobson),[8] but they have tended to break up into schools and to offer successive generations of critics incompatible or unpalatable paradigms for the analysis of speech and meter: structural linguistics, generative grammar, and intonational theory, among others. And with their narrowing focus on technical questions of stress placement, linguists have scanted the skill and artistry of poets. As a rule, they have seemed slow to understand that in some expressive poetic lines our metrical expectations often overbear to some extent the speech rhythms we might elect for the same words in a prose setting, and are overborne in turn by speech rhythms we cannot suppress. After Jespersen, even linguists sensitive to the rhythms of spoken English have rarely been attuned to verse rhythms. The New Critics' readings could be arbi-

6. See, e.g., Yvor Winters, "The Audible Reading of Poetry," in *The Function of Criticism: Problems and Exercises* (Denver: Alan Swallow, 1957), pp. 79–100; Arnold Stein, "Donne's Prosody," *PMLA* 59 (1944): 373–97; Robert Bridges, *Milton's Prosody* (Oxford: Oxford University Press, 1921); S. Ernest Sprott, *Milton's Art of Prosody* (Oxford: Basil Blackwell, 1953); Edward R. Weismiller, "The 'Dry' and 'Rugged' Verse," in *The Lyric and Dramatic Milton,* ed. Joseph H. Summers (New York: Columbia University Press, 1965), pp. 115–52; and W. K. Wimsatt, Jr., and Monroe Beardsley, "The Concept of Meter: An Exercise in Abstraction," *PMLA* 74 (1959): 585–98. For other work by these writers, see the bibliography in *SMA.*

7. Marina Tarlinskaja, *Shakespeare's Verse: Iambic Pentameter and the Poet's Idiosyncrasies* (New York: Peter Lang, 1987); Henri Suhamy, *Le vers de Shakespeare* (Paris: Didier-Erudition, 1984).

8. Otto Jespersen, "Notes on Metre," in *Linguistica: Selected Papers* (Copenhagen: Levin and Munksgaard, 1933), pp. 249–72; Roman Jakobson and Linda Waugh, *The Sound Shape of Language* (Bloomington: Indiana University Press, 1979).

trary, but the best of them listened to verse much better than linguists have.

My own aims have been practical and pedagogical, not philosophical or scientific. I want to entice students, readers, critics, and actors to follow and enjoy the technical artistry of poets. My purpose is not to study metrical patterning as a theoretical aspect of language but to understand how a poet uses his or her palette or keyboard for significant effects. My subject is aesthetic, formal, rhetorical, dramatic—"applied prosody," as the late O. B. Hardison reasonably called it,[9] and I can't disown the phrase, though it makes my precious discernments sound like a sort of prosodic engineering.

This distinction between what I try to do and what more linguistically oriented metrical scholars are about was not clear to me when I started, but little by little the terrain I had stumbled into became familiar ground. Here and there within its borders appeared a quaint and curious volume of forgotten lore—such as Ants Oras's admirable technical study, complete with fascinating graphs and charts, of "pause patterns" in Renaissance verse.[10] But the more I read, the clearer it became that I had been learning some things about the expressive uses of meter that weren't turning up in the literature on the subject, partly because New Critical perceptions of metrical artistry were usually not grounded in a thorough understanding of historical metrical practice, as I hoped mine would be. My original intention was to survey all English poetry and write a brief, technical, aesthetic history of its iambic pentameter; but this proved unworkable, and I narrowed my subject to Renaissance verse, interpreting "Renaissance" generously to include every major poet from Chaucer to Milton. The first version of my book tried to cover them all in some detail, but since what I chiefly had to say concerned Shakespeare most of all (a long essay on Wyatt having appeared separately),[11] I cut two hundred pages, including a lengthy essay on Donne's metrics, in order to focus on the poet whose intricate system of metrical variation and deviation, it seemed to me, had never been adequately set forth.

Among other things, I learned that the study of meter is laborious;

9. O. B. Hardison, Jr., *Prosody and Purpose in the English Renaissance* (Baltimore: Johns Hopkins University Press, 1989), p. xiv.

10. Ants Oras, *Pause Patterns in Elizabethan and Jacobean Drama: An Experiment in Prosody* (Gainesville: University of Florida Press, 1960).

11. George T. Wright, "Wyatt's Decasyllabic Line," *Studies in Philology* 82 (1985): 129–56.

it involves the reading of a whole library of theory and commentary as well as of masses of English poems and verse plays; and it changes one's views and one's life. In the course of writing on meter, my ideas about the proprieties of metrical analysis, my scruples about proper procedures, and my doubts about the methods of other critics (and even my own) have crystallized considerably. When I looked back recently at early notes for my book on Shakespeare's meter, I marveled at the naïveté that gleamed through early stages of this grandiose enterprise. I had started more or less as a formalistic critic, but in time I learned to modulate into a newer sort, not quite a poststructuralist (though I have come to see meter as often undermining and unsettling the words it rides and drives), yet I still remained partly the dogged delver for data that older historical scholars had often been. Such delving is justified (to the worker) by two enormous rewards: the intense, partly musical pleasures of the journey, and the flashes of understanding that keep lighting up a crooked and troubled road.

THE TROUBLE WITH LINGUISTS

Most scholars understand the meter of a poem or passage to designate its basic—that is, its recurrent—accentual, syllabic, or quantitative pattern. That definition seems acceptable to me, so long as we understand that the pattern is either a sounded pattern or one that is silently "heard," not one that is merely represented graphically on a page, void of sound or virtual sound. Still, in practice I use the term to mean not only (1) the paradigmatic pattern but also (2) the set of variations from it that can be found in the poem or passage in question.[12] And implicit for me in this looser definition is (3) the range of expressive functions served by this complex of sounded pattern and variations. To study such a system—of paradigm, departures, and purposes—one has to have some feeling for (and technical understanding of) the style with which sentences and arguments unfold in English and rhetorical

---

12. Latin metrists, after all, do this, too. The difference is that in English the number of (stress) variations that lines may exhibit while still belonging to a given iambic meter is far larger. Because I include acceptable variations in my definition of a meter, I understand individual lines not as having started from the paradigmatic base and having then been changed (as all talk of substitution, promotion, and similar terms implies), but as realizing in their different ways the general form, as different members of a species all realize its paradigmatic form in their individual ways.

schemes and tropes (such as irony, metaphor, and all the figured ar-
rangements of language that Renaissance poets and audiences exulted
in) affect the intonation of lines and sentences. But because the subject
is not just linguistic but aesthetic as well, a knowledge of linguistics
and of rhetorical pattterning is not sufficient.

One queerness of metrical study is that linguists who interest themselves in it care little, as a rule, about how poems sound. What they
care about is the extent to which, in a given poet's work, the stress
patterns of speech phrases correspond to the stress patterns of metrical
lines. That sounds like sound, but it isn't—or it leaves out much that
is. The interest is in *whether* the stresses in a phrase conform to the
stresses in a line, not in *how* they do or don't, not in the style or force
or flair with which they fit or fail to fit. Many linguists find themselves
at a loss to understand why literary metrists such as myself maintain
that the metrical technique of poets consists less in the extent to which
they put stressable syllables in stressed positions and minor ones in
unstressed positions (the deviations from norms submitting to strenu-
ous tabulation and empirical generalization) than in the artistry with
which poets interweave the metrical pattern and the linear and syntactical schemes to provide another dimension of emphasis to the sheer
prose sense of phrases and sentences. Typically, the pleasure of the
metrical text resides in the perception of fluid shifts in the variation
schemes forced on the meter by natural phrasing, usually over a passage of several lines.

> Thus was | Ĭ, sleep|ing, by | ă bro|ther's hand,
> Of Life, | of Crown, | and Queen | at once | dispatch'd;
> Cut off | even in | the Blos|soms of | my Sin,
> Unhous|l'ed, dis|appoint|ed, un|anel'd,
> No reck|oning made, | but sent | to my | account
> With all | my im|perfec|tions on | my head;
> Oh hor|rible, | Oh hor|rible, | most horrible
>
> (*Hamlet* 1.5.74–80)[13]

Scansion marks recognize some of the accentual variety in feet and
lines, but the phrasal segmentation, too—only partly registered by
punctuation—is different in every line and often in the syntactical con-

13. The wording and punctuation are from *The First Folio of Shakespeare,* prepared
by Charlton Hinman (New York: Norton, 1968); the spelling is that of *The Riverside
Shakespeare.*

nection between one line and the next. Lines can also give pleasure by exhibiting an unexpected congruence between metrical pattern and authentically speechlike phrasing: "Methought I was enamor'd of an ass" (*A Midsummer Night's Dream* 4.1.77), or "I think it was to see my mother's wedding" (*Hamlet* 1.2.178), or by showing mildly or wildly unexpected disparities between them:

> (As Ĭ | foretóld | yŏu) wēre | all spí|rĭts and . . .
> (*The Tempest* 4.1.149)

> Rȋng thĕ | alárum-bell! | Múrthĕr | and treason!
> Banqŭo | and Donalbain! | Málcŏlm, | awake!
> (*Macbeth* 2.3.74–75)

Sometimes we enjoy the meter's surprising but satisfying direction of emphasis toward what are usually minor syllables in English and away from major ones:

> Ŏn thís | sìde mý | hànd and | ŏn thát | sìde yóurs . . .
> (*Richard II* 4.1.83)

There seem to be, in Renaissance verse, no limits to the ingenuity and inventiveness with which poets—Shakespeare is by no means alone in this—use the accentual patterns of speech and verse to modify each other and compose an authentic verse speech.

THE TROUBLE WITH TIMERS

If meter's connection with language can be overstated, so can its connection with music. Though we speak of the musical qualities of verse, and though meter is a musical as well as a poetic term, it does not really function in poetry as it does in music. This is especially true of iambic pentameter, which scholars agree in calling an unusually speechlike meter. As with free verse, there may be moments when musical analogies can clarify effects, but neither of these verse modes, free or blank, is subject to the strict time counting that is essential to most music. And if the time requirements are more relaxed, so are the pitch and duration—and even the accent—requirements. Actors or readers have far more discretion in producing and spacing the words than singers ever have. Furthermore, when words are set to music, they almost always forfeit their speech rhythm, but much of the art of the skillful poet, especially in iambic pentameter, and most of all in the best Renaissance verse drama, consists in negotiating the interplay between natural speech rhythms and a minimal metrical observance of pattern. It is clear that different metrists may interest themselves in different sides of this complex subject, but for me its soul is this interplay: how the elements of metrical pattern display themselves in a poet's or playwright's work, and how the strong rhythmic currents of spoken English submit to and strain that pattern.

THE TROUBLE WITH ACTORS

If linguists tend not to listen to meter but to decide by abstract considerations which syllables in a sentence merit stress, people in the theater often distribute stress in obedience to their sense of prose sentences and let the meter shift for itself. In recent decades, however, some directors (notably John Barton)[14] have begun to insist that one key to the sense of Shakespearean utterances can be found in the meter. But even well-intentioned actors can hardly follow the metrical clues without a better feel than most of them have for the variant and deviant lines that Shakespeare uses. My own work has been done partly in the hope of helping actors to master Shakespeare's complex system of norm and variation and use their richly timbred voices to make the most of the dramatic opportunities offered by that system's rich linear designs.

Some time ago, after a lecture, I was asked how a knowledge of Shakespeare's complex metrical system can help an actor find more effective ways to speak verse lines on the stage. I gave then a not very helpful answer, but was spurred to compose this practical advice: In preparing a speech, study the sentence and study the metrical line, and work out a way of speaking the words that is consistent with the stress requirements of both, that seems to spring from both, and that fits with your whole reading of the character and the dramatic situation. Then take advantage of your own voice and its special powers of timbre, volume, pitch, and pace to register nuance and expression.

But a professional meter reader has always to keep in mind that we

14. See John Barton, *Playing Shakespeare* (London: Methuen, 1984).

can hear lines silently, too, though not all readers do. When I read poetry, I hear it in my head, the successive pulses tapping out the meter in my skull (or so it seems). I depart from this way of reading verse (and much prose) only when skimming, yet even then my insuppressible internal scanner may pick out lines here and there to "listen to." I read most lines metrically, without scanning or formulating their meter in prosodic terms, but I know instantly (and may look more closely to see why) when a line is odd or deviant.

If I "hear" poetry as I read it soundlessly, then the sound I hear from actors in the theater I "read" as falling into lines. Normally this just happens: for Shakespeare's earlier plays, it happens without effort because of the frequent rhymes and the high incidence of endstopped verse; in later plays, where the verse is more often blank and enjambed and the lineation much more difficult to detect by ear, listening to the meter exacts a higher cost. One doesn't want to be distracted from the stage action by compulsive searching for the frequently submerging verse (although its problematic character mirrors the problematic later themes and plots). Still, even there I hear the surfacing verse whenever I can, again without analyzing but enjoying the flow of the syllables, the pulsing speechscape, sentences plunging forward on the currents of time and feeling which usually flow unobserved but are here marked and measured into paradoxically invisible lines by more or less equal sets of more or less periodic accents—and are thereby intensified, given additional weight and force, made more expressive.

Sometimes an actor's voice will bring out special rhythmic effects that silent readers may not have noticed. Yet all too often, in my experience, particularly of American performances, the rhythm of lines is abused, sense and emphasis are blurred, and the tune of a speech is distorted by an actor's or director's greater concern with making some visual or doctrinal point. No matter that the meter *might* serve a production's other purposes if the director and actor could take advantage of it. Their audiences rarely expect them to do so. On the British stage, actors are often uncomfortable with high-sounding verse rhetoric and work to flatten its tunes. In the American theater, metrical verse itself is suspect and may be concealed by those who speak it, as if it were a shameful relic of a distant age, like anti-Semitism, imperialism, melodrama, or patriarchal attitudes toward women. Indeed, some critics connect it with one or more of these ensigns of infamy.

The unhappy truth is that most American listeners to plays are deaf to metrical verse. It is poorly read to us by the parents or teachers or actors from whom we first hear it. We rarely find chances to practice reading it ourselves. Few American theater companies relish the verse; actors, like teachers, are more deeply stirred by other elements in Shakespeare's dramaturgy than by the movement, the sweep, the strength, the drama of the verse. Most of them have come late to the speaking of verse, and they have not really taken to it. They make adjustments and compromises; they deal with it as they can.[15] But they have not grown up with it, it is foreign to them, and this shows in their manner of evading or slurring the pulses, of fouling the metrical line.

In part the problem is that the blank or rhymed iambic pentameter that Shakespeare wrote most often is indeed a foreign verse, and most of the strongest American poets of our time have found it uncongenial—of our language but not of our speech. They have not heard in the old British line a suitable vehicle for the cadences of American talk. Some poets have successfully practiced a looser form of iambic verse, and a group of New Formalists have achieved some prominence, but for much of the century it has seemed that if you write iambs instead of the now canonical free verse, your work will be either derivative or comic.

Under these conditions, it isn't easy for an American reader or actor to form the habit of listening to Shakespeare's metrical verse as verse, of hearing how the meter makes or reinforces rhetorical emphases, deepens or shifts a mood or tone, powers an emotional sentence or period, and intensifies not only the speech but the action.[16] Not that British readers acquire these skills with ease, but they do have a better chance: the rhythms are native rhythms; their voices and intonational systems are closer in wavelength to those of Shakespeare's players and watchers; and they hear more often (not always, of course)—in the theater or on the BBC—actors and actresses who do indeed know

15. As Marlon Brando did in the film of *Julius Caesar,* trying to make up for a lifetime of metrical innocence by seeking the advice of an old hand (or voice), John Gielgud.

16. What we have lost is not merely the ability to hear verse as verse but the ability to hear it as rhetoric, just as we have lost our ear for the more recondite figures and schemes of the classical repertoire. The repetitions of meter are more closely connected to those of traditional figures than we usually recognize, even when we discuss differences between Renaissance prose and verse. I don't quite suggest that prose is a form of verse, but when we speak of Renaissance writing the idea is less crazy than we might think.

how to hold a metrical current and clinch a metrical emphasis in a line, a passage, or a scene.

THE TROUBLE WITH READERS

To some extent, I confess, this situation has driven me back to private and silent reading or to making a point of speaking the verse in the classroom, which I do rarely just for the sake of the verse but rather as an aid to analysis of motive or action. I try to give the speeches the animation, spirit, and semantic emphasis appropriate to the speaker's situation and emotion, avoiding two extremes: excessive excitement and lifeless mouthing of the words. But even when a line or a phrase of some length is repeated frequently in a class discussion, it should be cited, by student or teacher, in a voice that at least intimates its dramatic feeling. To be sure, there are instances—Lear's "Howl's" and "Never's"—which can hardly, in a classroom, be given their full force without absurdity. But nothing is deadlier to an understanding of metrical verse, more academic in the worst sense, than the pusillanimous speaking of a strong Shakespearean line. To treat an expressive line as mere idea, mere content, mere image, is to treat poetry not simply as if it were prose (because the principle applies as well to expressive prose), but as if it were fossilized speech, a piece of dead language that had broken off and crumbled on the tongue. For a teacher to do this encourages the student to do the same, to lose all sense of the distinction and of the special powers of poetry.

In our own speech we can say with genuine feeling, "I don't *want* you to do that" or "*Love!* his affections do not *that* way tend." But, faced with such words in print (and in class or on a public platform), readers regularly tone down the feeling and mitigate the italics, as poets often do nowadays in reading their poems, apparently as part of a half-century-long reaction against Victorian and modernist over-statement. It's as if they wouldn't be caught dead being eloquent—and they won't be. But one result is a serious weakening of the union between speech feeling and metrical verse that is close to the heart of traditional English poetry. The New Critics themselves, by empha-sizing poetry as a means of providing structures of cerebral experience (of tension, paradox, imagery, and textual decoding), may have helped to compromise the immediacy of expressive speech as a crucial element in poetry. And students have been further encouraged to think

English poetry a meager and precious (and silent, if not absent) affair by the notorious, even ghostly, abstraction of contemporary theoretical criticism and its chronic remoteness from texts and performances.

Ultimately, in its fullest embodiment, the language of poetic drama is sounded and needs to be heard. For the verse, as for the dramatic action, the text is not the work of art. To see the text arranged in lines is, for modern readers as for Shakespeare's company of actors, a covenience only, although, to be sure, the silent text silently audited still offers an eloquent mute image of spoken words actually heard. It remains for the reader, the actor, the teacher, the scholar, over and over again—like Pygmalion on Cyprus—to bring that mute image to life.[17]

THE TROUBLE WITH THEORISTS

> When I see verses bend from left to right,
> I have to think some bard's been swinging them.

Perhaps the severest problem for a metrist of my stripe is to resist claiming too much for the role of meter in constructing the meaning of texts. In my book on Shakespeare's meter, I had occasion to glance at Antony Easthope's suggestion that iambic pentameter can be identified with "bourgeois liberal capitalism" and accentual meters with collective political economies.[18] This seems to me, on the face of it, preposterous—another moralistic attempt to see every feature of every past age as fatally implicated in its shame, to which it is the mission of the correcting critic to hold our guilty muzzle. But I see less difficulty in proposing that there is some structural similarity between the way even a loose meter such as English iambic constrains natural English speech rhythms and the Renaissance view of how individual heroic aspiration must yield to temporal and divine authority and ultimately succumb to a universal mortality (*SMA*, p. 260). Such suggestions must be made very tentatively because they stretch the connections between verse speech and other social institutions and be-

17. Cf. J. Hillis Miller's contention, in *Versions of Pygmalion* (Cambridge: Harvard University Press, 1990), that Pygmalion can serve as a figure for the act of reading, in which we bring the suggestions of the printed page to life.

18. Antony Easthope, *Poetry as Discourse* (London: Methuen, 1983). See *SMA*, p. 321, n. 8.

liefs quite far; but, if proposed with tact, they can forge a link between my old aestheticism and some new historicism.

On a smaller scale, one has to be wary of attributing determinate meanings to specific metrical practices. It seems reasonable to draw inferences about which devices of sound or form Renaissance poets and attentive listeners found appropriate to certain subjects or dramatic behavior. But one never claims that pyrrhic variations (or trochaic or spondaic) always carry an identical content. Ironically enough, before my book was published, one critic took Easthope and me to task for allegedly having read specific meanings into literary devices: Easthope for that view of iambic pentameter I had already deplored, and myself for an earlier article on Shakespeare's use of the rhetorical figure hendiadys.[19] I had thought my analysis avoided the flaw this critic now found in it and suggested only that the evident meanings in a large number of passages described a range of meanings which after a while began to be recognizable as a range and could be used as a presumptive (and only a presumptive) instrument in the interpretation of others. That is, once you establish a range of effects in a good number of appearances of a literary or metrical device, you have the right to presume that further instances encountered in the same author's work will probably convey meanings within that range, but you recognize that such a range of meanings is not determined: there is always a chance that at the next occurrence of the device the meanings may fall outside the author's usual practice and either extend the theorized range or prompt a changed description.

On this view, I have felt justified in suggesting, for example, that Shakespeare's practice in writing variant lines of several sorts is not entirely mysterious, but that some kinds of aberrant lines—short or long or with missing or extra syllables—have effects that fall into perceptible patterns. You don't want to pursue such claims too far, or to imply that "often" means "always," but if patterns appear to be purposeful, you want to hear them.

Shakespeare's management of his resources results in departures from the norm (or realizations of it that seem notable in some way— for their energy or timidity, for their muted or commanding tone, for their grace under pressure) which fit with the meanings or feelings of the passage. But what is this "fit"? It certainly appears that the poets themselves understood some Elizabethan departures from metrical

19. Ellen Spolsky, "The Limits of Literal Meaning," *New Literary History* 19 (1988): 419–40; George T. Wright, "Hendiadys and *Hamlet*," *PMLA* 96 (1981): 168–93.

regularity as part of a code of metrical conventions which was never extensively formulated. Once we catch on to the system and are set to identify new designs within it, it begins to train us to accept some variations as intensifying, reinforcing, or qualifying semantic or dramatic meanings, just as musical dynamics does—getting louder or softer or faster for expressive purposes, alterations which listeners accept as they internalize the code. Shakespeare's metrical practice operated as a system of conventions, of understandings (by poets, actors, and initiates in the audience) about the relations of rhythmic sounds, stage action, and concepts which governed their perceptions of the world. Editors, I take it, try to adopt conventions of text presentation that will give alert readers every chance to read these conventions accurately.

THE TROUBLE WITH EDITORS

The terms I use in metrical analysis are inevitably different from those employed by editors in explaining their editorial procedures and the impact metrical considerations have on their textual decisions. Editors usually want to make sure that the lines they provide for us are, on the whole, the lines that Shakespeare wrote for his actors, and they have to decide whether and where the lines of Folio and Quarto need emending. So long as a line meets the expected requirements, they are understandably not much concerned with expressive motions within lines or passages. It is important to me, however, that their commendable wish to present an authoritative text not lead them needlessly to "regularize" aberrant lines that fall within Shakespeare's acceptable range of variation. Not all of these will have clear expressive force, but some will, and the ideal text, from my point of view, is one that offers opportunities for forceful performance that are consistent both with our textual sources and with Shakespeare's common metrical practice.[20]

THE TROUBLE WITH METER READERS

When critics analyze meter, they have to adopt some system of graphic notation that makes clear to readers what goes on in Shakespeare's

20. I have seen an unpublished early version of an essay by Gary Taylor, titled "Metrifying Shakespeare," which shows an admirable grasp both of Shakespeare's

verse. One point at issue is whether analysis of a line's meter should
use the old Latin measures which represented what took place in a
quantitative meter and were later adapted to describe an accentual-
syllabic system like Shakespeare's. Analyzing metrical lines into feet
is a curiously artificial custom, but it is no more so than the printing
of plays or libretti. Neither the metrical foot nor the visible text has
any audible reality. This circumstance has made many metrists uneasy
about conventional foot-bound analysis. After all, a line is visible on
the printed page, but a foot is not. Isn't it, therefore, a fiction? Yes, of
course it is. But onstage, isn't the line a fiction, too? When I watch
Hamlet being performed, I never see a single line of verse. We hear, in
this play about a ghost, only the ghosts of lines. When I listen in the
theater to a metrical "line," a string of syllables heard and measured
by the ear, I may not hear the feet one by one (except in unusual lines,
such as "Will praise a hand, a foot, a face, an eye, / A gait, a state, a
brow, a breast, a waist, / A leg, a limb—" [*Love's Labor's Lost* 4.3.182–
84]), but as a passage continues (if the actors speak it well), I will normally have a sense of five somewhat similar stress units recurring to
my ear again and again—the tramping of ghostly feet, perhaps, and
sometimes as difficult to detect as the position of galloping horses'
feet before photography stilled them. When I look more closely at the
words, I can see, in retrospect at least, that what I have heard is a kind
of rippling current made up repeatedly, though with variations, of a
relatively unstressed syllable followed by a stronger one. The foot,
understood in this way, is no more a fiction than the bar in a musical
score, which during a performance no one in the audience sees or hears
or leans on. It is prudent, in a classroom, to make clear the provisional
and heuristic nature of this "foot," but the term and what it stands for
are still defensible.

Both foot and play text are comparable to a musical score. Although sophisticated musicians claim to be able to hear a musical work
from the score alone, no blare from the page will ever pain their ears.
Both the text we read and the foot we distinguish are guides to performance; and, as the score may give silent pleasure to the trained
reader but cannot be fully heard until its music is carried by instruments, so neither the foot nor the dramatic text is fully realized until

---

metrical options and of the principles that ought to guide an editor's treatment of the
metrical evidence.

it is embodied in a voice or voices uttering speechlike English sentences that somehow describe metrical designs.

A difficulty with metrical analysis, with scansion in particular, is its seeming rigidity. When you scan a line, you seem to be saying, "Here is the way it must be read," when you usually mean only, "here is one likely reading." In class you sometimes must add, "There are certain ways it cannot be read": for example, miscounting the number of syllables, or not realizing which syllable of a disyllabic word conventionally receives stress in the scanner's own English—frequent beginners' mistakes, and they are mistakes, not just unpersuasive readings. What makes the subject more difficult to *write* about is that you cannot use your voice to exhibit a line. The delicate negotiation between stresses that goes on in Renaissance poetry can be conveyed in print only by, first, accurate notation (italics or scansion marks that offer at best a rough image of what we hear); and, second, lucid explanatory prose. What I try to do in the written metrical analysis of a passage is to make a reader or actor aware of the kinds of considerations that might guide our listening or speaking, not to close off options but to open up additional ones, to let the language move and engage as actively as—in our common personifying metaphor—it appears to have wanted to do.

The metier of the metrist (of *my* kind, at least) is to keep asking questions about poetry, in text or performance, that expose its stylish motions and the human issues they bring into play. I imagine all the elements of dramatic poetry (visible action, verse, characters) as held in a moving suspension before and within the enchanted reader or audience. If we readily submit to the theatrical illusion that the persons onstage are deeply involved in the world the play presents, we can also assent to the parallel illusion that the verse has a life of its own. Along with the stage action, it constructs the characters and action as it goes along, making its nuanced adjustments to suit (and keep inventing) the personages it speaks through. Even in a drama that has moved far from the highly stylized mask technique of the Greek theater or the Renaissance use of allegorical identities, Shakespearean dramatis personae are indeed masks through which the lines and speeches emerge.

So it is the verse that alters, not the character who selects a style or a meter (see *SMA*, pp. 254–56). The text changes metrical modes (or shifts to prose) as a landscape changes, not whimsically but in response to pressures: the winds of feeling, volcanic violence, the warming and cooling of passion as weathers strike, confront, and dissolve. The play needs to shift as it does in order to present the tumult and harmony it is after, not to accommodate the personal styles of characters. Rather, the poetic drama *uses* Isabella or Hamlet or Leontes, as music—a Beethoven symphony, say—uses the voices of the orchestra. They are instrumental to their formal cause, which words such as *work* and *play* conceptualize better than *text*. But poetry's medium is words, and what poetry of this strength and complexity provides is an aggrandized speech, the language we utter raised to a higher power, made to express more than we thought it could, to give form and heightened feeling to visions, images, revels that could not be realized, and ended, without it.

Is this bourgeois, regressive, patriarchal? Does it make too much of the words? Does it tempt us to forget the issues in favor of the audited design? Not really. But it does participate in that achievement of oral culture, or of traditional oral elements that survive in a literate culture, of making us feel that the words themselves sacralize something, keep for us some ghostly, culturally meaningful utterance that is sure to return to life if only our actors, our voices, can speak it.

Part Two

Reading Reflexively

4

Hydra and Rhizome

HARRY BERGER, JR.

The roots from which this essay on the Henriad grows are tangled
together in the plot containing the following seeds of wisdom, anxiety, and fantasy:

> A rhizome as subterranean stem is absolutely different from roots and
> radicles. Bulbs and tubers are rhizomes. . . . Even some animals are, in
> their pack form. . . . The rhizome includes the best and the worst: po-
> tato and couchgrass, or the weed. Animal and plant, couchgrass is crab-
> grass.
> —Gilles Deleuze and Felix Guattari
> *A Thousand Plateaus: Capitalism and Schizophrenia*

> hydra[2] . . . A multifarious source of destruction that cannot be eradi-
> cated by a single attempt.
> Hydra[1] . . . A many-headed monster . . . growing back two heads for
> each one cut off.
> —*American Heritage Dictionary*

> Hydra . . . A genus of Hydrozoa . . . [whose] name was given it by
> Linnaeus (1756), in allusion to the fact that cutting it in pieces only
> multiplies its numbers.
> —*Oxford English Dictionary*

> The camomile, the more it is trodden on the faster it grows.
> —Sir John Falstaff

Hand-pulling may be a perfectly good way of removing some weeds, but this isn't true of crabgrass if it's an established growth—hand-pulling actually pulls buried crabgrass seed into sprouting position.

"Sunset" Introduction to Basic Gardening

Our trip through this imaginary garden begins with the irruption of the most evolved of its monsters in the text of the *Henry IV* plays.

THE HYDRA

"And yet new *Hydraes* lo, new heades appeare / T'afflict that peace reputed then so sure": so writes Samuel Daniel in the third of his *First Foure Bookes of the Civile Wars*. The editor of the New Arden *1 Henry IV* notes in his comment on Henry's opening speech that "the irony of Henry's deluded hopes is present" in Daniel's image.[1] "Head" in various senses crops up all over the text of the play, but the Hydra itself does not appear until act 5, scene 4, after the raging Douglas has killed two of Henry's decoys at Shrewsbury ("The king hath many marching in his coats") and confronted what he takes to be a third:

> *Douglas.* Another king. They grow like Hydra's heads:
> I am the Douglas, fatal to all those
> That wear those colors on them. What art thou
> That counterfeit'st the person of a king?
> *King.* The King himself, who, Douglas, grieves at heart
> So many of his shadows thou hast met,
> And not the very King. . . .
> *Douglas.* I fear thou art another counterfeit,
> And yet, in faith, thou bearest thee like a king.
>
> (24–35)

Daniel's "heades" are rebellious factions and their armies, whereas Douglas's are kings, but Henry's tainted succession jeopardizes the distinction, and Douglas's language makes the most of the uncertainty. In the readings that follow I try to connect the generation of Hydra heads with the transgression of the official lines of battle, and convert the Hydra to a figure of the continuous process of displace-

1. A. R. Humphreys, ed., *The First Part of King Henry IV,* 6th ed. (London: Methuen, 1974), p. 3. All quotations from this play are taken from this edition; quotations from *2 Henry IV, Richard II,* and *Henry V* are taken from the Arden editions by Humphreys, Peter Ure, and J. H. Walter, respectively.

ment from the discourses at war within language to the interlocutory, military, and political conflicts that unfold in narrative time and theatrical space. I begin with an analysis of the scene of displacement that surrounds the first mention of the Hydra in *1 Henry IV.*

Thinking that Sir Walter Blunt, the second royal counterfeit, is Henry, Douglas says, "Some tell me that thou art a king," and, after he kills Blunt, "A borrow'd title hast thou bought too dear" (5.3.5, 23). Regardless of what the speaker may be taken to intend, his comments target Henry's illegitimate possession of the title he "borrow'd." They brighten the eyes of the ethical reductionist in search of the ironic little nuggets of Henry-bashing he assumes Shakespeare to have salted away in odd textual corners, unbeknownst to the guilty king himself. But they can also convey a more interesting message if one construes the nuggets as clues to the lurking presence of the sinner's discourse in Henry's language—clues, that is, to the Henry-bashing of which Henry seems capable, and desirous, and afraid.[2] Then they may remind us of the anxiety that motivated him in act 1, scenes 1 and 3 to behave in a manner guaranteed to provoke his supporters to insurrection. In the political economy of the Henriad, the Northumberland rebellion would dissociate him from his allies in usurpation and make him more legitimate. But in the ethical and psychic economy, it would create a faction that could uphold Richard's cause and administer his and God's revenge on Henry's mistreadings. Worcester's complaint, however self-interested, accurately characterizes the relation of the private war Henry wages against himself to the factious Hydra heads of public war:

> We were enforc'd for safety sake to fly
> Out of your sight, and raise this present head,
> Whereby we stand opposed by such means
> As you yourself have forg'd against yourself.
> (5.1.65–68)[3]

2. The sinner's discourse is one of a set of interrelated and interactive discourses or language games circulating through the speech community of the Shakespeare text. I discuss these discourses, which I call ethical (to distinguish them from positional language games such as discourses of gender, generation, social hierarchy, and so on), in "What Did the King Know and When Did He Know It? Shakespearean Discourses and Psychoanalysis," *South Atlantic Quarterly* 88 (1989): 811–62. Throughout the present essay I rely on and presuppose that discussion.

3. The logic of displacement suggests that this emendation would make the complaint conform to Henry's scenario: "We were enforc'd for your safety to fly / Into your sight."

Douglas's military victories give Henry temporary relief from his private war in that they divert him from the conflict between the sinner's discourse and those of the victim/revenger and generous donor he mobilizes against it. To achieve the objective of the sinner's discourse he needs eventually to lose, not win, the public war; the effect of the royalist victory at Gaultree in *2 Henry IV* is a strange deflation of Henry's morale that seems only to hasten his death. At the end of *1 Henry IV* he seems on the way to defeating the rebels, but under conditions not calculated to ensure a satisfactory resolution of the private war. If Douglas accommodates him by embodying the threat of public war in the convenient narrative form of a physical encounter, the more dangerous battlefield to which the private war is displaced is that of Henry's interlocutory struggles with his "nearest and dearest enemy" (3.2.123), Harry. The strange set of episodes that concludes the play binds these three figures together in transgressive conflict.[4]

The real battle at Shrewsbury picks up where it left off in act 3, scene 2, where Henry attacks his son with the example of Hotspur, whose "more worthy interest to the state" he oddly ascribes to the martial energy that makes him politically unstable. Henry especially admires him for having

> Discomfited great Douglas, ta'en him once,
> Enlarged him, and made a friend of him,
> To fill the mouth of deep defiance up,
> And shake the peace and safety of our throne.
>
> (114–17)

The invidious contrast that follows testifies to the success of Harry's plan to influence "men's hopes"—lower their opinion of him—by his display of "loose behavior" (1.2.203–6), and Harry's response to his

---

4. In what follows I strongly disagree with the assessment of D. A. Traversi, to whose sensitive reading I am nevertheless strongly indebted for numerous insights into the play. In *Shakespeare from "Richard II" to "Henry V"* (Stanford: Stanford University Press, 1957), Traversi asserts that Henry and Harry "alike belong to the public rather than the private sphere" and that the efforts "they make to move out of it are not always dramatically convincing. The relation between them is, at its most interesting moments, of another kind, akin to tragedy," but what is expressed in this scene "belongs to the inherited conception on which the action is based, true and necessary, but scarcely forming part of the deeper content of the play" (pp. 103–4). My argument is that Henry and Harry "belong" to the dialectical process in which private and public spheres are termini of displacement, and therefore that what is expressed in this scene does belong to the play's deeper content.

father is both a promise and a deferral of the reformation that will glitter over his fault:

> I will redeem all this on Percy's head,
> And in the closing of some glorious day
> Be bold to tell you that I am your son.
>   (132–34)

But not yet; Henry will have to wait until his son is ready and thinks the time is ripe to falsify men's hopes.

Harry's acerb mimicry of his father's opinion, "This gallant Hotspur, this all-praised knight, / And your unthought-of Harry" (140–41), suggests that his challenge to Hotspur will also be a challenge to Henry. Thus, when he offers to meet Hotspur in single combat at Shrewsbury, the terms of the challenge he aims at Hotspur glance at the king:

> Yet this before my father's majesty—
> I am content that he shall take the odds
> Of his great name and estimation,
> And will, to save the blood on either side,
> Try fortune with him in a single fight.
>   (5.1.96–100)

Although Percy is the obvious antecedent of "he," a slight effort is necessary to keep it from veering toward Henry. The king's response is politic: "So dare we venture thee," he begins, arrogating some of Harry's daring and venturing to himself, and he adds what at first appears to be only a counterfactual objection: "Albeit, considerations infinite / Do make against it" (101–3). But he then proceeds to ignore the offer and turns to Worcester with his own stratagem for saving blood. The prince, eager for his chance, predicts, "It will not be accepted, on my life" (115), at which Henry foils his son's scenario by unwrapping his backup plan: "Hence, therefore, *every* leader to his charge" (118).[5]

Falstaff's comment to Harry two lines later crystallizes the ambivalence of this interchange and anticipates the second moment of father-son conflict: "Hal, if thou see me down in the battle and bestride me,

---

5. And when Harry does get to perform his glorious deed, he is denied the audience he wanted: no one sees it but Falstaff.

so; 'tis a point of friendship." The "point" flashes in scene 4, when
Harry, announcing himself in full regalia as "the Prince of Wales . . . /
Who never promiseth but he means to pay" (41–42), beats Douglas
away from his endangered father, and then shows top-class behavior
by making conspicuously little of his accomplishment:

> Cheerly, my lord, how fares your grace?
> Sir Nicholas Gawsey hath for succour sent,
> And so hath Clifton—I'll to Clifton straight.
>   (43–45)

This gives Henry a chance to delay Harry long enough to lavish thanks
on his savior. He takes, but doesn't exactly seize, the opportunity; his
thanks are carefully measured out in terms that remind Harry of what
he owes while limiting his own obligation:

> Stay and breathe a while:
> Thou hast redeem'd thy lost opinion,
> And show'd thou mak'st some tender of my life,
> In this fair rescue thou hast brought to me.
>   (46–49)

Harry responds with an outburst that effectively lays claim to a larger
share of gratitude:

> O God, they did me too much injury
> That ever said I hearken'd for your death.
> If it were so, I might have let alone
> The insulting hand of Douglas over you,
> Which would have been as speedy in your end
> As all the poisonous potions in the world,
> And sav'd the treacherous labor of your son.
>   (50–56)

Warding off Douglas's "insulting hand," Harry replaces it with something close to an insulting speech. Henry can meet this thrust only by
turning abruptly to other matters—"Make up to Clifton, I'll to Sir
Nicholas Gawsey" (57)—and hurrying off.

Douglas's role and fate symbolize the functional subordination of
the public to the private war. As Stephen Booth remarks, Douglas is
a parody of Hotspur, and he provides a service similar to that which

Harry expects from Hotspur: "Percy is but my factor . . . / To engross up glorious deeds on my behalf" (3.2.147–48).[6] In the economy of honor he fulfills the demand for a General Chivalric Factor, a feared and famous warrior whose sole function seems to be to get beaten so that the victors may become more feared and more famous. His win-loss ratio in the play is mediocre: he kills two or three royal decoys (only one onstage) and threatens the king. But he is twice captured, and sent flying once by Harry, who later reports his humiliating last stand, or stumble: when Douglas saw "the noble Percy slain, and all his men / Upon the foot of fear," he

> fled with the rest,
> And falling from a hill, he was so bruis'd
> That the pursuers took him.
>
> (5.5.19–22)

This makes him a pawn in the next move of the private war. "I beseech your Grace," Harry continues, "I may dispose of him," and Henry replies, "With all my heart" (23–24). I don't think it improbable to assume that the king might hear "dispose" as an offer to imprison or execute the man who endangered his life. If so, the prince's response is unexpected:

> Then, brother John of Lancaster, to you
> This honorable bounty shall belong;
> Go to the Douglas and deliver him
> Up to his pleasure, ransomless and free:
> His valors shown upon our crests today
> Have taught us how to cherish such high deeds,
> Even in the bosom of our adversaries.
>
> (5.5.25–31)

Another show of top-class behavior; another insult to the king, whose person and decoys were the only apparent objects of Douglas's "valors."[7] The gesture recalls, mimics, and responds to Henry's praise of

6. Stephen Booth, *"King Lear," "MacBeth," Indefinition, and Tragedy* (New Haven: Yale University Press, 1983), p. 176.

7. Compare Kenneth Muir, who, after noting that Shakespeare departs from Holinshed in shifting this act from Henry to Harry, thinks the change was made to give the latter "a final touch of magnanimity"; see Kenneth Muir, *The Sources of Shakespeare's Plays* (London: Methuen, 1977), p. 98. That such a touch is undeniable at the level of manners justifies the act and "covers" its aggressiveness. Readers (including actors) whose interpretation transforms the speaker of Harry's lines into a character

Hotspur for having captured and "enlarged" Douglas (3.2.114–17). In imitating Hotspur, Harry both competes with him and replaces him as the king's adversary.

"I'll so offend to make offense a skill": the offensive skill of this gesture ambiguates Harry's final line, his last words in the play, and gives them a resonance that sustains the father-son conflict beneath the comedic resolution of the public war. Thus, descriptions that focus on the latter but ignore the former don't quite ring true: "*1 Henry IV* is designed toward the release of combat. We watch the opponents quarrel; lay their plans, and gather their forces; march toward Shrewsbury and fail in last-minute negotiations, until by Act v, scene iii, we are ready for that discharge of tension which of itself seems to create a sense of order."[8] This reading misses the extent to which the public war provides a medium of displacement for the struggle between Henry and Harry which is itself a covert displacement of the private war, the conflict of discourses, within each. Those "inward wars" are conspicuously latent, conspicuously damped down by the forward push of the public war. By "conspicuously" I mean that when we pay attention to the play of discourses, we can see them being damped down; indeed, we can see how they are empowered and kept in force by displacement to the manifest circumstances of a narrative order "designed toward the release of combat."

One of the major theses of this essay is that the conflict and play of discourses invest the language of speakers with performative energy, the energy of emplotment that drives the narrative forward and motivates the sequence of public actions constituting the "history" the Henriad represents.[9] "Performative" denotes what a speaker's language is *doing* apart from what he may be doing with it, and this objective force can be explored even when the language does not provide the evidence for deciding whether the actions and strings of action it produces appear to be intended or unintended. From my reading of the performative and discursive aspects of language, I derive a sense

---

may agree as to the ambivalence of this speech act but disagree as to its subsequent analysis with respect to Harry's intention, awareness, motivation, and so on. See my discussion in the next two paragraphs for a profile of the performative dimension, the dimension of emplotment, within which or about which readers may be more likely to agree.

8. Sigurd Burckhardt, *Shakespearean Meanings* (Princeton: Princeton University Press, 1968), p. 149.

9. On discourse as emplotment, see Berger, "What Did the King Know?" pp. 847–53.

not only of the speaker's contribution to the dramatic or "historical" plot but also of the *scenario* that motivates the contribution; the scenario is what the speaker wants to happen, but "wants" in the register of desire, which is to say, what he wants whether he knows it or not. So, in confronting *1 Henry IV*, I try to elicit the scenarios of Henry, Harry, Hotspur, and Falstaff by discursive analysis of the private war within each, and I trace their patterns of convergence or collision as they gear into the action of speech and event, the interlocutory and narrative sphere to which inner conflicts are displaced. Viewed in the perspective of displacement, the relation between the private and public wars, between the discourses and historical drama, resembles that between latent and manifest content in Freudian analysis. The public war appears as the anamorphic projection or representation of the private war; the contradictions, ambiguities, fissures, and dislocations beneath the smooth resolution of the former may be accounted for by the pressures of displacement. It is this process and product of anamorphic projection that I encode in the figure of the Hydra.

This approach to the Henriad has more explanatory power than one that is content to describe closures, symmetries, and antitheses, and then show that they are problematized; for example:

> Loose ends are apparent at the end of *1 Henry IV*, to be sure, for history is open-ended even in a play that achieves brilliant closure. After all, even *Henry V* concludes, for all its triumphs in war and marriage, on a reminder of the failures of Henry VI that are to follow in the course of history. In *1 Henry IV* rebellion is never wholly quelled, and the introduction of the Archbishop of York in 4.4 is a reminder of unfinished business. . . . The uneasy relationship between Hal and his father attains a moment of trust appropriate to Hal's emergence as his father's son, but there is unfinished business here too. The actions in *Part 2* that involve repetition—the second rebellion of the Percys, the second long tavern scene, the second interview of father and son—all arise from the perception that what seemed so easy of solution is in fact deeply problematic.[10]

But what makes it problematic? To attribute failures and loose ends to the open-endedness of history is to ignore their textual source in the conflict of discourses, as the reference to the "moment of trust" sug-

10. David Bevington, ed., *Henry IV, Part 1*, The Oxford Shakespeare (Oxford: Oxford University Press, 1987), p. 41.

gests. The closure of *1 Henry IV* is brilliant precisely because it is already problematic and its easy solution inadequate. I don't merely mean that it is circumstantially inadequate, which is obvious; the final scene falls away from the conclusive certainty of Henry's opening line, "Thus ever did rebellion find rebuke," to the provisionality of his final sentence, "Rebellion in this land shall lose its sway" if the troops press on, therefore, "Let us not leave till all our own be won." Rather, I mean that this military project is traversed by the contradictory desires and conflicting discourses which, as I have noted, divide Henry's scenario against itself, and which are anamorphically registered in the first line of his concluding speech: "Then this remains, that we divide our power." Harry's freeing of Douglas adds bite to this irony, especially when the king states, "Myself and you, son Harry, will towards Wales" (39). Teaming up with Harry is one way to keep his power divided and continue the private war in which Harry's function is "to punish my mistreadings" (3.2.11).

When the division is alluded to in *2 Henry IV,* the relation between latent conditions and manifest circumstances has decisively altered. Hastings follows his report that the king's divisions "are in three heads" with this assessment: "So is the unfirm King / In three divided, and his coffers sound / With hollow poverty and emptiness" (1.3.70–75). This is meant as a comment on the king's military circumstances, and as such it is false. But the statement also contains an unintended description of the king's ethical condition, and as such it is true. The rebels continually misjudge situations and talk themselves into losing—almost, indeed, as if the need to lose is their hidden ethical agenda as well as Henry's. In doing this, the fate they solicit increases the king's infirmity, as I suggested earlier. The manifest circumstances of *2 Henry IV* everywhere fail to contain the latent grief, the pressure of the sinner's discourse challenging the repeated claims of victimization and the assertive displays (whether serious or comic) of villainy. In saying this I am not criticizing the play but stating its theme. Until Harry takes over in act 5, the apparently casual ramble through tableaus of social misrule and political disorder composes into a "rude scene" (1.1.159) which is an anamorphic shadow of the unseen grief that produces it. A. R. Humphreys justly observes that the fluent energies of the play's language are "more important, dramatically, in that the narrative content is not greatly compelling."[11] What actually

11. A. R. Humphreys, ed., *The Second Part of King Henry IV,* Arden edition (London: Methuen, 1966), p. lxii.

happens in castle, tavern, palace, battlefield, and country orchard is conspicuously anticlimactic. Since the manifest circumstances of emplotment and narrative are *represented* as inadequate displacements of the latent grief, we may expect the repetition mentioned by David Bevington to take the form of a proliferation of Hydra heads.

The Hydra that presides over *2 Henry IV* is not named until act 4, scene 2. But it is prepared for by several anticipatory allusions. The first appears in the Induction, whose speaker, Rumor, gleefully claims to specialize in the wholesale distribution of "smooth comforts false, worse than true wrongs" (40). Rumor describes herself/himself/itself (the gender of this personification is as uncertain as everything else about her/him/it)[12] as a pipe

> Blown by surmises, jealousies, conjectures,
> And of so easy and so plain a stop
> That the blunt monster with uncounted heads,
> The still-discordant wav'ring multitude,
> Can play upon it.
>
> (16–20)

With characteristic shiftiness she selects an image that traditionally—under Platonic influence—represents at once a psychic and a political source of disorder, and exercises her gift for metonymy in a dazzling series of displacements. She links the monster to the psychic referent in line 16, then redirects it outward to hoi polloi in the appositional clause. The source of false report is displaced first from Rumor's own uncounted tongues—which in turn represent displacements of cause from the ears of all those whose mishearing empowers Rumor—to the general apprehensiveness and mistrust that will plague the aristocratic leaders of faction, and then from this to their political scapegoat, the mob.

This metonymic contagion itself rhetorically enacts the process of false report by which true wrongs are replaced by "smooth comforts false." The blunt monster is the instrument of avoidance in a moral economy in which, as Jonathan Goldberg has argued, "the starving poor and the criminals are misrepresented as 'the cankers of a calm

---

12. See my "Sneak's Noise, or, Rumor and Detextualization in *2 Henry IV*," *Kenyon Review*, n.s. 6, no. 4 (Fall 1984): 58–78. I choose to refer to Rumor as "she" because Shakespeare's personification reminds me of both Virgil's Fama and Erasmus' Moria. On the latter, see my "Utopian Folly: Erasmus and More on the Perils of Misanthropy," in *Second World and Green World: Studies in Renaissance Fiction-Making,* ed. John P. Lynch (Berkeley: University of California Press, 1988), pp. 229–48.

world,' as if they were solely responsible for their poverty, as if, save
them, the world would be secure and at peace."[13] Shifting responsibility for what Henry calls "inward wars" (3.1.107) outward to Rumor's
"stern tyrant War" (Ind. 14) and downward to the blunt monster is a
formula for fabricating rather than eliminating "new Hydraes" and
"new heades." Several lines later, one of the false reports Rumor
boasts of is "that the King before the Douglas' rage / Stoop'd his
anointed head as low as death" (31–32). This reference to the Shrewsbury episode catches the many-headed monster in a web of purely
associative filaments which include Douglas's mention of the Hydra
and the sheer mnemonic trigger "blunt" (that is, "blunt monster" reminds me of Douglas's victim, Blunt). Rumor spreads this false report
"through the peasant towns" (33), another reference to the blunt-
headed lower class she contemptuously commandeers.

Rumor seeds potential Hydra heads throughout the play text. Thus,
the Archbishop of York identifies the blunt monster with the "commonwealth," which he reduces to a "common dog," and dispenses
false comfort by citing its wavering taste in kings as a reason for taking
arms (1.3.85–108). Later he argues that the king will accept the rebels'
bill of grievances, "For he hath found, to end one doubt by death /
Revives two greater in the heirs of life" (4.1.199–200); another smooth
comfort false. The Hydra lurking under this figure surfaces in the next
scene when the same speaker complains that the court's previous rejection of the bill is part of "the time misorder'd" that "doth . . . /
Crowd and crush us to this monstrous form / . . . Whereon this Hydra son of war is born" (4.2.33–38). Rumor has anticipated this particular comfort when she takes responsibility not only for false reports
of peace but also for

> fearful musters and prepar'd defence,
> Whiles the big year, swoln with some other grief,
> Is thought with child by the stern tyrant War,
> And no such matter?
>
> (12–15)

The unclarity of the image (pregnant from some other cause or not
pregnant but swollen with disease?) is part of the tease, and its vague-

---

13. Jonathan Goldberg, "Table Manners: Engrossing Shakespearean Histories,"
lecture delivered at the University of California, Santa Cruz, spring 1988. Quoted
with the permission of the author.

ness, its dark reaches, its conspicuously withheld reference provoke our own "surmises, jealousies, conjectures" about those that hide behind the maddeningly noncommittal "some other grief."[14]

The Archbishops's bill of grievances and Hydra son of war are circumstantial displacements of deep-rooted conditions. To shift the source of anxiety from grief to grievance, inner structure to outer event, to alienate it to some more manageable scapegoat or monster in whose direction bad humors can be vented, offers the relief of action, purgation, and closure. As a personification Rumor embodies, represents, and presides over this process by which the uncanny is domesticated—is given a local habitation, a name, a talking head—and it is within this thematic network that the Hydra raises its heads. When it issues forth from the Archbishop's mouth, the logical implications of the figure begin to insinuate themselves subversively into the argument he is trying to make. Whether the genitive phrase "son of war" is subjective or objective, whether "stern tyrant War" is father or son, the inherent Hydra logic—"killing" one war will generate two others—suggests something contrary to what the speaker seems to intend. Hence he is forced in the next line to replace the Hydra with Argus, "Whose dangerous eyes may well be charm'd asleep / With grant of our most just and right desires" (4.2.39–40). But this smooth comfort harks back to the more "jealous" (i.e., suspicious)—and truer—surmise of Worcester in the preceding play, "Supposition all our lives shall be stuck full of eyes," in other words, "Interpretation will misquote our looks" (*1 Henry IV* 5.2.8, 13).

When Hastings proceeds to unpack the Archbishop's Hydra figure, his attempt at smooth comfort also falls prey to the monster's logic:

We have supplies to second our attempt:
If they miscarry, theirs shall second them;
And so success of mischief shall be born,
And heir from heir shall hold this quarrel up
Whilst England shall have generation.

(4.2.45–49)

As a figural embodiment, the Hydra congeals and thus conceals a dia-

14. The image is further ambiguated by the fact that in the phrase "the big year," "year" can function as a dialectal variant of "ear" (cf. 1.2.193–94, along with the texual variants and the Arden note). The ambiguity is consistent with the others that waver between inner and outer, small and large, conditional and circumstantial references.

chronic structure whose "baneful or destructive character" *(OED)* only a Hercules can overcome. Hastings's language projects an endless series of quarrels, and the undesirable alternative, "mischief of success shall be born," vibrates in the many-headed meaning of "success of mischief." Reading it as "succession of mischief," we can construe the whole phrase (and not only "success") as the subject of the verb. Taking "success" as "royal succession," the words intended to characterize the persistence that will lead to success at the same time predict the Wars of the Roses, which dramatize the violent operations of the "combat model" of succession. As Hastings develops and loses control of the figure, England becomes the Hydra whose heads are not only wars and fears but also expendable kings. The blunt monster is not only the many-headed "beastly feeder" the Archbishop complains of but also the sick "commonwealth"—in Henry's words, the foul and diseased "body of our kingdom" (3.1.38) which, Hydralike, thrives on the disorder symbolized by decapitation. This political version of the Hydra principle is enunciated by Richard II when he prophesies to Northumberland that

> The time shall not be many hours of age
> More than it is, ere foul sin gathering head
> Shall break into corruption: thou shalt think,
> Though he divide the realm and give thee half,
> It is too little, helping him to all;
> He shalt think that thou, which knowest the way
> To plant unrightful kings, wilt know again,
> Being ne'er so little urg'd, another way
> To pluck him headlong from the usurped throne.
> *(Richard II 5.1.57–65)*

One of the first acts of the new regime is head-gathering: six freshly cut heads are sent to London by Northumberland and Fitzwater (5.6.6–16).

The Hydra logic refuses to yield to the intentions of those who use it to explain, visualize, and cope with the civil and political problems to which they attribute "the times misorder'd" (4.2.33). After Rumor's takeover in *2 Henry IV* it comes to express the desperation of the victim's discourse mingled with the sinner's—the desire for helplessness and for just deserts—which underlies and erodes their hope. This logic cannot be explained in terms of politically reductive schemes such as Jan Kott's "Grand Mechanism," the "image of history" as "a great staircase," a self-perpetuating system of rising and falling kings.[15] The Hydra's body lies concealed not in the autonomous working of the mechanism but in the fluid medium of "some other grief." From its flourishing root system in "buried fear" and "inward wars" it shoots forth "new Hydraes, lo new heades" to afflict the peace, and these heads always appear in the wrong place, which is to say they appear in *place:*

> And 'tis no little reason bids us speed,
> To save our heads by raising of a head . . .
> > (*1 Henry IV* 1.3.277–78)

> A mighty and a fearful head they are,
> If promises be kept on every hand,
> As ever offer'd foul play in a state.
> > (3.1.167–69)

> If we without his help can make a head
> To push against a kingdom . . .
> > (4.1.80–81)

> And in conclusion drove us to seek out
> This head of safety . . .
> > (4.3.102–3)

> > the King hath drawn
> The special head of all the land together . . .
> > (4.4.27–28)

> We were enforc'd for safety sake to fly
> Out of your sight, and raise this present head . . .
> > (5.1.65–66)

> Whether our present five and twenty thousand
> May hold up head without Northumberland.
> > (*2 Henry IV* 1.3.16–17)

> For his divisions, as the times do brawl,
> Are in three heads . . .
> > (1.3.70–71)

Think you not that the powers we bear with us

15. Jan Kott, *Shakespeare Our Contemporary,* trans. Boleslaw Taborski (Garden City, N.Y.: Anchor Books, 1966), pp. 10 and 3–55 passim. For a concise and shrewd criticism of Kott, see Jonathan Dollimore and Alan Sinfield, "History and Ideology:

Will cut their passage through the force of France,
Doing the execution and the act
For which we have in head assembled them?
                                (Henry V 2.2.15–18)

The last excerpt is Harry's question to one of the three traitors who
will shortly lose their heads, and the brief abstract of his intention to
make stern tyrant War impregnate the big year may be linked to the
Hydra's final appearance in the tetralogy. This time the monster has
turned and is closer to home. The Archbishop of Canterbury is mar-
veling at the suddenness and violence of Harry's conversion:

Never was such a sudden scholar made;
Never came reformation in a flood,
With such a heady currance, scouring faults;
Nor never Hydra-headed wilfulness
So soon did lose his seat—and all at once—
As in this king.

                        (1.1.32–37)

The reappearance of "heady" in "Hydra-headed" suggests that in spite
of their contrary impulses the same Herculean violence may fuel both
the willfulness and the "currance" of reform, leaving it unclear
whether the effect of scouring faults is to get rid of them or to nourish
their root structure so that they can put forth more heads. Canterbury
and his interlocutor, the Bishop of Ely, are trying to persuade themselves that since the king has reformed and is "a true lover of the holy
Church" (23), they can persuade him to forestall dispossession of
church lands in exchange for their support of the cause against France.
It is because Canterbury is so obviously a worldly ecclesiastic skilled
in the art of pietistic euphemism that the strangeness and wonder in
his words stand out. The language of exorcistic violence so conveys
the hero's self-purging fury that it transgresses the speaker's apparent
intention to praise. Canterbury wants to believe in Harry's reformation, has an interest in believing it, but the effect of the repeated
"never's," inflating the "faults" to monstrous proportions (the Augean
stable, the Hydra), is to stress his incredulity. And if we remember
the Prologue's heraldic image of "the warlike Harry" at whose heels,

The Instance of *Henry V,*" in *Alternative Shakespeares,* ed. John Drakakis (New York:
Methuen, 1985), p. 208.

"Leash'd in like *hounds,* should famine, sword, and fire / Crouch for employment" (Pr. 6–8), the "cur" in the nonce word "currance" strains forward to touch up the ferocity of Canterbury's image. The hidden cur externalized and idealized in the hounds waiting to be unleashed implies that some motive other than the "inward wars" of the body politic lies behind the bearing of "civil swords and native fire / As far as France" (*2 Henry IV* 5.5.106–7) and behind the rhetorical violence with which Harry will scour many faults during the course of the play, but none of them his own.

In my imagination I never see the Hydra's body, only its heads gnashing about like those of so many brontosaurs hidden from the neck down in earth, mud, or water. And if I try to imagine the body, it takes on the aspect of a densely tangled intertwining root structure creeping laterally in every direction and sending up capital shoots that work like crabgrass, offering its enemies the wrong targets so that efforts to curb its growth not only will fail but will invigorate the root structure and multiply its heads. The point about the Hydra, however, is that as a mythological pest, it does not exist until someone brings it into being by desiring targets of decapitation, that is, by making heads. Decapitation is futile because it is the masked form of its opposite, capitation. The Hydra is born from the head of the decapitator.

Another name for the Hydra's hidden body, as I visualize it, is *rhizome,* whose roots Gilles Deleuze and Felix Guattari have extended into language:

> In a rhizome . . . semiotic chains of every kind are connected . . . according to very diverse modes of encoding, chains that are biological, political, economic, etc., and that put into play not only regimes of different signs, but also different states of affairs. . . . A semiotic chain is like a tuber gathering up very diverse acts—linguistic, but also perceptual, mimetic, gestural, and cognitive. . . . Language stabilizes around a parish, a diocese, a capital. It forms a bulb. It evolves by means of stems and underground flows. . . . Language can always be broken down into its internal structural components, an activity not fundamentally different from a search for roots.[16]

Another name for *rhizome* might be *text.*

16. Gilles Deleuze and Felix Guattari, *On the Line,* trans. John Johnston (New York: Semiotext[e], 1983), pp. 11–13, an augmented version of the authors' *Rhizome: Introduction* (Paris: Editions de Minuit, 1976). I use this translation here because it is a little closer to the original than Brian Massumi's (Gilles Deleuze and Felix Guattari, *A*

THE RHIZOME

Among the various mirroring devices and "ways of recording the progress of inward 'action'" Maynard Mack found in "The Jacobean Shakespeare," the one that took root in subsequent criticism was the concept of "umbrella speeches," so called because "more than one consciousness may shelter under them." Thus Lear's Fool "serves, to some extent, as a screen on which Shakespeare flashes, as it were, readings from the psychic life of the protagonist," and through Lady Macbeth's sleepwalking Shakespeare keeps Macbeth "before us in his capacity as tragic hero and sufferer." Some umbrellas are larger than others: Mack argues that Edmund, Gloucester, and Lear are all partly sheltered under the Poor Tom umbrella put up by Edgar. And perhaps there are also choric umbrellas under which the playwright and the play as a whole—its world view or moral order—huddle together. At least it used to be thought so, and Mack observes that he is not the first to have sought shelter under the concept.[17]

But why it should be an umbrella remains puzzling to me. Why a manufactured defense against bad weather, against what comes down from above, opened up by one character but companionably shared by another, or others? And why can't the character who is or holds the umbrella also be the "other" who shelters under it? Why can't several such speakers and umbrellas converge into one? Mack's concept is both powerful and serviceable, but the gratuitous details of his image are distracting. It is the playwright who manufactures the umbrella and the critic who opens it up, and what they collaborate in producing is an article whose perimeter is congruent not with individual speeches or the speeches of individual characters but with the language of the play as a whole, that is, with the text. Individual speeches may well be defenses against textual bad weather, but I think it would be better to invert the image and conceive of bad weather as coming up from below. For this, mushrooms are preferable to the umbrellas they vaguely resemble: they spring up out of the tangled, dark weblike mycelium of the text like Hydra heads, and they bear the darkness in their substance. Mushroom speeches growing from textual mycelium: an image whose time may come. But for now I shall resist its

Thousand Plateaus: Capitalism and Schizophrenia [Minneapolis: University of Minnesota Press, 1987]).

17. Maynard Mack, "The Jacobean Shakespeare," in *Jacobean Theater*, ed. J. R. Brown and Bernard Harris (1960; rpt. New York: Capricorn Books, 1967), pp. 24–26.

appeal in favor of another organic image more deeply rooted both in the language of the Henriad and in its genealogical themes.

In the opening lines of act 1, scene 2 of *Richard II,* John of Gaunt complains to the Duchess of Gloucester, widow of the murdered Thomas of Woodstock, that "the part I had in Woodstock's blood" impels him to avenge his brother's murder, but that since he cannot stir against God's deputy, who "made the fault," he leaves it to "the will of heaven" to "rain hot vengeance on offenders' heads." The Duchess retorts that he should act anyway because he and Woodstock are among "Edward's seven sons" and are as "seven branches springing from one root" (1–13). In this connection I register my support for the Quarto's "Woodstock's blood" in preference to the Folio's "Gloucester's blood." This is because one botanical root of the Duchess's genealogical metaphor is the (wood)stock—not in its first *OED* sense of a *lifeless* stump but in the second sense of a *living* trunk or stem (*OED* entry 2c equates "stock" with "rhizome," and the *American Heritage Dictionary* mentions "rootstalk" and "rootstock" as synonyms of "rhizome").

We recognize, of course, that the second *OED* sense is metaphorically even less accurate than the first, since Edward III is no more alive than Woodstock. It is only when his living descendants adopt the botanical fiction as a call to action that the "root" is resurrected, and the call is usually, as here, a response to some rupture or break which itself becomes the rootstock or woodstock of the resurrective project. Edward III is not the rootstock of this play; Woodstock, or rather his murder, is. A lifeless subterranean stump, a dead brother, a murder, seeds the genealogy and text of the buried fear transmitted through the Henriad. From this progenitor no *linear* succession can descend, or ascend, for the genealogical positions are continually being shuffled, exchanged, reoccupied in the Henriad's symbolic economy: brothers fill in as sons, cousins as fathers and sons, sons as cousins and fathers. The genealogical narrative, with its lineality and linearity, moves over the surface of a very different kind of structure, one that "always has multiple entrances" like a burrow, one that is "reversible, and susceptible to constant modification," one that Deleuze and Guattari at times depict less as a structure than as a vortex:

> A rhizome can be cracked and broken at any point; it starts off again following one or another of its lines, or even other lines.

Always follow the rhizome by rupturing, lengthening, prolonging,
. . . making it vary, until it produces the most abstract and tortuous
line in *n* dimensions and scattered directions. Combine the deterritorialized flows.[18]

Deterritorialized flows are textual flows; they go off the line. Reterritorializing the flows brings them back on the line of events and bodies
that compose into the space-time of dramatic narrative and theatrical
performance. Reterritorializing thus detextualizes. It makes heads.

PASSING SHOW: THE LAFEW PRINCIPLE

My parabolic reflections on the Hydra and rhizome were intended to
join them in a figure that faces two ways: toward a particular reading
of the Henriad and toward a general approach to Shakespearean dramaturgy. The point of the exercise was to suggest that the Henriad
and its dramaturgy are linked by isomorphism in their structure of
relations and by homology in the transformational dynamic that acti-
vates the structures. The dynamic is reflected in these passages of text:

1. The shadow of my sorrow? ha! let's see—
   'Tis very true, my grief lies all within,
   And these external manners of lament
   Are merely shadows to the unseen grief
   That swells with silence in the tortur'd soul.

   (*Richard II* 4.1.294–99)

2. . . . a plague of sighing and grief, it blows a man up like a bladder.

   (*1 Henry IV* 2.5.327–28)

3. And who but Rumor, who but only I,
   Make fearful musters, and prepar'd defence,
   Whiles the big year, swoln with some other grief,
   Is thought with child by the stern tyrant War,
   And no such matter?

   (*2 Henry IV* Ind. 11–15)

4. This tempest will not give me leave to ponder
   On things would hurt me more.

   (*King Lear* 3.4.24–25)

18. Deleuze and Guattari, *On the Line*, pp. 17–18, 23.

5. They say miracles are past; and we have our philosophical persons
to make modern and familiar, things supernatural and causeless.
Hence it is that we make trifles of terrors, ensconcing ourselves
into seeming knowledge when we should submit ourselves to an
unknown fear.

(*All's Well That Ends Well* 2.3.1–6)

6. But I have that within which passes show,
These but the trappings and the suits of woe.

(*Hamlet* 1.2.85–86)

These passages have one thing in common: they piont to a distinction
and relation between "internal" and "external" representations of grief
or anxiety—between what passes show and its expression in the passing show—and they mark the passing show as either an inadequate or
a diversionary expression.

One of my objects in this study is to try to demonstrate by close
reading that the passing show is formally, or tropically, an *anamorphosis* of what passes show. As its etymology suggests (the Greek
means something like "shaping up" or "shaping back"), the trope of
anamorphosis presents a conspicuous distortion or deviation from
some other form and thereby encourages us to recuperate its original
form through corrective adjustments. This is "scientifically" possible
in the case of visual anamorphoses; it may or may not be possible when
the figure is tropologically mapped onto a representational field only
part of which may be visual—the field, for example, constructed by
the interaction of the textualized signifiers of reading with the detextu-
alized signifiers of performance, or between the language of words
and the language of bodies. Anamorphosis may function in a manner
similiar to pastoral—as an instrument of control through simplifica-
tion, domestication, or reduction of textual obscurity to visual clarity.
So with the anamorphosis of grief. "If you observe your own grief,
which senses do you use to observe it? A particular sense, one that
feels grief? Then do you feel it *differently* when you are observing it?
And what is the grief that you are observing—is it one which is there
only while it is being observed?"[19] And, to follow Wittgenstein's questions with another, is there a grief you don't actually "feel" but suspect
is there?

19. Ludwig Wittgenstein, *Philosophical Investigations,* trans. G. E. M. Anscombe,
2d ed. (Oxford: Basil Blackwell, 1958), p. 187e.

Of course, the citational form of the passages I have quoted reduces them to my passing show; snippetotomy diverts them from their contexts, diminishes their ability to express or adumbrate what lies within and passes show. Many of them rhetorically enact the problematic relation they state by parading themselves as inadequate or obscure or misleading expressions. Thus, passages 1 and 6 are but the trappings and the suits of what lies all within. Richard's statement, for example, undoes itself because it is another external manner of lament. As shadows or players of his unseen grief, his words fall short in that their rhetorical embodiment falsifies it. For he appears to be harping on his victimization and loss of power at the hands of others while clearly enjoying his theatrical control over Bolingbroke in a flaunt that belies his words. And as I tried to demonstrate in *Imaginary Audition* (1989), his control over both his own undoing and Bolingbroke's ethical condition is more than theatrical. What the local strings of utterance cannot adequately express is the volatile interplay of the sinner's, the saint's, and the victim/revenger's discourses in his language, the power of his "still-breeding thoughts" to inseminate Henry's conscience and ultimately swell with silence in his tortured soul. It is very true, then, that Richard's grief lies, just as Hamlet's show traps, sues, and pursues. To notice this is to begin to see the kind of adequacy of which their inadequate expressions—an inadequacy flagged by endstopped iambics and jingling rhyme—are capable.

We might pause over passage 2 long enough to appreciate the metaleptic density of Falstaff's caricature, at once an insight into the symbol of corpulence and a scoff at the canny reductiveness of medical explanation, which domesticates the dis-ease of "some other grief" so as to submit it to the cure of pneumatic or hydraulic pathology.[20] A similar move occurs in passage 5, which is the old courtier Lafew's philosophical observation on the dubious knowledgeability of the doctors trying—pretentiously and without success—to diagnose the king's mysterious illness. Lafew's comment is itself pretentious and seemingly knowledgeable, and it thus fails to keep the folly assigned to the third-person plural from penetrating the show of wisdom that pales in the first-person singular. Anyone who chooses to appropriate and utter Lafew's insight, present company not excepted, is subject to the same penetration. Nevertheless, as the hapless Duke of Albany

20. On this point, see the related discussion in Berger, "What Did the King Know?" pp. 823–25. Passage 4, from *King Lear*, is discussed in my "*King Lear*: The Lear Family Romance," *Centennial Review* 23 (1979): 362–63.

would say—does say—"That's but a trifle here," and I plan to elevate
Lafew's comment to a dramaturgical principle that will make modern
and familiar things supernatural and causeless.

The first step in this plan is to identify what passes show with the
rhizome and the passing show with the Hydra, and to list some of the
relational pairs whose polarities provide the site of the transformations
I explore:

Rhizome	*Hydra*
semiotic chains	narrative chains
latent conditions	manifest circumstances
discursive action . . . interlocutory action . . . dramatic action	
text, language . . . script, speech . . . events, bodies, performance	
inward wars	stern tyrant War
grief	grievances
terrors	trifles
unknown fear	seeming knowledge
"some other" within	external manners, trappings, suits

My thesis is that this transformational matrix can serve as a model for
both the specific structure and thematics of the Henriad and the general structure and thematics of Shakespearean dramaturgy. I view the
general model as something Shakespeare's text represents, and I distinguish it from the literary model of stage-centered reading which
guides my approach to the text. The latter is a heuristic device, a property of interpretive practice, but the former is a virtual property of the
interpreted text. Barry Weller remarks of Shakespeare's characters that
they "frequently manifest the desire to be recognized as something
other than they 'seem,' that is, to belie the visible and audible evidence
of their presence onstage by suggesting that it does not and cannot
adequately represent what they are."[21] I submit that Shakespeare's
plays manifest the same desire, and I shall try to show that the way
they do so in the Henriad conforms to the Lafew principle.

To begin with some definitions of terms in Lafew's statement: a
sconce is a fortification, a defense, and a *trifle* is not only something
trivial but also, in one of its older senses, a false tale or lying fable told
to deceive or divert. I want to explore and test a particular hypothesis

21. Barry Weller, "Identity and Representation in Shakespeare," *ELH* 49 (1982):
342.

about Shakespearean dramaturgy, which is that the play text represents its dramatic and theatrical circumstances as forms of defensive trifling. As I noted earlier, the hypothesis is based on a modern and familiar theory of the relations between latent and manifest content, and of the dynamic mechanisms—condensation, displacement, visualization, dramatization—that preside over their transformations.[22] Redirecting Freud's model to plays does not mean reducing them to dreams or jokes, since the dynamics of the model give shape to the economy of many other representational activities. Dream work, joke work, and play work are different expressions of the same general field of forces. In applying the model to Shakespeare's writing, I center on the passage from latent psychological *conditions* or relationships to the manifest *circumstances* of narrative, dramatic, and theatrical performance.

My reason for choosing the two terms emphasized in the previous sentence is based on several etymological considerations. In using *circumstance* I mean to activate not only senses such as "factors that modify a course of action" and "additional or accessory information" but also those implied in the phrases "circumstantial evidence" and "pomp and circumstance."[23] Buried in my use of the word *condition* is the Latin verb behind its Latin cognate, *condere,* which means, among other things, to write or compose, to collect, to preserve, to bury, to conceal. The meanings collected under this sign (one of the meanings of the Latin root of *collect* is "to read") allow me by a happy coincidence to bind together two kinds of latency: the latency of what may be called deep-structural *psychological* conditions and that of *textual* conditions, that is, the rhetorical, syntactical, and lexical play of meaning most fully accessible when the system of verbal signs is committed to writing and offered to readers for interpretation. Superimposing psychological and textual conditions in this manner implies, on the other side, the superimposition of two kinds of manifest content: that of the unfolding circumstances of dramatic narrative (story or *mythos*

22. I got the idea of relating these mechanisms to Shakespearean dramaturgy from Joel Fineman. See his brief but brilliant comments in "Fratricide and Cuckoldry: Shakespeare's Doubles," in *Representing Shakespeare: New Psychoanalytic Essays,* ed. Murray M. Schwartz and Coppélia Kahn (Baltimore: Johns Hopkins University Press, 1980), pp. 72–73.

23. For some related comments on "circumstances," see Patricia Parker's discussion in "Shakespeare and Rhetoric: 'Dilation' and 'Delation' in *Othello,*" in *Shakespeare and the Question of Theory,* ed. Patricia Parker and Geoffrey Hartman (New York: Methuen, 1985), pp. 54–74, esp. pp. 55–58.

and its organizing emplotment) and that of the theatrical play of bodily and phonic signs in which meaning is circumstantially conveyed through kinesic, proxemic, and speech patterns.

In regard to the specific relationship of textual conditions to theatrical circumstances, I think it obvious that it is polarized and conflictive. The polarity arises from the different aims and structures of literary and theatrical interpretation. To borrow some terms from the Chorus of *Henry V,* theatrical interpretation—by spectators, not by the director, whose relation to the text is that of a reader—asks for winged thought, while literary interpretation is "cripple tardy-gaited" thought that meanders painfully about the text and leaves filthy little tracks like a snail. Or, to put it in the language of corpuscular theory, theater induces quick motions that heat up the mind, while reading induces slow motions that make it pale, cold, and melancholic. Actors and spectators display the symptoms Falstaff attributes to the "two-fold operation" of sack: it makes them "full of nimble, fiery, and delectable shapes . . . delivered o'er to the voice" and ear (and eye); and it makes the blood "course from the inwards to the parts' extremes" until "it illumineth the face." And yet, because readers are more "sober-blooded" and eschew "inflammation," they suffer from the anemia of "demure boys" who imbibe thin potations and get wenches. Or so it seems to those who insist that "the foolish and dull and crudy vapors" environing the text be burnt off in accordance with the criteria of performability—of what can be digested in a staged play—and who think the "learning" of armchair interpreters to be "a mere hoard of gold kept by a devil" (*2 Henry IV* 4.3.85–115).

These are relatively obvious and mundane observations, even more trivial if all they refer to is a polarity between text and performance, or reading and playgoing. How can empirical statements of this sort be made to converge on thematic claims about the relation of psychological or textual conditions to dramatic or theatrical circumstances? Responding to this question in *Imaginary Audition,* I began by resituating the polarity *within* reading and treating it as a conflict between stage-centered and text-centered reading, and I then complicated the scheme by introducing a *via media* which I called the literary model of stage-centered reading, distinguished from the theatrical model. One effect of these moves is to shift the locus of the representational medium from the mutual presence of theatrical performance and audience to that of text and reader. Thus displaced, theatrical performance no longer has pride of place as the actual medium that "imitates," communicates, and interprets a dramatic fiction, and the relation be-tween them is no longer an empirically fixed prior condition that es-capes and determines interpretation. Rather, theater joins drama as one of the absent *representata* of the text. Its use and meaning, its rela-tions to dramatic fiction and text, are now among the variables whose interplay is open to the reader's interpretive decisions. From here it is only a short step to a second move, one that will allow me to state my claim in its strongest and most controversial form. Situating the text-performance dialectic within reading produces this consequence: whether and why reading should or should not be constrained by the structural characteristics of theatrical performance become (at least potentially) substantive problems that affect the meaning of the dra-matic fiction. These are the problems whose existence T. S. Eliot accu-rately discerned, but whose thematic status he misunderstood, in his discussion of the "objective correlative." My claim is that this prob-lematic is built into the Shakespeare text as a critical thesis about the-ater in particular and theatricality in general, that the critique can be extended to the theatrical model of stage-centered reading, and that it is fully accessible only to the literary model of stage-centered reading, which provides an interpretive standpoint outside the direct or indi-rect influence of the stage.

5

Othello and *Hamlet*

DILATION, SPYING,
AND THE "SECRET PLACE" OF WOMAN

PATRICIA PARKER

The lap or privity dilated or laide open . . .
—Helkiah Crooke
Descried and set forth the secretes and privities of women . . .
—Eucharius Roesslin

Some time ago, in an essay that argued for the convergence in *Othello* of narrative or rhetorical structure with the contemporary apparatus of judicial power, I began with one of the play's most controversial textual cruxes—the lines in act 3 whose "close dilations" Dr. Johnson tantalizingly suggested might be read as "close delations" ("secret and occult accusations") rather than simply as "dilations" in the current senses of either amplifications or delays.[1] I argued there that the rea-

A slightly different version of this essay appeared in *Representations* 44 (Fall 1993), ©1993 by the Regents of the University of California, reprinted by permission. Thanks are due to the generous readings the present essay received in earlier drafts from David Bevington, Margreta de Grazia, Andrew Gurr, Michael Neill, and Catherine Gallagher, Stephen Greenblatt, and the Editorial Board of *Representations*. Its errors, as always, are my own.

1. See *Othello* 3.3.123, and Patricia Parker, "Shakespeare and Rhetoric: 'Dilation' and 'Delation' in *Othello*," in *Shakespeare and the Question of Theory,* ed. Patricia Parker and Geoffrey Hartman (London: Methuen, 1985), pp. 54–74, and Arden editor M. R. Ridley's rejection of the "close dilations" of the Folio (and Q2) in favor of the "close denotements" that appears only in Q1 (London: Methuen, 1974). Except where noted, *The Riverside Shakespeare,* ed. G. Blakemore Evans et al. (Boston: Houghton Mifflin, 1974), is the text used here, and italicization is mine.

sons given by at least one modern editor of the play for excluding the resonance of "secret accusation" from the "close dilations" of the Folio text were indefensible, for they assumed the nonexistence of "dilation" (or its alternate "delation") in the sense of "accusation" in Shakespeare's day, when even the most cursory search of early modern texts yields an embarrassing abundance of uses of the term in exactly this judicial sense, as well as instances of a paronomastic crossing of the two—delation and dilation, that which accuses and that which opens and amplifies.[2]

In this essay I return to this subject anew in order to consider the implications of reading both Shakespeare and the texts of early modern culture with an awareness of the historical resonance of their terms, not just for the purposes of interpretation but as a way of perceiving links between the plays and larger contemporary discursive networks. The two contexts set beside *Othello* and then, in diptych fashion, *Hamlet,* are first, the function of the delator or informer as a secret accuser, associated both with spying and with bringing something "hid" before the eye; and, second, the language of uncovering, dilating and opening the "privy" place of woman, in the quasi-pornographic discourse of anatomy and early modern gynecology which seeks to bring a hidden or secret place to light.

❑

Let us begin with the "close dilations" of the Temptation Scene. It is here that Iago, the figure who will become "virtually an archetype of the informer"[3] in this play, introduces the hints and inferences that set Othello "on the rack," creating a sense of something needing to be brought forth to "show":

> *Othello.* Think, my lord? By heaven, thou echo'st me,
>   As if there were some *monster* in thy thought

2. See Ridley in the Arden *Othello,* p. 99, and the *OED*'s citing of early modern English "delate" for "to accuse, bring a charge against, . . . inform against" (including 1536 "dilatit of adultry"), Stow's 1598 "delators or informers" (s.v. "delator" and "dilater" in *Survey of London,* 2 vols. [Oxford: Oxford University Press, 1908]), and Bishop Hall's "dilaters of errors, delators of your brethren" from 1640.

3. Robert B. Heilman, *Magic in the Web* (Lexington: University of Kentucky Press, 1956), p. 63.

Too hideous to be shown. Thou dost mean something.
I heard thee say even now, thou lik'st not that,
When Cassio left my wife. What didst not like?
And when I told thee he was of my counsel
In my whole course of wooing, thou criedst, "Indeed!"
And didst *contract and purse* thy brow together,
As if thou then hadst *shut up* in thy brain
Some horrible conceit. If thou dost love me,
Show me thy thought.

(3.3.106–16)

These central lines—forging their famously punning links between "monster" and "show," "hideous" and "hid"—lead to Othello's suspicion of "close dilations, working from the heart" (123) and then to hunger for information from one he assumes "sees and knows more, much more, than he unfolds" (243).[4] Beyond their immediate resonance in the Temptation Scene, the lines also forge links (through "contract and purse . . . shut up . . . show") with the opening of the play or theatrical "show," which begins with an enigmatic reference to something not to be told ("Tush, never tell me!") and to a "purse" whose mouth can be opened or shut (1.1.1–3).

In the semantic field of early modern English, the "close" of "close dilations" here means "secret" or "private"—the opposite of what is displayed or "shown"—as in Claudius' "we have *closely* sent for Hamlet" (3.1.29) in a context that clearly means "privily" or "secretly."[5] But it also manages to suggest the sense of something constricted or closed, a sense that echoes the scene in act 1 where Othello narrates his response to Desdemona's entreaty that he might "all [his] pilgrimage dilate" (1.3.153), opening to her "greedy ear" what had previously been known only in "parcels," or in part (149–55). "Close dilations" conveys the sense of partial opening and partial glimpses of something closed or hid, just as the resonances of "accusations" in Johnson's "oc-

---

4. On these puns, see Michael Neill, "Unproper Beds: Race, Adultery, and the Hideous in *Othello*," *Shakespeare Quarterly* 40 (1989): 383–412. Randle Cotgrave's *Dictionarie of the French and English Tongues* (London, 1611) gives for "monstre" "view, shew, or sight; the countenance, representation, or outward appearance of a thing." Both "contract and purse" and "unfolds" (or "unfoulds") appear in the Folio and Quarto texts.

5. See Barret's *Alvearie or Quadruple Dictionarie* (London, 1573) and John Minshieu's *Ductor in Linguas* (1617) for "close" and "secret" as synonyms.

cult" or "secret" sense surround Iago with hints of the informer who works behind doors.[6]

"Dilation" as "delation" also carried with it implications of a specifically *narrative* relation or report, just as dilation as *rhetorical* opening had to do with uncovering and bringing before the eye.[7] And "dilation" in the sense of "accusation" was a charge made "privilie" or "secretlie," a "delator" a "privie" or "*secret* accuser" or bearer of report.[8] The "close dilations" of the Folio's Temptation Scene, therefore, need not even be altered to the "close delations" of Johnson's emendation in order to convey an already overdetermined sense of "secret accusations," the activity of an informer carried out privately, without the knowledge of others, which comes in *Othello* only after the damage of accusations made in secret has been done. To look closely at the "close dilations" of this controversial text, then, is to discover the implications of "dilation" in the multiple senses of opening and informing, discovery and indictment, of bringing forth to "show" something privy or "close"; and its range of meaning is a reminder of the inseparability of the rhetorical and the judicial in early modern discourse, of opening a "case" and bringing a "cause" to light.

❑

6. "Dilate" is the term that appears in both Folio and Quarto texts of Othello's narrative before the Senate in act 1. The other complex pervading Iago's "informing" is that of the "index" (2.1.257–58), a term that retains its compound Latin sense of forefinger, informer, and index to a book. See Minshieu, *Ductor,* s.v. "index," "*ab indicando,* of showing," and Barret, *Alvearie,* s.v. "index" "an accuser or appeacher: an utterer; a discloser of himself and other; the forefinger; the table of a book." *OED* comments on the links between "index"/"indicate" and "indite"/"indict" (*indicare,* "to give evidence against") through "confusion of the L. verbs *indicare, indicere, indictare;* thus in It., Florio has '*Indicare,* to shew, to declare, to utter; also to endite and accuse, as *Indicere*'; '*Indicere,* to intimate, denounce, manifest, declare; . . . also to accuse, to appeach or detect.'" "Indite" as "write" is linked with *delatio* through Latin *deferre.*

7. For "delate" in this period as "narrate" or "report" (from *deferre,* "convey, deliver, report, indict, accuse"), see Jonson's *Volpone* 2.6 ("They may delate my slackness to my patron") and the *OED*'s "He . . . delated the matter to the Queen," under *delate.*

8. Apart from its English uses, see "dilation" in Richard Huloet's *Abcedarium* (London 1552) as "Accusation secretly made"; Barret, *Alvearie,* "delator" as "secret accuser" and "delatio" as "accusation or complaynt *secretly* made, a tale tolde *privily*"; Thomas Thomas's *Dictionarium Linguae latinae et anglicanae* (1587), s.v. "delator," "secrete accuser . . . a tell tale," "delatio" as "an accusation . . . secretlie made, a tale told privilie" as well as a "bill of complaint, or inditement"; "delateur" as "*privie* accuser" in Claude Desainlien's *Dictionary French and English* (1593), and in Cotgrave's *Dictionarie* as "such a one, as either in love unto Iustice and the State, or in hope of reward or gaine, prosecutes offendors, or *publishes Concealements.*"

That the "close dilations" of the scene in which Desdemona's accuser begins the secret work of his informing should summon the more ominous judicial sense of "information" is far from surprising in a play where reminders of the judicial loom so large, both in the domestic sphere and in the affairs of state—from the Moor's summons to answer the charge of "witchcraft" before the Venetian Senate in act 1 to his invocation of a justifying "cause" ("It is the cause, it is the cause . . .") as he prepares to be judge and executioner in the scene of Desdemona's death.[9] But in order to convey a fuller sense of the historical myopia of excluding an informer's "delations" from the resonances of the "close dilations" of all the authoritative texts of the play but one, we also need to set the language of this passage and its informing beside the contemporary context of delation, spying, and "privy" intelligence.

Here we encounter a wealth of contemporary reference to delators as "secret" or "privie" informers—those who inform *about* the secret and inform *in* secret—as part of what historians of the period describe as the "floating population" of informers and spies in the years before more full-scale development of the police and policing apparatus of the state.[10] G. R. Elton emphasizes the importance of "delations and informations" in the development of the means of "discovery," or bringing a hidden crime to light, as early as the regime of Cromwell.[11] Even more acutely in Elizabeth's reign, in the wake of the 1581 act against reconcilation with Rome and the papal bull *Regnans in excelsis* forbidding her subjects, under pain of excommunication, to obey "her orders, mandates and laws," the workings of Iago as accuser and informer have their counterpart in the multiplication of "delators" and spies encouraged by the need to ferret out recusants and harborers of

9. See Winifred M. T. Nowottny, "Justice and Love in *Othello*," *University of Toronto Quarterly* 21 (1952): 330–44; and Katharine Eisaman Maus, "Proof and Consequences: Inwardness and Its Exposure in the English Renaissance," *Representations* 34 (1991): 29–51.

10. The phrase "floating population" is from Alison Plowden, *Danger to Elizabeth: The Catholics under Elizabeth I* (New York: Stein and Day, 1973), p. 226.

11. See G. R. Elton, *Policy and Police: The Enforcement of the Reformation in the Age of Thomas Cromwell* (Cambridge: Cambridge University Press, 1972), chap. 8, on the "primitive police system" that depended on informing, and his "Informing for Profit: A Sidelight on Tudor Methods of Law-Enforcement," *Cambridge Historical Journal* 11 (1953): 149–67. Elton is less certain of its early central organization than Cromwell's biographer, Roger B. Merriman, in *Life and Letters of Thomas Cromwell*, 2 vols. (Oxford: Clarendon Press, 1902); see, e.g., 1:99, 360, which also stresses the importance of the development of espionage in the period.

secret treason to the queen.[12] In the context of this paranoid atmosphere of spying and being spied upon, one text from the decade before *Hamlet* and *Othello* reports on the omnipresence of "secret spies"
who "do insinuate themselves into our company and familiarity" with
such pretense of "zeal, sincerity, and friendship" that they are able
both to "inform" and to "give intelligence" of the most *"secret* intents." Francis Walsingham—the secretary of state who so enlarged
the Elizabethan network of intelligence—was described in his obitu-
ary notice as "a most diligent searcher of hidden *secrets.*"[13]

   The business of detection and informing, of espial and bringing
"privie secretes" before the eye, was part of the obsession in early
modern England with things done "privilie" or in secret, in the
confessional, the "secret chamber" of the heart, or the "closet" of a
monarch.[14] And echoes of this network of informers, agents, and "in-

   12. See Lowell Gallagher, *Medusa's Gaze: Casuistry and Conscience in the Renaissance*
(Stanford: Stanford University Press, 1991), pp. 71, 294; Conyers Read, *Mr. Secretary
Walsingham and the Policy of Queen Elizabeth,* 3 vols. (Oxford: Clarendon Press, 1925),
e.g., p. 336; R. A. Haldane, *The Hidden World* (New York: St. Martin's Press, 1976);
Alison Plowden, *The Elizabethan Secret Service* (New York: St. Martin's Press, 1991),
and John M. Archer, *Sovereignty and Intelligence: Spying and Court Culture in the English
Renaissance* (Stanford: Stanford University Press, 1993). The increase in informing for
money inspired denunciations such as Bishop Hall's later one against "delators, and
informers" as "infamous and odious" (1649).
   13. See, respectively, "Father Richard Holtby on Persecution in the North" (1593),
in *The Troubles of Our Catholic Forefathers,* ed. John Morris (London, 1877), 3:121, and
Neville Williams, *Elizabeth I, Queen of England* (London: Sphere Books, 1971), p. 261;
also L. B. Smith, *Treason in Tudor England: Politics and Paranoia* (Princeton: Princeton
University Press, 1986).
   14. For different manifestations of this preoccupation, see Patricia Fumerton, "'Secret' Arts: Elizabethan Miniatures and Sonnets," *Representations* 15 (Summer 1986):
57–97; Elizabeth Hanson, "Torture and Truth in Renaissance England," *Representations*
34 (1991): 53–84; Maus, "Proof and Consequences"; Christopher Pye, *The Regal Phantasm: Shakespeare and the Politics of Spectacle* (New York: Routledge, 1990); Gallagher,
Medusa's Gaze, p. 79, for Francis Bacon (himself a spy) on the "secret" and "insinu-
ative" confessional, with Archer, *Sovereignty and Intelligence,* chap. 5; the related language of "discovery" in accounts of the New World and other "hidden" territories in
Patricia Parker, *Literary Fat Ladies: Rhetoric, Gender, Property* (New York: Methuen,
1987), chap. 7; Timothy J. Reiss, *The Discourse of Modernism* (Ithaca: Cornell Univer-
sity Press, 1982), esp. pp. 189–90; and Louis Montrose, "The Work of Gender in the
Discourse of Discovery," *Representations* 33 (1991): 1–41. Parts of the foregoing work
call into question assumptions in Francis Barker, *The Tremulous Private Body* (London:
Methuen 1984), as does, *avant la lettre,* Stephen Greenblatt's *Renaissance Self-Fashioning*
(Chicago: University of Chicago Press, 1980). On secrecy more generally, see Sissela
Bok, *Secrets* (New York: Pantheon, 1982), and Frank Kermode, *The Genesis of Secrecy*
(Cambridge: Harvard University Press, 1979).

telligence" are everywhere in Shakespeare, from the "suborn'd informer" of Sonnet 125 and the "poursuivant" of *Richard III* (part of what Elton calls the "primitive police system" of sixteenth-century England) to the "smiling pick-thanks and base newsmongers" (*1 Henry IV* 3.2.25) who bear against Hal what Holinshed termed "informations that *privilie* charged him with . . . demeanor unseemelie for a prince" and the "tales and informations" gathered by Cromwell in *Henry VIII* (5.2.145). Especially resonant for *Othello* and the figure of "birdlime" applied to Iago (2.1.126) is the description of such "lynx-eyed" men as having the faculty of a "lime twig," able to "catch" anything that comes close.[15]

Things done in secret that depended on "intelligence" or report—crimes, such as adultery and witchcraft, beyond the access of ocular proof[16]—are very much part of the atmosphere of espial and informing in the period before *Hamlet,* itself filled with attempts to ferret out an "occulted guilt" (3.2.80), and *Othello,* which introduces early on a bearer of reports who puts the Venetians in "false gaze" (1.3.19). But the contemporary world of informing and "espials," of the "close" or secret both brought to light and judged, is also joined by an equally resonant context for both plays, one that involves a form of disclosure or espial concerned with the "secrets" of women and a female "close" or privy place. It is to this context that we now turn before returning to the language of these two plays.

◻

15. Elton, *Policy and Police,* p. 345. See "A Yorkshire Recusant's Relation," in Morris, *Troubles,* 3:69; Gallagher, *Medusa's Gaze,* pp. 94–95; and Geoffrey Bullough, *Narrative and Dramatic Sources of Shakespeare* (London: Routledge and Kegan Paul, 1973), 4:195. These are only a few of many Shakespearean instances, which include "espials" (*1 Henry VI* 1.4.8) and informers (*Richard II* 2.1.242) in the early histories, Parolles's informing in *All's Well* (4.3), "information" in *Measure for Measure* (e.g., 3.2.198), and also *King Lear* (4.2.92) and *Coriolanus* (1.6.42). See also Jonathan Dollimore, "Transgression and Surveillance in *Measure for Measure,*" in *Political Shakespeare* (Ithaca: Cornell University Press, 1985), pp. 72–87.

16. For witchcraft, see Maus, "Proof and Consequences," p. 38, and Karen Newman, *Fashioning Femininity and English Renaissance Drama* (Chicago: University of Chicago Press, 1991), pp. 73–93. On the general problem of evidence, see Barbara J. Shapiro, *Probability and Certainty in Seventeenth-Century England* (Princeton: Princeton University Press, 1983); and on slander and the problem of proof, see Kenneth Gross, "Slander and Skepticism in *Othello,*" *ELH* 86 (1989): 819–52; J. A. Sharpe, "Defamation and Sexual Slander in Early Modern England: The Church Courts of York," Borthwick Papers no. 58, University of York (1981); and W. S. Holdsworth, *A History of English Law,* 9 vols. (Boston: Methuen, 1927), 3:409–11, 5:205–12.

Like the letter, o, small and wondrous narrow . . .
Too obscoene to look upon . . .
                    —Helkiah Crooke

In order to link this sexualized and gendered context to the world of
informing and spying out secrets, we need to consider once more the
"close dilations" of the Temptation Scene, not simply as secret accusations but in their other sense as rhetorical *opening*. To "dilate" in early
modern usage came with a sense of widening, stretching, or enlarging
something "closed." Hence it meant both to "make large" and to
speak "at large," expanding or discursively spreading out something
originally smaller or more constricted.[17] In the rhetorical and narrative
sense introduced into the play in Othello's reference to the request that
he might "*all* [his] pilgrimage *dilate*" (1.3.153), the link with dilation
made rhetoric itself a form of opening, illustrated by the figure of the
open palm in contrast to logic's closed fist.[18] One of the most famous
of early modern descriptions characterizes rhetorical dilation as an enlarging or unfolding through which the eye is enabled to see things
previously "folded" or closed ("But if you *open up* those things which
were included in a single word, there will appear flames pouring
through houses and temples"). To "dilate," then, was directly related
to a *visual* sense of opening up to "show"—"like displaying some object for sale first of all through a lattice or inside a wrapping, and then
unwrapping it and opening it out and displaying it *more fully to the
gaze*." Descriptions of such rhetorical opening manage to suggest an
eroticized, voyeuristic, or even prurient looking, not just a way to
"spread abroad" something hidden or closed but a means by which
"to open the bosom of nature and to *shew* her branches, to that end
they may be *viewed and looked upon, discerned and knowen*."[19]
    It is this dimension of "dilation" that made possible the easy move-
ment between rhetorical and sexual opening, between the open palm
of rhetoric and the open hand or palm taken (as in *Othello* or *The
Winter's Tale*) as sign of the openness of a woman and her sexual appe-

17. See, for example, Thomas's *Dictionarium* (1587), s.v. "dilato," "To stretch out
in breadth, to extende or enlarge, to delaie"; and Cotgrave, *Dictionarie,* s.v. "dilater,"
"To dilate, widen, inlarge, extend, stretch out, spread abroad, make broad."
    18. See William G. Crane, *Wit and Rhetoric in the Renaissance* (New York: Columbia
University Press, 1937).
    19. See, respectively, the discussion of "Abundance of Subject Matter" in Erasmus,
De Copia, bk. 2 ("ac totam oculis exponat"); and Henry Peacham, *The Garden of Elo-
quence* (1593; rpt. Gainesville, Fla.: Scholars' Facsimiles, 1954), pp. 123–24.

tite, a "frank" and "liberal" hand that argues a licentious or a "liberal heart" (*Othello* 3.4.36–46).[20] In Shakespeare, this link between opening a "matter" rhetorically "at large" and the sexual opening or enlarging of a woman is already familiar from the so-called Dark Lady sonnets of a "large" and "spacious" female "will" (Sonnet 135), a closed or "private" female place become the "wide world's *common* place" (Sonnet 137).[21] Concern that this secret or "privie" place might become instead a "common" place characterized in particular anxieties about adultery, the fear that a virgin, once opened, could not have her "opening" controlled. To open or "dilate" a virgin, the term used routinely in the period for such sexual opening, involved the threat of "enlargement" in every sense: the opening of a formerly closed and "privie" place which simultaneously opened up the possibility that a woman might be at large in a more threatening sense—that, as Othello puts it, "We can call these delicate creatures ours, / And *not their appetites*" (3.3.269–70).

"Close," then, in the "close dilations" of the Temptation Scene, carries the implication of "private" and "secret" in a sexual sense, a hidden place which only through opening can be displayed or "shown." And this sense of "close" as "secret" or "hid" in relation to the sexual "privitie" of woman informs the network of associations between this private female place and the language of espial and informing central to *Othello* and to *Hamlet,* including the scene in a queen's "closet" to which a secret informer, or delator, comes as spy. Before we turn more directly to the plays, therefore, let us consider the particular contemporary discourse that combines both the dilating or opening of the "privitie" of woman and the sense of bringing something hid before the inspection of the eye. This is the gynecological discourse of a contemporary anatomy dedicated to the "ocular" discovery or exposing of a woman's "privity" or "lap."

The language of the "close" or "secrete"—of a hidden "matter" or "matrix" that might be dilated, opened, and displayed—pervades the literature on the "privities" of woman in contrast to the exteriorized sexual parts of man. Helkiah Crooke's "Of the Lap or Privities" ("in

20. See the Riverside edition's note on "frank" (p. 1223); *OED,* s.v. "frank" a2.2.b; and the play in *Love's Labor's Lost* 3.1.120–21 on "enfranchise" and "Frances," a name that appears in the form of "Frank" in John Marston, *The Dutch Courtesan* (1605), in relation to female sexual appetite.

21. On "private place"/"common place," see Parker, *Literary Fat Ladies,* p. 104, and p. 251 n.12.

Latine *pudendum muliebre,* that is, the woman's modesty") treats, for
example, of "the outward privity or lap" of a woman as a "cleft"
which like a "doore" might be "opened" or "shut"—a sense of the
"close" or of something closeted behind a "doore" which pervades
medical as well as popular references to this secret place. The orifice
of the matrix or womb—in ways highly suggestive when placed beside the familiar Shakespearean euphemism for the female sexual orifice, the "O" or "nothing" printed in early Shakespeare texts as a
graphically smaller "o"—is described in this same medical text as "like
the letter, o, small and wondrous narrow," yet capable of being *"more
open"* according to "the womans appetite."[22]

Crooke's and other discussions of this "privy" place repeatedly treat
of its capacity to dilate—first in the initial opening of a "closed" virginity (where it is rare that "the Membranes are dilated with little or no
paine") and thereafter "in Copulation" and "in childbirth." Renaldus
Columbus—the anatomist who claimed, like another Columbus, to
have brought a previously hidden place to light—spoke of the "mouth
of the womb" or matrix as being *"dilated with extreme pleasure* in inter-
course."[23] The sexual dilation of a virgin, or of a more experienced
woman, was thus in every sense an opening to "increase," the enlarging of something "close" or closed whose opening was essential to
fulfilling the command to increase and multiply. In ways resonant beside the "close dilations" of the Temptation Scene and its "contract
and purse," the image used repeatedly in contemporary discussions of
this "privie" female place was of something "dilated and shut together
like a purse," a figure that appears in the work of the physician
Thomas Vicary ("open" or "shut togeather as a Purse mouth"), as in

22. See Helkiah Crooke, *Microcosmographia: A Description of the Body of Man* (London, 1615), pp. 232–34, 237; subsequent references are cited in the text.
23. See, respectively, ibid., p. 236, and Audrey Eccles, *Obstetrics and Gynaecology
in Tudor and Stuart England* (Kent, Ohio: Kent State University Press, 1982), for passages on the "opening" of the cervix "in Copulation and in childbirth"; Renaldus Columbus, *De re anatomica* (Venice, 1559), bk. 11, chap. 16, p. 445; and (including on the
links between the two Columbuses) Thomas Laqueur, *Making Sex: Body and Gender
from the Greeks to Freud* (Cambridge: Harvard University Press, 1990), pp. 64ff. "Dilation" is, of course, still the term for the opening of the cervix in childbirth. For its
sexual cognates, see also the repeated Shakespearean image of the chevril glove, for
example, its capacity for "stretching" used for the ambivalent "capacity" of Anne Bul-
len in *Henry VIII* (2.3.31–33). Stretching in order to "serve" in a sexual (including
homoerotic) sense also crosses with the "service" of artisan players in the highly sexualized language of class difference in *A Midsummer Night's Dream* 5.1.78–81 ("Extremely
stretch'd and conn'd with cruel pain, / To do you service").

such popular texts as *De secretis mulierum,* or *On the Secrets of Women.*[24] The privity or "lap" itself was understood as something "folded," and hence needing to be unfolded in order to be available for "show"[25]— a sense of unfolding exploited not only in Othello's suspicion that his informer "sees and knows more, much more, than he *unfolds*" (3.3.243) but also in the obscene play on "lap" in *Hamlet,* as we shall see.

As with rhetorical dilation as an unwrapping or unfolding to the eye, the female "lap" or privity was thus something folded or closed as well as something secret or "close." And here, in the impulse of anatomical discourse to open up to "show," the links are even clearer between the language of the informer exposing something secret to the eye and the discourses surrounding a woman's "secrete" place, not only brought to light but indicted and judged. In his discussion "Of the Lap or Privities," Crooke not only speaks of the little "o" which is "more open or more contracted" according to the "womans appetite"; he also provides an anatomical diagram of this secret place in which "the cleft of the lap or privity" is described as "dilated or laide open" to the gazer's view (p. 220). The "dilating" of a woman figures, therefore, in these texts both sexually and visually, both as opening and as bringing a secret place before the eye.

This sense of "dilation" as visual opening is of course part of the ocular impulse of anatomy more generally—its preoccupation with what William Harvey called "ocular inspection," with what can or cannot be opened up to "shew," an impulse that has led recent commentators to align it with the specularity of theater. Like informing or espial, the vogue for anatomy in the early modern period involved a fascination with the ocular, with exposing what lay hid to the scru-

24. See Thomas Vicary, *The Anatomie of the Bodie of Man* (1548; London 1888 ed.), chap. 9, p. 77; Laqueur, *Making Sex,* pp. 63–64, and *The Works of Aristotle the Famous Philosopher* (New York: Arno Press, 1974), p. 81 ("which may be *dilated and shut together like a purse;* for though in the act of *copulation* it is *big enough* to receive the glands of the yard, yet after conception it is so *close shut,* that it will not admit the point of a bodkin to enter; and yet again at the time of the woman's delivery it is opened so extraordinary"). The link between this "purse" and the mouth is exploited in the double-meaning "delivered" of *Two Gentlemen of Verona* 1.3.137: "Open your purse, that the money and the matter may be both at once delivered"; see also the "purse"/"person" play in *2 Henry IV* 2.1.127 and in the homoerotic context of the Antonio-Bassanio relationship in *Merchant of Venice* 1.1.138.

25. See Huloet's *Abecedarium* s.v. "lap," and Minsheu, *Ductor,* who gives both "lappe" and *gremium* and "to Lappe, or fould up." "Lapped" as "folded" is a common meaning in the period.

tiny of the gaze.[26] The impulse to open and expose as an epistemological hunger to "see and know" is, in the case of the "privitie" of
woman, however, a much more complicated impulse, a desire both
to see and not to see, to display to the eye and to discourage or refrain
from looking. Crooke's text both calls attention to the diagram displaying "the lap or privity dilated or laide open" to the view and warns
that this place is *"too obscoene to look upon,"* a warning it shares with
other descriptions of the "occult" or hidden parts of women. Beside
the exposed anatomy of a man, its title page sets the more modestly
opaque and closed body of a woman, covering her private parts.[27] The
text speaks particularly of the "o" or "fissure that admitteth the yard"
as "a part thought too obscoene to look upon," adding that this is the
reason, "sayth Pliny, that the carcasses of women do floate in water
with their faces downeward, contrary to mens which swimme upward; even Nature itself yeelding to modesty" (p. 239)—a claim to
which we will need to return in the case of the "o" of Ophelia and her
more immodest drowning.

A sense of this secret female place as something too "obscene" for
"show" recurs repeatedly in anatomical discourse. John Banister's *His-
torie of Man,* a text of anatomy published in 1578, claims that "there is
nothing so highe in the heavens above, nothing so low in the earth
beneath, nothing so profound in the bowels of Arte, *nor any thing so
hid in the secretes of nature,* as that good will dare not enterprise, *search,
unclose or discover*" (Epistle Dedicatory). But when he comes in book
6 to speak, after the sexual "instruments" of man, of the corresponding parts of women, he writes: "Because I am from the beginning
persuaded, that, by lifting up *the vayle of Natures secretes in womens
Shapes,* I shall commit more indecencie agaynst the office of Decorum

---

26. See *The Anatomical Lectures of William Harvey,* trans. Gweneth Whitteridge (Ed-
inburgh: E. & S. Livingstone, 1964), p. 4[lv], with among others, Laqueur, *Making
Sex;* Luke Wilson, "William Harvey's *Prelectiones:* The Performance of the Body in
the Renaissance Theater of Anatomy," *Representations* 17 (Winter 1987): 69–95; and
Devon L. Hodges, *Renaissance Fictions of Anatomy* (Amherst: University of Massachusetts Press, 1985), esp. chaps. 1 and 6.

27. For continental references, both medical and literary, to this "obscene" place,
see, for example, Thomas Johnson, trans., *The Workes of that famous Chirurgeon Am-
brose Parey* (London, 1637), p. 130, and Barthélemy Aneau, *Picta Poesis* (Lyons, 1552),
p. 52, on the *obscoena lama* ("obscene bog") of the *cunnus,* in relation to female sexual
appetite. On Crooke's title page and other such illustrations, see Newman, *Fashioning
Femininity,* pp. 2–5.

than yeld needefull instruction to the profite of the common sort, I do here ordein the vi rest of these my labours." The marginal text records: "Why the partes of women are not here spoken of." The sense of a female "privity" too "obscoene" to be seen also lies behind the warnings against and simultaneous stimulation of the gaze in anatomical treatises aware of bringing before the eye what otherwise would be lapped, folded, secret, hid. Crooke warns in relation to the "obscoene parts" of woman that caution must be exercised in describing and hence displaying them vicariously to the eye: "We will first describe the parts of generation belonging to men, and then proceede to those of Women also; of which wee would advise no man to take further knowledge then shall serve for his good instruction" (p. 199). A kindred sense of the pornographic dangers of opening and displaying "close" and "secret" female parts sounds through Eucharius Roesslin's *Byrth of Mankinde* and its warning that some "wold have hadde this booke forbidden" because it "descried and set forth the secretes and privities of women" in ways that allowed "every boy and knave" to view them "openly."[28]

Ambivalence, then, about opening up to "shew" this "secrete" part produces what might be called the anatomical text's pornographic doubleness, its simultaneous opening up and denying to the eye. In this sense, exposures of a female "lap" or "privitie" are part of the more general hunger in the period for pornographic or quasi-pornographic display, not just in gynecological description or anatomical illustration but in the extraordinary growth of a "monster" literature—the word itself (as in *Othello*) forging a link between "showing" or "de*monstra*ting" and the "monstrous" as the previously unknown or hidden from vision.[29] Crooke's text presents a female "lap" or privity "dilated or laide open" to the eye while warning its readers against the uses to which this dilation or unfolding might be put—in a way not unlike the pandering and pornographic doubleness

28. See Eucharius Roesslin, *The Byrth of Mankinde, otherwise named the Woman's Booke,* trans. Thomas Raynolde (1560).

29. On the vogue for this literature, see among others Katharine Park and L. J. Daston, "Unnatural Conceptions: The Study of Monsters in Sixteenth- and Seventeenth-Century France and England," *Past and Present* 92 (1981): 20–54; on *monster/ monstrare,* see Ambroise Paré, *On Monsters and Marvels,* trans. Janis L. Pallister (Chicago: University of Chicago Press, 1982), p. 196.

of Iago's simultaneous invitation to and prohibition of the "ocular."[30] In a metaphor that already linked the opening of a woman to the opening of a book, texts of anatomy that exposed such "secretes" encountered the problem of *publishing,* in the sense of making "public," the double of the impulse to "display" (*displicare,* "unfold") which in the instance of opening a woman up to "show" risked turning a "private" into a "common" place.

❏

> an essence that's not seen.
> —*Othello*

To return to the "close dilations" of *Othello* from the contemporary context of both judicial uncovering and the desire to see and not to see an "obscoene" and private female place is to become aware of the simultaneously sexual, judicial, and epistemological impulses of opening, dilating, or uncovering to the view that combine so powerfully in this play. It might indeed be said that *Othello* trains the domestic *political* activity of the delator or informer on the domestic *private* sphere of this "secrete" female place, in ways that involve not just the language of a crime to be uncovered but a simultaneously prurient and deeply ambivalent fascination with the "close" or privy locus of female sexuality, opened, "unfolded," brought forth to "show." The already cited passage of Iago's "close dilations" is resonant with the sense of something too "monstrous" or "hideous" to be shown, while the sexual suggestiveness of "queynte" lurks within the lines on Cassio as one "acquainted" with Othello's wife (3.3.99). And the partial glimpses that lead to the Moor's suspicion that his informer "sees and knows more, much more than he unfolds" (243) culminate in the demand for "ocular proof" (360) from an informer whose "report" and circumstantial evidence promise to lead him to a "door of *truth*" (3.3.407) linked with the privy "chamber" of a woman.

Within the almost unbearably protracted Temptation Scene, the "close dilations" that lead to this demand for "show" find their echo in a later passage whose terms are also both epistemological and sexual:

> *Iago.* My lord, I would I might entreat your honor
>   To *scan this thing no farther;* leave it to time.

30. On *Othello* in relation to the rise of pornography in the period, see Lynda Boose, "'Let It Be Hid': Renaissance Pornography, Iago, and Audience Response," in

> Although 'tis fit that Cassio have his place—
> For sure he fills it up with great ability . . .
>
> (3.3.244–47)

Hidden within an informer's advice to "scan this thing no farther"—in lines whose "thing" appears to designate simply the matter under discussion (Desdemona's adultery)—is a "matter" that elsewhere in this scene is the "thing" or "common thing" (301–2) Emilia offers to her husband, the female privity or *res* that Iago vulgarly sexualizes when she intrudes to offer him what turns out to be the "trifle" of the handkerchief.[31] The advice against "scanning" this "thing," appearing to speak only to an epistemological hunger to "see" and "know," introduces into the lines that follow the double meanings of the "place" Cassio "fills up" with "great ability," a "place" whose sexual inference is joined by the threat to Othello's "occupation" through the more obscene sense of "occupy."[32] "Scan this thing no farther" resonates with a *res* that is at once epistemological and sexual, as with a sense of scanning as the inspection of a matter or "thing" brought before the eye.[33]

Hunger to "know" as desire to "see" pervades the scene of Iago's partial or "close dilations" and Othello's "if thou dost love me / *Show* me thy thought" (115–16), in lines that link hunger to see what is hidden within Iago's mind to an increasingly obsessed fascination with what lies "hid" within Desdemona's "chamber."[34] "Show," as in *Hamlet,* is a term that already reverberates with overtones of female sexual-

---

Autour d'Othello, ed. Richard Marienstras et al. (n.p.: Presses de l'UFR Clerc Université Picardie, n.d.).

31. See Erik S. Ryding, "Scanning This Thing Further: Iago's Ambiguous Advice," *Shakespeare Quarterly* 40 (1989): 195–96.

32. The lines appear in both Folio and Quarto texts, as does this "common thing" and references to Othello's "occupation." For "occupy," see Parker, *Literary Fat Ladies,* p. 132; Marlowe's *Massacre at Paris* ("till the ground which he himself should eccupy" [4.5.4–9]), in *Christopher Marlowe: The Complete Plays,* ed. J. B. Steane (Harmondsworth: Penguin, 1969); Peter Stallybrass, "Patriarchal Territories: The Body Enclosed," in *Rewriting the Renaissance,* ed. Margaret W. Ferguson et al. (Chicago: University of Chicago Press, 1986).

33. My argument is meant both to intersect with and extend that of Stanley Cavell on the play, in, for example, his "Othello and the Stake of the Other," in *Disowning Knowledge in Six Plays of Shakespeare* (Cambridge: Cambridge University Press, 1987), pp. 125–42.

34. On the homoerotic implications of this passage and the corresponding imagery of penetration through the ear, see my essay "Fantasies of 'Race' and 'Gender': Africa, *Othello,* and Bringing to Light," in *Women, "Race," and Writing in the Early Modern Period,* ed. Margo Hendricks and Patricia Parker (London: Routledge, 1994).

ity—as in the pun on "shoe" and "shew" in *Two Gentlemen of Verona,*
where the "shoe with the hole in it" is taken to be the mother as the
"worser sole" (2.3.14–18).[35] What is secret or unseen here, like the
"dark and vicious place" of begetting in *Lear,* is the ambiguous "place"
of all the double-meaning references to the "place" Cassio might occupy as Othello's "place-holder" or lieu-tenant.[36] At the same time,
the almost tortuously condensed senses of "some *monster* in thy
thought / Too *hide*ous to be *shown*" register a double impulse, as in
Crooke's presentation, "dilated and laide open" to the view, of something simultaneously "too obscoene to look upon." "Hideous," as Michael Neill has brilliantly argued, is in this complex pun "virtually an
Anglo-Saxon equivalent for the Latinate 'obscene,'" as that which,
according to a powerful though false etymology, should be kept "offstage"—forging a link of sound between the *scaenum* or stage and the
obscene as what should be hidden, unseen, not "shown."[37]

As has often been remarked, however, *Othello* provokes a constant,
even lurid fascination with the offstage, hidden or in this sense obscene. Much of its language, from the visually evocative rhetoric of
Iago and Roderigo at its opening ("an old black ram . . . tupping your
white ewe" [1.1.88–89]) keeps attention centered on an unseen sexual
coupling, or imagined coupling, that also involves the sexual opening
of Desdemona as a virgin on her wedding night or, once Iago's inferences and "close dilations" begin, as an already "open" and too "liberal" woman. The fact that this opening is happening offstage and
hence is barred from more direct ocular access prompts what mounts
in the play both as a hunger for yet more narrative or report—the
desire of now another "hungry ear" that an informer might "*all* [his
narrative] *dilate*"—and as a desire that the hidden, "close," or secret be
brought forth to "show." The audience of the play—and its critics—
get caught up in its obsessive reference to this hidden scene, inacces-
sible to what Lacan called the eye's *invidia.* Obsession with what is
available only in "close dilations" or partial glimpses—and the hunger
to have dilated "at large" what has been glimpsed only in "parcels" or
in part (1.3.154)—becomes in *Othello* the powerful dramatic counterpart of the obsessive scopophilia of jealousy, its obsession with

35. See Eric Partridge, *Shakespeare's Bawdy,* rev. ed. (New York: Dutton, 1969),
p. 121.

36. On "place"/"lieu-tenant," see Michael Neill, "Changing Places in *Othello,*"
Shakespeare Survey 37 (1984): 124, 127–28; and Julia Genster, "Lieutenancy, Standing
In, and *Othello,*" *ELH* 57 (1990): 785–809.

37. See Neill, "Unproper Beds," p. 394.

glimpses possible only through a tantalizing *jalousie,* a link also forged
in the language of rhetorical dilation as showing first through a "lattice" before opening more fully to the gaze.[38]

Desire in this play to bring the hidden forth to "show" emerges
most clearly in the substitute fetish object of the handkerchief, introduced first as the "thing" Emilia offers to show her husband after
Othello's "Show me thy thought" and his demand to "see" and
"know." Through a pun on "matter" and female "matrix," which
runs through *Hamlet* as through *Othello,* this "thing" is paired syntac-
tically with something that is "the matter" ("*Des.* I will so. What's the
matter? / *Oth.* That handkerchief . . ." [5.2.48–50]). "Spotted" with
strawberries (3.3.435), it is linked with Desdemona's sexuality, blood-
stained wedding sheets, and hence with the "show" that signals a virgin's opening.[39] As a "thing" that *can* be "scanned" and "seen," it
makes the invisible visible, standing, as "trifle," for a female "particular" otherwise out of the field of vision, forging links of sound with
the open "hand" of Desdemona that argues something else too open
and too "liberal." As the visible counterpart to the *rhetorical* uncovering of the lines on Cassio and Desdemona "naked in bed" (4.1.1–
5)—narrative that appears to bring something offstage before the
eye—it is associated with the exposure of secrets, standing in for "an
essence that's not seen" (4.1.16) and figuring a magical ability "almost
[to] read / The thoughts of people" (3.4.57–58). As a form of "show"
that renders the private public, it appears to expose the "villainous
secrets" for which Emilia is the "closet lock and key" (4.2.21) and thus
to *publish* Desdemona's crime, offering a "thing" or "common thing"
that makes this "privie" female place into a "common place," pro-
voking Othello's "O thou *public commoner*" (4.2.73) as he delivers the
judgment Iago's informing finally brings him to.

In the desire for "show" or "ocular proof" that begins with the
"close dilations" of act 3, Iago plays both informer on a hidden crime,
invoking all the language of judicial "proofs" (3.3.430), and pander to
the simultaneously horrified and fascinated gaze. The partial glimpses
offered by his informing lead toward the offstage "chamber" of Des-

---

38. *Gelosia* as both "jealousy" and "a Lattice Window" appears in Richard Perci-
vale, *A Dictionarie in Spanish and English* (London, 1599). See also Minsheu, *Ductor,*
"Lattises, *a latendo,* of hiding," and Cotgrave, *Dictionarie,* "Ialousie: f. Iealousie, sus-
pition, mistrust; also, a lattice window, or grate to looke through."

39. See Lynda Boose, "Othello's Handkerchief: The Recognizance and Pledge of
Love,'" *English Literary Renaissance* 5 (1975): 360–74.

demona's sexuality and assumed offense. But the double impulse which in an anatomist such as Crooke involves both the exposure of a "privity dilated or laide open" to the view and the sense that it is a place "too obscoene to look upon" also informs the desire in *Othello* at once to see and to avert the eye. The sense of disgust conveyed in Othello's "She with Cassio hath the *act of shame* / A thousand times committed" (5.2.211–12) and the metaphorical displacements of his description of Iago as an "honest man" who "hates the slime / That sticks on filthy deeds" (148–49) resonate, as Edward Snow has argued, with disgust at the sexual act itself, with what Crooke terms "so obscoene a businesse" in a text that also describes the female orifice in particular as something "obscoene."[40]

We have already noted the ambivalence involved in the sexual as well as rhetorical opening or "enlargement" of a woman, as well as its relation to the anxieties of adultery, the fear that a "closed" virgin, once "opened," might be enfranchised or "at large." In this sense the dilation or opening of a "privie" female place also involves something threatening to the privy or private as sole possession or private property, to closure and *en*closure at once. The sense that a woman can be either "closed" or dangerously "open" hovers in *Othello* around the association of Desdemona with the women of Venice in particular, simultaneously a "Virgin Citie" and the "wide world's common place," famous for its courtesans.[41] But it also underlies the exploitation in *Othello* of links between the two traditionally associated female orifices—closed or silent mouth and female "lap" or "privitie"—both suspect, and threatening, in their potential liberality. Desdemona's "parleying" early in act 2—in a scene filled with reference to the too "liberal" female tongue, mouth, and "lips," and to women's proverbial propensity to "disclose" secrets (2.1.156)—links her with the topos of the too open and unsecret female mouth (as will her resolution, later, to "talk Othello out of patience" [3.3.23]), while the attendant suggestion of sexual openness, her "parley to provocation" (2.3.23), as Iago tellingly puts it, is a link made sotto voce in the climaxing of this exchange with the hint of "strumpet" in "The Moor! I know his trumpet" (2.1.178). In relation to this threatening openness of "o" and

40. See Edward A. Snow, "Sexual Anxiety and the Male Order of Things in *Othello,*" *English Literary Renaissance* 10 (1980): 384–413, and Stephen Greenblatt's reading in *Renaissance Self-Fashioning,* pp. 232–54.

41. On Venice, see Ann Rosalind Jones, "Italians and Others: Venice and the Irish in Coryat's *Crudities* and *The White Devil,*" *Renaissance Drama,* n.s. 18 (1987): 101–19.

mouth, Desdemona is silenced as well as made more passive-obedient in order simply to affirm her chastity as the play proceeds, in contrast to the frankness of her speech at the beginning, when, asking for an "ear" to her "unfolding" (1.3.244), she had expressed desire for the "rites" of a marriage resulting from her own will. The form of her death, then—in a striking departure from the play's source—becomes the closing or stifling of her mouth, an act that makes explicit the links between the two orifices throughout, a symbolic "close" both to her speech and to the assumed crime of sexual openness enacted on her wedding sheets.

The sense of closing, or attempting to close, what has been "opened," in this linking of the "o" of a woman's "secrete" place with the openness of her mouth, gathers force as the tragedy moves to its own close, in the increasingly insistent references to the stopping of women's mouths: in the desire to keep Bianca from railing "in the streets" (4.1.163) and in Iago's command to Emilia to "speak *within door*" and "charm" her tongue before she finally, too late, determines to be "liberal" in her speech (5.2.219–22). In relation to the stage directing of Iago as the Moor's sole informer, the attempt to charm or stop female tongues and other tongues as the play proceeds toward its "bloody period" (5.2.357) parallels this informer's need to prevent what is called a further "unfolding" (5.1.21). In this sense, the closing down that takes over as the tragedy rushes toward its end involves a closing off of further dilation or "increase," not just stopping mouths but putting an end to Desdemona's threateningly open sexuality, along with the nightmare of increase ("a thousand times committed") glimpsed through the *jalousie* of Iago's informing. As a foreclosing of "increase," the scene of her death (with all its images of symbolically regained virginity) echoes the desire for closure and perfection already expressed in the scene of "parleying" in act 2, where Othello's yearning for death ("If it were now to die . . ." [2.1.191]) stands in striking contrast to Desdemona's "The heavens forbid / But that our loves and comforts should *increase* / Even as our days do *grow*" (2.1.193–95).

The impulse to "see" and open up to "show"—driving obsession with what is offstage and hidden from the eye—is countered correspondingly as *Othello* moves to this close by the impulse to close off or hide from sight. The play repeatedly eroticizes the offstage "chamber" linked with Desdemona's sexuality and hidden behind a "door" before that chamber, and its bed, are finally uncovered to vision in the play's last scene. But when what has been offstage, ob-scene, and hidden is finally brought forth to "show," it is only after this privy/ob-scene female place has been indicted. *"Enter Othello, [with a light,] and Desdemona in her bed"* is the stage direction in the Folio—supplemented by the "light" of Q1—reproduced in most modern editions. But what is in this almost literal sense finally exposed or brought to light—the hidden place of Desdemona's sexuality and her "crime" (5.2.26)—is, almost as soon as it is shown, rehidden and reclosed. The lines simultaneously bespeak the desire to "put out the light, and then put out the light" (5.2.7), a sense that emerges in the gesture of repressing which extends to the whole of the spectacle the play has exposed, in the lines addressed by Lodovico to Iago, the simultaneous informer and pander responsible for this "show": "Look on the tragic loading [Q1, lodging] of this bed; / This is thy work. The object *poisons sight,* / Let it be *hid*" (5.2.363–65).

The final scene that leads to Desdemona's stifling in the "bed" she has "defil'd," one that invokes the satisfying of a "justice" ("The justice of it pleases" [4.1.209]), begins with Othello's "It is the cause, it is the cause, my soul; / Let me not name it to you, you chaste stars," and then repeats "It is the *cause* . . ." (5.2.1–3). The judicial resonance of this repeated "cause" summons the judicial language so pervasive throughout the play, here invoked to authorize a husband as final judge and executioner of a too open or too "liberal" wife ("Yet she must die, else she'll betray more men," [5.2.6]). But the "cause" that cannot be named to these "chaste stars" also hides a language that has lurking within it the threateningly open "case" of an unchaste woman, through a complex interlingual pun linking "cause," "case," "chose," and "thing," the obscene, unnameable "case" of a woman whose opening provides the justifying "cause" of her death and the judicial proceeding of a husband against a female "chose" or "thing" that cannot be named to stars figuring the virginal coldness of a closed perfection.[42] Female "case" and legal "cause" are linked elsewhere in

42. The English "cause" descends from the same Latin *causa* as French *chose,* or "matter" (a sense that *causa* has in Salic Law) and so easily crosses with the sexual meaning of *chose* or "thing" (as in the "bele chose" of Chaucer's Wife of Bath). In the legal sense it is "a matter before a court for decision," and hence often used for "case." On the virginal/perfect here, see Janet Adelman, *Suffocating Mothers* (New York: Routledge, 1992), chap. 3. Both "chaste starres" (or "Starres") and the repeated "cause" (Q1) and "Cause" (F) appear in Quarto and Folio texts here.

Shakespeare, before and after the staging of this scene.[43] But in this tragic context, what began as the opening of this case in the "close dilations" of Iago's informing here in the lines that move from "It is the cause" to "Put out the light" becomes, in every sense, a final closing of the case, an opening of the closed "chamber" of Desdemona's sexuality, only to execute upon it the "foregone conclusion" of a predetermined justice. Othello's "It is the cause, it is the cause" summons the sense throughout the play of a monstrous parallel between a process of judgment, where the information laid by a secret accuser is enough to result in the death of the accused, and the suppressed, subliminal language of the sexual "cause," or "case," as something—secret, close, occult—always indicted in advance.[44]

The tragedy that leads from Iago's tantalizingly partial or "close dilations" to Othello's demand for "ocular proof" ends with a gesture of repression and re-closing expressed not only by the desire that something that "poisons sight" be "hid," but by this informer's "Demand me nothing" (5.2.303), its verbal or rhetorical counterpart. The play that began with "Tush, never tell me" and with reference to the opening of a "purse" both opens up to "show" and then recloses, as if there were an underground link between the dilating or opening of a secret place to view and the theatrical "show" which, as in the root of "*thea*trical," depends on the sense of something viewed or "seen."[45] Before we consider the fuller implications of this link, however, let us

43. In Mistress Quickly's "my exion is ent'red and my case so openly known to the world" (*2 Henry IV* 2.1.30–31) and in *Cymbeline* ("I will make / One of her women lawyer to me, for / I yet not understand the case myself," [2.3.73–75]).

44. On the "preposterous" order of "foregone conclusion" (3.3.428), reversing effect and "cause," accusation and crime, see Joel B. Altman, "'Preposterous Conclusions': Eros, Enargeia, and the Composition of *Othello*," *Representations* 18 (1987): 129–57, and Parker, *Literary Fat Ladies,* pp. 67–69, 93, 112; and, on this perverse logic in relation to female sexuality, Patricia Parker, "Preposterous Events," *Shakespeare Quarterly* 43 (1992): 186–213.

45. See Joel Fineman on the links between Greek *epideiknunai* (to show, display), *deiknunai* (to bring to light, show forth, represent, portray, point out), and the "*thea*trical" as "the seen" in *Shakespeare's Perjured Eye* (Berkeley: University of California Press, 1986), pp. 102–3; and Barbara Freedman, *Staging the Gaze* (Ithaca: Cornell University Press, 1991), esp. pp. 48, 70, with Harry Berger, Jr., *Second World and Green World* (Berkeley: University of California Press, 1988), esp. pp. 145–46 on "theatrical experience" and "optical perception." Fineman's essay "The Sound of O in *Othello*: The Real of the Tragedy of Desire," *October* 45 (1988): 77–96, is similarly attentive to the etymological resonances of sound in this play, though its quasi-allegorical reading elides crucial gender and racial differences.

now turn to *Hamlet,* which draws an explicit link between the spying
out of secrets, dramatic spectacle, and female "show."

❑

Her clothes spread wide . . .
                    —*Hamlet*

In the midst of *Hamlet,* in the scene meant to "catch the conscience of
the king," Hamlet initiates an exchange with Ophelia filled with obscene double entendres, first on "lap" and then on "shew" or "show."
The exchange begins with "Lady, shall I lie in your lap?" (3.2.112), a
question made more bawdy by the reference in both Folio and Second
Quarto to "country matters," obscenely invoking a female "matter,"
count or "cunt," and the "nothing" that lies "between maids' legs"
(116–19). It continues as this "nothing" is iterated in Hamlet's "For
O, for O, the hobby-horse is forgot,"[46] and then, following the Dumb
Show and its "show of protestation" made by a queen, in the concluding double entendres on the meaning of this "show":

Oph. What means this, my lord?
Ham. Marry, this'miching mallecho, it means mischief.
Oph. Belike this show imports the argument of the play.
                                             [*Enter Prologue.*]
Ham. We shall know by this fellow. The players cannot keep
        counsel, they'll tell all.
Oph. Will a' tell us what this show meant?
Ham. Ay, or any show that you will show him. Be not you
        asham'd to show, he'll not shame to tell you what it means.
                                                      (136–46)

The obscene play on "show" or "shew" here exploits, once again, the
links between dramatic "show" and female "show," heightened (as in
Two Gentlemen) by the possibility of a pun on "shoe," referring to a
woman's sexual part.[47] Both the initial reference to a female "lap" and

46. See the 1604 (Second) Quarto ("for o, for o, the hobby-horse is forgot") and the
1623 Folio ("For o, For o . . ."). "Hobby-horse" is also Elizabethan slang for "whore."
47. Harold Jenkins's Arden edition of *Hamlet* (London: Methuen, 1974), p. 297,
cites *Trivium* 4.108–11. The link between dramatic "show" and female "show" also
appears elsewhere, e.g., in Ben Jonson's *Conversations with Drummond* (1.140.292–94),
cited in both John Dover Wilson's edition of *Hamlet* (Cambridge: Cambridge University Press, 1934) and the G. R. Hibbard edition (Oxford: Oxford University Press,
1987), p. 256: "One lay divers times with a woman, who shew[ed] him all that he

"o" and the obscene sense of a place Ophelia may be "ashamed to show" hovers, then, around the dumb show of a play designed both to "catch the conscience of the King" (2.2.605) and to bring his "occulted guilt" (3.2.80) to light.

The lines that feature both the obscener sense of female "show" and a "shew of Protestation" (F) by a Player Queen also include concern that a secret will be let out, that "players" who "cannot keep counsel" will "tell all." Hamlet's "The players cannot keep counsel, they'll tell all" just before Ophelia's "Will 'a tell us what this show meant?" bespeaks an inability to keep "counsel," or secrets, which elsewhere in Shakespeare, as in other early modern writing, is most often the proverbial inability of women in particular to keep from disclosing what should be hid, a clear link with the secret sexual place they are to guard from "show." The "shew" of the Dumb Show authorizes a whole play here on "show" and "tell" as different forms of revealing secrets, telling "all" or opening to view what is otherwise "hid," linking players whose art is to make things public or expose to "show" with an assumed female inability to keep things "close" or secret.[48] The links established in this scene, designed both to catch the "conscience" of the king and to bring to light the information and reliability of the Ghost, continue into the immediate aftermath of this onstage "show"—first in Hamlet's exchange with Rosencrantz and Guildenstern, informers sent to "pluck out the heart of [his] mystery" (3.2.365–66), then in the aborted confession of Claudius in the Prayer Scene, unable except in secret to disclose his guilt, and then in Gertrude's interview with Hamlet, not in the public, open space of the earlier dramatic "show" but in the private space of a mother's "closet," where the woman whose sexuality and secrets are so much the focus of the play is warned by her son that she must not reveal what transpires privily within it.

In the Closet Scene itself, the link between a female "matter" and revealing secrets from a "closet" is suggested first in the harping, just before, on "matter" and "mother" *(mater)*—in Hamlet's "but to the

---

wished except the last act, which she would never agree to." The playing on "show" (Q2) or "shew" (Q1,F) appears in all three texts of *Hamlet* here, as does the juxtaposition with "tell," made even more striking in Q1's "Be not afeard to shew, hee'le not be afeard to tell."

48. See, for example, *Julius Caesar* 2.4.9 ("How hard it is for women to keep counsel") and *1 Henry IV* 2.3.108–11 ("Constant you are, / But yet a woman, and for secrecy, / No lady closer, for I well believe / Thou wilt not utter what thou dost not know").

matter: my mother" (3.2.324), as Rosencrantz and Guildenstern deliver their message that his mother "desires to speak with [him] in her
closet ere [he goes] to bed" (331), and in his repeated, "Now, mother,
what's the matter" (3.4.7) as he enters it.[49] The link is even more strikingly suggested in the tortured syntax of Hamlet's desire that his
mother not "ravel" a secret "matter" out, in lines that evoke both her
sexuality and her bed.

> Not this, by no means, that I bid you do;
> Let the bloat king tempt you again to bed,
> Pinch wanton on your cheek, call you his *mouse;*
> And let him, for a pair of reechy kisses,
> Or paddling in your neck with his damn'd fingers,
> Make you to ravel all this *matter* out,
> That I essentially am not in madness,
> But mad in craft.
>
> (181–188)

"Mouse" here—a more privy term for "woman"—and Hamlet's reit-
erated concern for the keeping of secrets (in the "sense and secrecy"
that might "such dear concernings *hide*," 191–92), forge clear verbal
links between the "matter"/"mother" of this Closet Scene and the description of players who cannot "keep counsel" in the scene of the
"*Mouse*-trap" set to disclose or ravel out a secret or "occulted guilt."
The scene in Gertrude's "closet" picks up echoes from this earlier
scene of "show" and "tell," just as it anticipates the language of Claudius' attempts to ferret precisely this woman's secret out ("There's
matter in these sighs, these profound heaves— / You must *translate*"
[4.1.1–2]). For it is in this same closet that Polonius, come as a spy, is
silenced as a potential exposer of its secrets, now not to be revealed by
a "counsellor" or keeper of official secrets who as "a foolish *prating*
knave," has been rendered "most still, most secret, and most grave"
(3.4.213–15) by the thrust that keeps him from informing on or telling
all of what he has come to spy upon.

---

49. On "matter"/"mother," see, inter alia, Avi Erlich, *Hamlet's Absent Father*
(Princeton: Princeton University Press, 1977), p. 215; Margaret W. Ferguson, "Hamlet: Letters and Spirits," in Parker and Hartman, *Shakespeare and the Question of Theory,*
p. 295; Adelman, *Suffocating Mothers,* p. 6, and her extraordinarily rich reading of *Hamlet* in chapter 2. The "mother"/"matter" wordplay appears in both Q2 and F, while
Q1 has a repeated "Mother, mother" at the beginning of the closet interview. The
"mouse"/"matter" play also occurs in Q2 and F.

The sense of keeping "counsel" or secrets, begun in the exchange around the Dumb Show and its female "show," has reverberations both before and after the Closet Scene. Its echo sounds immediately after Polonius' death, when Rosencrantz and Guildenstern come to inquire where the body is hid ("*Ham.* Do not believe it. / *Ros.* Believe what? / *Ham.* That I can *keep your counsel* and not mine own" [4.2.10–11]) and then, at the threshold of the mad scene of Ophelia, in the queen's aside on the spilling of her own "occulted guilt" ("To my sick soul, as sin's true nature is, / Each toy seems prologue to some great amiss, / So full of artless jealousy is guilt, / It spills itself in fearing to be spilt" [4.5.17–20]). In the mad scene itself, Ophelia's bawdy songs, linked from the outset with a speech that is "nothing" (7), treat obsessively of something opened or let out. Warned earlier by Laertes that she must not her "chaste treasure open" (1.3.31), O-phelia sings of the opened "chamber doors" of maids ("And dupp'd the chamber-door, / Let in the maid, that out a maid / Never departed more" [4.5.53–55]), just after lines whose "When they ask you what it means" (46–47) echo her "Will 'a tell us what this *show* meant?" (3.2.144) in the scene of the Dumb Show which played repeatedly on a female "o," and was her last appearance onstage. In contrast to the "natural modesty" of women reported in Pliny and repeated in Crooke, Ophelia, in the "melodious lay" (4.7.182–83) of her drowning, floats more openly, face up, "her clothes spread wide" (175), in lines the ear may hear, given other such Shakespearean instances, as the spreading "wide" of her *"close."*[50]

Ophelia's "close," or clothes, "spread wide" display or open to the view what in the passage from Pliny cited by Crooke on the "Lap or Privities" should more modestly be hid. The "spreading wide" of a "close" in this sense joins the language of Polonius' "I'll *loose* my daughter to him" (2.2.162) and the innuendos of sexual enfranchisement in Hamlet's "Let her not walk i' the sun" (184). It picks up the hints of sexual opening and closing in the double entendres of her songs, as in the description of "long purples / That *liberal* shepherds

50. See also Juliet's "Spread thy close curtain, love-performing night" (*Romeo and Juliet* 3.2.5), and Frankie Rubinstein, *Dictionary of Shakespeare's Sexual Puns and Their Significance* (London: Macmillan, 1984), p. 251, which glosses "spread" here as "open for copulation." In early modern English "spread" carries the sexual sense of enlarging or widening which makes it a synonym for "dilate." See *OED*, s.v. *spread* (v.)1 and 5b. On the "clothes"/"close" quibble, see Helge Kökeritz, *Shakespeare's Pronunciation* (New Haven: Yale University Press, 1953), p. 321.

give a grosser name, / But our *cull-cold* maids do dead men's fingers call" (4.7.169–71). Whether or not this buried sense of the opening of a "close"—with its echoes of Hamlet's double entendres on what Ophelia might be "asham'd to show"—gives support to Rebecca West's thesis of an already unchaste Ophelia is here beside the point. What matters is not the prior or offstage history of a single character but the play's pervasive harping on opening something "closed," the attempts everywhere within it to ferret out secrets and disclose what is hid. As with the possibility of the queen's adultery (or Desdemona's in *Othello*), what is at issue is fascination with unseen events, the obsession everywhere in *Hamlet* with spying and being spied upon linked with the secrets of women that can be exposed to "show,"[51] a fascination that makes women, marginalized as *characters* within the play, paradoxically central to it.

❑

> How all occasions do inform against me.
> —*Hamlet*

We need, therefore, to note more concretely how closely bound up both the plot of *Hamlet* and its obsessive language of "seeing" are with the visual preoccupations of the world of informer and spy. Editors of the play routinely gloss Hamlet's "I see a cherub that sees them" when Claudius says to him, "If thou knew'st our purposes" (4.3.47–48), by reference to the cherubim that have the gift to "see truly" in *Troilus and Cressida* (3.2.70), the order of angels identified with knowledge and keenness of vision, as later in *Paradise Lost* (11.128–31: "Watchful Cherubim; four faces each / Had, like a double Janus, all their shape / Spangled with eyes more numerous than those / Of Argus"). These angelic intelligences, however—and with them an older imagery of divine vision and intellection—had, by the time of *Hamlet,* already been accommodated to the new context of "intelligence" as espial, to the "eyes" of statecraft as the "Argus eyes" of spies. Among the prayers to be read in churches upon the discovery of Dr. William Parry, an informant (and double agent) executed in 1585 for designs

51. For Rebecca West's argument, see *The Court and the Castle* (New Haven: Yale University Press, 1957), pp. 3–84. The sexual double entendres on "show" following the Dumb Show are also, for example, anticipated when Rosencrantz and Guildenstern are first sent to spy on Hamlet, in the obscene byplay on female "shoe"/"show"/"privates"/"secret parts" (2.2.229–36) and the "button" on "strumpet" Fortune's "cap" (which appears in Q2 as *"lap"*).

upon the life of the queen, was one that praised the "vigilant eye" of Providence for the "sudden interruption of his endeavour," when the vigilance in question was clearly that of a spy (he was informed against by a fellow conspirator), and the "vigilant eye" of Providence a euphemism for state intelligence. We need here to recall the description from 1593 of the sheer omnipresence of "secret spies" who "give intelligence" of "secret intents," or Walsingham's network of informers, set up to "draw secrets from the conscience of the body politic."[52]

Hamlet comes at this crucial historical juncture, the point where an older language of divine or angelic intelligence was being converted into the new lexicon of espial and the "privy intelligences" provided by a progressively more organized network of informers and spies. Spying is everywhere in *Hamlet,* adding to the sense of claustrophobia that pervades the world of the play (it may be one of the resonances in the name Claudius) and giving to it the sense at its end, in the advent of Fortinbras, of the arrival on stage of something like the beginnings of the modern state. Claudius sends Polonius, and then Rosencrantz and Guildenstern, to "pluck out the heart" of Hamlet's "mystery," to spy into the causes of his "antic disposition." Polonius sends Reynaldo to spy on Laertes in Paris and extract a narrative from acquaintances in order to "make inquire" (2.1.4) into the private life of his own son. He demands to know of his daughter what was "between" her and Hamlet, reporting the results of this intelligence dutifully to the king and queen ("This in obedience hath my daughter *shown* me, / And more above, hath his solicitings, / As they fell out by time, by means, and place, / All given to mine *ear*" [2.2.125–28]). The play on "show" and "tell," eye and ear, exploited in the Mousetrap Scene, echoes throughout in these dual modalities of "informing." Spying with the eye and ferreting out a narrative are combined within the Closet Scene, where Polonius, come as spy, hides behind the arras in order to "hear" the "process" (in early modern English "narrative") of what transpires. And the play ends by promising, beyond its own theatrical spectacle, the narrative of Horatio/*oratio* that is to report Hamlet's story faithfully to those who could not see or ocularly witness it.

---

52. See Gallagher, *Medusa's Gaze,* pp. 96–97, with "Father Richard Holtby on Persecution in the North," in Morris, *Troubles,* 3:121, and for the citation from the Parry case (also reported in Holinshed), see John Strype, *Annals of the Reformation,* 4 vols. (Oxford, 1824), 3:1, pp. 378–79. On the transforming of the language of angelic or divine intelligence, see Archer, *Sovereignty and Intelligence,* e.g., pp. 1–3. The gloss from the "Cherubim" of *Paradise Lost* appears in G. R. Hibbard's edition of *Hamlet.* The seeing "Cherub(e)" appears in both Q2 and F.

"How all occasions do *inform* against me," laments Hamlet, using "inform" in the sense of impeach or accuse, in a soliloquy (4.4.32–66) not long after the scene of players who "tell all" (3.2.142). "Who is't that can *inform* me?" asks Marcellus in the opening scene, opening the way to Horatio's exposition of a prior offstage history, the "source of this our watch, and the chief head / Of this post-haste and romage in the land" (1.1.79–107). So much of the play is in the "interrogative" mode—to invoke, but in a politically more resonant context, the familiar phrase of Maynard Mack. The impulse that stands behind such questioning as Hamlet's address to the Ghost ("Say *why* is this? *wherefore? what* should we do?" [1.4.57]) frequently verges on what elsewhere in Shakespeare are called "interrogatories," forms of interrogation in a more aggressive sense, determination to bring a "mystery" to light that involves the attempt to extract information or a narrative, to get a "questionable shape" to "speak" (1.4.43–44). Once again, the emphasis on questioning, espial, and informing crosses with an epistemological hunger to "see" and "know": the play is filled not just with spies but with what Polonius expresses as the desire to "find / Where truth is hid, though it were hid indeed / Within the centre" (2.2.157–59), a hunger to ferret out mysteries shared, as with *Othello,* by the whole history of its criticism.

The sense of opening something hid to a "show" that will "tell all" links the play on "show" and "tell" around the Dumb Show with the iteration throughout *Hamlet* of the sense that secrets, or the hid, will finally out—from Hamlet's "Foul deeds will rise, / Though all the earth o'erwhelm them, to men's eyes" (1.2.256–57), after Horatio tells him of the appearance of the Ghost, to his description of the "purpose" of players and the play meant to "catch the conscience of the King" (2.2.605):

> I have heard
> That guilty creatures sitting at a play
> Have by the very cunning of the scene
> Been strook so to the soul that presently
> They have proclaim'd their malefactions:
> For murther, though it have no tongue, will speak
> With most miraculous organ.
>   (2.2.588–94)[53]

---

53. The link with "confession" is explicit in Q1's corresponding text ("Hath, by the very cunning of the scene, *confest* a murder / Committed long before").

The "show" presented by players Hamlet predicts, when the Prologue appears, "cannot keep counsel" but will "tell all"—publishing secrets to both onstage and offstage audience—is one that is to bring out into the open this "occulted guilt." The collocation of the two—bringing to light a hidden guilt and a "prologue" that indicates in brief what the "show" will present "at large"—sounds again in the lines in which Gertrude envisions the spilling of her secret "guilt" ("To my sick soul, as sin's true nature is, / Each toy seems *prologue* to some great amiss" [4.5.17–18]).[54] The sense that the "secret" or "occulted" will come finally to light is countered within the play, however, by a powerful contrary sense of opacity, of an inability to penetrate to the "show" beyond the "show," of mysteries that cannot be uncovered or made visible to the eye.[55] This is the language of the Ghost's "But that I am forbid / To tell the *secrets* of my prison-house, / I could a tale *unfold* whose lightest word / Would harrow up thy soul" (1.5.13–16), or the soliloquy "To be or not to be" with its evocation of death as an "*undiscover'd* country, from whose bourn / No traveller returns" (3.1.78–79). The Ghost, warning that "this eternal blazon must not be / To ears of flesh and blood" (1.5.21–22), goes on to a narrative unfolding or blazon meant to counter the "forged process" or lying

54. In *A Midsummer Night's Dream,* Quince's prologue promises his players' similarly doubled audience that by this "*show, / You shall know all, that you are like to know*" (5.1.116–17), before a performance that features obscene play on the little "o" of the "crannied hole or chink" of a "Wall" suggestive of the hymeneal one.

55. *Hamlet* is full of spectacle, verbal/visual tableaux, and references to "show" as early as act 1's royal spectacle and Hamlet's "I have that within which passes show, / These but the trappings and the suits of woe" (1.2.85–86)—in lines suggesting in their "actions that a man might *play*" something beyond the "show" of theater—as well as in the Dumb Show of the mousetrap scene and its "show of protestation" in a spectacle whose "Mutes" call attention to a mute or dumb "show" that has to be translated or "interpreted" (3.2.246). The promise of revelation beyond "show," "trappings," or spectacle is, however, countered by the deflections suggested in the "trap"/"trope" play on "mousetrap" and "tropically" in that same scene (3.2.237–38, the term in F and Q2 for which Q1 has "trapically"), as if there were tension between a "trap" that might "catch" (as in "catch the conscience of the King") and a tropic deflection or turning which means that the players' "show" fails in its purposed revelation, either of this "occulted guilt" or of the Ghost's veracity. The harping on "show" in *Hamlet* is, of course, joined by that in *Othello*—the explication of "Ensign" in Iago's "I must show out a flag and sign of love" (*Othello* 1.1.156), the lines on the deceptions of women who "let heaven see the pranks / They dare not show their husbands" (3.3.202–3), the sense of demonic "show" in "When devils will the blackest sins put on / They do suggest at first with heavenly shows" (2.3.358–59), and the "demon" that also lurks within the sounds of both "demonstrate"/"monstrate" and the Desdemona Othello calls "Desdemon" (5.2.41).

narrative with which the "ear of Denmark is . . . / Rankly abused"
(36–38). But the play never offers any perspicacious or unambiguous
sense of a revelation beyond "forgery," not even in the player's
oblique "show" of a hidden scene its commissioner seeks to bring un-
ambiguously to light.

This sense of both the withholding and the spilling of secrets in
Hamlet is what makes Jonathan Goldberg's investigations of the office
and function of the early modern "Secretary" (or "Secretorie") so suggestive when placed beside this play, even apart from the more obvious links between the new emphasis on script and writing and a plot
obsessed with both. The link between "secrets" and "secretories" is
everywhere emphasized in the world contemporary with *Hamlet,* in
contexts that overlap with secrecy in the realm of espionage and spies.
The "secretorie," as Angell Day puts it in *The English Secretorie,* is the
keeper of "secrets or counsels," a trust that linked the office of Principal Secretary with the monarch's "closet" or "secret Cabinet."[56] As
"the closet, wherof another hath both the key, use and commande-
ment," he ought to be "as a thicke plated doore, where through, without extraordinarie violence no man may enter, but by the locke which
is the tongue" and "of such efficacie, as whereof no counterfeit key
shoulde bee able to make a breach" (p. 124). The opposite of this faithful keeping of "secrets or counsels" is the untrustworthiness of those
with "as little secrecie as silence," counselors whose "loosenes" of
tongue means that they are incapable of keeping "close," but, as with
the players (or Polonius), will tell all (p. 123).[57]

What this description of the "secretorie" does when placed beside
Hamlet is to evoke not only the link between secrets and their potential
disclosers but, again, the emergent world of statecraft contemporary
with the play, one that historians describe as increasingly involving
the mediation of agents, go-betweens, and representatives across bu-
reaucratic as well as geographic distances, along with the correspond-

56. See Angell Day, *The English Secretary,* ed. Robert O. Evans (Gainesville, Fla:
Scholars' Facsimiles, 1967), facsimile of the 1599 edition containing "Of the partes,
place and Office of a Secretorie" (pp. 101–33), subsequently cited in the text, and Jonathan Goldberg, *Writing Matters* (Stanford: Stanford University Press, 1990), esp. pp.
265–72.

57. The passage is reminiscent throughout of contemporary strictures on women's
assumed looseness of tongue, and injunctions to silence. For early modern texts that
undercut any potential gender essentializing of references to this loquacious "female"
tongue in the period, see Patricia Parker, "On the Tongue: Cross-Dressing, Effemi-
nacy, and the Art of Words," *Style* 23 (1989): 445–65.

ing multiplication of informers and spies.[58] What the language of passages like this one from Day's *Secretorie* also demands, however, is to call attention to the sexualizing of an office associated with "closets" and "secrets" and with standards of "fidelitie," with a "key" and "doore" only a "Lord and Master" might "breach." The "secretorie" is the "closet" of his lord, the place where this master deposits "secrets," a description whose language of opening and entry recalls the "secret matters" of which women traditionally figure as ambiguous keepers, or more dangerously disclosers, part of an imagery that figures—here homoerotically—between men, in the affairs of state.[59] The secretary's keeping of "counsel" or secrets, including the secrets of power, is bound up with an imagery of the closeted or "close," of silence and fidelity, which runs throughout the language of these descriptions, just as it does through the scene in *Hamlet* that links the players' inability to "keep counsel," or secrets, with a female "lap" and "show." It is to this, therefore, that we once more return.

◻

The Queen, the Queen's to blame.
　　　　　—Janet Adelman

The exchange on "show" as female "show" in the Dumb Show of the play-within-a-play includes exploitation of the "nothing" or "o" of

58. See, among other works, Plowden, *Secret Service;* G. R. Elton, *The Tudor Revolution in Government* (Cambridge: Cambridge University Press, 1959) and *The Tudor Constitution* (Cambridge: Cambridge University Press, 1986); and the critique of parts of Elton's arguments in Christopher Coleman and David Starkey, eds., *Revolution Reassessed: Revisions in the History of Tudor Government and Administration* (Oxford: Clarendon Press, 1986). The link between "secretories" and the world of spies and espionage emerges in references to "secrett intelligencers" in Nicholas Faunt, who was also secretary to Walsingham. See "Nicholas Faunt's Discourse touching the Office of Principal Secretary of Estate," *English Historical Review* 20 (1905): 501–3.

59. The male-male eroticism in Day's text (accompanied by the analogy of joining in matrimony used by Faunt for the relation of master and secretary) is confirmed in an essay directed not to Shakespeare but to Spenser, though it is everywhere evocative of *Hamlet,* including in its reminder that this relationship was also described through the analogy of father and son. See Richard Rambuss, "The Secretary's Study: The Secret Designs of *The Shepheardes Calendar,*" *ELH* 59 (Summer 1992): 313–35, which also draws on Goldberg's "Colin to Hobbinol: Spenser's Familiar Letters," in *Displacing Homophobia: Gay Male Perspectives in Literature and Culture,* ed. Ronald R. Butters et al. (Durham: Duke University Press, 1989), pp. 107–26. The homoerotic implications of "close" need also to be explored in relation to this "closet."

female sexuality, in the "lap" and "country matters" of Hamlet's obscenely suggestive lines. So concentrated is the evocation of a female "matter" exposed to "show" in this scene of doubled spectatorship that one of the variants an eighteenth-century commentator suggested for the "miching mallecho" of its most puzzling lines was "Malbecco," the figure of Gelosia, or Jealousy, whose specular obsessions involve not just spying generally but spying on a woman.[60] However inappropriate the suggestion at the level of acceptable textual variants, the sense of spying into specifically female "matters" or secrets hovers around the doubling meanings of this Dumb "Shew," within a play which focuses relentlessly on the "frailty" and suspected adultery whose name is "woman."

Hamlet's fascination with seeing or uncovering the secrets of his mother has been the focus of much psychoanalytic criticism of the play—indeed, one of the founding texts of psychoanalysis itself.[61] This queen is the woman who betrays her son first, as a mother, a woman whose sexuality is something secret or withheld from him, and then in the opacity and ambiguities of her complicity with Claudius, the man who killed his father and lay with his mother, whether before or after is unclear. It is this that produces the sense in *Hamlet* that the play turns on the pivot of an offstage primal scene beyond the reach of vision, a scene on which gazing is forbidden, even in the deflected representation of the players' "show"—the reason, perhaps, why this *dramatic* show includes its bitter double entendres on the "o" or "nothing" that is woman. This desire to open up to "shew" involves the sense of a crime that, at least as centrally as Claudius', involves an offstage secret the entire play comes belatedly after and then attempts recursively to bring to light. In a pun on "lap" and *lapsus* that joins the punning on "fault" and "fall" linked to the play's fallen Edenic imagery—the sin of origin in a frail and "faulty" mother[62]—the "o"

---

60. See Zachary Grey's *Critical, Historical, and Explanatory Notes on Shakespeare* (London, 1754).

61. For the sense of psychoanalysis as historically following from Shakespeare and the early modern rather than as a privileged mode of transhistorical analysis, see, among others, Stephen Greenblatt, "Psychoanalysis and Renaissance Culture," in *Literary Theory/Renaissance Texts*, ed. Patricia Parker and David Quint (Baltimore: Johns Hopkins University Press, 1986), pp. 210–24, and Parker, "Preposterous Events," p. 212.

62. On "fault" and "fall," see Adelman, *Suffocating Mothers*, esp. pp. 23ff.; on "lap"/*lapsus*, see Mary Nyquist, "Textual Overlapping and Dalilah's Harlot-Lap," in Parker and Quint, *Literary Theory/Renaissance Texts*, pp. 352–54, 371.

or "lap" of woman in the Mousetrap Scene invokes the *lapsus* or falling off of woman more generally, the sexual cleft or "fault" which is both the "frailty" of woman and her crime. Critics of *Hamlet* have sensed the centrality of Gertrude and Ophelia to this play even when, as characters, they are marginalized by what appears to be taking center stage—the reliability of the Ghost or Hamlet and Claudius as "mighty opposites."[63] Criticism informed by psychoanalysis has focused especially on Gertrude. I prefer to return to this female "matter," however, in ways more historicized than the suggestive but universalizing and transhistorical paradigms of psychoanalysis, through a historically more immediate model in which the mother in particular represents a "matter," lapse, or fault that comes *between,* one related to the importance of "secretes" in the play, as well as the contemporary world of agents and intermediaries, go-betweens and spies.

Hamlet swears Gertrude, in her "closet," to secrecy against her husband, in lines that underscore the link between a female "matter" and a "close" or secret matter not to be revealed or "ravelled out." When Claudius presses her to disclose what has transpired in that private place ("There's matter in these sighs, these profound heaves, / You must translate" [4.1.1–2]), the terms of his questioning echo Hamlet's invocation in the Mousetrap Scene of the translator or "interpreter" (3.2.246), the figure who goes between *(inter-pres)* in a different sense. The play draws repeated attention to something that is not just "the matter" but the "matter *between,*" as in Polonius' "What is the matter, my lord?" in act 2 and Hamlet's responding "Between who?" (2.2.193–94). "Matter" here is something that comes "between," just as the play on "country matters" and matter/*mater*/mother before the "closet" scene is linked with a female "matter," the matrix of both sexuality and increase.

This female "matter" also, moreover, "comes between." Hamlet's "Now, *mother,* what's the *matter?*" comes just after Polonius counsels this mother to remind her son that she has "*stood between* / Much heat and him*" (3.4.3–7). There is an even more striking juxtaposition of "woman" and a frail or "baser matter" that "comes between" in the commission Hamlet-father delivers to Hamlet-son:

> thy commandement all alone shall live
> Within the book and volume of my brain,

63. See, for example, Marjorie Garber, *Shakespeare's Ghost Writers* (New York: Methuen, 1987), p. 193.

Unmix'd with *baser matter*. Yes, by heaven!
O most *pernicious woman!*

(1.5.102–5)

Beyond the generalized Oedipal paradigm of a mother who "comes between" a father and son as the object of rivalry (elicited more readily from *Hamlet* by the shift from brother to nephew as the murderer in the Mousetrap Scene), the reference here to mixture with a "baser matter" summons the specific historical resonance of Aristotelian notions of female "frailty" as a "matter" or *materia* that "comes between" father and son in a different sense.[64] In a generative context, this female "matter" is the "woman's part" in man (*Cymbeline* 2.5.20) that undermines and adulterates the perfect copying or reproduction of parthenogenesis—a lapse in what might otherwise be the replication of Hamlet-father in Hamlet-son. In the influential tradition of woman as imperfect and secondary, a *lapsus* or falling off from the more perfect male, she is both "baser matter" and adulterating mixture, a frail or "weaker vessel" whose coming between involves an aberrant and translative detour, a creature whose status is also figured by sexual parts that are secret, "occult," or hidden from the eye.[65] In this historically contemporary model of the female *matrix,* the "matter" of woman thus "comes between"—as *lapsus,* error, detour, frailty—the generative reproduction of a paternal original in a son who might be a faithful copy or representative, perfect instrument of a father's will.[66]

64. For the complex reflection of the Aristotelian hierarchy of (male) form and (female) matter elsewhere in Shakespeare, together with the conflation of Aristotelian and Galenic notions in a text such as the influential Elizabethan medical guide known as *The Problemes of Aristotle,* see Louis Adrian Montrose, "'Shaping Fantasies': Figurations of Gender and Power in Elizabethan Culture," *Representations* 1, no. 2 (Spring 1983): 61–94, esp. pp. 72–74, with the discussion of the female "matrix" and "materiall cause" in *The Problemes of Aristotle, with other Philosophers and Phisitions* (London: Arnold Hatfield, 1597), esp. sigs. E3v-E4r. The juxtaposition of "baser matter" with "woman" occurs in both F and Q2 texts of the play.

65. For fuller accounts of this tradition, including Aristotle and Saint Paul on the Genesis Eve, see R. Howard Bloch, *Medieval Misogyny and the Invention of Western Romantic Love* (Chicago: University of Chicago Press, 1991), and Patricia Parker "Coming Second: Woman's Place," in *Literary Fat Ladies,* pp. 178–233. On this adulteration and disruption of parthenogenesis, see chap. 2 of Adelman, *Suffocating Mothers.*

66. The obvious Mosaic and Christological echoes in this "commandment" and father's will have led to strenuously theological readings of *Hamlet,* though the play's extraordinary variations on fathers and sons, as well as on copying, replicating, and acting as agent or representative, go so far beyond that context.

Angell Day's faithful "secretorie" as the bearer, conveyer, or translator of messages is also to be the perfect copyist ("His pen in this action is not his owne"), "utterlie to relinquish anie affectation to his own doings" or admixture of his own will, avoiding "all maner of delaies" in the interest of "speedie conveyance" or "dispatch" (p. 130). The baser "matter" or mother who comes "between" opens, by contrast, a space of "error" or "increase" not just between father and son, but between a paternal script, commandment, or commission and its fulfillment. This is perhaps why Hamlet in his own delay as his father's agent, "secretorie," or messenger castigates himself for the "woman's part" within:

> This is most brave,
> That I, the son of a dear father murthered,
> Prompted to my revenge by heaven and hell,
> Must like a whore unpack my heart with words,
> And fall a-cursing like a very drab.
>
> 2.2.582–86

Hamlet actually begins with reference to the conveyance or faithful transmission of a message, not only in the commission to Hamlet to represent his father's will—a commission not to be "mixed" with "baser matter"—but in the commission of the new king to *his* agents or representatives, with a command (like Hamlet's to the players) that they not deviate from their script: "Giving to you no further personal power / To business with the King [of Norway], more than the scope / Of these [Q2: *delated;* F: *dilated*] articles allow" (1.2.36–38). Claudius' commission thus introduces into *Hamlet* the very complex we began from in *Othello,* the link between "dilation" (F) and "delation" (Q2), in lines that have provoked a similar editorial controversy. When the Second Quarto's "delated articles" appear as the text in most modern editions, it is as a simple variant in spelling for the sense of something rhetorically amplified or set forth "at large."[67] This is the form of dilation echoed in Claudius' commission to the King of England in act 5 ("An exact command, / Larded with many several sorts of reasons" [5.2.19–20]) and parodied in Hamlet's amplifying "As's" in the commission (5.2.38–47) that sends Rosencrantz and Guildenstern to their death.

67. See, for example, the Riverside edition: "*Delated:* extended, detailed (a variant of *dilated*)."

The suggestion of "accusations" in Q2's "delated"—counterpart to Dr. Johnson's for the "close dilations" of *Othello*—was made for *Hamlet* by John Dover Wilson, in a reading whose controversial history led to its rejection by most editors. Claudius' articles are clearly "dilated" here, part of the amplified or "larded" style of this "bloat" king which Hamlet copies in act 5. But portmanteau words like these in Shakespeare work routinely in excess of their immediate context; and the overtone of "accusation"—whether or not appropriate for the message sent to accuse a rebellious nephew—is not at all inappropriate at the beginning of a play heavy with the sense of secrets and of hidden crimes. Claudius' commission to his messengers—giving them "no further personal power" than "these delated/dilated articles allow"—appears in Q1, moreover, as no more power than these "*related* articles do *shew,*" lines that convey the combination of "show" and narrative relation or "tell" that will surface in the "show" and "tell" of the Mousetrap Scene, where a play designed to bring forth to "show" this same king's "occulted guilt" has as the very "purpose of playing" delating or informing upon a hidden crime.

❏

>   the play's the thing
> Wherein I'll catch the conscience of the King. . . .
> The king is a thing . . . / Of nothing . . .
>   —*Hamlet*

In *Hamlet,* this language of "dilation" and "delation"—amplifying and indicting—also comes to focus, though in a different arena than in *Othello,* on the "matter" of woman. Spying, opacity, and the language of a secret female place or "privitie" inform the obsessive circlings of this play around a mystery that only obliquely, or ambiguously, is ever brought to light, an ob-scene or offstage tableau the play attempts, but finally fails, to bring forth to show, displacing it at the end to still more narration, relation, or report. Both explicitly in the Mousetrap Scene and covertly in other scenes of dilation as opening, publishing, and exposing an "occulted guilt," the more obscene sense of the secrets and "faults" of women combines with the play's striking preoccupation with spying, but also with what James Calderwood calls go-betweens and get-betweens, with delays, and with opacity.[68]

68. See James Calderwood, *To Be and Not to Be: Negation and Metadrama in "Hamlet"* (New York: Columbia University Press, 1983).

Women in *Hamlet* are repeatedly associated with this interposed "between," as with the space of dilative and potentially dangerous "increase." Not only does Gertrude "come between" Old Hamlet and his brother Claudius, as a "jointress" (1.2.9) in several overdetermined senses; she also falls victim, finally, in an act of coming between or intercepting the poison Claudius means for Hamlet. Ophelia is "loosed" by Polonius as a means of policy (2.2.162), part of the emphasis in the play on the interposing of women into affairs between men, in lines that lead to Polonius' "What is the *matter?*" and Hamlet's "*Between* who?" Players whose "show" and "tell" are linked with the female mouth and the privity or "o" that O-phelia may be "ashamed to show" fail as messengers as well as "secretories," unable not only to "keep counsel" but also (unlike Claudius' messengers to Norway) to bring about the hoped-for "end" (2.2.85).

The multiple eyes of the Mousetrap Scene, with its doubled onstage spectators, are focused not just on this theatrical show but on a king who is himself both watcher and watched, spectator and anxious object of Hamlet's eye. In a context of gender crossings that include the incestuous syllogism making Claudius into Hamlet's "mother" (4.3.49–52), the scene of the play-within-a-play designed to "catch the conscience of the King" also elicits the "con-," *count,* or euphemistic "country matter" lurking within this monarchical "con-science" and its closeted secrets, in a "*Mouse*-trap" whose name will soon be echoed in the pet name for Gertrude in the Closet Scene.[69] Spying into the secrets or "occulted guilt" of a king who in the "union" of one flesh is both "father" and "mother" is thus already, in the "shew" of Dumb Show and "Mouse-trap," associated with the language of spying into a female "privity," the secrets of the closeted and the hid. The fact that the cross-gendering performed by this collapsing syllogism comes just after Hamlet's invocation of the figure of spying and "intelligence" ("I see a cherub that sees them" [4.2.28–30]) further links this king's secret, occult or hidden designs to the "matter" of a woman to be spied upon. And the lines in act 4 that begin by invoking the Two Bodies of a king and then move to "The King is a thing . . . / Of nothing" (4.2.28–30)—repeating the earlier rhyme of "king" and

69. See Erlich, *Absent Father*, pp. 188, 229–30, with the "conscience" of Sonnet 151 and the "capacity" of Anne's "soft cheveril conscience" in *Henry VIII* 2.3.31–33; Stephen Booth, *Shakespeare's Sonnets* (New Haven: Yale University Press, 1977), p. 526; and Adelman, *Suffocating Mothers,* p. 255, which emphasizes the shifting focus of the Play Scene from Player King to Player Queen.

"thing" (2.2.604–5)—explicitly assimilate the watched and watching king to the "o" or female "nothing" that was the focus in the Mouse-trap Scene of all its obscene play on "lap" and "show."

Such gender crossing or confusion was of course part of the "secret" of English transvestite theater in particular, itself suggestive of more hidden from the eye than could be "shown." In the antitheatrical literature that condemned such confusions as "monstrous," the very term of opprobrium evoked both the threat posed when outward signs failed to provide what Philip Stubbes termed a "signe distinctive" of the unseen and the polemicists' own obsession with making the hidden visible.[70] Shakespearean exploitation of what can and cannot be de*monstrat*ed or brought forth to "show," as well as of the doubled spectatorship of on- and offstage audience, needs also to be set against the controversy over a public or "common" as distinguished from a private theater, and the relation of such public playing to a different kind of sexual "show." The greater threat posed by public playing and the public stage—as contrasted with "playenge or shewing in a pryvate place"—is part of what prompted the 1574 Act of the Common Council of London and attempts to regulate and restrain the license of the "Liberties" *Hamlet* would refer to in its Players Scene, in the context of references to a War of the Theaters that also involved this public/private tension.[71] Both civic pronouncement and antitheatrical polemic were directed not only toward the stage itself as a place of "unchaste, uncomelye, and unshamefaste" words and actions but toward the public space of a theater which, according to Andrew Gurr and other historians of the English stage, women were attending in significant numbers.[72] The anxiety in such texts seems to be that

70. See Philip Stubbes, *The Anatomie of Abuses* (1583), ed. F. J. Furnivall, 2 vols. (London: Trubner, 1877–79), p. 73; and, on the implications of this uncertainty, Laura Levine, "Men in Women's Clothing: Anti-Theatricality and Effeminization from 1579 to 1642," *Criticism* 28 (1986): 121–43; and Stephen Orgel, "Nobody's Perfect, Or, Why Did the English Stage Take Boys for Women?" in Butters, *Displacing Homophobia*, pp. 107–26.

71. For the 1574 act, see E. K. Chambers, *The Elizabethan Stage*, 4 vols. (Oxford: Clarendon Press, 1923), 4:273–76; on *Hamlet* and the War of the Theaters, see Joseph Loewenstein, "Plays Agonistic and Competitive: The Textual Approach to Elsinore," *Renaissance Drama* 19 (1988): 63–96. For a different Shakespearean instance of offstage/onstage audiences combined with play on "show," see note 54 and Freedman, *Staging the Gaze*, pp. 180–83.

72. See Andrew Gurr, *Playgoing in Shakespeare's London* (Cambridge: Cambridge University Press, 1987); and the discussion of the problem posed by the presence of

women playgoers—and not just courtesans—were made "common" in the public theater by the gaze of many men, no longer subject to the exclusive surveillance and control of father or husband but open to the taint of sexual license or liberty that in an onstage context would provoke Othello's "O thou public *commoner.*" Women in the public theater were made "common" by being opened indiscriminately to the view, just as in the more promiscuous license and loosened state control of the "Liberties," both "greatness" and kingship could be made "common" or familiar on the public stage.[73]

The contrasting sense of opacity—of what could not, even on stage, be brought to "show"—is also, finally, part of what Jean-Christophe Agnew and others have identified as the more general "crisis of representation" in the period, a crisis of which the public theater functioned paradoxically as revelatory instrument.[74] The obsessively staged desire to see or spy out secrets, or in the absence of the directly ocular, to extract a narrative that might provide a vicarious substitute—not only in *Hamlet* and *Othello* but in plays contemporary with them— implicates both "show" and "tell," eye and ear, in the broader sixteenth- and early seventeenth-century problem of testimony and report, the complexities of the relation between "ocular proof" and what in *Lear* is termed "auricular assurance" (1.2.92), a theatrical problem shared by the law courts and other contestatory sites of epistemological certainty and "evidence," of what might be reliably substituted for what could not be directly witnessed.[75]

women playgoers in Jean Howard, "Scripts and/versus Playhouses: Ideological Production and the Renaissance Public Stage," *Renaissance Drama*, n.s., 20 (1989): 31–49.

73. See Howard, "Scripts," pp. 32–37; Stephen Orgel, "Making Greatness Familiar," *Genre* 15 (1982): 41–48; Steven Mullaney, *The Place of the Stage* (Chicago: University of Chicago Press, 1988), esp. chaps. 1 and 2; and, on the implications of the English transvestite stage, Orgel's "Nobody's Perfect," in Butters, *Displacing Homophobia*, pp. 15–17.

74. See Jean-Christophe Agnew, *Worlds Apart: The Market and the Theater in Anglo-American Thought, 1550–1750* (Cambridge: Cambridge University Press, 1986), pp. 97–98, on the "national, if not global, crisis of representation, one wherein traditional social signs and symbols had metamorphosed into detached and manipulable commodities," a crisis in which "professional theater offered itself, ironically, as the most credible instrument with which to visualize, so to speak, the lost transparency" of other acts.

75. See Barbara J. Shapiro, *Probability and Certainty in Seventeenth-Century England* (Princeton: Princeton University Press, 1983), on the problem of evidence across several fields in this period, including law; and on the complicating of the relation of eye and ear, Peter Stallybrass, "Reading the Body: *The Revenger's Tragedy* and the Jacobean

❑

In the case of *Hamlet,* what emerges in these buried linkages involves not so much what is embodied in the characters of Gertrude and Ophelia as something independent of embodiment,[76] the spilling of obsession with female "shew" into the obsession in *Hamlet* with secrets, spying, and "intelligence," producing what might be called analogously the Two Bodies of woman in this play, or perhaps the Queen's Two Bodies, given its staging late in the reign of a queen who emphasized her own tantalizing gender uncertainty—father and mother to her people, "frail" body of a woman and body of a king—as well as the controlled display but finally the opacity of her "closet," her privy "chamber," and her "secretes."[77] What this intersection raises are the possibilities of what Joel Fineman elliptically suggests as the more political than psychologized reading of the proliferating eyes and ears of the famous Rainbow Portrait of this same Queen, a portrait whose sexual inference is unmistakably invoked by the placing of an ear (another organ "lapped" or folded) over the locus of her "secrete" part.[78] What is important in eliciting from *Hamlet* or *Othello* their complex evocations of spying, informing, and exposing secrets in a context that also involves fascination with the hidden "privity" of woman is the way the private in this sense crosses with the political in early modern England, linking the language of the plays and the discourses—anatomical, medical, theatrical, judicial—of the culture that forms the broader context for their demand to "see" and "know."

When Elizabeth delivered her famous pronouncement on the spectacle of monarchy ("We princes are set on stages in the sight and view

Theater of Consumption," *Renaissance Drama,* n.s., 18 (1987): 121–48, with the discussion of *evidentia* in Parker, *Literary Fat Ladies,* pp. 138–40. For another dramatic instance of obsession with the secret and the hid, see Michael Neill, "'Hidden Malady': Death, Discovery, and Indistinction in *The Changeling,*" *Renaissance Drama* 22 (1991): 95–121.

76. Jacqueline Rose, "Sexuality in the Reading of Shakespeare: *Hamlet* and *Measure for Measure,*" in *Alternative Shakespeares,* ed. John Drakakis (London: Methuen, 1985), pp. 95–118.

77. In addition to the instances in Fumerton and other works cited in note 14, see the explication of the occult meanings of a royal "show" in "the hole matter opened" (as it is phrased in the almost simultaneously published text) of *The Quenes Maiesties Passage through the Citie of London . . . the Day Before her Coronation* (1559), ed. James M. Osborn (New Haven: Yale University Press, 1960), p. 40.

78. See Joel Fineman's suggestive "Shakespeare's Ear," *Representations* 28 (1989): 6–13, and Christopher Pye's analysis of the Rainbow Portrait in *The Regal Phantasm,* pp. 68–73. For "lappe of the eare," see Huloet, *Abecedarium,* s.v. "Lappe."

of the world"), or when James warned his son that kings are placed on a stage "where all the beholders' eyes are attentively bent to look and pry into the least circumstances of their secretest drifts,"[79] both were addressing the circumstances of an England that included not only an increasingly elaborated secret service as the dispersed eyes and ears of state but also increasingly extended networks of mediation and representation, of go-betweens who simultaneously conveyed and enfolded messages and "secretes," as well as not infrequently interposing their own "will" between. It was also, in striking relation to both monarchs, an England that had frequent recourse to the language of a hidden "chamber," closeting, or secrets as a complexly deflected (or as in *Hamlet* "troping") cover for the simultaneously hidden and "open" secret of a homo-sexuality tied selectively to the visibility, culpability, and detection of other "monstrous" things.[80] This, too, along with a homoerotics of the desire to "see" and "know," the self-consciously "thea-trical" theater of Shakespeare—its "show" and "tell"—folds into its metaphorics of spying, of showing, and of opacity or withholding from vision.

Far, then, from perpetuating an earlier agenda of close reading which separated Shakespeare artificially from this history (and which, ironically, often resulted in an inability to read even the most fundamental verbal resonances of the plays) or abandoning more careful

---

79. See J. E. Neale, *Elizabeth I and Her Parliaments, 1584–1601*, 2 vols. (London: Cape, 1965), 2:119, and *Basilikon Doron* (1609) in *The Political Works of James I*, ed. Charles H. McIlwain (Cambridge: Harvard University Press, 1918), p. 5, with Pye, *Regal Phantasm,* chap. 2, which starts from Stephen Greenblatt's "Invisible Bullets," in *Political Shakespeare,* ed. Jonathan Dollimore and Alan Sinfield (Ithaca: Cornell University Press, 1985), p. 44.

80. I hyphenate "homo-sexuality" here to signal the crucial distinctions which Alan Bray and others have drawn between post-nineteenth-century understandings and early modern practices. See Alan Bray, *Homosexuality in Renaissance England* (London: Gay Men's Press, 1982), also on "monster" as a sixteenth-century designation (pp. 13ff.): Bray's "Homosexuality and the Signs of Male Friendship in Elizabethan England," *History Workshop* 29 (Spring 1990): 1–19; and on the "open secret" and "lieu," Jonathan Goldberg, *Sodometries: Renaissance Texts, Modern Sexualities* (Stanford: Stanford University Press, 1992), esp. p. 48 and chap. 3. On the multiple contradictions involved in the simultaneous denunciation of sodomy among unforgivable "crimes" (James I, *Basilikon Doron*) and the practices of figures as prominent as Francis Bacon and the king himself, see Bruce R. Smith, *Homosexual Desire in Shakespeare's England* (Chicago: University of Chicago Press, 1991), esp. pp. 14, 26, 176. For the relation of *Othello* to this "monstrous" possibility, and its racial counterpart in the union of Othello and Iago, see my essay in Hendricks and Parker, *Women, "Race," and Writing.*

reading altogether in reaction to that bracketing, we need to attend to the characteristic terms both of the plays and of the culture contemporary with them. Striking examples of such simultaneously textual and contextual study have already been initiated, no longer attached to simply formalist or politically more conservative aims. My own reading starts in part from the premise that elements such as the Dumb Show in *Hamlet* (or the "delations" of Claudius' scripted message to another king) operate in ways very different from the anachronistic assumptions of logical, psychological, or chronological plausibility on which so much critical energy has been spent,[81] and from the conviction that the plays of Shakespeare—like other early modern texts—themselves offer us terms that, if read historically, would provide keys to the language of the culture they complexly demonstrate or hold up to "show." To read with care in this sense is not simply to add to the resources of cultural studies or cultural "poetics" those of a cultural semantics or philology, but to explore the network of terms that shaped politics, institutions, and laws as well as discourses of the body and all that we have subsequently come to think of as "literature." To approach a culture as important to and yet as distant from us as that now termed the "early modern" must be to take its own developing language seriously, not just in ways that would oppose to a dehistoricizing formalist literary criticism the resources of a Spitzerian historical semantics, or even a version of Empson's "structure of complex words," but something that begins from a more detailed examination of what Raymond Williams called clusters of "key words,"[82] heuristic approaches to the complex relations of culture and society.

81. On these assumptions as post–sixteenth-century historical productions, see, among other work, Margreta de Grazia's pathbreaking *Shakespeare Verbatim* (Oxford: Oxford University Press, 1991).

82. See William Empson, *The Structure of Complex Words* (London: New Directions, 1951); and Raymond Williams, *Key Words: A Vocabulary of Culture and Society*, rev. ed. (London: Fontana, 1983), originally begun as an appendix to his *Culture and Society*. Evelyn Fox Keller, in *Secrets of Life, Secrets of Death: Essays on Language, Gender, and Science* (New York: Routledge, 1992), pp. 56–72 (a discussion with obvious relevance to the present one) also begins from the importance of "key words" for any study of gender in early modern science.

6

"To You I Give Myself, For I Am Yours"

Erotic Performance and Theatrical Performatives in *As You Like It*

SUSANNE L. WOFFORD

More than almost any other of Shakespeare's comedies, *As You Like It* is the play of proxies, of actions enacted in or undertaken by an alternative persona. Whereas in *The Comedy of Errors* Shakespeare's Adriana says, "I will attend my husband . . . for it is my office / And will have no attorney but myself" (5.1.98–100),[1] in *As You Like It* one can woo, marry, and even die by attorney—indeed, at least in the case of wooing and marrying one not only can but must, or so the play suggests. This essay explores the effect of using a proxy on the performative language necessary to accomplish deeds such as marriage, considering first the purposes of the erotic performance of Rosalind/ Ganymede, especially the question of whether it serves to ward off threats to the comic ending, and if so what those threats may be.

The emphasis in Shakespeare studies of the last decade or so on social structure, and its connection to the sexual politics implicit in *As You Like It,* has led to a concern not only with the attitudes a play may express or represent, but also with the extent to which a play acts as an agent in society (in Shakespeare's own or in ours) either to change beliefs and social possibilities or to reconfirm them. In his 1981 essay "'The Place of a Brother' in *As You Like It*: Social Process and Comic

---

1. Quotations throughout are taken from the Arden editions of Shakespeare's plays, notably the New Arden edition of *As You Like It,* ed. Agnes Latham (London: Methuen, 1975), and are subsequently cited in the text. The title quotation is from *As You Like It* 5.4.115–16.

Form," Louis Montrose suggested some avenues by which to pursue the difficult project of discussing how theater as an institution may *act*: by providing "compensation," serving as a "projection," and mediating ideological contradictions, he argues, the play performs valuable psychological and ideological work. Since it both reflects social conflict and provides "a theatrical *source* of social conciliation," the play serves a social function, in this case, to provide apparent resolutions that confirm or strengthen the patriarchal order.[2]

Many political interpretations, however, have tended not to discuss how theatrical language may gain the power ascribed to it. If it indeed has the power to act beyond the boundary of the stage, perhaps that action can be understood better through an examination of those speeches that have such power invested in them linguistically—illocutionary and perlocutionary speech acts in general and, in particular, performative utterances that, by definition, participate in social action such as the performing of a marriage. The question of how marriages should be arranged and who had the right to perform them was, of course, a matter of much argument in early modern England.[3] Plays

2. See Louis Montrose, "'The Place of a Brother' in *As You Like It*: Social Process and Comic Form," *Shakespeare Quarterly* 32 (Spring 1981): 28–54; the quotation is from p. 54. Many writers have drawn similar political conclusions about Shakespearean comedy. See Sara Claiborne Park, "As We Like It: How a Girl Can Be Smart and Still Popular," in *The Woman's Part: Feminist Criticism of Shakespeare*, ed. Carolyn Ruth Swift Lenz, Gayle Greene, and Carol Thomas Neely (Urbana: University of Illinois Press, 1980); Peter Erickson, "Sexual Politics and Social Structure in *As You Like It*," *Massachusetts Review* 23 (1982): 65–83, reprinted in Peter Erickson, *Patriarchal Structures in Shakespeare's Drama* (Berkeley: University of California Press, 1985). For feminist studies of the comedies as affirmative of female power or disruptive of the patriarchy imposed in the ending, see Catherine Belsey, "Disrupting Sexual Difference: Meaning and Gender in the Comedies," in *Alternative Shakespeares*, ed. John Drakakis (London: Methuen, 1985), pp. 166–90, and Barbara Bono, "Mixed Gender, Mixed Genre in Shakespeare's *As You Like It*," in *Renaissance Genres: Essays On Theory, History, and Interpretation*, ed. Barbara Kiefer Lewalski (Cambridge: Harvard University Press, 1986). See also Lynda Boose's thoughtful review essay "The Family in Shakespeare Studies; or—Studies in the Family of Shakespeareans; or—The Politics of Politics,"*Renaissance Quarterly* 40 (1987): 707–42; and the helpful introduction to Marilyn Williamson, *The Patriarchy of Shakespeare's Comedies* (Detroit: Wayne State University Press, 1986).

3. See Keith Wrightson, *English Society, 1580–1680* (New Brunswick, N.J.: Rutgers University Press, 1982), pp. 71–84, 87–88. See also appendix B of the New Arden edition, in which Agnes Latham summarizes the legal evidence concerning private bethrothals to suggest that "I take thee Rosalind for wife" (4.1.137) is a statement that transforms the mock marriage into something "very near to being a real one" (p. 133). She cites F. Pollock and F.W. Maitland, *The History of English Law before the Time of Edward I* (London, 1898), II:364ff., on the contemporary validity of the "sponsalia per verba de praesenti," which takes place if the man and woman "declare that they take

such as *As You Like It*, with its invocation of the wedding performative ("I take thee Rosalind for wife" [4.1.137]) and its potentially subversive representation of a wedding onstage (a wedding which is not "true"), may in fact be participating in a complex way in a cultural debate about the power of fathers and of the state to control the language that gives such actions a social reality—in other words, that makes the language truly performative. Shakespeare's theater contests the control of the performative utterance by the crown, implicitly claiming for itself the right to do things with words.

These issues can best be addressed through strategies of close reading sometimes sidestepped in criticism that defines its aims as explicitly political or sociological.[4] Without closer attention to the workings of language and to rhetoric, such political readings risk duplicating the older thematic approaches they first set out to correct, except that they place a different set of themes in the critical foreground.[5] To focus on the rhetorical structure and social force of words uttered in a play is, in contrast, to link a concern with the play's assertions about gender and cultural authority to the kinds of power such assertions have. Moreover, close reading is essential to criticism that aims to indicate the participation of a text in its culture's ideological work, or that aims to find those moments of fissure and disruption where the text marks the limits to the culture's attempts to resolve social and moral contradiction.

---

each other as husband and wife now, at this very moment." For an account of the validity of such marriage contracts at the time of *As You Like It*, see Ernest Schanzer, "The Marriage-Contracts of *Measure for Measure*," *Shakespeare Survey* 13 (1960): 81–89, who cites Henry Swinburne's *Treatise of Spousals* as evidence of the way the law was interpreted around 1600. Here is the heart of Latham's conclusions: "Marriage *per verba de praesenti* was still valid in the sixteenth century. The Church disapproved, unless its blessing was subsequently asked, especially if the marriage was consummated before the couple came to church. . . . Nonetheless, the troth-plight marriage, provided the couple were careful about their tenses, was legally valid. They were not free thereafter to divorce or to marry again and the children were legitimate" (p. 134).

4. I have singled out the work of Louis Montrose precisely because it stands out as an exception to this tendency. Catherine Belsey, in "Disrupting Sexual Difference," similarly proves an exception, arguing for the importance of close reading in political criticism: "But I want to propose that a close reading of the texts can generate a more radical challenge to patriarchal values by disrupting sexual difference itself" (p. 180). Also, the work of feminist critics such as Madelon Sprengnether Gohlke and Janet Adelman, drawing on an alternative tradition of psychoanalytic interpretation, provides instructive examples of the value of close reading in feminist criticism.

5. Examples of this more thematic approach can be found in Erickson, "Sexual Politics," and Bono, "Mixed Gender, Mixed Genre." I intend here not an attack on these writers for having identified a project different from my own but rather an articulation of the directions in which their work now points us.

My use of the terminology of performative utterances comes in part out of a critical engagement with J. L. Austin,[6] whose theories most notably exclude precisely the kind of language under study here: "A performative utterance will, for example, be *in a peculiar way* hollow or void if said by an actor on the stage, or if introduced in a poem, or spoken in soliloquy. . . . All this we are excluding from consideration."[7] Austin excludes such "parasitic" or "etiolated" examples of the performative because they meet neither the first condition for all performatives—that the act be a conventional act understood as such by all parties—nor the condition of sincerity, for performative expressions onstage cannot be thought to be meant seriously by the speakers. It is precisely these conditions, however, that one might interrogate in order to consider the value of the theatrical performative, and, more precisely, in order to find a language to describe how power is appropriated or challenged in a given society. This essay briefly reconsiders not just the felicity conditions Austin lays out for successful performatives but also the ways in which they are ideologically constrained.[8]

6. I distinguish my project, then, from that of Joseph A. Porter in *The Drama of Speech Acts: Shakespeare's Lancastrian Tetralogy* (Berkeley: University of California Press, 1979) and Mary Louise Pratt, *Toward A Speech Act Theory of Literary Discourse* (Bloomington: Indiana University Press, 1977). See Wolfgang Iser, "The Reality of Fiction: A Functionalist Approach to Literature," *New Literary History* 7 (1975–76): 7–38, for an analysis of the extent to which Austin's conditions for illocutionary speech acts fit literature; and, in response, the criticism by Stanley Fish of such extended applications of Austin in "How to Do Things with Austin and Searle: Speech Act Theory and Literary Criticism," *Modern Language Notes* 91 (1976): 983–1025. Fish criticizes Iser for implying that a speech act can "create" meaning: "The only thing that performative or illocutionary acts produce is recognition on the part of the hearer that the procedures constitutive of a particular act have been invoked. . . . It is simply wrong to think of an illocutionary act as producing meaning in the sense of creating it. Indeed, the meaning the act produces (a better word would be presents, as in presents a compliment) necessarily pre-exists it; or, to put it another way, in Speech Act theory, meaning is prior to utterance" (p. 1003). One could argue about this claim, but it suffices to note that Fish sees the limits of speech act theory as definitive, whereas I use them to indicate ways in which the theory can be challenged and extended.

7. J. L. Austin, *How to Do Things with Words*, 2d ed. (Cambridge: Harvard University Press, 1962), p. 22. Subsequent quotations will be cited in the text.

8. It is noteworthy that the argument in print between Jacques Derrida and John Searle (in *Glyph* 1 and 2) centers in part on precisely this exclusion by Austin of the "non-serious" citation (onstage, in a poem, or in soliloquy). In "Signature Event context," *Glyph* 1 (1977), Derrida argues that "what Austin excludes as anomaly . . . is the determined modification of a general citationality—or rather, a general iterability—without which there would not even be a 'successful' performative" (p. 191). Derrida's focus on the ways in which the citation exemplifies the structure of language more generally, and his study of the problems in Austin's concept of limiting context, tend

The speech acts Austin describes in *How to Do Things with Words* take place in the context of what appears to be a completely static and unchanging society: his is a synchronic analysis (though he makes convincing diachronic arguments elsewhere). Certain people—judges, for instance—are described as possessing the institutional power to perform particular speech acts. Those speech acts are considered more dubious if others try to pronounce them; but Austin is not engaged in describing how one might question the source of that institutional power or the ways in which new institutions might take on such power. Thus, Austin requires for a felicitous performative that "the particular persons and circumstances in a given case must be appropriate for the invocation of the particular procedure invoked" (p. 34), without analyzing the ways in which such people come to be "appropriate." The word he uses to describe inappropriateness is "incapacity," yet he limits his account of this incapacity to stating that the person was not "duly appointed." Austin's concern is to show that there is no such thing as unconstrained intentionality, as he sees whatever power may arise from such utterances as institutionalizations of linguistic commitments, and the power they commit us to. Nonetheless, he is not directly concerned with the ways in which institutions gain power, nor is his theory about the regulation of action by law or by authorities; rather it treats these questions as an extension of linguistic commitments that precede any individual intention. His taxonomy of speech acts thus needs to be extended if one wishes to describe how the power to perform a given speech act is instituted or modified in society. Since Shakespeare's plays are filled with examples of moments when characters either lose or claim for the first time the capacity to perform certain speech acts, they call for some theorizing about the origin of this "capacity."

Austin's first requirement—"There must exist an accepted conventional procedure having a certain conventional effect" (p. 14)—presents similar problems, especially with the question of the meaning of the word "accepted." If it means more than simply "conventional," then it raises the difficult question of the extent to which people affirm a given legal or social custom. The example he picks here is telling: "Consider 'I divorce you,' said to a wife by her husband in a Christian country. . . . In this case it might be said, 'nevertheless he has not

---

in a different direction from my essay (toward a general theory of language and meaning), but they nonetheless helpfully indicate how very problematic is Austin's attempt to exclude the kind of language at issue in a Shakespearean play.

(successfully) divorced her. . . . We do not admit any procedure at all for effecting divorce—marriage is indissoluble.' This may be carried so far that we reject what may be called a *whole code* of procedure" (p. 27). It is not surprising that Austin's difficult case comes from the debates about who controls and defines the limits of marriage. His example could be interpreted differently, as describing how social or institutional shaping of meaning may eventually be changed if "we reject . . . a whole code of procedure." The question arises how to adjudicate moments when the linguistic commitments implied in performative utterances conflict with legal or governmental regulation, or when the institutional constraints on meaning conflict with other kinds of conventional constraints, such as moral ones. Austin describes how a performative may fail because of social constraints or law, but he does not explicitly focus in *How to Do Things with Words* on those explosive cultural moments when the felicity conditions of a performative utterance are challenged and perhaps redefined. It is precisely such a moment that *As You Like It* is concerned to dramatize—"There's a girl goes before the priest," as Rosalind will put it in act 4 (4.1.131–32).

The question of what is the "accepted" procedure and who is the "proper" person to perform it leads into historical obscurity and to a (logically) ever receding origin, for Austin does not discuss who has the power to make the speech act "I appoint you as someone who has the power to use the performative in this case," or "I appoint you as someone who may appoint her as someone duly appointed to use the performative in this case." The moment of empowerment precedes his theory just as the struggle against disempowerment seems to fall beyond its purview. His examples thus consistently evade any explanations that might concern those moments of self-instituting power, or any case in which there may be a contest of power.

Austin's concern is to a large extent with the given, then, and not with the origin of the system, and yet he does seem to imply that the origin of such "capacity" is in language itself and the way people use language, rather than in the codifications that make legal regulation possible. He imagines that institutions determine meanings, and that meanings and successful performatives do not take place as an instance of individual free choice or self-origination. But the range of these institutionalizations of linguistic commitment is large, and the theory leaves open the possibility that differing conventions defining the capacity to utter successful performatives may conflict. Thus, the operative phrase in many of his examples is "it might be said"—but how, one may ask, is it determined whether or not "it might be said"? In this essay I extend Austin's theory in ways that I believe are in sympathy with his project, though not articulated expressly within it.

Austin's exclusion of theatrical language fits well with the way his theory, as worked out in *How to Do Things with Words*, necessarily marginalizes those moments in which cultural conventions and social expectations are being challenged or reshaped, for art defines one of the cultural spaces in which such challenges are stated and such changes are given palpable form. A theatrical performative presumably functions on at least three levels: within the play, a performative utterance is understood to have its conventional force,[9] while the audience understands the staged speech act as a representation of a performative utterance. It does not have a direct power outside the action of the play. The same language, however, pronounces simultaneously a second-order performative, in which the play or the theater as institution claims the right to speak with performative power: "I, the theater, appropriate the power to appoint those who will have the power to say 'I do,'" or "I, the theater, name myself as an institution that has the power to use the performative," or even "I, the theater, appropriate the power to take cultural action." Through its own focus on the kind of validity Rosalind's similar use of the performative may have, *As You Like It* provides an exemplary text for considering the ways in which the play and popular theater more broadly may contest the implicit claim of the crown to be the sole arbiter of who is the "proper person" to pronounce a culturally powerful speech act.

In interpreting the erotic performance of Rosalind, I consider the ways in which acting can effect a cure, or, to put it another way, the extent to which performance itself takes on performative power. Apotropaic signs or gestures and other representations intended to ward off evil themselves fit the felicity conditions for a performative utterance in all but one sense: the immediate addressee cannot be named as a person who could be judged to recognize or to fail to recognize the

9. When it does not have that conventional force within the plot, the loss of royal power thereby indicated leads to tragedy, as we see most notably in *King Lear* and *Richard II*. This is an old argument, expounded most eloquently and persuasively by Sigurd Burckhardt in "*King Lear*: The Quality of Nothing," and "The King's Language: Shakespeare's Drama as Social Discovery," in *Shakespearean Meanings* (Princeton: Princeton University Press, 1968), pp. 237–59 and 260–84. I note in particular the value of Burckhardt's early focus on the importance of the performative power of language in Shakespeare.

conventionality of the acts. They indicate, then, why the presence of the audience of those who can understand such conventional and social force is essential to the "success" of protective signs, for the audience is the addressee of the "serious" second-order performative at issue in the case of ritual or of theater. Thus, Austin's assumption that the audience, "overhearing" (as it were) the speeches made onstage, will always remember that these actions are neither "serious" nor "sincere" is belied in the case of apotropaic representation, the function of which is clearly "serious" in Austin's sense, although independent of an individual subject-enunciator and a self-conscious addressee. A study of the social force of theatrical language can thus link the theory of performative utterances, to which I return explicitly in the final section of the essay, to the dialectic of protection and contamination that studies of ritual, as well as the documents of the sixteenth- and seventeenth-century debate about the theater, have led us to see at work on the Shakespearean stage.

EROTIC PERFORMANCE AS CURE

In Shakespearean comedy, enacted scenes often serve an apotropaic function: they work to ward off the danger that they represent, the representation itself ostensibly protecting the fictive characters (and by extension the actors and audience) from the dangers that usually give the plot its interest. This is notably true in such plays-within-plays as "Pyramus and Thisbe" in *A Midsummer Night's Dream*, where the latent tragedy in the story of the four lovers is represented in unintentionally comic form, in order that such a tragedy might be averted. It might be said to be a generic characteristic of comedy that it allows this warding-off function to appear successful, but such plays also generate a dialectic of protection and contamination, to the extent that the enacted scene or representation may express an unspoken threat or complication, inadmissible by the plot but significant nonetheless for the play's cultural force. These admissions are acknowledged by critical insights such as that, for *A Midsummer Night's Dream*, the play within the play may express the nightmare or tragic aspects of the main action—aspects ostensibly dismissed by the comic conclusion.

As You Like It speaks of "curing" an "infection" ("Why do you infect yourself with them" [3.2.111–12]) rather than of warding off an evil—an infection associated with the disease of love and manifested in bad love poetry and in the lovers' tendency to literalize Petrarchan conceits—witness the debate between Phebe and Silvius (act 3, scene 5) about whether or not eyes are murderers.[10] The actions of warding off and curing are related but distinct: that which needs to be "cured" cannot be precisely the same as that which needs to be warded off, for in the latter case the threat is only potential, and the play need never openly acknowledge its efforts to protect against it. The need for a displacement from the infection that must be cured to the threat that must be averted is indirectly admitted when Ganymede describes the "cure" s/he has in mind: by playing what s/he considers the woman's part, Ganymede explains, "I drave my suitor from his mad humour of love to a living humour of madness, which was, to forswear the full stream of the world and to live in a nook merely monastic. And thus I cured him" (3.2.405–9). This claim understandably provokes Orlando to say, "I would not be cured," and indeed the play does not intend to lead the principal characters to the monastic cell (or to the cave of the convertite). Since Rosalind, if anything, wants to test Orlando's love, not cure him of it, it can be argued that neither of them is in fact engaged in a curing. Interpretation has emphasized the importance of Rosalind's teachings, and of her weaning of Orlando from his narcissistic love—"as loving yourself than seeming the lover of any other" (3.2.373–74)—but whether Orlando changes very much remains in doubt. Such "curing" of the "infection" of lovers' clichés takes a second seat to the more difficult task of warding off the threatening images that Rosalind enacts in the wooing scenes, images that would truly dispel any possibility of a comic ending. The circularity of such imagery of "curing" is enacted in the chiasmus of "his mad humour of love to a living humour of madness": if this is to be the result of Ganymede's erotic performance, the play wants nothing of it. The pretense that this performance is all a cure for love, then, may serve rather as a figure for the kind of warding off or protecting against contamination that may be under way. The mirroring in the chiastic phrase strengthens the warning conveyed by the words ("to a living

---

10. For an account of the way the play treats romantic love as social sickness, see Thomas McFarland, "'For Other Than for Dancing Measures': The Complications of *As You Like It*," in *Shakespeare's Pastoral Comedy* (Chapel Hill: University of North Carolina Press, 1972), pp. 112–13. The imagery of infection in the play, and the notion put forward playfully that bad poetry is infectious, echoes the language of the antitheatrical tracts which speak of theater itself as spreading its contagion among the audience, adding a metatheatrical dimension to the dialectic of infection and cure.

humour of madness") that such a "cure" may be more contaminating than beneficial, and figures the dialectic of "curing" and reinfecting which will engage the action in the courtship scenes.

In the case of *As You Like It*, the erotic performance of Rosalind/ Ganymede as Rosalind indeed seems to ward off several threats to her promised union with Orlando. Given the allusion to the Ganymede story in her self-naming as male, readers have responded to the not-so-submerged homoerotics of her performance as marking one such threat. The enactment of a homosexual wooing scene—if it works successfully as an apotropaic representation—may thus seem to ward off, by representing it, the danger that either lover might actually be attracted to the "wrong" sex and thus make the comic conclusion of marriage impossible. Indeed, the play does seem concerned to break the close, passionate ties between Rosalind and Celia ("never two ladies loved as they do" [1.1.112]; "whose loves / Are dearer than the natural bond of sisters" [1.2.265–66]; "We still have slept together / . . . And whereso'er we went, like Juno's swans, / Still we went coupled and inseparable" [1.3.69–72]), whereas it favors and advances the apparently homoerotic tie between Orlando and Ganymede, finally concluding in the traditional marriage pattern in which the women's friendship is subordinated while male bonds are reaffirmed (ties between brothers and between suitor and father). Especially given the use of a male actor to boy Rosalind's greatness, critics have seen the play as expressing an unacknowledged but powerful homoerotic aesthetic, if not desire. The breaking of the close bonding of women in the affirmation of a patriarchical order which is itself dependent on an unacknowledged homoerotic bonding between male characters could be described as constitutive of comic closure in Shakespeare—exemplified, again, in *A Midsummer Night's Dream*.[11]

If this model is correct, it applies in a somewhat unusual way to *As You Like It*, where the enactment of what appears to be a homosexual liaison becomes the means to the concluding marriage, as if to literalize and radicalize the pattern. Here homosexuality is denied only at the last moment—or, indeed, made a central component of the resolution—so that the erotic performance seems less to ward off the threat

11. See Shirley Nelson Garner, "*A Midsummer Night's Dream*: 'Jack Shall Have Jill: / Nought Shall Go Ill,'" *Women's Studies* 9 (1982): 157–76, on the breaking of female bonds in the conclusion of Shakespearean comedy; and Montrose, "'The Place of a Brother,'" on the importance of bonds between men, and on the actions of purging and strengthening them in *As You Like It*.

of a homoerotic block to the marriage than to indicate the way in which this marriage system depends precisely on such ties between male and male. The homoerotic performance, then, functions apotropaically at the level of plot—the marriages are not undermined by the homoerotic subtexts thereby engaged—while at the same time it represents the play's unadmitted but (at the level of plot) fundamental allegiance to such ties between men.[12]

The principal threat that is warded off by Rosalind/Ganymede's erotic performance is of a different nature. What Rosalind/Ganymede acts out specifically are the vagaries of a woman being wooed or a woman won: s/he stresses the stereotypical attacks on women that characterize the literature of misogyny.[13] Functioning in an apotropaic manner, then, the play put on by Rosalind/Ganymede could be said to avert the threat that Rosalind herself, once married, will play any of these stereotypical female roles so threatening to men, including most notably that of the scold (the woman who talks too much, who develops a kind of female eloquence in order to extend her power), the flighty, changeable woman with no constancy, and the woman who cheats her husband (especially sexually).[14]

The allusions to what we might call homoerotic subtexts serve rather to define this other female threat more clearly. In describing the attire she will wear as Ganymede, Rosalind somewhat improbably says that she will carry "a boar-spear in [her] hand" (1.3.114). Although this part of her disguise never appears again, the allusion suggests that the boy Ganymede is also the boy boar hunter Adonis, and leaves open to question whether Rosalind/Ganymede will be wounded by the boar or, in a rewriting of the myth, be victorious over it. In Shakespeare's *Venus and Adonis*, in either case, Adonis is

12. One sees a similar treatment of a homosexual subtext in plays such as Lyly's *Gallathea* and *The Maydes Metamorphosis,* in which love between two women is authorized while the threat of homosexuality is evaded by an actual transformation in the conclusion of one of the lovers into a man.

13. One possible source for Rosalind's love cure, noted by Agnes Latham, is Lyly's play *The Woman in the Moon,* where Pandora cures the shepherds of their love by actually behaving as Rosalind says she will behave (see the New Arden edition, p. lix). This source can help a modern reader remember that Rosalind/Ganymede's claims about women were not so far from what could, in another context, seem an acceptable representation of the behavior of a woman.

14. Thus, this play could be said to protect against the dangers to which Rabelais devoted his third book: whether, when he gets married, Panurge will be beaten, cuckolded, and robbed. In Rabelais, the question of female eloquence does not arise as such, though other kinds of noises become associated with femininity.

clearly a young man who, like the Bertram of *All's Well*, scorns love, especially, by implication, love of women: "Hunting he loved, but love he laughed to scorn" (*Venus and Adonis*, 4). The overpowering, maternal Venus of the poem makes heterosexual seduction into something closer to incest than to love, and female desire into a destructive force that, like the boar, wounds men.

Rosalind/Ganymede's erotic performance may serve, then, to distance or at least contain the threat of this powerful female figure, a threat that is indeed of significance to a play in which a woman takes control over both her own marriage and the resolution of the plot. The unacknowledged force of this female threat also explains in part the many allusions in the play to cuckoldry, which, according to a strict reading of the plot, should not be at issue here. One of the scenes in which Rosalind/Ganymede most explicitly lays out the threat posed by the uncontained, powerful woman begins with a series of exchanges about cuckoldry:

> *Rosalind.* I had as lief be wooed of a snail. . . . For though he comes
>   slowly, he carries his house on his head; a better jointure I think
>   than you make a woman. Besides, he brings his destiny with him.
> *Orlando.* What's that?
> *Rosalind.* Why, horns—which such as you are fain to be beholding to
>   your wives for: but he comes armed in his fortune, and prevents
>   the slander of his wife.
>
> (4.1.50–59)

These lines laugh ironically at the very activity undertaken by Rosalind/Ganymede, for her performance could also be described as arming the participants against their fortune and preventing the slanderous accusations of cuckoldry. The play plays with the possibility that such enactment (including apotropaic replaying through witty analogy) can actually ward off such a fate, and suggests that another way to read the seasons of love correctly ("men are April when they woo, December when they wed" [4.1.139–40]) is to be forearmed against fate by wit—that wit has an apotropaic function.

Wit is indeed the central culprit in Rosalind/Ganymede's pseudo-indictment of women. The discussion of a woman's wit centers on its power to find excuses to cover sexual wandering but serves also to suggest the ways in which the play's own ambiguities are implicated in the discussion of the threat of adultery. Rosalind first presents a woman whose wit (and, by extension, whose self) cannot be contained:

> *Orlando.* But will my Rosalind do so?
> *Rosalind.* By my life, she will do as I do.
> *Orlando.* O but she is wise.
> *Rosalind.* Or else she could not have the wit to do this. The wiser, the
>   waywarder. Make the doors upon a woman's wit, and it will out at
>   the casement; shut that, and 'twill out at the keyhole; stop that,
>   'twill fly with the smoke out at the chimney.
>
> (4.1.149–56)

The double reference at the beginning of Rosalind's speech—"to do this" refers both to the changeable roles that Rosalind/Ganymede claims women perform and to the performance at hand—alerts us to the application of this wafting wit to the play's own status. The description of wit escaping enclosure through any and all available exits reflects uneasily similar descriptions of the deeds of witches, a repressed figure of female power, whose souls were said to leave their houses through the windows or chimneys, spending the night far from their bodies. Here, however, the wit of the passage turns on whether the body is imagined to follow:

> *Orlando.* A man that had a wife with such a wit, he might say, "Wit,
>   whither wilt?"
> *Rosalind.* Nay, you might keep that check for it, till you met your
>   wife's wit going to your neighbour's bed.
> *Orlando.* And what wit could wit have to excuse that?
> *Rosalind.* Marry to say she came to seek you there. You shall never
>   take her without her answer, unless you take her without her
>   tongue. O that woman that cannot make her fault her husband's occasion, let her never nurse her child herself, for she will breed it
>   like a fool.
>
> (4.1.157–67)

The excuse that Rosalind puts in this imagined woman's mouth works in two quite contrary ways: the intended joke is evident, but behind it hover several suppressed homosexual scenes. Since neither the husband nor the wife could be imagined to go to the neighbor's bed if both neighbors were in it, the scene must be reimagined twice, producing either the image of two women or of two men in bed—two men if one imagines the wife coming to meet her male neighbor and finding her husband there instead; two women if the wife's wit is not to be at fault ("she came to seek you there" suggests that it must be the neighbor's wife with whom the wife is dallying, or else she herself has imagined a scene of two men). Rosalind/Ganymede's imagined excuse hints, then, at a different waywardness (or wisdom?) from that of the simple sexual betrayal of cuckoldry jokes, and it also comes to serve as a figure for the workings of metaphor (and dramatic figuration), connected here as always with promiscuity, and specifically with the threat of cuckoldry.[15] Wit involves, then, the capacity of one meaning to move from its proper "house" to a neighboring "house," where it makes new combinations that are "improper." But a woman's wit specifically claims to be going after the man, going to the nearby house "to seek [him] there," and thereby leaving no one "at home" in his or her own "proper" house at all—or else the man's efforts to seek out the woman in her improper relation, to contain or control it, itself results in a similar "improper" stance, for again no one is left at home in his or her own bed. The project of control itself leads to impropriety.

If this "waywardness" is to be warded off, then, the play will have to make some fast turns, for the very capacity that allows the woman to escape confinement and that poses the greatest threat to the husband (cuckoldry) is intimately connected to metaphor, and to the imaginative doubleness that characterizes all of the playacting scenes (and, by extension, all theater). By virtue of its wit, the erotic performance of Rosalind/Ganymede is thus threatened by the very figure that it at a different level works to ward off—the figure of the powerful, "improper" woman who will dominate and cuckold her husband. The language points to an unending oscillation between protection and contamination, between apotropaic representation and the return, in imagery that bespeaks a submerged ideological assumption, of that which was averted. If this warding off is fictionally successful, then, it is so only at the cost of implicating the play's symbolic action in a related, "female" metaphoric impropriety.

Rosalind/Ganymede goes on to evoke a rather disturbing image: the only way to control such a woman is "to take her without her tongue." In one sense, this "taking" is precisely what cannot and does not happen here—Rosalind is never to be without her tongue—and

15. See Patricia Parker, *Literary Fat Ladies: Rhetoric, Gender, Property* (London: Methuen, 1987), pp. 103–13.

yet "Rosalind" only gains her tongue with her disguise, as she becomes Rosalind/Ganymede. She loses her tongue as she relinquishes her disguise: except for the Epilogue, she has no lines after she has given herself to father and husband, and the previously marginal male characters such as the Duke Senior step forward to take command and finish the action. The lines evoke the alternative story of Philomela, a woman who was literally taken without her tongue and who found nonetheless a way to describe her victimization. If her erotic performance wards off the figure of powerful female language by evoking it, it also presents the threat that this enactment will become contaminated with what it represents—that Rosalind will become this dominating woman—at which point the only way to control her would be "to take her without her tongue."[16]

This line also resonates in surprising ways with the cultural ideal of woman, which was, after all, one of silence.[17] Rosalind/Ganymede's joke creates a literalized version of this ideal: women should be without tongues; they should all always be taken without their tongues. The literalization makes evident the way in which this "ideal" depends on a lack or an excision, which might be considered a female version of castration, a cutting off of that defining and "improper" thing ("improper" in being associated with the woman's wit). Rosalind/Ganymede's erotic performance serves to ward off the threat of the excision, for as long as s/he is a man, s/he does not need to fear the loss of her tongue. In this latter case, the performance averts the threat in a paradoxical way, for by becoming a man, s/he becomes a "man" without his sexual parts. The hovering sense of the youth as castrated man is brought out in the allusion to the Adonis story, for the wound that the boar leaves in Adonis' "thigh" can be interpreted as a castra-

16. The story of Philomela provides an etiological myth for art, suggesting that rape and excision of the tongue can be interpreted as the horror that generates great art, or the beauty in nature (the beauty of the nightingale's song) that becomes a figure for human art. It has been seen as a myth defining the human capacity to create beauty out of suffering, yet such interpretations tend to sidestep the fact that it is a myth of beauty made from female suffering. The suggestion here that women should be taken without their tongues to forestall their wayward wit thus suggests the congruence between the cultural ideal of the silent woman and such myths locating beauty as the aftermath of violence against women. On the Philomela myth, see my essay "The Social Aesthetics of Rape: Closural Violence in Boccaccio and Botticelli," in *Creative Imitation*, ed. David Quint et al. (Binghamton, N.Y.: Medieval and Renaissance Texts and Studies, 1992), pp. 189–238.

17. See Catherine Belsey, *The Subject of Tragedy: Identity and Difference in Renaissance Drama* (London: Methuen, 1985), pp. 149–92, esp. pp. 178–92.

tion wound. Again, the enactment that wards off this threatening alternative becomes itself contaminated by that which it is designed to avert.

The doubled imagery of excision or of castrating wounds—the excised tongue for the woman, the wound of Adonis for the boy—suggests that the roles of Ganymede and Rosalind have become inseparable. The same threat presents itself in both cases, and the question remains whether Rosalind can succeed at averting it through this performance. The doubled threat of excision suggests, then, that although Rosalind thinks she has freely chosen the role of Ganymede and can drop it at will, she in fact becomes contaminated by what it represents in ways that the play measures. Moreover, women who must act as men to have a voice have effectively lost their tongues as women. The character Rosalind as a woman loses her tongue during the scenes in which she must speak as Ganymede even as she averts the threat of the "roaring" or witty woman. The dialectic of protection and contamination leaves the social actor nowhere to stand in gender terms. Being either one gender or the other would leave one open to this threat, so the only solution—the only performance that can be apotropaic—is to remain both genders at once.[18] Indeed, Rosalind/Ganymede is in many ways both, and she sports a male tongue in a female body. The many unanswerable questions and comments about identity made in the playacting scenes point to the play's uncertainty about Rosalind/Ganymede's gender: "And I am your Rosalind" (4.1.61); "Am I not your Rosalind?" (4.1.84); "By my life, she will do as I do" (4.1.150). The play needs to reaffirm a form of enacted gender undecidability to avert the threats to the desired ending that it itself evokes. The only way for Rosalind not to become the kind of woman s/he enacts is never to be only a woman, while to the extent that she becomes fully a woman in the conclusion, her erotic performance cannot be seen as successfully apotropaic. *As You Like It* can perhaps be

18. This same gender undecidability associated with female loudness can be seen in *The Roaring Girl* by Middleton and Dekker, where the principal character cannot be pinned down by gender and switches roles and costumes throughout the play. As Sir Alexander puts it, "It is a thing / One knows not how to name: her birth began / Ere she was all made. 'Tis woman more than man, / Man more than woman, and—which to none can hap— / The sun gives her two shadows to one shape." Thomas Middleton and Thomas Dekker, *The Roaring Girl*, ed. Paul Mulholland (Manchester: Manchester University Press, 1987), 1.2.128–32. *The Roaring Girl* also provides an example of the problem posed by female eloquence—association of female eloquence with the monstrous and also with the bizarre, the uncategorizable.

distinguished in this way from a tragedy such as *Macbeth*, in which the unspeakable threat, suppressed and repressed in various ways by the protagonists, may well be precisely this undecidability of gender.[19] The comedy seems, in contrast, willing to countenance such a doubleness, or in any case requires it for its erotic performances to have their desired end.[20]

This doubled gender in its turn defines the self as already troped, already a performance. The self protects itself by enacting an "other" that also "infects" it or parasitizes it, gaining and losing a tongue in the same moment. This troped self suggests not only that the "I" can never be neutral in phallocentric discourse—for the woman has no unified position of "I" from which to speak—but indeed that the female "I" always must be double in precisely this way, both and yet neither alone. It also suggests why the stage provides a particularly complex space within which to consider the rhetorical status of the "I," most notably whether and how it takes on the status of a figure, since all identities onstage are proxy identities, and yet the gender of the actor—the actor's body—as well as the gender of the character remain crucial determinants of this proxy self.[21]

"THERE'S A GIRL GOES BEFORE THE PRIEST": THEATRICAL PERFORMATIVES

The principal performative speech acts of *As You Like It* are the vows taken in the betrothal and wedding ceremonies (though Jaques, too, as we shall see, has his performative moment). The moment in which

19. For gender undecidability in *Macbeth*, see Marjorie Garber, *Shakespeare's Ghost Writers: Literature as Uncanny Causality* (London: Methuen, 1987), pp. 87–123.

20. In *The Roaring Girl* the comic "happy ending" seems also comfortably to depend on the principal character's continuing ambiguity of gender. There too this ambiguity is necessary for the plot resolution, though in a more blatant and less problematic way—less problematic because the roaring girl herself is finally not one of the lovers who gets married off in the end.

21. On the ways in which *As You Like It*, and Shakespearean comedy more generally, call into question the audience's knowledge of sexual difference "by indicating that it is possible, at least in fiction, to speak from a position which is not that of the full, unified, gendered subject" (p. 180), see Belsey, "Disrupting Sexual Difference," pp. 177–89. See also Mark Bracher, "Contrary Notions of Identity in *As You Like It*," *Studies in English Literature* 24 (1984): 225–40, on the play's promotion of an "inclusiveness" of character in which the self accommodates itself to otherness "so as to include the other as *other*" (p. 225).

Rosalind gives herself away both allows the play to end and poses a number of difficulties about what kind of action this troped or doubled self can take. Rosalind reenters the scene with Hymen, and immediately turns to her father and says, "To you I give myself, for I am yours" (5.4.115). This line might not seem problematic, were it not repeated immediately in ritual fashion to Orlando. Giving herself to her husband apparently entails giving herself to her father, and vice versa: although Rosalind earlier had commented, "But what talk we of fathers, when there is such a man as Orlando" (3.4.34–35), now the two seem to imply each other, her relation to each being defined in identical terms. The line conveys something different in each case, something centering on the status of each "I." To what extent "is" Rosalind her father's? The line might be read as meaning "to you I give myself, for I (the possibility of being an I, or being a subject, especially the subject of a performative utterance) am yours," a reading marking the marginal position of the female subject in patriarchal discourse. This position is indicated by a simpler thematic interpretation: the only kind of performative that Rosalind as woman can utter is to give herself away to the men who already possess her. The statement is in effect a kind of tautology: if I am yours, then there is no sense in which I am actually "giving" you something you did not already possess. Rosalind's performative utterance can thus be seen as an affirmation of her father's control of her. The repetition of the line—to father, to husband—might thus seem to emphasize what has already been argued in other contexts, that the marriages at the end of such comedies reinforce a restrictive patriarchal order and reinscribe the otherwise rebellious females within it. The repetition also gives an incestuous cast to the final resolution, pointing to the structural dependence of patriarchy as a system on the incestuous doubling of father/husband.[22]

As we know, however, from research on the capacity of children to decide whom to marry, the power Rosalind appropriates here is certainly significant. Not only does she select her own spouse, using the structure of the drama to ensure that her father will not object, but she gives herself away. The play comments on the unusual nature of this move in the person of Sir Oliver Mar-Text, who, uneasy about the

22. One might note also the fairy-tale solution to the financial worries and to the inevitable problem for a sixteenth- or seventeenth-century audience: the younger son. On the role of primogeniture and the social and plot difficulties it poses, see Montrose, "'The Place of a Brother.'"

projected marriage of Touchstone and Audrey, reminds Touchstone, "Truly she must be given, or the marriage is not lawful" (3.3.63–64). Agnes Latham, the editor of the New Arden edition, has pointed out that "Christian marriage required no more than the consent of the two persons concerned," though the custom of "giving in marriage" went back to Saxon times and had its roots in the patriarchal system (p. 134). Rosalind's failure to fulfill this custom seems to go unnoted in the ending of the play, but Mar-Text's comment certainly helps to underline the unusual power exercised by a woman in this final scene—and thereby, perhaps, to emphasize as well the ways in which the comic ending may resemble the structure of wish, dream, or desire. Rosalind's power is real, then, even if it is carefully circumscribed by the fact of male possession and priority.

Moreover, the fictional context gives rise to the question whether the enacted marriage vows of Orlando and Rosalind/Ganymede can be understood to have performative force.[23] Both of the characters know that they are only "playing"—that they are not speaking "seriously" in Austin's sense—yet for both Rosalind and Orlando the scene seems to mark a shift in their relation and an end to their "courtship." In addition, a performance can complicate the scene by raising questions in the audience's mind of whether Orlando has begun to suspect the "true" identity of "Ganymede." If this enacted performative of act 4, scene 1 is only fictional, and does not carry performative force, it undermines Rosalind's concluding performatives, which also are theater, after all, suggesting perhaps a woman can speak only in troped performatives which indicate the secondary nature of her power to accomplish deeds in the world, especially with words (while she still has her tongue). And yet, the play seems to affirm the performative force of such enacted vows, as if to emphasize that troped performatives nonetheless carry cultural force, and may be the only performatives that most subjects can pronounce.

Rosalind "is" Orlando's in another sense too, then, for in act 4, scene 1 the same ceremony that will conclude the play is enacted as

---

23. As my notes to Latham's edition suggest, she concludes that such lines had performative force legally in sixteenth- and seventeenth-century English society. See appendix B, pp. 133–34, of the New Arden edition. On the father-daughter bond, and the significance of the linking of father and husband in Rosalind's performative, see Lynda E. Boose, "The Father and the Bride in Shakespeare," *PMLA* 97 (1982): 325–47, esp. 326–27.

part of the erotic performance of Rosalind/Ganymede. Thus Rosalind
has already given herself to Orlando:

> *Orlando.* I take thee Rosalind for wife.
> *Rosalind.* I might ask you for your commission; but I do take thee Or-
>   lando for my husband. There's a girl goes before the priest, and cer-
>   tainly a woman's thought runs before her actions.
>
> (4.1.129–34)

These enacted performatives indicate that the performative that closes
the play—"To you I give myself, for I am yours"—was already in
effect a repetition, at least in the case of Orlando. The line could then
be construed as reading: "To you I [Rosalind] give myself, for I [Rosa-
lind/Ganymede] am [already] yours." This reading again suggests that
some sort of troping or doubling of the self is effected by the doubly
repeated performative.

With the double repetition of the line we are already speaking of a
fragmented subject, an "I" that is divided and multiple, a ghostly ironizing of the "I" which generates an "I" that cannot easily serve as the
subject of a performative utterance. The repetition itself evokes an
ironizing, or at least a questioning, of the value of the performative,
for, if one repeats a performative, what status does the first statement
have? Is it undone by the repetition or reinforced by it? Sense can be
made of this repeated performative only if either the "I"s are different
or the act of giving is meant differently in each sense. The necessity
of this difference suggests that the subject itself—the "I"—is a trope
or figure, marking the space of at least two different subjects, possibly
of two different genders. Or, to put it another way, the performative
itself may be understood as being already troped (though, as we see in
the action of the play, in which Rosalind is successfully "given" to her
husband, this does not mean that it lacks performative force).

Beyond the problematic status of a woman's power to make
performative utterances, the enacted marriage scene (symmetrical
with both man and woman vowing, unlike the final scene) raises the
broader question of the theatrical performative. Onstage, within the
fiction, the line "To you I give myself, for I am yours" has a performative power: Rosalind is understood fictionally as having "given" herself with these words. From the perspective of the audience, however,
this performative utterance is understood as being spoken within quotation marks, just like her earlier statement to Orlando ("I do take thee

Orlando for my husband"). The potentially radical nature of the scene may seem to be contained, then, by the understanding that this is a representation, and therefore that no woman has in fact achieved this performative power, that no woman goes before the priest (or before the father's legal right to select the husband and give away his daughter).

The limitation on the more socially innovative gestures of the play established by the containing power of theatrical representation is nonetheless not the final level at which this question can be posed. One might speculate that with these performative utterances onstage the theater as institution also claims for itself a performative power, a power to shape or create social norms simply by performing them. What the theater performs in doing so may conserve social norms—as when Rosalind locates herself so clearly as the object, not the subject, of patriarchal discourse—but it need not, as when Rosalind first takes Orlando as her husband. The theater institutionally preserves the power to say that the girl may go before the priest, and this power itself is potentially more disruptive (the power of theater as social institution, appropriating the king's language) than the specific ending that the play represents. Following this logic, one might argue what, indeed, many viewers may feel about the exchange of vows between Orlando and Rosalind/Ganymede in act 4, scene 1: that it can be taken as in some degree a real action, that their troths are plighted by this enacted performance, that Orlando is in some sense agreeing to marry someone who is partly a man, that performance can indeed be performative.

The words spoken, when directed toward the right person ("I take thee *Rosalind*," not "Ganymede"), come, then, to serve as tropes of themselves. They are both true and fictional at once, just as Rosalind and Ganymede are the same character but exist separately at the same time. The statements Rosalind/Ganymede makes are simultaneously valid for both, but not as man or woman. Neither, one might add, is fully present or absent as man or woman, a situation that offers a critique of the distinction of presence/absence itself. This staged performative thus returns us to the idea of the contagion of role: the comedy affirms generically that the roles played in a wooing game are freely chosen, that one can play them or drop them at will, but the structure of the exchanges between Rosalind/Ganymede and Orlando suggest that, for the woman at least, this is not the case. (The role Orlando plays is equally contagious and necessary for him, though it

remains less evident because it is given the same name, "Orlando.")
The prosopopoeia of the subject—the taking of someone else's face
or mask—rhetorically reveals itself to result in the contamination of
the "I."

The doubling of the wedding performatives suggests, then, a more
disruptive cultural statement: that all performatives are staged, pronounced by multiple or troped selves. Embracing this cultural and
theatrical contamination of the self need not lead to marginalization
or lack, the play argues, but rather to the kinds of empowerment the
action seems to present, which, appropriately enough for the institution of theater, draw precisely on those modes of self-presentation
(with their accompanying speech acts) that have to do with endorsing
and putting into action the capacities of this multiple self.

One final performative utterance deserves a brief, concluding comment, since in fact it concludes the play. As the couples prepare to go
happily offstage together, Jaques is left unwilling to join the celebration, and he marks his departure by "bequeathing" to the others his
best wishes along with that which, in most cases, they have already
attained. His bequest, then, like Rosalind's gift, adds Jaques's best
wishes to what is otherwise a tautology. Jaques's statement is odd in
that it implies that he possesses these qualities of plot resolutions to
bequeath, making him momentarily a figure of the author, who be-
queaths the consequences of his plot as a closural gesture. A bequest,
moreover, becomes valid only upon death, so Jaques's words suggest
that, in turning to the convertite's cave, he "dies" to the social world
of the play. From this figuratively soon-to-be-dead Jaques, the plot
resolution can be established, as if Jaques takes on himself the costs of
the happy ending. Jaques, then, may be said to be the true recipient of
Ganymede's cure for love: on him is projected the "intended" ending
of the erotic performance of Ganymede and Orlando, that the "cured"
person would "forswear the full stream of the world and . . . live in a
nook merely monastic" (3.2.407–9). Orlando's fate is thus projected
onto Jaques, while Orlando is allowed to remain in love (which, as
we have seen, is not only to remain mad but to remain in fiction, or
in trope).

Jaques's bequest can also be said to provide the model for the female
performative, since, as we have seen, a woman cannot use language
performatively without being at least partly a man. The only form in
which a woman *as woman* can "give" herself is in a bequest, when she
has, as it were, died as a woman and taken on a male tongue. Other-

wise she can only return herself to those who already possess her, enacting in her performative the social possibility that preceded her utterance. Indeed the humor of melancholy was thought particularly to typify women, so that, like Hamlet, Jaques can be seen to be overtaken by a female mood. Jaques, then, becomes the closing example of the play's penchant for mixed gender, of its structural reliance on an undecidability of gender to pull off its conclusions and to perform them in society.

7

Pushing the Envelope
SUPERSONIC CRITICISM

DAVID WILLBERN

Malvolio. What employment have we here?

[Taking up the letter.]

Fabian. Now is the woodcock near the gin.

Sir Toby. O, peace, and the spirit of humors intimate reading aloud to him!

Malvolio. By my life, this is my lady's hand. These be her very c's, her u's, and her t's, and thus makes she her great P's. It is, in contempt of question, her hand.

Sir Andrew. Her c's, her u's, and her t's: why that?

(*Twelfth Night* 2.5.82–89)

A generation ago, in 1966, Alfred Harbage remarked that "in general, Shakespeare's puns shade into his serious word-play by such imperceptible degrees that we cannot pinpoint the place where joking ends and poetry begins."[1] This view of a rhetorical continuum from low to high, base to sublime, has value, yet its assumption of *classes* of language and intent undermines its perception. A better idea may be to consider Shakespeare's language not as a hierarchy or spectrum— however shady the threshold between levity and gravity, crude joke and serious poetry—but as an arena of linguistic play in which pun and profundity coexist: a field of deep wit, wherein the nature of particular

1. Quoted in *The Reader's Encyclopedia of Shakespeare*, ed. O. J. Campbell (New York: Thomas Crowell, 1966), p. 831b.

rhetorical events is as much a function of our attitude toward them as of their intrinsic semantic qualities, or Shakespeare's inferable intent. This essay aims to test some boundaries in our rhetorical attitudes: to draw provisional lines around licit and illicit uses of Shakespeare's language and to propose some models of close reading. One might call them pilot projects.

Nowhere have the hazards of close reading been more effectively and hilariously dramatized than in *Twelfth Night,* in the scene of Malvolio and the forged letter, where, as a result of his ambitious efforts at literary criticism in the service of personal advancement and sexual adventurism, the humorless steward transforms himself into a cross-gartered fool, to be treated as a lunatic. The moment offers itself as an emblem: both joke and enigma, a moment of deep wit staged clownishly, obscenely. It may be that the crudity of the joke disguises the depth of the wit. Before examining Shakespeare's scene of Malvolio's employment, however, I should set my own.

My academic training as a reader and scholar occurred during the 1960s, near the end of the dominance of New Criticism, and before the institutionalization of postmodern interpretive styles and challenges to them. Using a blend of Empson and Freud, I honed what the psychoanalyst Theodore Reik termed the "third ear" for linguistic response: hearing over and under the manifest words, listening for latent senses. In the 1970s I began to publish my marginally maverick findings, usually on Shakespearean topics. Now, Shakespeareans are by and large a kindly, tolerant sort, occupying a large territory with flexible boundaries, whose tribal disputes rarely flare into real antagonism (rather like an extended family). Still, I found lines to cross. One trespass occurred when I delivered a paper, "Shakespeare's Nothing," to a meeting of the Northeast Modern Language Association, wherein I proposed that underlying a primary sense of Cordelia's fateful "Nothing" in her answer to Lear's demand in the rhetorical love test is the same meaning of the term in Hamlet's bawdy byplay with Ophelia: *no thing,* or female genitals. From this immodest observation I proceeded to develop some ideas on the paradoxical interplay of negativity and generativity within the profoundly sexualized imagination I find in Shakespeare.[2] After my paper, a fellow rose and sputtered from the audience: "You can't do that! Shakespeare won't let you do

2. An amplified version of this paper was published in *Representing Shakespeare: New Psychoanalytic Essays,* ed. Murray Schwartz and Coppélia Kahn (Baltimore: Johns Hopkins University Press, 1980), pp. 244–63.

that. What?! Are you proposing that, as she speaks, Cordelia throws up her skirt?" Startled by such vehemence, I composed myself and responded on three fronts. First, I allowed that the bit of stage business he proposed was unlikely to work well in performance, and that I had not thought of it at all. Second, I noted his Foucauldian use of "Shakespeare" as an author-effect to limit permissible readings. Last, and most important, I sketched out an essential element of my own approach to Shakespeare: namely, that we might think of two plays occurring simultaneously. One is the play of action and character: the evident phenomena of dramatis personae addressing one another and imitating actions (Aristotelian drama, in short). In such a scene, Cordelia is not likely to be referring to her genitals, by either her language or her gestures. The other play is what I call the *play of language*. The phrase refers not only to localized puns and wordplay, but to an entire circulation of linguistic meaning, within and without the drama, which subsumes characters, or in which characters participate but which they do not own or control. Outside of character, outside of action, there is another site of the play: the play of language. In this larger scene, language refers to—or encourages readers and hearers to respond to—other significances. After Freud and Lacan, this observation can hardly be startling.[3]

THE PLAY OF LANGUAGE

Another way to put the issue is in terms of character or agency. Does it make sense, for instance, to assert that Cordelia intends any genital significance in her word? As far as I can see, the only way to support such an assertion is to attribute unconscious intention to the character. Now, it is a great strength and a great weakness (like a "tragic flaw") of psychoanalytic criticism that it attributes unconscious intentions to literary characters. In this case, I think the weakness is more apparent. I, for one, would not want to have to defend such a contention about

3. Still, such naïveté persists. In his *William Shakespeare* (Oxford: Blackwell, 1986), Terry Eagleton refers to my published essay. In a footnote (p. 107) he discusses the possibility that the meaning of "no thing" *might* be allowable, but that in no case are we to think that when asked for her response to her father's "What can you say?" Cordelia replies "Female genitals, my lord." Right: she doesn't say that. But the language does, or, more precisely, the language puts the crucial term into play for resonance later with other, more specifically bodily meanings—for those with ears to hear.

Cordelia. But character, as a dramatic construct, has its own great strength and weakness. A weakness is that audiences and critics may come thoroughly to believe that each character owns his or her language, and that each dramatic moment provides a limiting context for the language. Of course the illusion of people walking and talking on a stage is powerfully compelling. And yet, a criticism that does not privilege character, and instead examines the linguistic matrix within which characters occupy positions from which they speak, need not be disabled or inhibited by ideas of intentionality localized in characters (whether conscious or unconscious).

There is little new here, of course. The history of criticism in the twentieth century, and especially of Shakespeare criticism, has variously argued the status of character versus language, or *parole* versus *langue,* or meaning versus metaphor. In the field of Shakespeare studies, A. C. Bradley and G. Wilson Knight may be taken as emblems of apparently oppositional styles of reading. Bradley's devotion to intricacies of character and specific details of dramatic action (such as, "Where was Hamlet when his father was killed?") contrasts with Knight's celebration of metaphor and image—what he termed "the Shakespeare universe." Contemporary versions of the argument may be found in modern analyses (including psychoanalyses) of characters as autonomous, ambulatory speaking fictions (dramatis personae) versus postmodern studies of such agents as literal figures in a (re)circulating system of supplementary signification.[4]

GATEWAY OR MIRROR

Before embarking on a few exercises in practical criticism (pushing the envelope), I want to examine an important and pivotal image in Shakespeare. It occurs in *Troilus and Cressida,* when Ulysses is trying to persuade Achilles to join the Greek forces against Troy. Ulysses, pretending to be reading philosophy, notes that virtue must demonstrate itself in order to be valued, and Achilles agrees:

4. An excellent essay on Shakespeare's relation to language is Geoffrey Hartman, "Shakespeare's Poetical Character in *Twelfth Night,*" in *Shakespeare and the Question of Theory,* ed. Patricia Parker and Geoffrey Hartman (New York: Methuen, 1985), pp. 37–53.

Achilles.　What are you reading?
Ulysses.　　　　A strange fellow here
　　　　Writes me that man, how dearly ever parted,
　　　　How much in having, or without or in,
　　　　Cannot make boast to have that which he hath,
　　　　Nor feels not what he owes, but by reflection;
　　　　As when his virtues, aiming upon others,
　　　　Heat them, and they retort that heat again
　　　　To the first giver.
Achilles.　　　　This is not strange, Ulysses.
　　　　The beauty that is borne here in the face
　　　　The bearer knows not, but commends itself
　　　　To others' eyes; nor doth the eye itself,
　　　　That most pure spirit of sense, behold itself,
　　　　Not going from itself; but eye to eye opposed,
　　　　Salutes each other with each other's form;
　　　　For speculation turns not to itself,
　　　　Till it hath travell'd and is mirror'd there
　　　　Where it may see itself. This is not strange at all.
Ulysses.　I do not strain at the position—
　　　　It is familiar—but at the author's drift,
　　　　Who in his circumstance expressly proves
　　　　That no man is the lord of any thing,
　　　　Though in and of him there be much consisting,
　　　　Till he communicate his parts to others;
　　　　Nor doth he of himself know them for aught,
　　　　Till he behold them formed in th' applause
　　　　Where th' are extended; who like an arch reverb'rate
　　　　The voice again, or like a gate of steel,
　　　　Fronting the sun, receives and renders back
　　　　His figure and his heat. I was much rapt in this.
　　　　　　　　　　　(3.3.95–123)[5]

Underlying Ulysses' speech is an analogy central to Shakespeare's art: that of theatricality, or acting on a stage. The phrase, "communicate his parts to others," opens a comparison made manifest in the terms "applause" and "arch" (of the sky or heavens, like the arch under which "Achilles" and "Ulysses" stand as actors before an audience at the Globe). Underlying the theatrical analogy is another simile, the *mirror*: "or like a gate of steel, / Fronting the sun, receives and renders back / His figure and his heat." Vividly sensual, the simile presents a

---

5. Quotations from Shakespeare are from *The Riverside Shakespeare,* ed. G. Blakemore Evans et al. (Boston: Houghton Mifflin, 1974).

brilliant sign of the reflected image ("figure") and power ("heat") of the eye of heaven as it gazes into the metal surface. It is a design perfectly suited to both Ulysses and Achilles, for it simultaneously models antagonism and mutuality (two styles of reciprocity). In Ulysses' production of the image—call it his reading—the primary meaning is a *mirror*, a shiny metal surface reflecting the shape and energy of the sun. But it is also a *gate*, alluding to the gates of Troy, which the Greeks seek to demolish, and perhaps even the Scaean Gates, before which Achilles will eventually meet his own fate. This simultaneous image of *gate* and *mirror* offers a way to construct or figure apparently opposed positions of literary response. That is, does/should the reader enter into the text and engage it on its own terms (text as gate), or does/should the reader find reflected in the text those familiar features he or she brings to it (text as mirror)? Having thus naively put the question, I propose that it, like the image, is only apparently oppositional. Shakespeare's figure is *both* gate and mirror, and so is my ideal reading. The choice between "the words on the page" and readerly interpolation (a.k.a. "reading into") is a false dilemma, since in practice the only way we *can* read is to engage the words from within various frames of reference that can never wholly exclude the "personal." That is, when we read, we make sense of what we read, and making sense is partly a constructive activity. Imagine looking through a window at an external scene: not only is your perspective framed by the architecture of the window (like a gate), limited by the angle of your view, and subject to your own qualities of apperception, but the scene may also be infiltrated through a reflection of your own image as you look out (a mirror). This is a sketch of the psychological and epistemological idea of a *frame of reference*.[6]

PUSHING THE ENVELOPE

If the text is partially a personal reconstruction, then how do we know if or when we are bending it to our own will, distorting its sense beyond recognition? Are there no limits to readerly re-creation? Rather

6. For helpful psychoanalytic and philosophical commentary on the question of individual frames of reference, see Heinz Lichtenstein, "Identity and Sexuality," *The Dilemma of Human Identity* (New York: Jason Aronson, 1978), pp. 49–122. The issue of readerly interpolation is especially acute in this passage from *Troilus and Cressida,* since one of the central lines is textually questionable. The line "Till it hath travell'd and is mirror'd" in both Quarto and Folio is actually: "Till it hath trauail'd and is

than belabor such familiar questions, let me turn to specific examples of Shakespeare in an effort to test the bounds of plausible interpretation: pushing the envelope, in test pilot idiom.

After Bassanio has accosted Shylock with his need for money, Antonio enters. The Jew thus greets the merchant: "Rest you fair, good signior," he says. "Your worship was the last man in our mouths" (*The Merchant of Venice* 1.3.59–60). Now, a necessary way to read this line is to translate it into its conventional equivalent (the necessary evil of paraphrase): "We were just speaking of you." Of course this is what the phrase does mean, and is the tenor of the typical editor's note. Yet to translate into common idiom is to veer away from the immediate and pervasive meaning of the words. How are we to respond? Can Shylock be voicing a wish to put Antonio into his mouth—that is, to eat him? Before any production of the pound-of-flesh contract, before Shylock begins to whet his knife and grind his teeth in vengeful anticipation of Antonio's sacrifice, can he be thinking of eating the Christian? Or should we consider the phrase an unconscious admission, wherein Shylock speaks no manifest intention to devour Antonio but betrays a latent cannibalistic desire? Or should we finesse the issue of Shylock as a character with an analyzable psychology and suggest that the phrase is part of the overall play of language: an early sounding of a theme and image that will echo throughout *The Merchant of Venice,* and that may arouse primitive fears of being attacked and devoured by a monstrous creature (similar to medieval Christian constructions of murderous Jews)?

If we accept that the greeting ("Your worship was the last man in our mouths") is a key moment in the play of language, further questions arise. I could argue, with substantial evidence, that a fantasy of Shylock carving and eating Antonio is "in" the play. But what if we were to press the image? For example, what if, given plausible homosexual readings of the play, and many modern performances, our associations led us into fantasies of oral sexuality? To many readers such a proposal would be unpalatable. Or, given the obvious theological registers of the play, what if a reader were to connect the term "worship" with that peculiar ritual of divine cannibalism known as the Eucharist (in which Christians symbolically eat a Jew), and find in

---

married." Modern editorial conjecture has emended reasonably, but changing "trauail'd" to "travell'd" dilutes the energy of the phrase by extracting the work (and *labor,* with its associations of pregnancy) from it, and translating "married" into "mirror'd" loses in erotic intimacy what it gains in ocular accuracy.

Shylock's greeting a keenly ironic allusion to that holiest of religious rituals which provides the reciprocal carnal analogy to the raw fantasy of the Jew eating the Christian? Or what if this emerging complex of carnality, sexuality, and theology were connected to the famous question of the pound of flesh, "to be cut off and taken / In what part of [Antonio's] body pleaseth [Shylock]" (150–51), and the standard psychoanalytic reading of castration were recalibrated as a central issue of cultural difference marked on the body—namely, circumcision?[7] I could argue that the cutting of flesh as a mark of difference is a crucial theme "in" the play, and that within the play of language, Shylock is honing his knife in order to turn Antonio into a Jew. (The Christian, of course, turns the tables by inflicting Christian charity on Shylock, demanding that he convert.) Shylock's language when he discovers his stolen treasure suggests that he feels the deprivation as much more than a material loss:

> My daughter! O my ducats! O my daughter!
> Fled with a Christian! O my Christian ducats!
>
> . . . .
>
> A sealed bag, two sealed bags of ducats,
>
> . . . .
>
> And jewels, two stones, two rich and precious stones.
>   (2.8.15–20)

(Shylock's own banker is named "Tubal.") Given this barely latent context of castration and circumcision, I might introduce the late medieval "cult of the holy foreskin" (Christ's prepuce), and such mystical visions as that of Catherine of Siena, who imagined marrying Christ with a ring of his holy foreskin, or the fourteenth-century Viennese nun who had a vision of receiving the sacred prepuce in her mouth, and who reported that it tasted like honey.[8] To me these are pertinent associations to the full play of language in the play; to others they may be impertinent, illegitimate readings, perverse distortions of Shakespeare's sense.

Another kind of example: the famous question of the origins of

---

7. See Leslie Fiedler, *The Stranger in Shakespeare* (New York: Stein and Day, 1972), pp. 124–25; and Marc Shell, "The Wether and the Ewe," in *Money, Language, and Thought* (New Haven: Yale University Press, 1982).

8. Caroline Walker Bynum, "The Female Body and Religious Practice in the Later Middle Ages," in *Fragments for a History of the Human Body*, ed. Michel Feher et al. (New York: Zone, 1989), 1:164.

Leontes' jealousy at the beginning of *The Winter's Tale*. Critics have
proffered various explanations for the sudden onset of the jealousy,
from the dramaturgical observation that the tragicomic events of the
play depend on the character's actions, and that a character can arrive
onstage without benefit of psychological coherence in the modern
sense, to psychoanalytic diagnoses of Leontes' displaced homosexual
affection for Polixenes, the suspected rival in the love triangle. I suggest that another source for the character's reaction may be found in
the play of language, apparently outside of any character's putative
agency. Here are Polixenes' opening lines:

> Nine changes of the wat'ry star hath been
> The shepherd's note since we have left our throne
> Without a burthen. Time as long again
> Would be fill'd up, my brother, with our thanks,
> And yet we should, for perpetuity,
> Go hence in debt. And therefore, like a cipher
> (Yet standing in rich place), I multiply
> With one "We thank you" many thousands moe
> That go before it.
>
> (1.2.1–9)

To my third ear, the references to nine months, to the moon as "watery
star," the images of "burden," "filled up," "standing in rich place,"
and "multiply" evoke highly suggestive associations to procreation
and pregnancy. Without pressing the point further into the scene,
where similarly suggestive language continues, I suggest that the origins of the *character's* jealousy lie in the *reader-audience's* associative responses to the language. Of course, a reader devoted to analysis of
character might argue that Polixenes' language indicates a wish to reveal his guilt to Leontes—a guilt he expressly does reveal in act 5, in
terms of deep fraternal sympathy (5.3.53–56)—but surely that would
be a strange speculation in a scene where the whole dramatic point is
that Leontes is sadly, horribly, wrong.

BREAKING THE BARRIER?

Isabella has come to Angelo to plead for her brother, who is condemned to die for the crime of fornication (*Measure for Measure* 2.2).

Her first words are not about Claudio but about her own views of sexuality and justice:

> There is a vice that most I do abhor,
> And most desire should meet the blow of justice;
> For which I would not plead, but that I must;
> For which I must not plead, but that I am
> At war 'twixt will and will not.
>
> (2.2.29–33)

Since Isabella's first words in the play concern the limits to her liberty when she joins the convent (she wants, in fact, more restraint than the already strict rules require), one reading of her initial words to Angelo reinforces a psychological view of the character as one who wishes to repress sexual energies. Her image of "the blow of justice" could be connected to her later notorious statement to Antonio that, rather than submit her body to shameful lust, "th' impression of keen whips [she'd] wear as rubies, / And strip [her]self to death as to a bed / That longing have been sick for" (2.4.101–3). Such a psychological reading could speculate about sadomasochistic ambivalences in Isabella, and call into question the posture of severe purity she maintains. A third-ear audition of her opening line ("There is a vice that most I do abhor") could hear the genital meaning of "vice" (used more directly in her charge to Claudio, "Wilt thou be made a man out of my vice? / Is it not a kind of incest, to take life / From thine own sister's shame?" [3.1.138–40]),[9] and an aural echo of the term she cannot say but which characterizes the flip side of the nunnery she intends to join (the play even has a character named "Abhorson"). But to really push the envelope, let me reform the lines in a way their form provisionally permits, but which many readers may judge out of bounds: "There is a vice which most I do abhor, and most desire." Period. Now, can I do that? Will Shakespeare let me? The syntactic moment evanesces, resolved into the succeeding clause. But for a moment the line captures the precise paradox of desire that energizes *Measure for Measure* and most of its characters, "at war 'twixt will and will not." But can she mean to have said this? Or is it unconscious? Or is it an aspect of the play of language? Or is it merely beyond the pale of permissible readings?

9. See Richard Wheeler, *Shakespeare's Development and the Problem Comedies* (Berkeley: University of California Press, 1981), p. 111; and Janet Adelman, "Bed Tricks," in *Shakespeare's Personality,* ed. Norman Holland et al. (Berkeley: University of California Press, 1990), pp. 169–70.

Now for the acid test. As the first interview is about to conclude, Isabella suddenly offers to bribe Angelo. "How?" he returns. "Bribe me?" "Ay," she says,

> with such gifts that heaven shall share with you.
> Not with fond sicles of the tested gold,
> Or stones, whose rate are either rich or poor
> As fancy values them: but with true prayers.
>
> (2.2.146–52)

Editors tell us that "sicles" derives from the Hebrew *shekel,* that "tested gold" is gold proved true on a touchstone, and that "stones" are precious jewels. Fine. And my third ear, by this time acutely attuned to the extraordinarily suggestive language of the entire scene, and further sharpened by Angelo's own quick response to Isabella's offer (in terms of his character's psychology, her answer may respond to his wish that she bribe him with sexual favors)—my third ear, now listening in supersonic registers, breaking sound and syntax barriers, hears Isabella referring to something that she cannot plausibly be referring to: these contiguous syllables, only slightly rearranged, evoke the term "testicles," immediately glossed by the common synonym of "stones." Now, what am I to do with this response? It's on the edge, marginal even for me. Does it make sense to construct an unconscious intention in the character whereby she produces a brilliant Freudian moment that discloses her own desires while appealing to Angelo's, in a kind of unconscious conversation such as real people may have but rarely become aware of outside of an analyst's consulting room? (Earlier she exclaims to Angelo, "I would to heaven I had your potency.") I could argue that the moment catches a radical ambivalence in Isabella, placed on the threshold between one state (the silence and repression of the nunnery) and another (sudden entry into the slippery sexual economy of Vienna). Or I could argue that the moment demonstrates how the sexually charged language of that erotic economy invades Isabella's speech even as she tries to deny it, as if it were unavoidable, a natural contamination by carnality (this is a condition common to characters in *Measure for Measure:* see, for instance, the Duke at 1.3.1–6). Or I might contend that Isabella's language, like the character herself, is a masculine invention, constructed with the purpose precisely of invading the privacy of her "true prayers" by a denied and displaced profanity. The textual moment replicates in miniature the large-scale project of the play, which is to move Isabella out of the nunnery and into the Duke's bed. The moment may be a prime instance of the play of language, beyond character, outside local intentionality. Or is it rather a prime instance of a reading distorted by what Timon of Athens, referring to another character's bawdy comments about procreation, calls "lascivious apprehension" (1.1.207)?

The two interview scenes between Angelo and Isabella are dramatized instances of the problem of *reading*. Both Angelo and Isabella are trying to read the other's character, to detect through language and gesture the other's intention, to discover underlying meaning. When senses and intentions that neither suspects gradually emerge, as when Angelo finds himself aroused by Isabella, who is the agent of this newly constructed meaning?

> What's this? what's this? Is this her fault, or mine?
> The tempter, or the tempted, who sins most, ha?
> Not she; nor doth she tempt; but it is I . . . .
> (2.2.162–64)

From the perspective of character, Angelo's location of meaning construction is apt and plausible. He is guilty of "reading into" Isabella's speech and gesture, of imposing his own wished-for sense on the text that she presents to him (rather like Malvolio and the forged letter). During the second interview, the readings of the situation by Angelo and Isabella become more obviously a struggle between competing meanings, as Angelo approaches the raw proposition of his scheme and Isabella seemingly is unable to comprehend. "Nay, but hear me," he says to her. "Your sense pursues not mine: either you are ignorant, / Or seem so, craftily; and that's not good" (2.4.73–75). At this point, both characters may be negotiating "lascivious apprehensions": Angelo is trying to bring them to the surface, while Isabella tries to keep them suppressed. What I suggest is that both characters are subsumed within a play of language wherein such meanings are already in play. Perhaps the characters arrive belatedly at understandings an attentive audience already entertains.

LANGUAGE, CARNALITY, AND THE FEMININE

By no accident are my examples predominantly sexual. It is an aspect of my reading style that my third ear is especially attuned to sexual meanings. It is also my theoretical conviction that the deep metaphoric core of language is carnal. At root, many terms relate to the body and to physical action, like Angelo's word "conception"; "genius" and "genital" have the same root. The phrase "lascivious apprehension" literally means to grasp or lay hold of wanton pleasures. Indeed, tracking the etymology of "lascivious" through Latin *lascivia* and Anglo-Saxon *lust*—both terms cognate with *ludere* (to play, to sport)—I realize that my personal and professional reading project is to conjoin the ludic and the lascivious. My own interpretive style involves a working compromise between literary learning and unconscious response, or (as a colleague has put it) a rhetorical co-production of my intellect and my primary process.

Yet I would argue that connections between language and sexuality in Shakespeare's texts are not only aspects of my interpretive style or of the carnal core of language. Feminist and psychoanalytic studies of Shakespeare suggest that masculine efforts to manage meaning and to control female sexuality (for instance, *Measure for Measure*) are powered by an anxiety about threats to the boundaries of conventional significance represented by the exorbitant surplus of "femininity." In an essay on *Hamlet* and *Measure for Measure,* Jacqueline Rose remarks that "slippage of meaning and sexuality as excess seem . . . to be the subtext of the critical focus on Isabella and Gertrude."[10] The figure of woman presents a destabilizing effect within the conventional system of representation known as "masculine hegemony" or "patriarchy." Femininity or female sexuality, as the site of excess, the ludic and lascivious realm of the infinitely marginal, may embody a powerful background against which traditional (masculine) critical projects enact their exegetical searches for stable meaning. Commenting on T. S. Eliot's famous remark that *Hamlet* is "the Mona Lisa of literature," Rose extrapolates her study of the place of sexuality in the plays into a hypothesis about the hermeneutic need for articulable meaning and recognizable aesthetic form as a defense against anxiety about destabilized, excessive feminine significance. This is a large and provocative claim, one that likely intimates Rose's personal notions of the power and place of her own interpretations. Traditional criticism of Shakespeare, however, as the poet of mixed metaphor and the all-too-willing victim of puns, suggests a similar point. For example, take Samuel

    10. Jacqueline Rose, "Sexuality in *Hamlet* and *Measure for Measure,*" in *Alternative Shakespeares,* ed. John Drakakis (London: Methuen, 1985), pp. 95–118.

Johnson, whose famous criticism of Shakespeare's wordplay is often quoted: "A quibble was to him the fatal Cleopatra for which he lost the world, and was content to lose it."[11]

Cleopatra, that occult agent of femininity who stretches the boundaries of passion and discourse, who figures infinite variety, who teases Antony and us with her "immortal longings," who makes men hungry even as they are satiated: the figure makes a powerful emblem of Shakespeare's language. And could there be (dare we hear it?) a pun in Dr. Johnson's own decorous objection to the "low" art of punning ("and was *cont*ent to lose it")? Does the ghost of the seventeenth-century Puritan Malvolio haunt the eighteenth-century guardian of reputable language? "These be her very c's, her u's, and her t's . . . It is, in *cont*empt of question, her very hand." We are back at Hamlet's byplay with Ophelia, and "country matters." If the pun is there, did Johnson intend it? Or is it an irruption of the good Doctor's unconscious associations? As editor, Johnson glossed the notorious lines in *Hamlet,* proposing to amend the phrase to "country *manners,*" as follows: "Do you imagine that I meant to sit in your lap, with such rough gallantry as clowns use to their lasses?" (Presumably by "rough gallantry" Johnson intended a sublime euphemism.) A later eighteenth-century editor rejected Johnson's emendation, attributing it to "casual inadvertence," and went on to state that "what Shakespeare meant to allude to, must be too obvious to every reader, to require explanation." Hilda Hulme, in whose study of Shakespeare's language I found these editorial opinions, remarks: "In this particular instance the post-Victorian student who notes the country pun will escape the charge of reading into Shakespeare's text some new obscenity, self-invented . . . It is likely also that the 18th-century editors were aware of some implications in the Shakespearean text which, because of the narrower code of verbal decency imposed in Victorian times, no longer have a place in the ordinary language of protected academic life."[12] Hulme wrote this in 1962. Today, not only post-Victorian but also post-Freudian, it is practically inevitable to acquaint the ordinary

11. Samuel Johnson, *A Preface to Shakespeare* (1765). In his *Dictionary* (1755), Johnson defines "quibble" as "a low conceit depending on the sound of words; a pun." At the entry on "punster," he notes: "a low wit who endeavours at reputation by double meaning."

12. Hilda M. Hulme, *Explorations in Shakespeare's Language: Some Problems of Word Meaning in the Dramatic Text* (London: Longman Group, 1962), pp. 92–93.

language of current unprotected academic life with those textual implications not traditionally noted in public.[13]

Let us return, therefore, to that gate of steel and reflect more on it. A deeper psychoanalytic reading of the passage notes Ulysses' appeals to Achilles' virility and exhibitionism: to his "parts" and their extension before an audience. As a corollary to the latent phallic play of the language, the arch or gate that receives and reciprocates masculine energies may plausibly be imagined as a body (vaginal) image. Underlying this traditional Freudian reading would be the traditional Shakespearean reading of besieged cities as feminine enclosures threatened by masculine force: the (sexual) rape of Helen, for instance, that spurs the (martial) rape of Troy, to which action Ulysses is slyly urging Achilles. Such an interpretation gestures toward those Freudian readings that have by now found a relatively acceptable place in Shakespeare criticism. I think the gesture can be extended.

Achilles' recital of conventional optics and the confrontation of forms relies on a naive assumption of accurate specular reflection in which the reciprocal circuit of mutual speculation leads to a clear picture. Ultimately the eye does "see itself" through the recognition of others. Achilles' beauty and prowess are evident, even self-evident, since they are always and obviously remarked by his admirers. Achilles' mirror is a narcissistic one.

Ulysses shifts the traditional position toward a skeptical challenge. It is no longer a mutual salutation of self-evident forms but an interactive process of re-cognition, in which the nature of a self is actually formed and echoed by the social matrix wherein that self communicates, extends, or performs itself. It is only a small step to reread these lines as a poetic evocation of a primary site and scene of identity formation: those repeated moments in infancy when a baby extends itself toward its mother and is met with echoing approbation. (A brief fantasy: The little Achilles reaches out to Thetis and grasps her finger. "Oh, how strong you are," she exclaims. "How beautiful! You're my hero." The infant's gesture, the mother's response, constituting his identity.) Ulysses reconfigures the narcissistic surface into a relational dynamic. From various psychoanalytic perspectives, then, the scene can be read in terms of exhibitionism, narcissism, and object relations.

13. The bawdy spelling lesson in *Twelfth Night* was evidently not noted publicly until 1933, by David Garnett in *The New Statesman*. See Eric Partridge, *Shakespeare's Bawdy*, rev. ed. (London: Routledge and Kegan Paul, 1968), pp. 160–61.

In my view, none of these perspectives is fully explicative, nor does one contradict another.

The model of reading Shakespeare that I am testing here, based on various responses to the gate/mirror/body image in *Troilus and Cressida,* is one that invites entry into a world of apparently autonomous characters (the Greek camp, the Viennese court), while offering frequent chances for self-reflection (I can see myself in Ulysses and Achilles, Isabella and Angelo, and, yes, Malvolio), and while arousing and shaping sexual energies. In short, reading Shakespeare is for me the nearest thing to the process of erotic identification that literature provides. Testing the limits, then—playing in the margins of Shakespeare's text—is a means of simultaneously questioning and validating the boundaries of language *and* of sexuality. At origin (if I may imagine origin), such an erotics of reading Shakespeare rests on a fantasized apprehension of the maternal body: Cleopatra's infinite variety, or Cressida's embodied discourse ("There's language in her eye, her cheek, her lip" [*Troilus and Cressida* 4.5.55]). "By my life," Malvolio says, "this is my lady's hand."

But Malvolio, of course, is mistaken: another critic taken in by a facsimile of re-presentation. The steward pushes the envelope until it tears. His reading, which exhibits his own private desires as he attends obsessively to the letter of the text, is metaphorically a rape. He opens the letter: "By your leave, wax. Soft! And the impressure her Lucrece, with which she uses to seal. 'Tis my lady" (*Twelfth Night* 2.5.91–93). The wax impression of Lucrece, the classic personification of both Chastity and Rape, marks the symbolic transgression: a rending of the virginal seal to know its contents, and when the contents prove intractable, a further forcing of Olivia's letter to his own will. What is hereby dramatized could be termed "The Tale of the Violated Letter," where the violated letter represents the alphabet ("M. O. A. I."), Maria's forgery of Olivia's writing, Malvolio's personal reconstruction, and ultimately our own readings of the scene and its cryptograms, in Shakespeare's text.[14] In order to render meaning, the text is rent. Perhaps Malvolio and we fellow critics are, like Feste, not so much fools as "corrupters of words" (3.1.40).

In the spirit of benign corruption, then, I propose three models

14. See my essay "Paranoia, Criticism, and Malvolio," *Hartford Studies in Literature* 11 (1979): 1–23. In some of his last work, Joel Fineman also addressed this figure of the violated letter: see, for example, "Shakespeare's *Will:* The Temporality of Rape," *Representations* 10 (1987): 70–71.

of critical reading based on these three emblems. One: the figure of Malvolio and the letter, which demonstrates the pleasures and perils of solitary monologic reading. Two: the figure of Isabella and Angelo, which offers a dramatic dialogic episode in which meaning is negotiated, or solicited, within a contest of opposed forces. Three: the figure of Ulysses and Achilles, which is not quite a dialogue but rather pedagogic, as one reader subtly instructs another in a hidden agenda. (Ulysses sets out to seduce Achilles, whereas Angelo is initially unaware of his motives.) Each of these interpretive moments blends understanding and obtuseness, arousal and inhibition, wish fulfillment and defensiveness within a play of language whose deepest strata are carnal, and whose layers of overdetermined meaning reach to the margins, and beyond.

CODA: CLOSE READING REDUX

The 1989 meeting of the Shakespeare Association of America, in Austin, Texas, highlighted a plenary session called "Close Reading." One of the profession's finest practitioners of that art, Stephen Booth, provided a dazzling demonstration of its possibilities while asserting a refutation of any theoretical grounding for the practice.[15] His initial example was the opening line of Edmund's soliloquy in *King Lear,* act 1, scene 2: "Thou, Nature, art my goddess." Booth pointed to the abrupt coupling in this opening line of two quintessential terms in *Lear* and in the largest philosophical quarrels of the Renaissance: "nature" and "art." Of course, in this instance "art" serves grammatically as verb, not noun, but once the acoustic-visual event is noted, such linguistic conventions may seem, to some very close readers, subordinate. The juxtaposition of the two words is an observable textual event. It may be an illegitimate, even "bastard" reading, but it is nonetheless an event. (To use Edmund's own argument, are ear and eye to be shackled by "the plague of custom?") What are we to do, Booth asks, with this event? Is it an accident of language? Did Edmund intend it? Did Shakespeare? Does it carry meaning? Booth went on to argue that it cannot be ignored (just try to forget it now), and that it need not carry characteral or authorial intention or thematic meaning. It's just there: a momentary phenomenon that we observe or bypass in

15. A version of Booth's remarks is published in Chapter 2 of this volume.

our readerly traversal of the line. He continued to state that his style of close reading is thus "merely academic," not tied to theoretical schools or hermeneutic assumptions.

At the conclusion of this session, someone in the audience asked Booth about the place of unconscious receptivity in his notions of literary response—and by implication in his presentation of a merely academic literary criticism. Booth's response was to rise from the panelists' table, walk to the podium, look at the questioner, and enact a lengthy moment of silence. He then joked, in his marvelous deadpan manner, about not having had time to explain the workings of the unconscious. Then he extended his arm to his side, turned his hand palm up, and stared at it—like Hamlet gazing at Yorick's skull, or like Macbeth interrogating his own vision. Finally, he spoke. "I don't know," he said. "I don't know [about the unconscious] any more than I know how I can do *this*." And here he closed his fingers in a grasping motion, a visceral apprehension that mimicked his acknowledged ignorance of the unconscious—literally, the un-known.

Of course, the gesture deflected the question. Both Booth and his questioner must have known it was unsatisfactory. Yet I thought it was a good move. It simultaneously disclosed Booth's inability to speak about "the unconscious" and the power of the unconscious to speak. For the gesture of sustained silence followed by recourse to pure physicality does display the unconscious. It is something apparently strange ("I don't know") yet fundamentally part of one's nature (like an extended appendage). It is a primary means by which we handle experience without thinking about it.

I liked the moment, yet I think its message, however interpretable, omitted a core issue. Booth's gesture evidently proclaimed that the workings of the unconscious are like the workings of the nervous system, or the ineluctable connections of synapse and muscle that enact articulations of the will upon the body. What the gesture omitted, and what Booth was unable to talk about, was the issue of *motivation* that underlies and in psychoanalytic theory defines "the unconscious." In Freud's original formulations, the "System Ucs." was the result of the dynamic repression of wishes: it was an arena of desire whose energies had gone underground but which continued to shape the acts and language of conscious life. The unconscious, in short, situates our most basic and personal wishes and fears, motives and anxieties. It grounds *why* we speak; it harbors imagos of *to whom* we speak; it adumbrates earlier moments and situations *when* we spoke. The proper place of the unconscious in psychoanalytic criticism is as the locus of primary, unacknowledged desire. So described, the concept of the unconscious has no place in the critical theory of Stephen Booth as he asserts it. A poetry and criticism of pure structure, of interacting patterns of potential coherence and subliminal significance, needs no concept of dynamically repressed unconscious motives. Booth's is a motiveless criticism—or so he insists.

Another prominent expert in Shakespearean close reading provides another kind of example: Harry Berger. Both Berger and Booth describe the moment-by-moment enactment of a text—in a dramatic production, or reading, or interpretation—as reifying latent possibilities within the text, possibilities that are simultaneously expressed and disguised. For Berger, Booth, and myself, a particular production or reading necessarily limits textual potential even as it enables some privileged significances to emerge. Berger refers to this process as "a defensive transformation of latencies in the text." Both Booth (implicitly) and Berger (explicitly) recognize the convention of dramatic character to be a linguistic and dramatic device, subsumed by and smaller than the larger play of language within which characters seem to live. Audiences reify and imagine as persons those characters they see onstage, or read on a page, but a prior and primary agency of audience evocation is not character but language, which refers beyond any single character's momentary articulation of it. Berger, for instance, brilliantly evokes ("excavates" is his favored term) the displaced Oedipal agon of the Bolingbroke-Gaunt relation in the opening scenes of *Richard II*. He demonstrates through meticulous attention to words and images how the unconscious contest between one father and son enacts itself in a scene of political rivalry. Using as well his earlier work on *King Lear,* he shows how intrafamilial contests get displaced onto contiguous nonfamily relationships. Berger speaks the sense of a scene that the scene itself can only hint at. For example, he says of the opening scene of *Richard II:* "Mowbray serves as the medium in which are condensed Bolingbroke's darker purpose, to accuse the king, and his darkest purpose, to rebuke his father."[16]

It seems to me that Berger has a working theory of the unconscious that Booth lacks—or displaces to deferred, absent explanation. Berger feels himself speaking for other characters in the play; he is "charmed"

16. Harry Berger, "Psychoanalyzing the Shakespeare Text: The First Three Scenes of the *Henriad,*" in *Shakespeare and the Question of Theory,* ed. Patricia Parker and Geoffrey Hartman (New York: Methuen, 1985), pp. 229, 226.

or "tempted" into an interpretive ventriloquism through which unheard meanings are articulated. Booth gestures toward the "undelivered meaning"; he notes the unheard echo in a line; but then he insists on deferring interpretation, since to fall into interpretation is to give up the momentary juggling of multiple meanings. Booth evokes possibilities but resists meaning: structure, not content, is all.

For Berger, as I read him, Shakespeare's text is a dark and mysterious place, in which meanings need to be excavated, disinterred; silent characters need to be given speech; repressions and displacements need to be undone. Light can be brought to the dark moments, but an attentive archaeologist of buried meanings can find motivations as well. This is a psychoanalytic style—a Freudian style—of listening to language as a symbolic expression of complex human relationships.

For Booth, as I read him, Shakespeare's text is both a beautiful puzzle of wondrously intricate patterns and a hazardous place. In his Shakespeare Association talk he described it as a "minefield," where meanings relevant or irrelevant, sensible or nonsensical, are likely to go off. Our best job, then, is to try to keep our wits about us amidst the melee of possible meanings, to traverse the territory (the mind-field minefield) without succumbing to the pitfalls of conclusion. (The Bible warns, "He who digs a pit will fall into it, and a serpent will bite him who breaks through a wall" [Ecclesiastes 10:8].)

Booth, I surmise, has no use for a theory of the unconscious. His practice assumes varying thresholds of subliminal apperception, building up accretions of sound and sense (he likes the musical analogy). The process is assertedly neutral: without active desire, without intention, without preferred result. The merely academic, motiveless criticism is like free association without tears. To repeat: the psychoanalytic idea of the unconscious is precisely that which partly motivates an action, a word, a reading, *and* that which responds to or makes possible interpretation, eventually achieving that privileged yet provisional moment called meaning.

Another question arises: that of psychoanalytic criticism releasing or taming subversive energies of a text or play by paradoxically making "the unconscious" available to knowing. Insofar as any conclusive criticism, by structuring such energies, thereby stabilizes and defensively transforms latent meanings into reified significances (such as "Freudian symbols"), psychoanalysis can be charged with complicity in such defensive management of the anxieties and emotions it excavates. (One might claim this as a function of literary criticism.) To quote Harry Berger in "Psychoanalyzing the Shakespeare Text": "The shifts described above [displacements of anger away from family and into politics] combine to mark the most fundamental process that structures this drama: the passage and transformation of conflict from the tongueless caverns of some 'hidden imposthume' to the safety of the sanctioned artifice and 'fair designs' of ritual combat and behavior."[17]

Meanings, like Robert Frost's slippery definition of a poem riding on its own melting, can be momentary stays against confusion. This is a point on which Booth and Berger and I agree (at least I think so). Yet insistently avoiding meaning can be as risky and dubious as too quickly falling into it. Stephen Booth steps warily through his mind field, pointing out potentially explosive moments, while Harry Berger happily and helplessly slides into any and all possible excavations. Perhaps one sees Ulysses' gate of steel as a mirror, reflecting intricate and fair designs at a distance, disclosing a quick glimpse of a figure, while the other sees the gate as an invitation to enter, in an ardent search for hidden energies. Together, both interpretive styles generate light and heat.

17. Ibid., p. 227.

Part Three

Reflexive Readings

8

The Taming of the Shrew, Good Husbandry, and Enclosure

LYNDA E. BOOSE

Readings of *The Taming of the Shrew* have always felt compelled to begin at the end, the site where happily-ever-after presumably begins and, in this play, the site/sight where the play produces its theatrical tour de force by offering up a prostrated woman's body to the eye— and the boot—of the stunned viewer. But whereas the play's stage history of repeated revisions clearly marks Kate's final speech as the site of textual excess,[1] what *Shrew* revisions have characteristically desired is not so much a way of undoing Kate's ventriloquization of male superiority as a way of making it more palatable. Kate's subjugation must be endowed with signs of resistance—but a resistance that Petruchio will not recognize. She must embody the illusion of subversiveness—but simultaneously be authorized to submit to whatever self-abnegation is imagined as necessary to preserve the heterosexual bond.

New Critical readings of *The Shrew*—even many feminist ones— have largely remained trapped within the revisionist conundrum, trying to resolve the play's contradictory desires from the already contained position of reading from "inside" the text and dismissing all considerations that lie "outside." Poststructuralist methodologies were probably necessary before this play could be read through a fully feminist perspective, for so long as readers adhered to the formalist

---

1. Ann Thompson's introduction to the New Cambridge *Taming of the Shrew* illustrates this phenomenon (Cambridge: Cambridge University Press, 1984), p. 24.

injunction to stay "inside," critique was tautologically restricted by assumptions that granted not only texts but also "good readers" the ideal status of artifacts somehow immaculately conceived outside history, ideology, and all the disunifying politics of historical contingency. But masked behind the presumption of being apolitical and hence "objective," formalism's impulse to universalize the particular has always tacitly subscribed to a politics that affirms the status quo. Reading *The Shrew* from inside the text dissociates the reader both from recognizing how the material conditions of early modern England might be implicated in producing its narrative and from any consciousness of the reader's own potential distance from the cultural location of insider-ness. Seduced into reading patriarchal texts from their center, the woman reader remains safely divorced from any recognition of her own resistance. When lured into such a position, the feminist critic has inevitably felt defensively compelled to take Kate's part, a course that by definition leads to rationalizing Kate's actions, usually by means of finding some hidden assurance of marital "mutuality" lurking behind the play's formidable show of patriarchal domination. And while such ameliorating scripts may format an unconscious working through of both the culture's and the critic's own relationship to the entangled symbiotics of patriarchal culture and heterosexual marriage, they are virtually incapable of emancipating either female or male readers from the relentlessly gendered experience that the dynamics of this play have constituted as inseparable from its fulfillment of comic desire.

Outside of such a (too) close reading, there is an "other" space from which to generate a potentially different understanding of this play, one that neither denies nor unwittingly validates the play's patriarchal premises but tries instead to consider how the text itself may offer a revealing narrative not only of its own production but also of the markedly compulsive needs for masculine dominance that underwrite it. Central to this strategy is a reading order which, by insisting on the diachronic structure of the narrative, firmly binds the play's often forgotten Induction to its more familiar woman-taming material. In the perspective I propose, the issues of gender and hierarchy are pushed outside the fictive frame of the Kate and Petruchio story in order to be searched out again among a variety of historicized construction sites, including, most prominently, an overdue consideration of the ways in which the material conditions of early modern England may be implicated in this text.

To begin such a historicizing, readers need first to recognize that there is a concrete historical analogue for the final scene and Kate's insistence that wives should "place your hands below your husband's foot, / In token of which duty, if he please, / My hand is ready, may it do him ease" (5.2.182–84). What needs to be recognized is that the (in)famous concluding spectacle of this play is itself a dramatized (and now correctly ordered) version of the parodic church wedding scene which had earlier occurred offstage. Within the invoked ritual framework, Kate's actions essentially replicate the script that appears in the Sarum, the York, the (Scottish) Rathen, and the (French) Martène manuals for the actions that the bride was to perform upon receipt of the wedding ring and her husband's accompanying vow of endowment. Following his pledge of worldly goods, the bride is directed to fall prostrate at the bridegroom's feet, and—in phrasings that vary from ceremony to ceremony but in both English manuals are contingent upon whether the groom had endowed his wife with *land*—the rite then directs that she is to "courtesy" his foot in gratitude before he stoops to raise her up into her new status as wife.[2]

For feminist scholars, recognizing this analogue (or discovering that Shakespeare is not the guilty party who invented it) does not resolve the issue. Rather, it compels the question of why Shakespeare chose to use so adamantly hierarchical and patriarchal a form of the wedding service when that model had been excised from the 1549 Book of Common Prayer and therefore had been, by the time *Shrew* was written, officially prohibited for some forty years. The invocation of a ritual service that the audience would almost certainly have recognized—but recognized as anachronistic—seems to me to work two ways at once: on the one hand, it inscribes the concluding Kate and Petruchio marital relation as an anachronism; and yet, on the other, by idealizing and romanticizing that model, it imbues it with the nos-

2. J. Wickham Legg, *Ecclesiological Essays* (London: de la More Press, 1903), esp. pp. 189–90; George Elliott Howard, *A History of Matrimonial Institution,* 2 vols. (Chicago: University of Chicago Press, 1904), 1:302–8; *Surtees Society Publications* 63 (1875): 20, note; Duncan MacGregor, ed., *The Rathen Manuel* (Aberdeen: Aberdeen Ecclesiological Society, 1905), p. 36 n. 1. In the York and Rathen rites, the bride was to kiss the husband's foot only if he had endowed her with land; a surviving "MS. Manual of Sarum Use," however, dictates that she must do so "whether there is land in the doury or not" (Howard, *A History,* p. 307 n. 1). The enactment of this ceremony of prostration and foot-courtesying seems to have been traditional throughout pre-Reformation Europe. For further details, see Lynda E. Boose, "Scolding Brides and Bridling Scolds: Taming the Woman's Unruly Member," *Shakespeare Quarterly* 42 (1991): 179–213.

talgic value of a vision of social order imagined as passing away. It is within this framework—the sense that this play both participates energetically in and yet nostalgically withholds itself from the world of its own contemporary modernity—that I hope, through a feminist-materialist reading, historically to situate the notably dislocated structural logic of *The Taming of the Shrew* and its obsessive investments in the reinstatment of a hierarchically gendered order.

Shakespeare's play is set in England. But in the unusual framing device with which it opens, the play literally dislocates its scene of action away from the setting it has first foregrounded: Christopher Sly's Burton-Heath (or William Shakespeare's Stratford-upon-Avon). By such relocation, the play situates the social and political landscape of small-town, rural, late sixteenth-century Warwickshire as the ground from which Signior Baptista Minola's "Padua" emerges as narrative displacement. Historically, the landscape from which the "taming" plot emerges was precisely the world where women defined as "shrews" or "scolds" became, during the late sixteenth century, an obsessive sign of monstrous disorder, and one in which—as I have elsewhere described[3]—a number of local Kates were being subjected to taming processes significantly more brutal than the proto-Skinnerian program of negative reinforcement which Kate undergoes in Shakespeare's play. The era's obsession with taming unruly women—which historian David Underdown has documented as a phenomenon peculiar to the "crisis of order" that he defines as having itself developed between 1560 and 1640 out of a "period of strained gender relations"[4]—is precisely what warrants the move to construct a reading from outside the text. For in terms of the history of gender during this era, the fixation on scolds, the substantial rise in both official punishments such as the cucking stool and extralegal ones such as the scold's bridle which were meted out to women defined by that term, and the marked increase during this period in defamation suits filed by women,[5] suggest not only a precipitous increase of male anxiety about authority but also the possibility that Kate and her sister scolds may

3. See Boose, "Scolding Brides and Bridling Scolds."
4. David Underdown, "The Taming of the Scold: The Enforcement of Patriarchal Authority in Early Modern England," in *Order and Disorder in Early Modern England,* ed. Anthony Fletcher and John Stevenson (Cambridge: Cambridge University Press, 1985), pp. 116–36, esp. pp. 116, 136.
5. J. A. Sharpe, "Defamation and Sexual Slander in Early Modern England: The Church Courts at York," Borthwick Papers no. 58 (1980), p. 24.

have been symbolically implicated in a larger network of cultural meanings than any that are immediately apparent within the Kate and Petruchio/Bianca and Lucentio story. My contention is that, despite its seeming lack of any of the "political" markers of the history plays, this play is every bit as much a dramatization of English history as are the *Henry VI* plays, which were written at very nearly the same time.

Obviously, many factors underwrite the gender crisis that Underdown defines. But beyond such anxieties that may have stemmed from the presence of the "female king" or the world of court politics, there was something else going on in England—something that may initially seem to bear no relation to issues of gender but that, in rapid increments, was the factor that was most dramatically changing the very basis of English social organization during these years. The events in question come from the history of English land use. To include them seems appropriate, for they effectively shift attention away from the sexual conduct of the Elizabethan upper classes, which has been the more frequent focus of *The Shrew's* literary historians, and relocate it inside the world and the issues which the Induction sets up as ground.

As scholars such as Raymond Williams and R. H. Tawney have eloquently discussed, it was during this era and in this world that the geographic, economic, demographic, and social landscape of England changed precipitously as the pattern of land use and tenancy, in addition to the way of life it had signified, was transformed from men working and living on land worked by their families for centuries and inherited in copyhold[6] into a system of rigidly demarcated private ownership for the few and dispersion and vagabondage for the many. During this transformation, England's social geography changed from a form of community space defined by common land on which manorial lord, yeoman, and peasant all grazed their livestock to a landscape of exclusive ownership quite literally etched by fences, hedges, and ditches across the face of England. It was during the Tudor years, with the decline of ecclesiastical authority, that lay landlords gained the necessary power, both in Parliament and at the county level, to outmaneuver the crown's rather desultory attempts to protect peasant tenancy. Through manipulation of the legal strategies of "ascertainment, enclosure, and the triumph of common law over clerical law

6. Richard Lachmann, *From Manor to Market: Structural Change in England*, 1536–1640 (Madison: University of Wisconsin Press, 1987), esp. pp. 100–149.

and manorial custom . . . a plurality of English peasants [were re-moved] from their tenancies, relegating them to positions as wage laborers or relief recipients . . . On Manors where the court and cus-tom had been abolished, a quarter of the original tenants, on average, retained their land rights. If the commons was enclosed, even fewer peasant farmers saved their holdings. Where manorial structures were preserved, more than a third . . . survived as independent farmers."[7]

By consequence, a few families (or one family) came to control all or most manors in a parish, while simultaneously, anywhere from one half to three quarters of the English peasantry were, by 1640 or so, left landless.[8] As the supply of landless laborers increased, their worth in wages declined. Whereas fewer than 15 percent of English peasants had been wage laborers at any time prior to the 1570s, by 1688 over

---

7. Ibid., pp. 118–19. See also R. H. Tawney, *The Agrarian Problem in the Sixteenth Century* (New York: Franklin, 1912), pp. 32–33, 64–65, and passim. The historians' debate over enclosure and the other land reallocations that initiated agrarian capitalism in sixteenth-century England has heated up again of late, spurred on by revisionist theses such as that of Eric Kerridge in *Agrarian Problems in the Sixteenth Century and After* (London: Allen and Unwin, 1969). To a poststructuralist literary scholar whose assumptions include recognizing a politics of the critic, the debate seems distinctly ideological. Although Kerridge never acknowledges a politics informing his own per-spective and instead sees it as a problem only in Tawney, a political perspective seems quite evident in his introductory comments: "In Tawney . . . a harmful prejudice was all too evident. Tawney the politician barred the way to Tawney the scholar. Time which he might have given to studying history was devoted instead to the Fabian Society and . . . socialist dogma. Hence his wholly untrue picture of early capitalism as cruel and greedy, destructive alike of social welfare and true spiritual values" (p. 15). Like "Shakespeare" in 1980s literary politics, the social history of the 1590s apparently locates a similar site for ideological contest among early modern British historians. Ian W. Archer's comments are instructive. While acknowledging the im-portant correctives that revisionist urban historians have offered to the so-called doom and gloom school of urban history, Archer points out that "because the stability of the city is always in view, these writers tend to be biased towards the success stories. Their attention is focused on upwardly mobile Londoners . . . . Consensual explanations are always favoured over those which recognise a degree of coercion, so that there is no discussion . . . of the repressive side to social policy." Ian W. Archer, *The Pursuit of Stability: Social Relations in Elizabethan London,* Cambridge Studies in Early Modern British History (Cambridge: Cambridge University Press, 1991), p. 15.

8. The wide variance in my figures reflects the apparent difficulty of finding a na-tional calculation based on tabulations that differ from county to county. Estimates of the number of those dispossessed by enclosure vary, sometimes greatly, among historians. Perhaps because the assessment is inextricable from an ideological perspec-tive it would appear to verify, history—whether of the sixteenth or twentieth cen-tury—seems to have a hard time counting up its homeless.

half had been reduced to that status.[9] Furthermore, in refutation of the 1970s–80s revisionist explanation that the primary rationale behind these massive dispossessions was improvement of the land for maximization of profits (and thus an end for the greater good), the data that historian Richard Lachmann amasses about the uses to which English landowners put the acquired land indicate that "the wage-labor market must be understood as the consequence of gentry strategies for land control, not profit maximization."[10] Whereas "the majority of landless peasants prior to the dissolution had been sons of landholding peasants who were awaiting the inheritance of the family farm . . . by the latter half of the sixteenth century, most landless peasants had no prospect of acquiring land at any point in their lives."[11] By then, the growing number of landless had only memories of claims to what had once been the land of their fathers and grandfathers—claims that at one time, in the old manorial court system, could have been substantiated by memorial recall of the genealogy from which such copyhold had been inherited. Whereas modern historians, commenting from hindsight, may view enclosure as merely a stage in the alteration of land use, for villagers of the late sixteenth century it was, as Roger Manning emphasizes, the "symbolic act [upon which] contemporary debate focused and it was upon the enclosing hedge that villagers with a sense of wrong vented their rage . . . Enclosure also was widely blamed for causing dearth [which] is why antienclosure riots were a much more widespread protest . . . than grain riots."[12] Likewise Joan Thirsk, who takes a more benign view of enclosure motives than does Lachmann, insists along with Manning that although the levels of catastrophe may seem exaggerated if measured retrospectively and from a national standpoint,

9. In Lachmann, *From Manor to Market*, p. 121 and table 1.1, p. 17, the sources for this figure are given extensive citation.

10. Ibid., p. 140. In seeing the strategies taken by the lords and gentry as designed to clear the land of a peasantry that had made gains both tenurially and materially during the fifteenth century and not as premeditated steps toward agrarian capitalism, Andrew Charlesworth essentially agrees with Lachmann. By enclosing the commons, raising rents, driving out the tenants, and subsequently leasing the property to graziers, the landlords increased their seigneurial power and prevented tenants from converting the land to freehold. See Andrew Charlesworth, "The Geography of Land Protests, 1548–1860," in *An Atlas of Rural Protest in Britain, 1548–1900*, ed. Andrew Charlesworth (Philadelphia: University of Pennsylvania Press, 1983), pp. 9–11.

11. Lachmann, *From Manor to Market*, p. 135.

12. Roger B. Manning, *Village Revolts: Social Protest and Popular Disturbance in England, 1509–1640* (Oxford: Clarendon Press, 1988), p. 23.

this was cold comfort to the husbandman of the sixteenth century
watching the progress of enclosure in and around his own village. Enclosure has first to be recognized as a social problem concentrated in the
Midlands. Seen in that narrower context, it cannot be lightly dismissed.
In Leicestershire alone, more than one in three of its 370 villages and
hamlets underwent some enclosure between 1485 and 1607. The motives and incentives to enclose . . . were many and complex. But they
worked their worst effects in one consolidated belt of country, stretching from the western half of Lincolnshire through Northamptonshire
and Leicestershire to Warwickshire and reaching south to include Bed-
fordshire and Buckinghamshire. The historian who tries to account for
trends and changes in a broad context recognizes different types of enclosures and different motives . . . [and] sees the problem of the sixteenth century as a temporary crisis only. But the Midland peasant lived
in the midst of events and saw only one widespread movement to enclose and convert the land to pasture. He saw more cattle and more
sheep in the closes. He saw rich farmers taking up more and more land
but giving less employment than ever before to the labourer.[13]

As enclosure began to effect the economic and demographic shifts
that enclosed the open fields and nearly depopulated areas in the Midlands such as the limestone and Cotswold hills[14] where Christopher
Sly's Burton-Heath is located, it was primarily the aristocrats and
lower gentry who improved their lot. The rise in status was also,
however, limitedly accessible to those yeomen and upper peasants
who could come up with either enough cash to buy a field and get a
corner on the land speculation market or enough determination to
marry the daughters of the lower gentry, both of which strategies
provided plausible routes upward. If Osric—the *nouveau* courtier
whom Hamlet says "hath much land, and fertile; let a beast be lord of
beasts, and his crib shall stand at the King's mess. 'Tis a chough, but,
as I say, spacious in the possession of dirt" (5.2.85–88)[15]—represents
(from Hamlet's aristocratic perspective) the first type of entrepreneur-

13. Joan Thirsk, *The Rural Economy of England* (London: Hambledon Press, 1984),
p. 81. For an excellent summary of the contradictory discourses in which enclosure
exists in even the sixteenth century, see James Siemon, "'Landlord . . . Not King':
Property and Propriety in the Heteroglot England of *Richard III*," in *Enclosure Acts:
Sexuality, Property, and Culture in Early Modern England,* ed. Richard A. Burt and John
Archer (Ithaca: Cornell University Press, 1994).

14. Thirsk, *Rural Economy,* p. 80.

15. All Shakespeare quotations are from *The Riverside Shakespeare,* ed. G. Blakemore Evans et al. (Boston: Houghton Mifflin, 1974).

ial good fortune, then William Shakespeare (like his father before him) represents the second group, the yeoman-class sons who married upward and then assuaged their apparent class insecurities by later purchasing bogus coats of arms. But as the few moved up, the greater majority of tenants became landless, leaving England with a suddenly sizable population of vagrants, who themselves accelerated the anxieties about ownership and material possession as they roamed the land in search of wage labor and squatted cottages on it. This is the England that suddenly became obsessed with laws against vagrancy; the England that, by the end of the sixteenth century, had established poor laws that instituted a system of compulsive charity as part of a design to control the mobility of the landless and thereby allay the fears of the landed. By the end of the seventeenth century, the poor had been successfully removed from public view, enclosed in workhouses.

Throughout the 1590s, however, before systems of social control had been fully implemented, and while peasant solidarity was still strong, popular protest was on the rise. Organized class rebellion and riots over enclosure were still perceived as a real threat; and local landowners were engaged in devising legal strategies to subvert peasant unity, to implement inexpensive ways to deflect and undermine the potential for protest, and, ultimately, to ensure that "peasant reaction to the loss of land tenure did not escalate beyond passive appeal for mercy from those landlords."[16] In London alone, between 1581 and 1603, Roger Manning counts "no fewer than 35 outbreaks of disorder";[17] Annabel Patterson, reflecting on these statistics, comments on "how unstable the social framework must have appeared to Shakespeare, beginning his analysis of Elizabethan history and culture in the early 1590's."[18] Moreover, it was the seven Midland counties, including Warwickshire, that lay at the center of the disturbances, and when the situation finally did explode, it did so in the 1607 Midland Revolt.[19] In Stratford itself, agitation against enclosure was apparently

---

16. Lachmann, *From Manor to Market*, p. 104; see also pp. 108–11.

17. Manning, *Village Revolts*, p. 187. Manning sees this concentration of disorder as primarily a crisis in urbanization, Annabel Patterson as one of economic distress, in *Shakespeare and the Popular Voice* (London: Blackwell, 1989), pp. 34–35.

18. Patterson, *Shakespeare and the Popular Voice*, p. 35.

19. Thirsk discusses how, long before the 1607 Midland Revolt, the authorities as far back as the enclosure commissions of 1548 and 1565 were already concentrating on the Midland counties. In 1548 the commission inquired into engrossing, enclosing, and emparking in Warwickshire and Cambridgeshire, and, in 1565, in Buckinghamshire and Leicestershire (*Rural Economy*, p. 72).

an integral part of village life: "In Stratford-upon-Avon, the enclosure of the town commons by Sir Edward Greville, the lord of the borough, provoked the burgesses to elect Richard Quiney as bailiff without seeking Greville's approval. Quiney and several townsmen then levelled the hedges and were prosecuted by Greville for riot . . . Their quarrels generated numerous cross-suits [and ultimately] Quiney, a friend of Shakespeare, died of head wounds inflicted upon him by one of Greville's servants while attempting to stop a brawl."[20]

Within the shire culture of small towns and villages, enclosure met with widespread resistance in the form of antienclosure riots. From surviving records of such resistance, it seems that women as well as men were participants, even staging some of the protests by themselves, as wives rounded up other wives in the dead of night to rip down the fences and hedges that had come to signify their own economic enclosure.[21] And although cross-dressing can be given too much symbolic emphasis if it is read primarily as a desire to invert the gendered order of things rather than recognized as a strategy for disguising the identity of male rioters, it is nonetheless true that the riots were often acted out on the stage of gender by men in cross-dress.[22] Yet despite the hints of an implied sexual egalitarianism in the various acts of resistance to enclosure, and despite the obvious shared interests that would argue for solidarity between men and women of a threatened social class, it was nonetheless during precisely this same period that the communities themselves began enacting newly harsh prohibitions and enclosures against women. Likewise at this time, female "disorder" and "unruliness" suddenly came to be viewed as a massive threat to community integrity. And though "misogyny" may

20. Manning, *Village Revolts*, p. 104. This Richard Quiney seems to have been not only William Shakespeare's friend but Judith Shakespeare's father-in-law.

21. Underdown comments: "The customary world has been turned upside-down by enclosers; the protesters symbolically turn it upside-down again (dressing as women, parodying the titles and offices of their social superiors) in order to turn it right-side-up." David Underdown, *Revel, Riot, and Rebellion: Popular Politics and Culture in England, 1603–1660* (Oxford: Clarendon Press, 1985), pp. 106–12. Charlesworth notes women's instrumentality in a number of the food riots in the era (*Atlas of Rural Protest*, p. 74), as does Buchanan Sharp, *In Contempt of All Authority: Rural Artisans and Riot in the West of England, 1586–1660* (Berkeley: University of California Press, 1980), pp. 11–42.

22. In *Revel, Riot, and Rebellion*, Underdown cites the 1598 riot at Datchet, Buckinghamshire, near Windsor, and discusses the use of cross-dressing under the figurative aegis of "Lady Skimmington" in the Braydon rebellions of the early seventeeth century (see esp. pp. 106–12). Also see Sharp, *In Contempt*, pp. 100–108, 129.

be accurately descriptive of the phenomenon, it is not very explanatory. The question to be asked is why, during an era when class relations had begun to shift precipitously, does the society undergo an epidemic-size outbreak of misogyny? With class anxieties breaking into public riot around England, to what extent does a play such as Shakespeare's *Shrew*—where the subjugation of resistance is played out on the battleground of gender—serve a culture's more amorphous desire for order by offering a displaced site for resolution of the other, more materially threatening issue of class conflict which is simultaneously always present and forever deferred inside the inverted master-servant dynamic of male relations so repeatedly played out in both this play's Induction and its inner text?

Through such questions I situate Shakespeare's comedy of circa 1592 squarely within what might be called a vast cultural circulation of the anxieties of displacement which arose from the enclosure era.[23] Within that circulation, the impetus for unchallenged proprietary ownership and culturally visible dominance was an issue foregrounded inside the increasingly pressured connection between class status and the privatization of land. Such desires were played out, however, within displaced forms of enclosure that concentrated on the public subjugation and private ownership of women. And although the equation between land and the female body which makes rape and imperialism homologous is a metaphor of masculine ownership that is neither peculiarly English nor new to England's enclosure period, the collocation of the two discursive fields clearly acquired new energy at precisely this historical moment of heightened land anxieties. The birth of England's colonizing impulse occurs within a discourse that repeatedly collapses the erotic and the imperial: the frank sexual desire of Donne's Elegy 19, "Going to Bed," for instance, is underwritten by the lust for land and imperial status that become the imaginary possible of "O my America, my new found land"; and Raleigh's *Discoverie of the Large, Rich, and Beautiful Empyre of Guiana,* while nominally a discourse on land acquisition, is equally inflected by a barely concealed incitement to rape: "Guiana is a Countrey that hath yet her Maydenhead, never sackt, turned, nor wrought, the face of the earth

---

23. Richard Wilson, in "*As You Like It* and the Enclosure Riots," *Shakespeare Quarterly* 43 (1992): 1–19, shows how certain central fictions of *As You Like It*—the relation between brothers and landownership, the band of latter-day Robin Hoods who reside defiantly in Arden Forest, and even the repeated motifs of deer and sheep—draw their impulse from the social realities of enclosure.

hath not beene torne, nor the vertue and salt of the soyle spent by manurance, the graves have not beene opened for gold, the mines not broken with sledges, nor their Images puld down out of their temples. It hath never been entred by any armie of strength and never con-quered and possessed by any Christian Prince."[24]

In terms of the sixteenth- and seventeenth-century discourse that was directly about enclosure, from More's *Utopia* onward, the debate over the moral and social consequences is starkly one-sided and weighted heavily in support of peasant claims. No one argued the ethi-cal or even the practical advantages of the England whose shape could be seen emerging into troubled form. Yet nonetheless, enclosure went relentlessly on, any guilt that the culture may have felt over the grow-ing ranks of the dispossessed ultimately displacing itself in a pattern that should seem familiar to present-day America: the demonization of the homeless vagabond who signified it. At this juncture, when one socioeconomic system was being replaced by another in a transition that was never inevitable, irreversible, or even very popular, a factor that may have made it possible for early modern capitalism to take root in the imaginations of even those Englishmen who did not themselves profit from it was the way that its model of private property played into and was conflated with the key terms and values of other highly invested discourses. As Annabel Patterson recognizes, the idea of "the common," for instance, carried considerable ideological force and "stood for customary practices and 'rights' that were clearly perceived as such at the time of, and because of, their rescinding."[25] Throughout the era, "the common" provided a powerful rallying cry for principles of fairness and community. Yet simultaneously, the way it could be fortuitously conflated with issues about women's sexuality made the term itself also ambiguous, if not downright suspect. The adjectival "common" routinely crops up, for instance, in utopias or descriptions of new world societies where "no one owns anything, but all things are common property. And the men have as wives those that please them, whether mother, sisters or friends; they make no distinctions

24. Sir Walter Raleigh, *The Discoverie of the Large, Rich, and Beautiful Empyre of Guiana* (London, 1596), p. 96. See also Philippe Galle's visual personification of *America* (ca. 1600), reprinted in Stephen Orgel's introduction to *The Tempest* (Oxford: Oxford University Press, 1987), p. 35.

25. Patterson, *Shakespeare and the Popular Voice*, p. 44.

among them."[26] Through this frequent association with sexual access, the primary meaning of the term as "possessed or shared alike by both or all (the persons or things in question)" (*OED* I.1) apparently began, through a process appropriate to an Empsonian analysis, to gravitate connotatively. Thus, by the early 1600s its association to female promiscuity (*OED* I.6[b]) was so widely presumed that Ben Jonson could simply depend on his audience to recognize the implications of a character named "Doll Common" (*The Alchemist*). By comparison, a figure named "Jeremy Common" would be referentially unintelligible, because "common" had by then become a gendered term.

Logically, the misogyny implicit in a usage such as Doll Common is unrelated to the issue of peasant rights abrogated by the enclosure of common lands. But the usage nonetheless seems to have infected the enclosure discourse and made the cry for "common" translatable—particularly to the ears of a London artisan class fearful of the spread of social upheaval—as the demand for the common ownership of wives, an association that itself played into the culture's already overinvested anxieties about cuckoldry and bastardy. Thus in *Edward IV (Part I)* (1599), Thomas Heywood inscribes history with contemporary anxieties by explicitly imagining the rebels as dispossessed products of enclosure ("hegebred rascals" and "filthy fry of ditches") and repeatedly characterizes the motives of the rebellion in the terms which his rebel Spicing invokes in the rallying cry: "Come on my hearts, we will be kings tonight, / Carouse in gold, and sleep with merchants wiues." Likewise, the motives of the city artisans who fight to keep the rebels out of the enclosure of London derive from this same fantasy. As Master Shore the goldsmith tells his wife, Jane, the reasons he fights are

> First to maintain King *Edward's* royalty;
> Next, to defend the city's liberty;
> But chiefly *Jane,* to keep thee from the toil
> Of him that to my face did vow thy spoil.
> Had he preuaild, where then had been our liues?
> Dishonourd our daughters, rauishd our fair wiues.[27]

26. From Hugh Honour, *The New Golden Land,* as quoted in Orgel, introduction to *The Tempest*, p. 33.

27. *The Dramatic Works of Thomas Heywood,* 6 vols. (London: John Pearson, 1874), 1:20,30,23. In a design that undercuts any potential sympathy for the rebellion, its leader, the bastard aristocrat Falconbridge, distances the rebellion both from legendary rebel-heroes and from the generally sympathetic causes of food shortage and enclosure:

Ironically, of course, while the artisans fight for the king primarily out of fear that their shops will be sacked by the desiring rebels, when the violation happens and Shore's shop is robbed of his most valued "jewel," it is the king, not the rebels, who makes Shore's wife "common."[28] In this linguistic mediation, a positively valenced term for affirming the claims of class equity became—by being routed through the discourse of gender—infected with negative, female-associated meanings from the other register. Once the male-female binary was piggybacked onto the enclosure-versus-common debate, the potency of the unrelated meanings could themselves then work to neutralize the cry against privilege and effectively marshall a certain affirmation back to the side of the enclosers. In George Gascoigne's use of this discourse for double entendre in *The Adventures of Master F.J.*, positive masculine success clearly accrues to the encloser: "The experiment she meant was this: for that she thought F.J.—I use her words—a man in every respect very worthy to have the several use of a more commodious common, she hoped now to see if his enclosure thereof might be defensible against her said secretary, and such like."[29]

Several other key terms for the collocation, recirculation, and eventual cultural displacement of class anxieties onto ones of gender appear in Joseph Hall's antiutopian fantasy voyage, *Mundus Alter et Idem* (1605), purportedly recording the discovery of "Antarctica."[30] Once again, the cultural fantasy involves the discovery of inhabitable land. "New Gynia" or "Vira-ginia," which Hall's traveler Mercurius Brittanicus discovers, is here, as in many discovery narratives, synonymous with woman. In Hall's parodic vision, however, the unexpected encounter with woman-as-shrew radically disturbs the traditional virgin/rape/dominance paradigm of conquest and converts it into one of male fear of subjugation. Controlled by unruly women who are

---

"We do not rise like *Tyler, Cade,* and *Straw,* / . . . . For mending measures or the price of corne, / Or for some common in the wield of Kent / Thats by some greedy cormorant enclos'd" (p. 9).

28. The connection to Heywood's play was suggested by a paper Jean Howard presented at a conference, "The European Renaissance: National Traditions," in Glasgow, August 1990.

29. George Gascoigne, *The Adventures of Master F.J.* (1573), in *An Anthology of Elizabethan Prose Fiction,* ed. Paul Salzman (Oxford: Oxford University Press, 1987), pp. 3–81; quote is from p. 26.

30. *Another World and Yet the Same: Bishop Joseph Hall's "Mundus Alter ed Idem,"* trans. John Millar Wands (New Haven: Yale University Press, 1981). See "Book Two: Viraginia, or New Gynia," pp. 57–67, esp. p. 57.

apparently so proud of their loquacity that cities have been named for parts of the mouth, in this upside-down society rather than dominating the woman/land as her master, Brittanicus is repeatedly enslaved by the authority of the woman/state. In the province of Amazonia (time-honored locus for male fantasies about female power), the extended satire on inverted authority exposes another key mediator linking the gendered deflection of class hostilities with the era's massive agrarian displacements. With men in Amazonia confined to housework and wives now tilling the fields, the houses for the first time, says Brittanicus sardonically, are actually getting clean. But the fields, alas, are "badly husbanded." Beneath the pun, the desired object of resentful dispute is a man's tenure over land; within the pun, as within Hall's dystopian narrative, the agent of his displacement from that status and from the respectability that came with it has been reconstituted from a cormorant landlord to an insubordinate wife.[31]

The newly intensified anxieties about women's self-sovereignty during this era and the discourse which Linda Woodbridge calls a veritable "storehouse of misogyny,"[32] that it produced all contribute, of course, to a reinscription of the very paradigm of the master-slave, possessor-dispossessed model of social relationship that lies at the root of the enclosure crisis. And although reenacting the hierarchical prin-

---

31. The OED sheds further light on the range of investments and desires that "husband" carries with it during this era. *Hus* (house) + *band* (bond) originates as a term of reference for a peasant who owned his own house and land—a freeholder, franklin, or yeoman; a man of rank in his capacity as head or master of a household. From "master of the house" it derives its meaning as a man joined to a woman in marriage. In its meaning as one who tills and cultivates, it had specific application to manorial tenants; and "husbandland" was a northern and lowland Scots term for a freeholder who held a "husband" of land. For "husbandman," the OED cites J. C. Atkinson's statement of "proof that . . . down to the first half of the seventeenth century, the appellation husbandman still distinguished the man of the class next below the yeoman, and that he was literally the holder of the orthodox husband-land consisting of two oxgangs." Stephen Booth, commenting on Sonnet 94 ("They rightly do inherit heaven's graces / And husband nature's riches from expense; / They are the lords and owners of their faces, / Others but stewards of their excellence"), notes how in the context of a love poem, the verb "husband" (to manage with thrift) "invokes unharnessed overtones of 'to husband' in its marital senses, 'to marry' and 'to get a husband for' . . . since 'to husband' is ordinarily used in reference to tilling and managing agricultural land, husband joins *inherit* to prepare the way for the estate metaphor of lines 7 and 8." Stephen Booth, *Shakespeare's Sonnets* (New Haven: Yale University Press, 1977), pp. 306–7.

32. Linda Woodbridge, *Women and the English Renaissance: Literature and the Nature of Womankind, 1540–1620* (Urbana: University of Illinois Press, 1984), p. 2.

ciple in the register of gender must only perpetuate its authority in the arena of class, this same illogical transfer does serve to produce the ego compensations of power, regardless of how limited and temporary such compensations may be. And because the prevailing anxiety from enclosure was itself invested in the amorphous fear of being literally displaced from one's land and deprived of the status of "husband," based on the constituting energies of language it makes a strange kind of sense that the cultural compensation produced in England would take the form of displaced hostilities enacted into new verbal, social, and ultimately legal enclosures of wives.

In addition to being the Shakespeare play that participates most overtly in the culture's need to assert a hierarchy of gender, *The Taming of the Shrew* is likewise a play peculiarly invested in the master-servant positions of social class. The play's only "authoritative" text appears in the Folio, where the play opens with the odd Induction, which seems itself to be the broken part of an enclosing frame from which the original conclusion (and perhaps additional segments) are missing. Including the Induction reconstructs the nature of the cultural story this comedy plays out: within the inclusive version, the Kate and Petruchio story occurs as "only" a play, fictionally located in Italy but actually being staged by a group of English players at the dictation of the local lord for the edification of a vagabond out in Shakespeare's Warwickshire.

By virtue of the array of particular details the Induction provides, this scene—situated indeterminately outside a tavern at the edge of some aristocrat's hunting preserve somewhere in Warwickshire—becomes in itself an abstract and composite of the conditions, the sites, the antagonists, and, ultimately, the means deployed for dispersing the threat of class conflict that rumbled beneath the surface of English life. The Induction opens as the drunken Christopher Sly is thrown out of a tavern by its hostess. In her first lines of the play, "A pair of stocks, you rogue" (Ind. 1.2), the hostess identifies Sly by the term that had arisen in the mid-sixteenth century as a specific pejorative for the newly created class of vagrants. What her remark prompts in Sly is a social-class discourse asserting the respectability and tenure of his family origins. Sly, as we will shortly learn, has in his time been a peddler, cardmaker, a bear-herd, and is now a tinker (20–22)—all of which reads like a veritable résumé and classic profile of the vagabond poor inside clay vale and/or wood pasture areas such as Warwickshire, the prototypical figure of the man dispossessed by enclosure and forced into piecemeal wage labor when shoved off the land by the entrepreneurial real estate class, itself predominantly composed of rich landlords who subsequently obviated the need for farm labor by converting tillage to pasture. At least one of Sly's occupations—a cardmaker, or one who carded the wool for spinning—specifically associates him with the cloth-working industry, the labor group most notoriously involved in the uprisings thoughout the era, especially those that had convulsed just four years earlier in a series of food riots in nearby Gloucestershire, the Cotswolds (where Burton-Heath is located), and the Severn River area. Moreover, the figures that populated those areas of deprivation likewise clearly populated Shakespeare's imagination. In a contemporary attack on the consequences of cloth-trade stoppages in the Cotswolds, for instance, it almost seems that we meet Autolycus in the observer's description of "infinite nombers of Spynners, Carders, Pickers of woll [who] are turned to begging with no smale store of pore children, who driven with necessitie (that hath no lawe) both come idelie abowt to begg to the oppression of the poore husbandmen, And robbe their hedges of lynnen, stele pig, gose, and capon . . . [and] being forced by povertie stele fish, conies, dere, and such like."[33]

This play begins with Sly's being thrown out of the alehouse for his inability to pay. The scene of the ejected beggar asleep onstage is then invaded by a lord with his hunting party, creating a signifying tableau that speaks to yet another bitter contemporary struggle over land use: the struggle over disafforestation and the nobility's enclosure of new deer parks for hunting. Onstage, the positional status of these two figures iconographically proposes precisely the conflict that the rest of the play must then disperse: the muted threat of class violence. For of all the various types of land conversions going on during this era, the conversion of forest land into private enclaves for the privileges of one aristocrat was the one that was most often and most intensely marked by violent popular protest.[34] As Roger Manning notes, "Scores of new

33. Sharp, *In Contempt*, pp. 13–16; quote on p. 34.

34. As attacks on symbols of seigneurial perquisites, those on deer parks were more specifically antiaristocratic than any other enclosure protests. Emparkment for aristocratic pleasure interfered directly in the local economy by taking away good farmland (Charlesworth, *Atlas of Rural Protest*, pp. 11–12), and it further restricted available game. As J. A. Sharpe comments about the poaching laws, "Whatever the provisions of individual statutes . . . the class basis of the game laws was obvious . . . . The first Jacobean game statute was specifically directed against 'the vulgar sort, and Men of

deer parks were enclosed during the Tudor-Stuart period . . . As
symbols of aristocratic arrogance, emparkments invited both antienclosure riots and widespread poaching. Where previously there had
been a tangible expression of a sense of community . . . the appearance of the enclosing hedge in the landscape served notice that henceforth the commodity of one individual was to be preferred."[35]

Even the alewife who opens the Induction is in several ways a historically specific player in an iconography of nascent social conflict.
As men were losing the traditional bases of their occupational security,
alewives—who, by the end of the sixteenth century, were still prominent in a trade that women had not yet been pushed out of—became
particularly subject to negative caricature.[36] They become stock figures of comedy, associated with an enraging kind of female independence and garrulous insubordination. But furthermore, as signifier of
the alehouse, the figure specifically suggests the site which, as Buchanan Sharp notes, was so traditionally understood as the space
where local uprisings were planned and initiated that it became
attached to popular protest and associated with the common folk's
"deep hatred of the people possessed of the power, social standing,
and landed wealth denied to them." So allied did the alehouse come
to be with sedition, in fact, that in the 1590s the crown ordered "suppression of superfluous alehouses in time of scarcity." Other officials,
however, more cynically contended that the alehouse and the alcohol

---

small worth.'" J. A. Sharpe, *Crime in Seventeenth-Century England* (Cambridge: Cambridge University Press, 1983), p. 168. Recognition of emparkment as a volatile,
highly contested social site provides suggestively interesting perspectives for reading
the attempted enclosure taking place in the famous "deer park" passage of *Venus and
Adonis*.

35. Manning, *Village Revolts*, p. 25.

36. Throughout the Middle Ages, women had traditionally been the brewers and
men the bakers. According to Alice Clark's analysis in *Working Life of Women in the
Seventeenth Century* (New York: Harcourt, 1920), by the end of the sixteenth century
the brewing trade had changed so as largely to exclude women (pp. 196–97, 234–35).
In *Annals of the Labouring Poor: Social Change and Agrarian England, 1660–1900* (Cambridge: Cambridge University Press, 1985), K. D. M. Snell shows the overall pattern
of gender in employment as connected both to the enclosures and to population
growth. As the population grew and agricultural jobs declined, prices rose and male
real wages also declined. When male unemployment rose, female labor was curtailed,
at which time women's marriage age fell further as a protection against the increased
possibility of their unemployment. A. J. Willis, in *A Calendar of Southampton Appren-
ticeship Registers, 1609–1740*, shows a drop during the seventeenth century from 48 to
9 percent in the percentage of Southampton apprentices who were female (quoted in
Snell, *Annals*, p. 274).

consumption it encouraged served a highly useful social purpose by deflecting the rage of the poor away from "more socially dangerous forms of expression"[37]—as the quiescent image of the drunken Sly would seem to confirm. And if indeed there was, as Annabel Patterson argues, a tradition of "memorial vocabulary" that worked like code to collate "the popular protests of the past, both with each other and with the issues of the day . . . [and] act as an incentive, an organizational credo, a symbol of radical claims that are themselves broadly defined,"[38] then even the otherwise unassimilated reference to "Marian Hacket," the "fat alewife of Wincot" may play a suggestive role in lacing this Induction with signifiers meant amorphously to evoke the scene of populist issues. For the chief rebel in the abortive 1591 London uprising at Cheapside—which had taken place perhaps only a year before *The Shrew* was written and would thus likely have been current in the populist genealogy of rebel history—was likewise named Hackett.[39]

As Sly falls asleep, a Lord enters onto the stage, ordering his huntsmen to "tender" his hounds, "sup them well and look unto them all" (Ind. 1.16,28), ostentatiously enunciating all the excesses of wealth in his boastful valuation of one of his dogs at twenty pounds (21). In all he says and does, the unnamed, presumably generic "Lord" provides a virtuoso dramatization of class position as he arrogantly plays out the privileges reserved for the aristocracy. Hard upon the heels of the Lord's solicitous concern for his hounds and his order to "breathe Merriman, the poor cur is embossed" (14)[40] comes his mildly contemptuous reaction to discovering Sly asleep on the ground: "What's here? One dead or drunk? See, doth he breathe?" (31). Deciding to have a bit of fun with this "monstrous beast [who] like a swine" (34) lies drunk before him, the Lord orders that the sleeping tinker be placed in the Lord's own bed, dressed in lordly raiment, and awakened to a world of exorbitant consumption, where he will be surrounded by servants who treat him as though he were the lord of the estate who has languished in sleep for many years, raving in his dreams as

37. Sharp, *In Contempt,* p. 42.

38. Patterson, *Shakespeare and the Popular Voice,* pp. 38, 39.

39. The information about Hackett's rebellion (although not the connection to *The Shrew*) comes from Patterson: see esp. ibid., pp. 32–51.

40. The Riverside edition places F1's wording, "brach Merriman," in parentheses and notes that most editors emend "brach" (bitch hound) to either "broach" (bleed) or "breathe" (allow to rest).

though he were a peasant. The world to which Sly awakens—which includes even the voyeuristic seductions of the Lord's private stock of "wanton pictures" depicting classical rapes—is one of luxurious excess that taunts rather than offers to fulfill the desires it solicits.

Initially, and with a pugnacious tenacity that configures class pride, Sly resists all enticements to being a lord, insisting that he needs no more clothes than he can wear, that he is "Christophero Sly, call not me honor nor lordship," and that he wants his pot of small ale, for "I ne'er drank sack in my life" (Ind. 2.5–6). To the Lord's assurance that he is "a mighty man of such descent, / Of such possessions and so high esteem" (14–15), Sly counters by invoking his pedigree as "old Sly's son of Burton-heath" (19)—a heritage that, as we learned from his contretemps with the hostess, Sly insists is an honorable and long-standing one that can be traced back to "Richard Conqueror" (1.4). But Sly, suddenly switching to unaccustomed blank verse, eventually comes around to believing "upon my life, I am a lord indeed" (2.72). Curiously, what finally persuades him is neither the material wealth, the sensory pleasures, nor the linguistic deference he receives from his supposed servants. It is the presence of the signified "wife." Once this fiction is in place—a fiction that correlates the audience's desires with Sly's, for the Lord's page Bartholomew is obviously no more a woman than is the actor who will play Kate—the inner play is ready to begin. As an entertainment especially designed to educate this lordly peasant, the Lord, who has produced the pretense of Sly's class superiority, has also arranged for a play to be put on by a band of traveling players—men who, because occupationally defined by the law as vagabonds, were themselves subject to arrest for vagrancy unless in service to a lord and thus constitute a group whose own status in society was scarcely more secure than the itinerant tinker's.

As I would propose to read the relation between opening frame and inner play, in its choice of central figures the frame has marked out the most extreme oppositions of class privilege, and thus quite literally foregrounds the potential for class conflict. But rather than dramatize the incipient opposition between the landed Lord and the landless tinker, before the Induction has ever introduced its plot line it has already inserted the paradigm of what the inner play will subsequently offer as substitute. In its opening conflict between Sly and the tavern hostess, the play offers a prologuelike scene of gender hostility that its Kate and Petruchio story will subsequently dramatize as the site for deflecting, absorbing, and relocating the conflict that the Induction embodies before us. To rechannel the implied class resentment into the arena of gender, the frame effectively transposes the woman's and the landlord's positional relations to Sly. What is thereby produced is a narrative in which the woman becomes the agent of dispossession who throws the impoverished Sly out of domicile and the Lord becomes the benefactor who welcomes him, makes him lord of the castle, and lavishes on him sumptuous food and soft bedding.

As the disgruntlements of class are being transferred into the space of gender,[41] the statuses that in reality quite strongly demarcate male class positions are simultaneously being made invisible by the pretense of their interchangeability: Sly can be the Lord and the Lord will be one of his servants; Tranio can be Lucentio and Lucentio change to Cambio; and, just as Sly can fill the Lord's position of "a mighty man," a Mantuan pedant can fill up the role even of Vincentio, the "mighty man of Pisa" (2.1.104). By means of such displacements and erasures, Sly, the lower-class male who has been dispossessed from all terms of husbandry, is set up as lord to a lady and husband to an estate, who sits by his lady to watch, in the story of Petruchio, a gendered model of male success. What he watches is an implicit pattern for obtaining social and financial prestige plus the domestic rewards of "peace . . . and love, and quiet life. / An awful rule and right supremacy; / And, to be short, what not, that's sweet and happy" (5.2.108–10). But all of this good fortune itself depends on a husband's ability to demonstrate that he "will be master of what is [his] own" (3.2.229), which, within the narrative of *The Shrew*, is a mastery whose demonstration lies in compelling "headstrong women" to know "what duty they do owe their lords and husbands" (5.2.130–31). These two terms, "lord" and "husband," which are at the end of the play again paired as they were by Sly's "Madam Wife" in the Induction, are, of course,

---

41. In positing a model of class-to-gender displacement as the appropriate lens for reading *The Shrew,* I am not attributing a fixed priority to the category of class. It likewise seems inappropriate to assign such status to either gender or race. Each of the three status categories is a social construction that can persuasively masquerade as something innate and organic, and the trajectory of displacement that occurs at any given time among the three will be dictated by the exigencies of the historical moment. Within such a paradigm, the category most likely to be displaced will be whatever category is currently on the hotplate. In the 1590s that issue was the potential for class conflict implicit in the threat of an uprising of the commoners. In the 1991 U.S. Senate's Supreme Court confirmation hearings for Clarence Thomas, the issue of gender that was raised by Anita Hill's testimony was successfully displaced by a selective focus on Thomas's race.

interchangeable cognates not in the world of male relations but only within the domestic sphere. All other venues being restricted by class and economic position, the statuses of "lord," "master," and "husband" are available to all men only through marriage. It is through Kate's public submission that Petruchio, having become a husband, becomes a lord indeed—and a "king," and "governor." And, as he reminds the disempowered Lucentio just before exiting the stage, it is Petruchio, alone among the men to have secured this entitlement, who exits "a winner."

Besides acquiring a dominant position in society through women, inside the compensatory fiction that *The Shrew* offers, all men—from the Lord to the tinker, from the the landed owner who produces and controls this fiction to the dispossessed vagrant who constitutes its target audience—are all bonded together by a common enemy: the shrewish female. Within that fantasy of egalitarian fraternity, distinctions of class get suspended and ultimately supplanted by the inner play's narration of woman taming. Through the comic mirror embedded in the play's conclusion, every man is made into potential lord in his own castle, confirmed in a status analogous to that of the landowner by the marriage covenant that guarantees him private husbandry over the wife/servant who is compelled to "serve, love, honor, and obey"—the wife/servant figure whom the Lord had placed next to Sly's bed as the reassuring sign of his status as an owner and the figure whose submission is literally staged in the inner play as the sign of Petruchio's public covenant with patriarchy. In the play's final scene, as all the players converge on Padua into the space of marriage celebration, the acting out of the shrew-taming scene transforms the celebration of "bridal" into a masculine arena of wager and competitive husbandry. Within this marketplace, disobedient wives, ironically enough, are by far the culture's most essential object. Like dragons to be conquered in medieval romance or maidens to be deflowered in love stories, the shrew appears in sixteenth- and seventeeth-century narratives as the test obstacle essential for positing the culture's terms for male dominance not only over women but over other men as well. Compelled during this era into an imaginatively heightened existence, the disobedient female is thrust into cultural centrality as a lightning rod to absorb and contain the society's amorphously circulating anxieties about the interlocked issues of dominance and subordination.

Inside *The Shrew's* narrative model of male success, Kate's ultimate function is to make Petruchio a winner, which status he achieves through the wager[42] he makes on his wife's proficiency in subjection. And, by the terms of his bet—"Twenty crowns! / I'll venture so much of my hawk or hound, / But twenty times so much upon my wife" (5.2.71–73), Petruchio acquires the preemptive privilege of a narrative entrance into the emparkment of superior status previously owned by the aristocratic Lord, who had entered the stage likewise venturing a bet beyond twenty pounds on his well-trained prize bitch.

For a theater audience, it is Petruchio who carries the middle- and lower-class male viewer's fused fantasies of erotic reward, financial success, and upward social mobility. What we know from the terms of the play is that, although Petruchio seems to have inherited a respectable amount of land, to guarantee an apparently otherwise precarious hold on upward mobility he has by necessity embarked on an openly acknowledged quest to wive it wealthily and, if wealthily, then well. As Gremio tells us, his master is flat broke and would marry an old trot if she had money enough. And although Hortensio can afford to insist that he would not marry a shrew for a mine of gold, Petruchio's financial exigencies make him assert, "thou know'st not gold's effect" (1.2.93). In the play's subliminal class structure, everything we know about Petruchio's situation suggests that he is in the predicament of a land-poor son whose father acquired enough land to stake a claim on the future, but who, like many others trying during this era to defend their newly won status, urgently needs ready cash to protect his gains against the various new fines, taxes, costs of enclosing, and other assessments that powerful and land-hungry owners kept successfully pushing into county legislation to force their less solvent neighbors to sell.[43] In wiving it wealthily, Petruchio manages to prove himself not only a good husband to his patrimonial inheritance but a better son-in-law than even Lucentio, the rich young Pisan whose class background announces itself in various ways throughout his opening speech of act 1, including the information he there pro-

42. As Carol Rutter pointed out in a personal communication, "wedding" is derived from "to wager" (German *vetten*).

43. For the elite strategies, see Lachmann's discussion in *From Manor to Market,* esp. his chapters "National-Level Elite Conflicts, 1536–1640" (pp. 66–99) and "Local-Level Class Conflicts, 1536–1640" (pp. 100–127). Against the presumption of a brewing social crisis during the 1590s, revisionist historians have made much of the stability of London. Ian Archer emphasizes, however, that this phenomenon should be attributed not to the absence of crisis but to the solidarity of the elite and the tightening of the machinery of social control in the face of the very real threat of potentially widespread disorder (*Pursuit of Stability,* pp. 18–57).

vides about his father, "A merchant of great traffic through the world, / Vincentio, come of the Bentivolii; / Vincentio's son, brought up in Florence" (1.1.12–14).[44]

In this play, the fantasy of a bourgeois (male) culture achieves a fully satisfying statement: upward mobility, displacement of one's supposed betters through the entrepreneurial success of deeds, and a new hierarchy of male relations no longer strictly defined by social class as birthright. The story is, essentially, a paradigm of the success story of the English yeomanry. And the fact of Petruchio's location in that class origin is strongly suggested through the connection the Induction sets up between Petruchio and the actor whom the Lord apparently singles out to play him[45]—the actor whom the Lord praises for his verisimilitude in playing "a farmer's eldest son" in a play "where you wooed the gentlewoman so well" that the "part / Was aptly fitted and naturally perform'd" (Ind. 1.84–87). The yeomanry was likewise the status group that defined Shakespeare's own origins and was the social class within which at least some—including both John and William Shakespeare—made significant gains during the shift to agrarian capitalism.[46] But furthermore, it was the class that in the early 1590s seems already to have evolved into something of a universal signifier, as capable as is the status of "middle class" in present-day America of carrying the projections of even the Slys of the world, as unmaterializable as their desires might ultimately prove to be.

In terms of this implied status, Petruchio actually belongs to a large group of aspiring hero figures who fill up the comic stage of the era: impoverished males like Bassanio, who may standardly appear in these fictions as down-on-their-luck young aristocrats with whom the upper tier of the audience can identify but whose penniless state none-

44. Whether or not an English audience would have classified Lucentio as "nouveau riche" rather than a "real" aristocrat because of his father's association to trade, Lucentio—unlike Petruchio—not only always speaks in aristocratic tones but also clearly has more than enough money to defend his claim to the upper echelon.

45. Although I am aware of the appearance of the speech prefix "Sincklo" before line 98 (Ind. 1), just where one would expect "player," I am not wholly persuaded by the conjecture or tradition that assumes that the prefix is an authorial error for the actor John Sincklo or Sincler. But see Thompson's introduction, p. 4.

46. In *Bingo* (1975), playwright Edward Bond takes an unflattering look at Shakespeare's own participation, upon his retirement in Stratford, in precisely the kind of land enclosures that had produced the world of "poor naked wretches" dramatized in *King Lear*.

theless simultaneously suggests an unspoken class differential that lurks beneath such male portraits and creates much of the desiring energy that drives their narratives. Inside such stories, success is defined by winning the golden fleece/wife, who signifies for not only Petruchio but also Bassanio (in *Merchant*), Orlando (in *As You Like It*), Claudio (in *Much Ado*), and Sebastian (in *Twelfth Night*) a thoroughly affirmed upward shift in economic and social status achieved through becoming "husbands." Placed onstage to act out that trajectory, such figures suggestively re-present a cultural unconscious being writ large and played out on the popular stage by playwrights and actors who were themselves prototypical of all the anxious class desires their fictions surreptitiously embody. Within the fiction that Petruchio enacts, "deeds" are in every way preeminent. It is a new world of opportunity and opportunism, one in which Sly's claim to being a "lord indeed" translates into Petruchio's entitlement to being a lord in deeds. For Petruchio is, as he several times says, the man who "would fain be doing" (2.1.74). And yet, as the dowry negotiations that so repeatedly enter into this play attest, "deeds" is never wholly separate from a reference to land titles.

Even the famous Kate and Petruchio battle of wills is waged through the vocabulary of class, most of which for an audience today no longer carry the same weight. At the moment Signior Baptista's elder daughter enters the stage, Petruchio greets her with an instant demotion from the aristocratic "Katherine" by which she defines herself to the distinctly common "Kate"—and "plain Kate, / And bonny Kate, and sometimes Kate the curst" (2.1.185–86). In her suggestion to Petruchio to "Remove you hence. I knew you at the first / You were a movable" (196–97) lies the disdaining insult by which Kate identifies her suitor as one of England's newly mobile social groups, either a vagabond or a social climber attempting to move up. In saying she is "too light for such a swain as you to catch" (204), she mocks his courtship as that of a country bumpkin. The tenor of most of the courtship consists, in fact, of a series of loaded class insults in which Kate repeatedly hits at the evident inferiority of Petruchio's status while Petruchio parries by repeatedly bringing Kate down to level terms and treating her more like a barnyard wench than a gentlewoman:

Pet.	What, with my tongue in your tail? Nay, come again.
	Good Kath, I am a gentleman—
Kath.	That I'll try. [*She strikes him.*]

Pet.   I swear I'll cuff you if you strike again.
Kath.   So may you lose your arms.
            If you strike me, you are no gentleman,
            And if no gentleman, why then no arms.
Pet.   A herald, Kate? O put me in thy books!
Kath.   What is your crest—a coxcomb?

                                             (2.1.218–25)

Likewise, Kate's complaint to her father

Call you me "daughter"? . . .
You have show'd a tender fatherly regard,
To wish me wed to one half-lunatic,
A madcap ruffian and a swearing Jack,
That thinks with oaths to face the matter out
                        (285–89)

is likewise grounded in terms that protest the class basis of the proposed match. And although Signior Baptista—happy that anyone will
marry Kate—never mentions such a class differential, it seems obvious
enough to the rich old nobleman Gremio, whose caustic observations
about Petruchio and comments to him throughout the play reveal a
distinct class disdain. On the wedding day, when Petruchio arrives
dressed as a vagabond in order to humiliate Kate and bring her to par,
it is Signior Gremio, for instance, who comments, "A bridegroom,
say you? 'tis a groom indeed, / A grumbling groom, and that the girl
shall find" (3.2.151–52).

But it is the term "gentle" and Petruchio's ability to manipulate it
that defines the ultimate weapon in the play's arsenal of class threats
and insults because slippage in this term was propelling it into an insidious link between the discourses of gender and class. When Petruchio says to Kate, "I find you passing gentle" (2.1.242), his
reference is to a term of gender, not class. When he denies her the cap
that all the "gentlewomen wear" by saying, "When you are gentle you
shall have one too, / And not till then" (4.3.71–72), he again switches
the reference from her assumption of entitlement based on class status
to one that makes it contingent on the exhibition of appropriately submissive female behavior, a standard of gender defined by male authority. And though it is most likely true, as Kate angrily exclaims, that
"your betters have endur'd me say my mind" (75), Petruchio has by

marriage acquired the power to manipulate the signifiers that define Kate's social status and determine just who her "betters" will be. For, as Pierre Bourdieu discusses extensively, class status is established through its own totemically self-conscious representations and is thus heavily dependent on the expenditure of cultural capital displayed through an intricate series of social signs: the vocabulary one uses, the fashion and the implied expense of the clothing one wears, and so on.[47] And whether Kate will ever show herself off in the class finery of the "silken coats and caps, and golden rings" (56) that Petruchio promises her or will be kept forever in the "honest, mean habiliments" (170) in which he forces her to return to Padua is a determination over which Petruchio, as the play demonstrates, has acquired complete control.

What has always been so especially disturbing about Kate's final speech is that it is staged as if it were a matter of her own joyful choice. Momentarily setting aside the matter of coercion, it is nonetheless true that for Petruchio to be uncontested lord and master, Kate must, at the minimum, agree to stop "crossing" his assertions. She does; but what she receives in return for her acceptance of patriarchal hierarchy is not, as many wishful readers have hitherto argued, anything that could ever be rightly equated with marital mutuality. Kate's submission to the hierarchy of gender is predicated on the retention of her social position in the hierarchy of class; and leading up to her final speech, Petruchio has employed a consistent strategy to compel her toward that trade-off. Beginning with her public humiliation at the wedding, every time Kate resists submission in the arena of gender, she is punished by degradation in the arena of class. Ultimately, what the play is designed to teach Kate is that, in the area of gender, the only privileges she may claim are the passive, receptive ones of femininity. She may, however, have access to the privileged signs of class; but as this play clearly demonstrates, by 1590 those signs were themselves in the midst of being reconstituted so that they were no longer separate from but were becoming co-implicit in the controlling norms of gender. Furthermore, the class privileges that Kate acquired through birth are now, ironically enough, privileges to which she has access only through her husband. Like the signifying cap and gown that Petruchio dangles in front of her own to whisk away, retention of her class status

---

47. See Pierre Bourdieu, *Outline of a Theory of Practice,* trans. Richard Nice (Cambridge: Cambridge University Press, 1971).

is a privilege that he has made contingent on her conceding male supremacy. In her final speech of the play, it thus may be said that Kate
"masters" a new understanding of the possible trade-offs of her situation. It may also be said that she sells out to the only vision of pleasure
that Petruchio will allow—a vision that is almost a comic prototype
of the consumerist, middle-class, bourgeois desires that will shortly
come to commodify the stage representation of the Restoration gentlewoman and thereby contain it as a comic stereotype.[48]

Within this emerging vision, Kate's rebellious demand for self-sovereignty falls prey to the substitute pleasures of a highly gendered,
patriarchally overlaid model of social class in which femaleness is conceived as a privileged object made to decorate male life, at once constituted so as to be wholly derivative of male status and yet always
defined inside a binary opposition to male subjectivity and male
power. To be female is constructed as the fine art of thinking one's
actions *from* the position of otherness while simultaneously always
seeing oneself *as* the other—of being careful to preserve one's attrac-
tiveness, not blot one's beauty with threatening brows or scornful
glances nor let anger muddy up the offered fountain lest that worst of
apparent eventualities occur and no man ever deign to drink of it.
Feminine achievement is conceived as making it successfully into
wifehood, and therein becoming the pampered object of a dedicated provider who, "for thy maintenance; commits his body / To
painful labour . . . Whilst thou liest warm at home, secure and safe"
(5.2.148–49, 151). Gone is the Katherina whom Hortensio described
as like to prove herself a soldier after she had quite literally broken the
lute on him; gone is the Kate who struck Petruchio and threatened to
comb old Gremio's noddle with a three-legged stool (1.1.64). In its
place in Kate's concluding vision is the model of physical helplessness
that will shortly become the romantic axiom for the eroticized feminine object. The speech thus marks a clear historical point at which
womanhood has been reconceived into the erotic fantasy of exqui-
sitely helpless fragility, of having a body that is "soft, and weak, and
smooth, / Unapt to toil and trouble in the world" (5.2.165–66); a body
whose "soft condition," being endowed with only "strength as weak,
[and] weakness past compare" (174) must physically yield agency to

48. See especially Margaret George, "From 'Goodwife' to 'Mistress': The Transformation of the Female in Bourgeois Culture," *Science and Society* 37 (1973): 152–77.
Alice Clark defines the ways that capitalist organization reconstructed the notion of
womanhood: "The wife of the prosperous capitalist tended to become idle, the wife

the mastery of those who are imagined as exact opposites to the soft, weak, and smooth of the feminine—to those opposites whose lances, in Kate's subtending fantasy, are (presumably) not just straws.[49]

The vision of true womanhood that Kate presents us with is, finally, the fantasy of being a gentle/woman—a putatively helpless object of leisure, enclosed and immured in masculine protection, born to shop and displayed forth in the fashionable signs of aristocratic status which Petruchio makes Kate realize he can and will withhold from her. Unless Kate becomes a gentle woman, she will remain in the low status of having to beg the servants for food, in every way infantilized, deprived of all authority, indefinitely dressed in "honest, mean habiliments," and thus signified with all the low-status cultural capital that announces her position in the world as perilously close to that of the beggar who watches this play.

The offered fantasies with which the play concludes are strongly gendered ones that exist in inverse relationship to each other. From the position of male desire, the fantasies that subscribe *The Taming of the Shrew* "work" through the unconscious displacement of class hostilities onto gender; for women, who are the locus of that displacement, the fantasies this play offers must "work" in precisely the inverse way, through a displacement of gender hostilities which ensures the dispersal of counterpart aggressions against men. For women, the invited trajectory is away from gender and onto anxieties about social class. Within the vision that Kate is constructed to dramatize, the trade-offs for which she settles exchange desire for equality in one hierarchy for the guaranteed material and social privileges of another.

What the play's various displacements contrive throughout to deny, of course, is the very site upon which the whole design is constructed: the enormous difference in the masculine positions of social class and the hostilities that such distributions engender. Despite such

---

of the skilled journeyman lost her economic independence and became his unpaid domestic servant . . . The alternatives before the women of this class were either to withdraw altogether from productive activity, and so become entirely dependent upon their husband's goodwill, or else to enter the labour market independently . . . in competition not only with other women, but with men . . . . At this time the idea that men 'keep' their wives began to prevail" (*Working Life of Women*, p. 276).

49. Barbara Hodgdon's essay "Katherina Bound; or, Play(K)ating the Strictures of Everyday Life," *PMLA* 107 (1992): 538–53, offers some valuable insight on the visual pleasures that performance of this play makes available to the female spectator.

avoidances, however, both the displacement and the difference it denies are historically collocated in the title noun that foregrounds them.
For the term "shrew" actually belongs to a whole class of words that
underwent a semantic shift that the pattern of this play—and, by inference, the culture in which it was constructed—actually duplicates.
Like the struggle over land tenure and the trajectory of displacement
which I posit, this semantic shift also occurred between the fourteenth
and seventeenth centuries. It was within those several centuries, which
frame England's transition from the late medieval to the early modern
world, from the feudalist agrarian economy to the capitalist one,
that a whole category of words such as "harlot," "shrew," "hoyden,"
"scold," "baggage," "brothel," "bordello," and "bawd"[50] were trans-
posed from their origin as contemptuous expressions for lower-class
males into terms that gendered such hostility, displacing it away from
the threat of male class revolt which remained real throughout the era
and redirecting it at women.

If we grant for the moment the Folio text of *The Taming of the
Shrew,* the Sly Induction works to lay bare a mechanism of social control that the play then retreats from exploring. Having exposed the
ground on which the Padua displacement is constructed, the text then
refuses to return to the scene in Warwickshire, withdraws from the
exploration of the class-gender nexus that it initially seemed poised
to query, and essentially abandons its audience suspended within the
displacement. Leah Marcus has argued for adopting an intertextual
approach that accepts Shakespeare as the author of *The Taming of A
Shrew,* the infamous other, "unauthoritative" text that exists in a historically undecipherable relationship to this play. In Marcus's analysis,
the two *Shrews* should be viewed "as a cluster of related texts which
can be fruitfully read together and against each other as 'Shakespeare.'"[51] With the use of *A Shrew*'s closing frame plus several of the
interruptions it stages within the taming story, the Sly plot narrative—in which issues of class difference remain active onstage and thus
become all but ineradicable—could work at strategic intervals to dis-

50. See Joseph M. Williams, *Origins of the English Language: A Social and Linguistic
History* (New York: Free Press, 1975), pp. 196–97.
51. In "The Shakespearean Editor as Shrew Tamer," *English Literary Renaissance* 22
(1992): 177–200, Leah Marcus offers a reading of the politics of textual editing. In the
steady demotion of *A Shrew* that began with Edmund Malone, editors were expressing
a decided preference for what Marcus classifies as the more authoritarian and patriarchal of the two *Shrew* texts.

rupt the otherwise seamless enactment that the authorized text provides of a social displacement that ends without waking its dreamer/
audience. In the closing frame of *A Shrew*, when Sly awakens on the
cold, hard ground, recalling his most rare dream of being a lord and
preparing now to go recuperate it by lording it over his own shrewish
wife, the return to reality works, at least in part, to collapse the ro-
manticized patriarchal fiction in which *The Shrew* leaves its audience
suspended. Moreover, one could also say that the ending of *A Shrew*
actually constitutes a morally damning critique of the way that *The
Shrew* ends, for what *A Shrew*'s return to Warwickshire dramatizes is
just how persuasively such representations of power and dominance
as that which the taming narrative has played out can work on the
disempowered to induce the kinds of aggressive displacements that
Sly, the modeled audience, departs the stage hoping to effect for
himself.

The only text available for teaching this play fails to unpack the
political narrative it produces. What that text does suggest, however,
is a clear recognition on Shakespeare's part of the class and gender
relations being constituted within his era and the potential manipula-
bility of the theater to become a stage for culturally reproducing only
those narratives that affirm the hegemonic and patriarchal.[52] It suggests an authorially conscious political reading of how, amidst the tur-
bulence of the class and gender crises of the early 1590s, such a thing
as a national ideology was being molded into shape, and what role
the theater was playing in that production. If *The Shrew* represents
Shakespeare's own pruned-down version of his original interplot narrative, as Marcus feels is likely, what such a re-vision seems to suggest
is a belated form of self-censorship, a second-thought stage in which
the author may have decided to excise the politically more radical line
of the Sly narrative, leaving behind only its fossil in the Induction. If
so, then it was a move that the writer of this play had already rehearsed
through his creation of Kate. For it is the move that Kate also chooses
when she, too, selects the hierarchical narrative and, dramatizing her
own disempowered relationship to it, tells women to "vail your stom-

---

52. Annabel Patterson makes a convincing case that the parody of court patronage
and the artisan's fear of offending court tastes in *A Midsummer Night's Dream*'s play-
within-the-play demonstrate precisely this sort of awareness (see *Shakespeare and the
Popular Voice*, esp. p. 58).

achs, for it is no boot" (5.2.176), as she prostrates herself before the represented sign of authority and its symbolic coercions of power.

In this play, as is frequently true in gender and class relations in general, beneath every asserted dominance is inevitably an unacknowledged, uncredited, and usually unpaid dependency of the higher on the lower. Like Sly, Petruchio moves from his initial status as a needy wanderer to the bed of a highborn wife; and, like Sly, Petruchio depends for his lordship on the signifying speech act of a madam wife who, positioned as she is within the gender hierarchy, is the one person who can make lord and husband interchangeable terms.[53] Sly's first anxious demand of his madam wife is that she call him husband. And obediently: "My husband and my lord, my lord and husband, / I am your wife in all obedience" (Ind. 2.104–5), intones Sly's wife. In her words, the play anticipates the parallel lines through which Petruchio's wife will elevate him into metaphoric peerage and women in the audience will be enjoined likewise to elevate their husbands: "Thy husband is thy lord, thy life, thy keeper, / Thy head, thy sovereign" (5.2.151–52), says Kate. But Sly's madam wife has always been, of course, little Bartholomew, the Lord's page, who has been commanded by the Lord to dress up like a lady and serve the Lord's voyeuristic desires by playing out a wifely acquiescence that will convince the hapless Sly that he, too, is a lord indeed. The play thus depends, in large, on Bartholomew's unchosen willingness to mediate the story of a class and gender nexus that is doubly represented in him. And it is Bartholomew/Madam Wife—the figure who embodies an intersection on the class-gender hierarchy and thus occupies the culture's most literal space for under-standing—who generically resituates *The Taming of the Shrew* and insistently removes it from the category of comedy. In doing so, he points toward new locations from which we might profitably consider the cultural fantasies constituted in and reproduced by *The Taming of the Shrew*. To Sly's query whether the Kate and Petruchio play at hand is a "comonty," a "Christmas gambold," a "tumbling-trick," or some "household stuff" (Ind. 2.138, 140) Bar-

---

53. See also Karen Newman's historicized approach, "Renaissance Family Politics and Shakespeare's *Taming of the Shrew*," chap. 3 in her *Fashioning Femininity and English Renaissance Drama* (Chicago: University of Chicago Press, 1991). As Newman comments: "By enacting Sly's identity as a lord through his wife's social and sexual (if deferred) submission, the induction suggests ironically how in this androcentric culture men depended on women to authorize their sexual and social masculine identities" (p. 38).

tholomew—speaking right at the juncture between frame and inner play, right between the Warwickshire ground and its Padua displacement—solemnly rejects all these farcical categories. Instead, he insists: "No, my good lord, it is more pleasing stuff . . . . / It is a kind of history" (Ind. 2.139, 141). And so, perhaps, it is.

9

"Word Itself against the Word"
CLOSE READING AFTER VOLOSHINOV

JAMES R. SIEMON

Every element of form is the product of social interaction.
—V. N. Voloshinov, "Discourse in Life and Discourse in Poetry"

The practice of close reading deserves reconsideration outside the confines of its appropriation by New Criticism and the political agendas to which its foremost American practitioners directed it.[1] Provisionally dislodged from its New Critical appropriation and considered according to certain underdeveloped implications of Bakhtinian sociolinguistics, the activity of close reading may yet prove useful to various forms of social analysis while, simultaneously and paradoxically,

Research for this essay was funded by the Graduate School of Boston University. Barbara A. Mowat provided generous assistance with documentation.

1. For an account of that theory attuned to differences between the micrological reading pioneered by Richards and Empson and the practice of the various New Critics who followed them, see John Paul Russo, *I. A. Richards* (Baltimore: Johns Hopkins University Press, 1989), esp. pp. 540–62. Russo traces American New Criticism to roots in the frustrations of the Fugitives and Agrarians of the twenties and thirties and differentiates their concentration on the "inside" of the poem from Richards's concern with "all utterance" (p. 545) according to his "continuity principle." For analysis of Richards's political agendas in relation to his valuation of mastery, see Paul Bové's chapter on Richards in *Intellectuals in Power: A Genealogy of Critical Humanism* (New York: Columbia University Press, 1986), pp. 39–77; also William V. Spanos, "The Apollonian Investment of Modern Humanist Education: The Examples of Matthew Arnold, Irving Babbitt, and I. A. Richards," *Cultural Critique* 1 (1985): 7–72.

suggesting a possible alternative to current interpretive modes. Specifically, close reading that investigates the formal elements of texts in
the light of socially and historically conjoined "utterances" deserves
consideration as a means of pursuing the volatile issue of social-evaluative orientation as defined by the Bakhtin circle.[2] Furthermore, a
critical practice that would conjoin substantial portions of text with
its own critical countertext in a dense encounter modeled on close
reading but extending its purview to the noncanonical might offer an
alternative to practices that, despite their avowal of "thick description"
in principle, often approximate the familiar literary-historical model
of critics such as E. M. W. Tillyard in the deployment of minimally
contextualized citation and paraphrase. As a practical instance, in the
argument that follows I offer a necessarily limited engagement with a
nexus of utterances constituted by four textual loci: the famous report
of Queen Elizabeth's conversation with William Lambarde in 1601,
Shakespeare's *Richard II,* John Hayward's *History of Henry IV,* and
documents concerning the abortive uprising of the Earl of Essex.

To assume the Bakhtin circle's model of utterance as the basis for
analysis is in part to consider certain pragmatic dimensions of any
communication, but such considerations are, finally, only components of a more fundamental inquiry into what V. N. Voloshinov calls
"evaluative orientation." "No utterance can be put together without
value judgment," Voloshinov writes. "Every utterance is above all an
evaluative orientation. Therefore, each element in a living utterance not
only has a meaning but also a value." In fact, "referential meaning is
molded by evaluation; it is evaluation, after all, which determines that
a particular referential meaning may enter the purview of speakers."[3]
This primacy of valuation in determining referential meaning may be
seen as at once Marxist and Nietzschean in grounding such evaluation
on conflict, on a "constant struggle of accents in each semantic sector

2. On social-evaluative orientation, see, e.g., V. N. Voloshinov, *Marxism and the
Philosophy of Language* (1929), rev. ed., trans. Ladislav Matejka and I. R. Titunik (Cambridge: Harvard University Press, 1986), p. 105, where Voloshinov discusses orientation in the "choice and deployment of the basic elements" of utterance. On "utterance"
as the fundamental category of Bakhtinian analysis, see Tzvetan Todorov, *Mikhail
Bakhtin: The Dialogical Principle,* trans. Wlad Godzich (Minneapolis: University of
Minnesota Press, 1984).

3. Voloshinov, *Marxism,* p. 105.

of existence."[4] Thus, a fundamental constituent of any signifying practice is the product of neither a unitary and stable social "context," since contexts of each utterance "are in a state of constant tension or incessant interaction and conflict," nor of the solitary creative consciousness, as it sometimes appears near to becoming, despite reservations about "completely free combination," in Bakhtin's own more lyrical, phenomenological moments.[5] Voloshinov, even in claiming that evaluative orientation "will be the determinative factor in the choice and deployment of the basic elements that bear the meaning of the utterance," insists that the grounds of such choice, like those of all experience, lie wholly on "social territory."[6]

Despite its crucial importance to any signifying practice, the "evaluative orientation" of the utterance is "least amenable to reification," a volatile "multiaccentuality" which ought to be "closely associated with the problem of multiplicity of meanings."[7] For the Bakhtin circle, such volatile phenomena are the very life of everyday discourse. Concrete discourse, as Bakhtin puts it, is populated with devices and deviations resembling those in the most complex verbal art: "We very sensitively catch the smallest shift in intonation, the slightest interruption of voices in anything of importance to us in another person's practical everyday discourse. All those verbal sideward glances, reservations, loopholes, hints, thrusts do not slip past our ear, are not

4. Ibid., p. 106; see also Sam Weber, "The Intersection: Marxism and the Philosophy of Language," *Diacritics* 15 (1985): 94–112, 105.

5. Voloshinov, *Marxism*, p. 80; cf. Weber, "The Intersection," p. 104. For Bakhtin's remarks on "our free speech plan," see Mikhail Bakhtin, *Speech Genres and Other Late Essays,* trans. Vern W. McGee (Austin: University of Texas Press, 1986), p. 80.

6. Voloshinov, *Marxism*, pp. 105, 90; cf. Bakhtin on choosing a "language" in Mikhail Bakhtin, *The Dialogic Imagination,* trans. Caryl Emerson and Michael Holquist (Austin: University of Texas Press, 1981), p. 295. Robert Young argues that Voloshinov resembles Althusser in seeing utterance determined by social relations, but the Althusserian subject is interpellated in the discourse of the other and allowed to speak only from that position, while for Bakhtin, as for Voloshinov, a speaker is not only able but indeed cannot fail to "accent words and to compete with other accentuations for his or her own purposes." Robert Young, "Back to Bakhtin," *Cultural Critique* 2 (1986): 71–92, 85. Bakhtin resembles Foucault in seeing society constituted by contradictory and competing discourses, but the stress on reported speech prevalent in any discursive practice, Young says, works against the Foucauldian notion of "rival and therefore distinct stratifications of discourses of truth," so that "reported speech makes it impossible to maintain distinctions between discourses in the first place; the struggle for power resolves into competing accents attached to individual words" (p. 85).

7. Voloshinov, *Marxism*, p. 81.

foreign to our own lips."[8] Acceptance of such basic priorities of the Bakhtinian metalinguistic enterprise entails recognizing the impossibility of ever coming to definitive and final terms with the warring accents and contexts present within each utterance. Thus, contextualizing might appear all the more nightmarishly difficult the further one moves—semantically, physically, culturally—from the concrete circumstances of utterance. Yet there is at least a provisional ground for optimism, insofar as the great "chain of speech communication" is said to stretch on, generating in the very necessity for "counter word[s]," the potential for new levels of understanding—and, not inconsequentially, misunderstanding.[9] To put it another way, considering critical writing as the encounter of utterance with utterance, as an attempt to embed the text's words in its contemporary counterwords as well as in our own paraphrases and indirect locutions, might further an archaelogical inquiry into the emergent and repressed, into those "rhetorical survival skills of the formerly unvoiced," those "lies, secrets, silences, and deflections of all sorts" that Barbara Johnson finds constituting "the routes taken by voices or messages not granted full legitimacy in order not to be altogether lost." At the same time, and nearer to home, such a critical practice might also further disclose—in the silences and indirections of our own struggles with the alien utterance of which we write—the openings and foreclosures we would not or could not name as our own, no matter how rigorous our rituals of self-situation.[10] That such a pursuit is posited on failure,

8. Mikhail Bakhtin, *Problems of Dostoevsky's Poetics,* trans. Caryl Emerson (Minneapolis: University of Minnesota Press, 1984), p. 201. Thinking about relationships of Bakhtinian imperatives to the emphases of New Criticism might begin with the fact that attention to tonality and dramatistic qualities of utterance, to ironies of "sideward glance" and ambiguities of words "with loopholes," are approached by the Bakhtin circle as inescapably social-ideological. Of course, a close reading of dramatic texts, especially the highly instable, multiple-texted plays of a playwright who was actor, shareholder, and more collaborator than author—to adopt Stephen Orgel's distinction—is from the outset the reading of situated and interanimated voicings. See Stephen Orgel, "What Is a Text?" *Research Opportunities in Renaissance Drama* 24 (1981): 3–6.

9. Bakhtin writes of this great chain in *Speech Genres,* p. 94; the "counter word" is discussed by Voloshinov in *Marxism,* p. 102.

10. Barbara Johnson, *A World of Difference* (Baltimore: Johns Hopkins University Press, 1987), p. 31. The encounter of relatively direct (since all utterance is marked by indirection) and relatively indirect discourses is a locus of primary interest for the Bakhtin circle, and it is also precisely what the written practice of close reading necessarily enacts, whether consciously or not; see Jon Klancher, "Bakhtin's Rhetoric," in *Reclaiming Pedagogy: The Rhetoric of the Classroom,* ed. Ellen Quandahl and Patricia

on a labor of analysis and response which would be, in Pierre Bourdieu's phrase, "strictly interminable," need not diminish the potential
implications of its practice. The attitudes and abilities potentially fostered by a worldly close reading so conceived need justification neither
from aestheticism nor from the academy. As Terry Eagleton has asked:
why do we assume that acuity and discrimination are any less appropriate to the analysis of that "nuance and particularity" found at large
beyond the self-imposed boundaries of traditional literary exegesis
and its high aesthetic text?[11]

In this light, arguments that both New Criticism and deconstruction are premised on related quietisms might appear true but limited.
Both movements offered, within certain historical circumstances and
in certain versions of their practice, the critical opportunity of surprise. Their power lay in renunciation of one kind of power—the
certainties of a dominant historico-literal sense in one case and of culturally dominant binarisms in the other—in order to suggest how little
one knew about the "known." If, in their domesticated, institutionalized forms, deconstruction and New Criticism tended to produce predictable instantiations of the already known—in the one case *différance,*
the abyss, and so on, and in the other irony, ambiguity, and paradox—
it is far from clear that such a fate is avoidable by any critical movement. If the work of the Bakhtin circle has something to offer, it is
not so much a case of something new, of some utopian escape from

Donahue (Carbondale: Southern Illinois University Press, 1989), pp. 83–96. As Dominick LaCapra notes: "Through the interaction of perspectives within the same utterance or text, langue becomes a site on which contesting and contested discourses
of different periods, groups, or classes engage one another as sociolinguistic forces.
Dialogized heteroglossia creates the space for critical and self-critical distance in language use, for it disrupts myth in the sense of an absolute fusion or bonding of a use of
words to a concrete ideological meaning." Dominick LaCapra, *Rethinking Intellectual
History: Texts, Contexts, Language* (Ithaca: Cornell University Press, 1983), p. 312.

11. Terry Eagleton, "The Subject of Literature," *Cultural Critique* 1 (1985): 95–104,
102. The implications of Eagleton's argument—that liberal humanism values only "a
sensitivity to nuance and ambiguity, a balanced discrimination, a capacity to entertain
imaginatively a variety of view points" in the isolated, readerly encounter of reading
subject and "literary" text and not in the socio-historical struggles of groups and indi-
viduals, where such values could oppose the demands of the capitalist state—should
be considered in relation to the analyses of Richards by Bové and Spanos cited in note 1.
For Bourdieu's use of Voloshinov, see Pierre Bourdieu, "The Economics of Linguistic
Exchanges," *Social Science Information* 16 (1977): 645–68. "Strictly interminable" describes Bourdieu's own analysis; see his *Distinction: A Social Critique of the Judgement of
Taste,* trans. Richard Nice (Cambridge: Harvard University Press, 1984), p.20.

the rhythms of institutional appropriation, as a serviceable reminder of unfinalizability, of how much there is always left to be done.[12]

Amid otherwise appropriate thoughts about loneliness, escape, Fortune, death, identity and timeliness, Shakespeare's Richard II takes a partly extrametrical detour into a discourse on textual interpretation, consciousness, and theology:

> And these same thoughts people this little world,
> In humours like the people of this world;
> For no thought is contented. The better sort,
> As thoughts of things divine, are intermix'd
> With scruples, and do set the word itself
> Against the word,
> As thus: "Come, little ones"; and then again,
> "It is as hard to come as for a camel
> To thread the postern of a small needle's eye."
> $(5.5.9-17)$[13]

The practice of interpretation is here made to stand synecdochically for thought itself. Consciousness is "like the people of this world" in its fundamental discontent: "For no thought is contented." Even the eternal self-identical significance of the biblical "word itself" is said to be subject to this divisive tendency on becoming the object of human cognition.

Within the confines of traditional close reading one might question the credibility of Richard's *aporia*. The New Critic might discuss intertextuality among canonical Renaissance tragedies and relate Richard's soliloquy to the opening soliloquy of *Doctor Faustus*. Both assert

---

12. On the institutional dimensions of this progress and its implications for recent criticism, see Murray Krieger, *Words about Words about Words* (Baltimore: Johns Hopkins University Press, 1988), esp. pp. 70–72. Frank Lentricchia was an early critic of deconstruction's quietism (*Criticism and Social Change* [Chicago: University of Chicago Press, 1983]) and has discussed continuities between New Criticism and poststructuralism in *After the New Criticism* (Chicago: University of Chicago Press, 1980). On Bakhtin's unconcluded dialogue between Marxism and formalism, see Tony Bennett, *Formalism and Marxism* (London: Methuen, 1979); also William Garrett Walton, Jr., "V. N. Voloshinov: A Marriage of Formalism and Marxism," in *Semiotics and Dialectics: Ideology and the Text,* ed. Peter V. Zima (Amsterdam: John Benjamins, 1981), pp. 39–102.

13. Citations are from Peter Ure's Arden edition of *Richard II* (1956; rpt. London: Methuen, 1969).

theological difficulties and buttress the assertion with distorted trun-
cations of familiar biblical quotations. Faustus' "The reward of sin is
death" (1.1.40)[14] leaves out the rest of Romans 6:23, "but the gift of
God is eternal life through Jesus Christ our Lord," while Richard's
instances of divine invitation and rejection do not mention that in the
Gospel, "children" are invited to come and a "rich man" is promised
difficulty in divine access.

Thus far a relatively intrinsic analysis according to New Critical
practice. But to define Richard's problem as an "ironic" misinterpretation revelatory of the "voice" of the "speaker," and to relate it to other
instances of "ambiguity" within the play in order to evaluate an overall
"tone," would be to limit analysis in a way that would preclude any
further sociohistorical definition of that tonality itself—or, rather, to-
nalities, since tone emerges only amid the differentiation of intona-
tions acting upon one another.

Remarkably, this passage shares the phrase "set the word itself /
Against the word" with lines occurring earlier in the Duchess of
York's contention with her husband's demand that their son be punished for treason. The Duchess's request that King Henry "pardon"
their son meets York's counterword: "Speak it in French, king, say
'pardonne moy,'" to which the Duchess herself counters:

> Dost thou teach pardon pardon to destroy?
> Ah, my sour husband, my hard-hearted lord,
> That sets the word itself against the word!
> Speak "pardon" as 'tis current in our land,
> The chopping French we do not understand.
>   (5.3.118–22)

Here it is the element of intonation which is said to offer the possibility
of purposefully, *rhetorically* setting the word against itself. Under the
pressure of conflicting purposes, and with the assistance of differing
linguistic usages "current," despite the Duchess's asseverations of national preference, in the England of the 1590s "pardon" can mean
either yes or no. In the case of Richard's final soliloquy, by contrast,
it is not a rhetorical intonational variance in the spoken word but consciousness itself that, no matter how presumptively unitary its object,

14. Christopher Marlowe, *Doctor Faustus,* ed. Roma Gill (Oxford: Clarendon
Press, 1990).

betrays an inevitable fractious tendency, setting word against itself.[15] One might find various points of agreement and disagreement with the assumptions and values expressed by the Duchess and Richard. The Duchess's assumed agreement among a national speech community that would disallow foreign usage or the "chopping" of a normative sense might appear less than compelling in an England of legal French, humanist Latinism, euphuism, or in a play that abounds in instances of politic ambiguity. But one might also object that a vestigial commitment to the assumption of normative senses operative in something like Stanley Fish's speech communities is what makes York's joke a joke rather than an unmarked alternative to "pardon." Conversely, although Richard's view of interpretation as divisive might be relativized in historical or social terms, his example suggests a more universalized notion such as may be found in Barbara Johnson's pronouncement: "Any utterance, if scrutinized sufficiently, *does* become problematic, like the dots in a newspaper photograph."[16]

But the differing treatment accorded by the Folio to Richard's utterance and that of the Duchess does not suggest their being *equally* problematic. The Folio alters Richard's phrase "the word itself against the word" to "the faith itself against the faith," while leaving the Duchess's utterance unmodified. Perhaps Richard's account of inevitably destabilizing interpretation carries more troublesome extratextual resonances than would a reference to intentional oratorical ambiguity. The Folio relocates divisiveness within the familiar battlefields of institutional division.

So one utterance is altered in print and the other not, though the "word itself" is semantically identical in both; yet Richard's utterance is revealing in another way as well. His elliptical utterance is not merely blind to its own creation of the discrepancy between word and word that it articulates insofar as it silently omits the distinction between rich man and child; it is also strategically limited by its abstract phenomenological form. "No thought is contented"—in such a formulation discontent is posited as free of social valuation, as a *human*

---

15. Cf. Voloshinov on the densely preinhabited status of the word confronting the poet (Todorov, *Mikhail Bakhtin*, p. 49) and Bakhtin on the contending languages and interpretations confronting the prose writer (*Dialogical Imagination*, p. 278).

16. Johnson, *World of Difference*, pp. 6–7. Compare Leah S. Marcus's relation of postmodern appreciations of textual rupture and self-division with her model of Elizabethan and Jacobean reading habits in *Puzzling Shakespeare: Local Reading and Its Discontents* (Berkeley: University of California Press, 1988).

characteristic natural to kind and found—slightly differentiated as to
its object, perhaps, but equivalent nonetheless—even in "the better
sort" of the clerisy. What such a generalized religious or "theoretical"
formulation forecloses, of course, is an analysis of the social genesis
and intergroup differentiation of entities such as "ambition" or "discontent," or, for that matter, "the word." One might consider the
particularly pious quality of "the Word" (cf. Ben Jonson's epigram
"On Reformed Gamester") or the embattled status of the practice of
biblical interpretation itself in post-Reformation England—quite aside
from particular interpretations. "Doe all interpret?" asks Oliver Ormerod in *The Picture of a Puritane* (1605), his rhetorical question expressing the exasperation of Anglican divines caught between centralized,
institutionalized authority, such as is embodied in bishops, convoca-
tions, and codified dogma, and the more radical impulses toward dispersion of authority among individual interpretive consciences as
sanctioned by the Reformation.[17]

In its limitations, then, Richard's analysis remains predictive of certain limitations of New Critical or poststructuralist exegesis, but these
very limitations might also suggest the potential usefulness of a close
reading that would turn its attention laterally to the choice of idiom
inhabiting each signifying act. Surrounded by the competing forms
and usages of "social heteroglossia," Bakhtin argues, the writer exemplifies the multivocal condition of any utterance: "Consciousness finds
itself inevitably facing the necessity of *having to choose a language.* With
each literary-verbal performance, consciousness must actively orient
itself amidst heteroglossia, it must move in and occupy a position for
itself within it, it chooses, in other words, a 'language.'"[18] Yet, to
follow this formulation in reducing the encounter with social heteroglossia to the necessity of *choice* among langv ages is to accept a potentially limiting line of Bakhtin's own emphases and to risk undercutting
Voloshinov's emphasis on form as the interactive expression of group
identities, differentiations, and struggles which themselves *produce* the
possibilities that appear as choice.

Every element of the utterance can be considered dialogically ad-

17. Oliver Ormerod, *The Picture of a Puritane* (London, 1605), p. 70. Robert Wei-
mann discusses this contention in "Discourse, Ideology, and the Crisis of Authority in
Post-Reformation England," *REAL: The Yearbook of Research in English and American
Literature* 5 (1987): 109–40; see also Robert Weimann, *Shakespeare und die Macht der
Mimesis* (Berlin: Aufbau Verlag, 1988).

18. Bakhtin, *The Dialogic Imagination,* p. 295.

dressive and responsive while still by no means to be understood as the exclusive product of some controlling transcendental *cogito* making its discriminations of finer tones and subtler harmonies and communicating them to an audience unified conceptually by either some shared cultural identity or aesthetically "disinterested" condition. Taken by itself, and despite its insistence on the oppositional elements of communication, the Bakhtinian pronouncement on choice of language might appear to sanction an analysis that would, after the fashion of E. M. W. Tillyard, identify in *Richard II* the linguistic elements of an official world view—or, as more recent usage might style it, "hegemonic" discourse—rather than attempting to examine the density of the play's social situatedness and the possible angles of its attack and reception within the concrete field of utterances. The "strictly interminable" analytical alternative proposed here would encourage looking *closely* at the formal elements of the aesthetic text and of the utterances with which that text coexists, agrees, struggles, and takes its very form and shape.

No New Critic himself, Tillyard made much of interconnectedness among texts: *Richard II,* for example, was said to share a discourse of Tudor providentialism with John Hayward's *History of Henry IV.* Hayward, Tillyard writes, "deals with history precisely as Shakespeare did," and Tillyard's treatment of this equivalence exemplifies the limitations of approaches that would isolate discourse from close reading of its concrete manifestation as utterance.[19] Granting that Hayward's book occasioned his imprisonment, Tillyard reasons that the cause lay in the extrinsic matter of a dedication to the Earl of Essex and in official misinterpretation of a single speech by the Archbishop of Canterbury detailing successful depositions. The *content* of Hayward's book Tillyard pronounces "perfectly orthodox" (pp. 243–44) in representing Henry Bolingbroke as a usurper and proclaiming providential judgment on his crime. But when Tillyard cites discourse Hayward shares with Shakespeare, he instances "Hayward's solemn setting forth of the prosperity of Edward III and his seven sons" (p. 244) in the initial sentence of his history: "The noble and victorious prince, King *Edward* the third, had his fortunate gift of a long and prosperous raigne ouer this realme of England, much strengthened

---

19. E. M. W. Tillyard, *Shakespeare's History Plays* (New York: Macmillan, 1946), p. 243; subsequent citations appear in the text.

and adorned, by natures supply of seven goodlye sonnes."[20] Characteristically, Tillyard's attention to content rather than occasion leads him to miss the very features that might warrant contemporary suspicion.

Sir Edward Coke's notes on Hayward's book, titled "his outward pretence and his secret drift" and intended for the author's trial in January 1601, record "a king described by these marks," and first of these is "without children" followed by citation from the paragraph Tillyard quotes.[21] Thus, in Hayward's opening sentence considered as an utterance rather than according to its "perfectly orthodox" content, there might appear to be one evaluative orientation interfering with another, as Tillyard's grand scheme of Tudor historiographic narrative meets Coke's local sense of the question of the Elizabethan succession. But further analysis of Hayward's utterance *as* utterance reveals how one discourse may articulate itself in the terms of another. Edward III is called "noble" and "victorious" in the opening sentence of a work that instances the *fortunate* deposing of his father as the culminating example in the Archbishop of Canterbury's attempts to "cleare this action [i.e. usurpation] of rarenesse in other countries; & noueltie in our."

Yet the official treatment accorded Hayward's history might suggest an even closer attention to form and circumstance of articulation, for in all copies of Coke's notes from 1600 to 1601 there survives his exact citation from the opening paragraph: "Neyther armyes nor strongholds are so great defences to a prince as the multitude of children, forts may decay, forces decrease."[22] Of course, such a sentence in the *form* of a general remonstrance to "a prince" concerning the benefits of secure succession might be more offensive to Coke's late Elizabethan official sensitivities than a specific historical reference to, say, Richard's own childlessness; but the concrete circumstances of

---

20. The citation is from John Hayward, *The First Part of the Life and Raigne of Henry IV* (London, 1599), STC 12997, with a slight modification of Tillyard's citation (*Shakespeare's History Plays*, p. 244). For an authoritative modern edition of Hayward's *History*, see John J. Manning, ed., *The First and Second Parts of John Hayward's "The Life and Raigne of King Henrie IIII,"* 4th ser., vol. 42 (London: Camden Society, 1991).

21. Coke's notes are from Public Records Office, State Papers Domestic (SPD), vol. 274, item 61; compare Calendar of State Papers Domestic (CSPD) 274, p. 405. The Hayward citation is from *Henry IV,* p. 67.

22. SPD 275, item 251; cf. SPD 274, item 61.

utterance in 1599–1601 should occasion further consideration.[23] References to "decrease" in troop strength and "decay" in materiel as points of hypothesized weakness in the heirless realm align Hayward's generalized historical apothegm with contemporary sources of friction. "He presupposed," Coke writes, "that there should be ill success in Ireland he writing his booke in 99 after the archtraitor was in his strenghe."[24] From Coke's perspective an utterance framed in a generalized language of mutability (all things are subject to "decrease" and "decay") could appear as a specific prediction that is itself, even in its very conditional form, of things that "may" decay and decrease—in fact a threat: a predicted collapse of Essex's Irish campaign not as a reflection of the weakness of his forces (or of the historical Richard's) but as a threat of potential mutiny led by the Essex faction in their "strenghe" and expressing disaffection (as their failings were pronounced in some circles). The general recommendation to "a prince" thus might appear a threat to *this* queen and, more specifically, to *those* Elizabethan officials who had opposed, and would continue to oppose, Essex and certain *values* with which he was associated.[25]

This brings us back to Tillyard's first sentence and the epithets "victorious" and "noble" applied to Edward III. The language of Hayward's account of the defeat of Richard II's Irish expedition attracts Coke's attention in his notes and in the actual proceedings against Hayward, but in both cases it is a connection between military failure and social division that Coke focuses upon. Coke's fragmentary notes read: "Many succors sent but scatteringly and droppinge, and neuer so many as were able to furnishe the warres if anything were attempted

---

23. On these circumstances and Hayward's problems, see Margaret Dowling, "Sir John Hayward's Troubles over His Life of Henry IV," *The Library*, 4th ser. (1930–31): 212–24; Evelyn May Albright, "Shakespeare's *Richard II* and the Essex Conspiracy," *PMLA* 46 (1931): 694–719; S. L. Goldberg, "Sir John Hayward, 'Politic' Historian," *Review of English Studies* 6 (1955): 233–44.

24. SPD 274, item 61.

25. Hayward's offending sentence is in fact derived from Henry Savile's edition of Tacitus (*The Ende of Nero and Beginning of Galba* [London, 1598], STC 23643, p. 165). Hayward, however, discusses the illusory nature of reliance on "fortes" and "forces" without dynastic security, while Savile's sentence criticizes the affectional ties binding "friends" as being weaker than bonds of blood: "For neither were Legions nor nauies so strong defences and rampiers of a Princes estate, as the multitude of children. Friendes with time and fortune, sometimes by vnaduised desires, or ouersights, decrease, fall from vs and fade, whereas a mans owne bloud cleaueth fast" (p. 165). Dowling's account of the Irish situation in "Sir John Hayward's Troubles" is helpful; cf. Hayward's remarks (*Henry IV*, p. 62).

happely acheued by any of the nobilitie it was by the kings base ha[.]"[26]
Which leads to this in the manuscript record of Hayward's interrogation: "And also that he [Hayward] gathered out of the actions of that
king recorded by Walsingham that matters of peace were managed by
menne of weakest sufficiency by whose counsell either ignorant or
corrupt. . . . That the kings counsel accounted ancient nobilitie a
vaine iest wealth and virtue the ready means to bring to destruction
which complaynt is extant in Hall and Polydore Virgill & many other
wrighters."[27] These observations are gathered from a passage in Hayward's book in which England's military failure is said (by the Archbishop of Canterbury) to exemplify its pitiful state—"a pitty to our
friends, and a verie ieast to our most base and contemptible enemies"—a state resulting from the fact that

> all our diligent and discreete leaders (the verie sinewes of the field) are
> either put to death, or banished, or els lie buried in obscurity and dis-
> grace: and the marshalling of all affaires is committed (without any re-
> spect of sufficiency or desert) to the counsaile & conduct of those, who
> can best apply themselues to the Kings youthfull delights. Among
> these, auncient nobility is accompted a vaine ieast, wealth, and vertue
> are the ready meanes to bring to destruction.[28]

Thus, in terming Edward III victorious and noble, Hayward merely
retails historical "fact"—Edward's victories and birth being public
knowledge—and simultaneously positions the values Edward stands
for as a positive ideal precisely in opposition to that "base" faction
controlling King Richard to the hindrance of "auncient nobility,"
"wealth," "vertue" and martial distinction. In this process, Hayward
might well appear to Coke to enlist Edward III in a socially defined
division of strategic import to Elizabeth's own day. Read closely and
laterally, considered as an utterance in struggle with other utterances,
Hayward's "perfectly orthodox" discourse betrays complicating fissures and discrepancies in evaluative orientation and allegiance.

Related complications riddle a text frequently appropriated in more
recent scholarship. Arguably the most widely cited "historical evidence" in discussions relating Elizabethan theater and society, the ac-

26. SPD 275, item 251.
27. SPD 278, item 17.
28. Hayward, *Henry IV,* pp. 62–63.

count of William Lambarde's exchange with Queen Elizabeth in East Greenwich dated August 4, 1601, has established itself as a documentary lynchpin of various readings. A reading that is at once close and laterally conjoined, however, suggests interesting potentials in this commonplace matter of truncated citation.

Most frequently cited as a single phrase—Elizabeth's "Know ye not that I am Richard II"—which is often conjoined with her subsequent observation, "This tragedy has been played forty times in open streets and houses," the anecdote has been enlisted as, in Walter Cohen's words, "historical evidence that such apparently orthodox plays as *Richard II*" seem to have "deeply troubled the Elizabethan and Jacobean upper classes."[29] Even when it has been evoked more fully, little

29. Walter Cohen, "Political Criticism of Shakespeare," in *Shakespeare Reproduced: The Text in History and Ideology,* ed. Jean E. Howard and Marion F. O'Connor (London: Methuen, 1987), pp. 18–46, 35. Cohen's essay is an excellent account of problems haunting recent political criticism. It is difficult to find discussions of the political situation of the Elizabethan theater that do not cite Elizabeth's remark to Lambarde as "evidence," and it is equally rare to find readings that cite the full sentence from which it is taken or convey *any* ambiguities concerning the identification of "this tragedy" with Shakespeare's play. For a few examples, see Marie Axton, "[Elizabeth's] famous remark 'I am Richard the Second. Know ye not that?' was made to William Lambarde . . . and its context makes clear that both Elizabeth and Lambarde saw the play's relevance to the Earl of Essex's rebellion" (*The Queen's Two Bodies: Drama and the Elizabethan Succession* [London: Historical Society, 1977], p. 2); Stephen Greenblatt, "In Elizabeth's bitter recollection the performance has metastasized: 'This tragedy was played 40tie times in open streets and houses'" (*The Power of Forms in the English Renaissance* [Norman, Okla.: Pilgrim Books, 1982], p. 3); Leah S. Marcus, "In 1601, a sudden rash of performances of Shakespeare's *Richard II* was taken by Elizabeth and her chief ministers (and not without reason) as propaganda for the Essex rebellion" (*Puzzling Shakespeare,* p. 27); David Scott Kastan, "Elizabeth bitterly remarked . . . when she was reminded of Essex's use of (what was presumably Shakespeare's) *Richard II* . . . 'this tragedy . . .'" ("Proud Majesty Made a Subject: Shakespeare and the Spectacle of Rule," *Shakespeare Quarterly* 37 [1986]: 468); Stephen Orgel, "[Elizabeth] paused at length over the reign of Richard II, and when Lambarde expressed his surprise, she explained, 'I am Richard II, know ye not that?' Lambarde acknowledged that he understood this to be an allusion to the drama of the late Earl of Essex, and the Queen continued, 'He that will forget God will also forget his benefactors; this tragedy was played forty times in open streets and houses.' . . . In her moving and baffling expostulation to Lambarde, she transformed the drama of *Richard II* into a piece of very dangerous civic pageantry" ("The Spectacles of State," in *Persons in Groups,* ed. Richard C. Trexler [Binghamton: Medieval and Renaissance Texts and Studies, 1985], p. 119). Historians have often treated Elizabeth's remark in similar fashion; see, for example, Lacey Baldwin Smith, *Treason in Tudor England: Politics and Paranoia* (Princeton: Princeton University Press, 1986), pp. 261–69, and 315n. For a strong counterstatement to such uses of the anecdote, see J. Leeds Barroll, "A New History for Shakespeare and His Time," *Shakespeare Quarterly* 39 (1988): 441–64.

attention has been given to potentially interesting features of the text taken as utterance, and above all to the evaluative orientations detectable in its formal and semantic features.[30]

Calling itself a "copy" of Lambarde's conversation with Elizabeth, and dated in the month of his death, the document represents Lambarde's presentation of the "Pandectae of all her Rolles, Bundles, Membranes and Parcells that bee repoased in her Maties Tower at London."[31] Elizabeth accepts the work "chearefully" and with a personal gratitude that is instanced as expressing a royal personalism: "You intended to present this Booke unto mee by the Countice of Warwicke, but I will none of that, for—if any subject of myne doe mee a Service, I will thankfully accept it from his owne hands." Then she reads and questions: "Then openinge the Booke, sayes, 'you shall see that I cann reade'; and soe, with an audible Voice, read over the Epistle, and the Title soe readily and distinctly poynted, that it might perfectly appeare, that shee well understood and conceaved the same." Although Elizabeth's readerly competence is remarked, a major component of the anecdote consists of her queries and Lambarde's explications.

Of the first page, Elizabeth "demaunded the meaninge of *Oblata, Cartae, Litterae clausae et Litterae Patentes,*" and Lambarde dutifully responds: "WL Hee severally expounded the Meaninge and layed out the true Differences of every of them; her Matie seeminge well satisfied, sayd that she would bee a Scholler in her Age, and thought it noe scorne to learne duringe her Life, being of the Minde of that Philosopher, who in his last yeares begann with the Greeke alphabet." After this initial exposition of terms and her reported self-characterization as perpetual scholar, unmindful of "scorne" from antihumanists, "shee proceeded to further pages, and asked (where she found cause of Stay) as were meant by *Ordinationes, Parliamenta, Rotulus Cambii,*

30. The readings in Greenblatt, *Power of Forms,* and Orgel, "Spectacles of State," amply repay investigation for what Jon Klancher terms a tendency to make "historical criticism a transhistorical echo of the politics of the present." Jon Klancher, "English Romanticism and Cultural Production," in *The New Historicism,* ed. H. Aram Veeser (New York: Routledge, 1989), p. 77.

31. British Museum Additional Ms. 15,664. f. 226. The version from which most criticism takes the anecdote is John Nichols, *The Progresses and Public Processions of Queen Elizabeth* (1823; rpt. New York: Burt Franklin, n.d.), 3:552–53. Nichols generally agrees with the British Museum Manuscript. The most noteworthy exception is that Nichols makes "benefactor" plural in the sentence concerning "this tragedy." The letter Nichols attributes to Lambarde in adjoining pages is of doubtful authorship.

and *Rediseisnes?*" It is these terminological queries that immediately bracket the famous self-comparison:

> WL Hee likewise expounded all these to theire originall Diversities, which she took in gratious and full satisfaction—Soe her Matie fell upon the Reigne of King Rich. 2d sayinge, "I am Richard 2d." know ye not that?
> WL—Such a wicked Immagination was determined and attempted by a most unkind Gent, the most adorned Creature that ever yr Matie made.
> *Her Matie*—Hee that will forgett God, will also forgett his Benefactor; this Tragedie was played 40tie times in open Streets and Houses.
> *Her Matie* then demanded, what was *Praestita?*

Abruptly the anecdote "then" returns to terminology, yet the conversation is not easily segmented; it is marked throughout by recurrences.

Lambarde's explanation of *Praestita* as "*Monies* lent by her Progenitors to their subjects for theire Good, but with assurance of good bond for repayment" occasions the first return to Richard II, by way of a remark concerning Henry VII: "*Her Matie* Soe did my good Grandfather Kinge Henry the 7th sparinge to dissipate his Treasure or Lands.—Then returninge to Richard 2d. shee demaunded whither I hadd seene any true Picture or lively Representation of his countenance or Person?" Upon Lambarde's remarking that he had seen "none but such as be in common Hands," Elizabeth mentions a portrait found in a "back room" that she has been requested to relocate "in order with my Auncestors and Successors" and says it will be shown to him. This is followed by another apparent change of subject: "Then she proceeded to Rolles." But the conversation circles once more, for Elizabeth returns to the terms immediately preceding her first turn to Richard II when, apparently unprompted, she "then" restates her understanding of "*Rediseisnes*": "*Her Matie* then demaunded againe if *Rediseisnes* were not unlawfull and forcible throwinge of men out of their lawfull Possessions?" Lambarde's confirmation of this understanding, occasions her final historical assessment:

> WL Yea, and therefore, these be the Rolles of Fines, Assesses and Levies uppon such Wrong Dooers, as well for the great and willfull Contempt of the Crowne and Royall Dignitie, as Disturbance of Common Justice.
> *Her Matie*—In those Days Force and Armes did prevaile, but now the Witt of the Foxe is every wheare on foote, soe as hardly a faithful or vertuoose Man may bee found. Then came shee to the whole totall of

all the Membranes and Parcells aforesaid, amounting to [blank space]
commendinge the Worke, not only for the Paynes therein taken, but
alsoe for that she had not receaved since her first comminge to the
Crowne any one thinge that brought therewith soe great Delectation
unto her; and soe beinge called away to Prayer, she put the Booke in her
Bosome, having forbidden mee from the first to the last, to fall upon
my Knee before her, concludinge—"*Farwell, good and honest Lambarde*"!

It is arguable that "those Days" in this paragraph constitutes another
return to Richard II, since Lambarde had elsewhere written of the sei-
zure of real property in Richard's day.[32] Most clearly, however, the
past is characterized by Elizabeth as exhibiting public, open violence
of "Force and Armes" which "now" has been replaced by the covert
"Witt of the Foxe" which "every wheare" corrupts the virtues of indi-
viduals and their bonds of faith. That past, as well as this present, are
both constructed in opposition to "good and honest Lambarde." And
here are places as good as any to pursue evaluative orientations and
social heteroglossia: oppositions of now and then, of open and covert,
of a good, honest individual and omnipresent foxlike wit, to be sure,
but also discrepancies among languages that are not reducible to oppositions—discursive heterologies, for example, between her account of
Essex's "tragedy" and his references to the "wicked Immagination" of
an "unkind Gent" and "adorned Creature."

If "now" is taken to be August 1601 rather than simply in the wake
of the Essex rebellion, then a rather specific light is cast on Elizabeth's
self-identification. Furthermore, if Lambarde is taken to be the
bureaucrat and judicial reformer, writer of legal and parliamentary
history, Protestant activist, and Cecil adherent rather than mere "antiquary," then yet other implications of that identification and of the
"Tragedie" that was "played 40tie times in open Streets and Houses"
bid for attention.[33]

In August 1601 Hayward's continuing imprisonment demonstrated

32. See William Lambarde, *Eirenarcha,* rev. ed. (London, 1592), STC 15167, pp.
154–67.

33. The phrase "in the wake of the abortive Essex rising" is from Greenblatt, *Power
of Forms,* p. 3. Greenblatt and Orgel ("Spectacles of State"), among many others, refer
to Lambarde as Elizabeth's "antiquary" and "archivist," respectively. On Lambarde's
life, see Wilbur Dunkel, *William Lambarde: Elizabethan Jurist, 1536–1601* (New Brunswick, N.J.: Rutgers University Press, 1965). A brief account is in Conyers Read's
introduction to *William Lambarde and Local Government* (Ithaca: Cornell University
Press, 1962).

that there could be infelicitous responses to a royal self-identification with Richard II—especially when an interlocutor shared Hayward's politically sensitive profession of historian. Although Lambarde's response appears to avoid problems—"WL Such a wicked Immagination was determined and attempted by a most unkind Gent, the most adorned Creature that ever yr Matie made"—it is not allowed to stand without recasting by Elizabeth: "Hee that will forgett God, will also forgett his Benefactor; this Tragedie was played 40tie times in open Streets and Houses." Lambarde's initial response conjoins the languages of legal and ecclesiastical clerisies: his "wicked Immagination" which was "determined and attempted" turns one legal designation of plotting as "imagination" toward what will be the King James Bible's characterization of human sinfulness as the wicked "imagination" of men's hearts and flexes it back again toward the courtroom in the lawyerly distinction between intention and action. But his subsequent phrasing offers other, less universalized evaluative orientations. The "wicked Immagination" Lambarde invokes is located neither in *man* nor in *subject* but in a doubly superlative epitome, "the most adorned Creature that ever yr Matie made." Here his phrasing follows the well-worn path of antiparasite polemic traditional to commons' complaints concerning courtly dependency. Yet this polemic is embedded in another narrative of much wider application—the dependent "Creature" "made" by the sovereign is an Elizabethan social recasting of the biblical creation narrative in the form of an assumed universality of patron-client vertical dependencies.[34] This story, however, commonplace of its age, is repositioned by Elizabeth in a horizontal orbit, as a counterutterance to other utterances adjacent to or even impinging upon it. A trace of these shadow utterances appears in Lambarde's designation of Essex as "a most unkind Gent," an equivocal utterance (like Hamlet's "less than kind") potentially implying individual unkindliness and/or violation of "kind"—an assumed, *natural* standard of conduct appropriate to a "Gent."

Elizabeth's reply at first appears to preclude such overtly social

---

34. On pervasive patronage relations, see Perez Zagorin, *Rebels and Rulers, 1500–1660* (Cambridge: Cambridge University Press, 1982), 1:70–71; Joel Hurstfield, *Freedom, Corruption, and Government in Elizabethan England* (Cambridge: Harvard University Press, 1973), pp. 150–58. For legal terminology of "imagination" applied to Essex, see "Calendar of the Contents of the Baga de Secretis," in *Fourth Report of the Deputy Keeper of the Public Records,* appendix 2 (London, 1843), p. 293. Cf. John Bellamy, *The Tudor Law of Treason* (London: Routledge and Kegan Paul, 1979), pp. 30–33.

orientation in that she responds only to the theological discourse in Lambarde's statement, making Essex's wrong and her virtue mere extensions of the larger, depersonalized, timeless, and estateless, indeed actionless, and most *human* frailty—forgetting God and "Benefactor"—rather than the more specific crimes either of a historically particular "wicked Immagination" and attempt, or of a socially particularized violation of "kind" by a "Gent." Yet the second half of her sentence seems quite specific in time and circumstance: "This Tragedie was played 40tie times in open Streets and Houses." This statement has often been read, of course, as referring to a play, perhaps Shakespeare's, about Richard II.[35] If, however, as syntax suggests, Elizabeth is speaking of the tragedy of Essex himself rather than that of Richard, other questions arise. Why might Elizabeth and her interlocutor and/or recorder of the anecdote have chosen to speak of the Essex uprising as a "Tragedie" of ingratitude "played" repeatedly in both "open Streets and Houses"? With and against what utterances might such an utterance take shape?

Seen from the wide perspective of discourse, the anecdote could easily be assimilated to the language of gratitude and ingratitude, benefactor and creature that permeates late Elizabethan official discourse in differing contexts of utterance. In her notes to the so-called Golden Speech to Parliament in 1601, for example, Elizabeth rejoices to be "a Queen over so thankful a people."[36] And, of all the matters for which Elizabeth might excoriate the late Philip of Spain in her final speech to the 1601 Parliament, she denounces him as one who "had as many provocations of kindness by my just proceedings, as by hard measure he hath returned effects of ingratitude."[37] John Croke's speech before her on October 30 stresses the thankfulness due from her subjects and the likely divine retribution if they begrudge that due.[38] Nor is this public discourse discontinuous with the terms of private exchanges,

---

35. The evidence and its problems are fully considered by Barroll ("A New History"). Shakespeare's *Richard II* was probably presented once on the eve of the rising. Some evidence suggests public readings of Hayward's book; see Ure's introduction to the Arden *Richard II*, p. lxi; cf. Mervyn James, *Society, Politics, and Culture: Studies in Early Modern England* (Cambridge: Cambridge University Press, 1986), p. 419n.

36. Paul Johnson, *Elizabeth I: A Biography* (New York: Holt, Rinehart, and Winston, 1974), p. 417.

37. J. E. Neale, *Elizabeth I and Her Parliaments, 1584–1601* (London: Jonathan Cape, 1957), 2:429.

38. Ibid., 2:373.

as is evident in the correspondence of the Earl of Essex. In his detailed advice for a letter to Elizabeth, Francis Bacon suggests, for example, that Essex explain his motivation for writing as "first and principally gratitude" and that he gently remind her of "anything that hath been grateful to her Majesty from you," while admitting that "princes' hearts are inscrutable."[39] The reply framed for Essex employs similarly combined rhetorics of gratitude and religion.[40] And yet the Lambarde anecdote is not merely an instantiation of such a culturally hegemonic discourse, nor is it simply expressive of a desire for generous patronage. Features of that discourse's deployment in this utterance, as well as in the exchanges surrounding the Essex affair more generally, register the anecdote's function in constituting a "counter word" addressed to certain other concrete utterances.

Official accounts repeatedly describe the personal threat of the Essex rising to Elizabeth, and in turn subordinate that threat to a larger sin of "ingratitude" to God. These accounts, furthermore, share the anecdote's language of dramatic form in typifying the uprising itself. Elements of this official line—with one noteworthy occlusion shared by the Lambarde anecdote—are exemplified in the accusations brought against Sir Christopher Blunt, who is said to be more culpable for conspiring against the "queen herself" than against the "State," and more heinous still for manifesting "ingratitude against God" in seeking "toleration of religion." Blunt's intention, furthermore, is said to have involved a resemblance to the "story of Richard II," and a royal assassination, which is likened to the "catastrophe, the conclusion" of Edward II's murder.[41] The language of dramatic form here employed is widely used elsewhere in the official pronouncements, with specific reference to tragedy. "Tragedy" is, of course, a term of wide provenance during the period, but particular uses in the polemic surrounding the Essex rebellion can be related to aspects of

39. *The Works of Francis Bacon,* ed. James Spedding et al. (1862; rpt. New York: Garrett Press, 1968), 9:195–96.

40. Ibid., 9:201. Essex's letter, Bacon says, should admit, "I know I ought doubly infinitely to be her Majesty's: both *jure creationis,* for I am her creature, and *jure redemptionis,* for I know she hath saved me from overthrow." For later use of the discourse of religion and gratitude against the court of James I, see R. Malcolm Smuts, *Court Culture and the Origins of a Royalist Tradition in Early Stuart England* (Philadelphia: University of Pennsylvania Press, 1987), pp. 34–35.

41. William Cobbett, *Complete Collection of State Trials* (London, 1809), vol. 1 (1163–1600), pp. 1421–22.

evaluative orientation in the Lambarde exchange and in the charges against Blunt.[42]

Bacon's *Declaration*,[43] which was sent to press April 14, 1601, and was, he says, "perused, weighed, censured, altered, and made almost a new writing" both by the "principall Councillors" and "the Queen herself," repeatedly refers to the uprising as a "tragedy"—complete with "preludes" (9:249), "platform," (9:264), "second act," (9:264), and a "catastrophe or last part of that tragedy for which he [Essex] came upon the stage" (9:253). Of the plot to seize the court by Sir Charles Davers, Sir Christopher Blunt, and Sir John Davies, one reads: "This being the platform of their enterprise, the second act of this tragedy was also resolved; which was that my Lord should present himself to her Majesty as prostrating himself at her feet, and desire the remove of such persons as he called his enemies from about her" (9:264). But the "tragedy" that Bacon, and apparently the queen and council, had in mind was of a particular sort.

After proclaiming its intent to counter "divers most wicked and seditious libels thrown abroad" (9:247), Bacon's *Declaration* opens with this assessment of the Essex story:

> The most partial will not deny, but that Robert late Earl of Essex was by her Majesty's manifold benefits and graces, besides oath and allegiance, as much tied to her Majesty as the subject could be to the sovereign; her Majesty having heaped upon him both dignities, offices, and gifts, in such measure, as within the circle of twelve years or more there was scarcely a year of rest, in which he did not obtain at her Majesty's hands some notable addition either of honour or profit.
>
> But he on the other side, making these her Majesty's favours nothing else but wings for his ambition, and looking upon them not as her benefits but as his advantages, supposing that to be his own metal which

42. Potentially relevant uses of "tragedy" might include Lambarde's lament over "what great Tragedies have beene stirred in this Realme by this our naturall inhospitalitie and disdaine of straungers" and his urging solidarity with foreign Protestants as "guestes and straungers in our Countrie." William Lambarde, *A Perambulation of Kent* (1576; rpt. London, 1826), pp. 323–24. Elizabeth herself translates from Boethius in 1593 such observations as "What does Tragedies clamour more bewayle, than a man turning happy Raigne by blynde fortune's stroke?" *Queen Elizabeth's Englishings*, ed. Caroline Pemberton (London, 1899), p. 23. Elizabeth also translates Plutarch in 1598 on the self-destructive nature of curiosity in Oedipus and the fate of "curious man" who "willingly may tragedies new made behold" (pp. 138, 128).

43. *A Declaration Touching Upon the Treasons of the Late Earl of Essex* (London, 1601), in Bacon, *Works,* vol. 9; subsequent citations appear in the text.

was but her mark and impression, was so given over by God (who often punisheth ingratitude by ambition, and ambition by treason, and treason by final ruin), as he had long ago plotted it in his heart to become a dangerous supplanter of that seat, whereof he ought to have been a principal supporter. (9:248)

Bacon offers commonplaces: a "creature" who forgets the "benefactor" who has "made" him and is providentially punished in a "tragedy" of self-love and ruin which follows in condign self-punishment. No matter the qualities and varieties of the historical participants and social particularities that might aid or retard the actors, the origin of evil is a self-generating discontent outside the fabula—perhaps, as Bacon hypothesizes, the product "of a nature disposed to disloyalty," yet ultimately beyond human explanation: "But as it were a vain thing to think to search the roots and first motions of treasons, which are known to none but God that discerns the heart, and the devil that gives the instigation" (9:249).[44] Possible alternatives to this homiletic "tragedy" of monarchical magnanimity, inexplicable human "ingratitude," and self-destructive "ambition" are subordinated within the account and addressed by it.

As Bacon's references to "oath and allegiance" suggest, one alternative would be to denounce Essex for violating the values of chivalric honor; another to accuse him of rending those ties of "subject" to "sovereign" as promulgated in Tudor accounts of consolidated monarchical authority. But Bacon's officially sanctioned choice of the rhetoric of theological tragedy over either of these evaluative alternatives should be considered according to other evidence within the *Declaration* which indicates its instantiation of social heteroglossia as a *response* to yet another social "language," against which either of these alternatives might have proven relatively ineffectual. Bacon's choice casts light on the heteroglossic dimensions of Elizabeth's own "Tragedie" of ingratitude "played 40tie times in open Streets and Houses."

Bacon's *Declaration* claims to respond to the fact that "there do pass abroad in the hands of many men divers false and corrupt collections and relations of the proceedings at the arraignment of the Late Earls of Essex and Southampton," and "divers most wicked and seditious libels thrown abroad" (9:247). He attempts the rhetorical neutralization of such voices by proclaiming them "partial." But already in the

---

44. Given this theological frame, the pervasive references to Providence in Bacon's account are not surprising; see, e.g., ibid., pp. 255, 257, 266.

fragmentary, unpublished records of the proceedings concerning Essex, held at York House in June 1600, well before the uprising proper of February 1601, similarly unauthorized "discourses" are mentioned as demanding official response. In this earlier instance, Bacon's providentialist rhetoric—distinctly Protestant in its emphasis on superabundant royal "grace"—specifically responds to the offending discourse and the *form* of its utterance:

> When Offence was grown unmeasurablie offensive, then did grace superabound, and in the heate of all the ill news out of Ireland, and other advertisements thence to my Lo: disadvantage, her Mate entered into a resolution, out of herself and her inscrutable goodness, not to overthrow my Lo: fortune irreparablie by publique and proportionable justice, notwithstanding, inasmuch as about yt time, there did fly about in London Streets and Theatres divers Seditious Libells, and Powles and Ordinaries were full of bold and factious discourses, whereby not onlie manie of her Maties faithful and zealous councillors and Servants were taxed, but withall the hard estate of Ireland was imputed to any thing rather than unto the true cause (the Earl's defaults).[45]

These threatening "publique" attacks in "London Streets and Theatres," "Powles and Ordinaries" are epitomized by a letter addressed to Elizabeth. This letter, arguing that Essex suffered under "passion and faction" and not under "justice mixed with mercy," though unfit to pass in "vulgar hands," was first divulged by "copies everywhere (that being as it seemeth the newest and finest form of libelling)" and then was committed to "press."[46] Thus, unofficial counternarratives to the official Augustinian tragedy of isolate evil inexplicably arisen to trouble "inscrutable," self-sufficient goodness and its superabundant "grace" appear officially represented as openly circulating "bold and factious" accusations. These are said to accuse "her Maties faithful and zealous councillors and Servants" for their own "passion and faction" as itself the origin of Essex's troubles. Such a discourse is, in the circumstances of its utterance, itself "factious," insofar as it publicly invokes factional contention within the official ranks of faithful, zealous servants and councilors rather than the individual "tragedy" of a subject's atheism, "ingratitude," or "wicked imagination" as the origin of Essex's actions. Furthermore, it offers an alternative evaluation of

45. Harleian Ms. 6854, f. 178.
46. Ibid.; cf. Bacon, *Works,* 9:178.

official "justice mixed with mercy" as instancing the same factional struggle. Thus, by its semantic choices, its practice of sociopolitical analysis, and the form and circumstance of its utterance—in "Streets and Theatres," "Powles and Ordinaries," and printed "copies every-where"—it invites open and public participation in such analysis.

These "factious" utterances that Bacon claims instigated the proceedings against Essex are also discussed by Fulke-Greville, the earl's relative and posthumous defender.[47] In describing his own self-censorship in destroying his unpublished tragedy of Antony and Cleopatra rather than risking having it "construed or strained to a personating of vices in the present governors or government," Fulke-Greville describes Elizabeth and Essex both as victims of "sect-animals" (p. 156) or "Party" (p. 160) among the "factious English" (p. 160). In this narrative Essex is trebly a victim. First, the "sect-animals" torment Essex alternatively with flatteries and minor vexations, which prompt in one of his "great heart" (p. 157) careless actions; then they forge libels in his name in order, finally, to propel him into the mills of the law, as predictably turned by "inferiour ministers of Justice":

> Into which pitfall of theirs, when they had once discerned this Earle to be fallen: straight, under the reverend stile of *Laesae Majestatis* all inferiour ministers of Justice—they knew—would be justly let loose to work upon him. And accordingly, under the same cloud, his enemies took audacity to cast libels abroad in his name against the State, made by themselves: set papers upon posts, to bring his innocent friends in question. His power, by the Jesuiticall craft of rumour, they made infinite; and his ambition more then equall to it. His letters to private men were read openly, by the piercing eyes of an Atturnie's office, which warrantes the construction of every line in the worst sense against the writer. (p. 157)[48]

47. Fulke-Greville citations are from *Works,* ed. A. B. Grosart (1870; rpt. New York: AMS Press, 1966), vol. 4; subsequent citations appear in the text. On faction, see E. W. Ives, *Faction in Tudor England* (London: Historical Association, 1979).

48. Compare Essex's remark to the queen in a letter of May 1600: "I am gnawed on & torn by ye vilest and basest creatures upon earth. The prating tavern-haunter speakes of me what he lists: the frantick libeller writes of me what he lists; already they print me, & make speak to ye world, and shortly they will play me in what form they list upon ye stage. The least of these is a thowsand tymes woorse then deathe" (SPD 274, item 138). On one engraved image of Essex circulating in 1600, see Richard C. McCoy, *The Rites of Knighthood: The Literature and Politics of Elizabethan Chivalry* (Berkeley: University of California Press, 1989), pp. 79–102.

Fulke-Greville consistently demeans the legal profession from its highest officials to the "inferiour ministers of Justice." His indirect discourse mocks the pretensions of their "reverend stile" and its strategic hypocrisy: they "warrant" the reading of "private" letters "openly," and they are said "justly" to be "let loose to work on him."

While Essex's enemies at court are said to encourage legalistic violence "as against an unthankfull favourite and traiterous subject; hee standing, by the law of England, condemned for such" (p. 158), Fulke-Greville defends the earl on the grounds of his martial accomplishments on England's and Elizabeth's behalf and of his immunity to the temptation to usurp the monarch's sovereign power of "creation" in cases that most immediately concerned him. In fact, Essex was such a loyal "favourite" that, true to values of chivalric honor, he "never put his soveraigne to stand between her people and his errors; but here and abroad, placed his body in the forefront, against all that threatened or assaulted her" (pp. 158–59). Far from affecting "absolute power," Essex avoided the abuses of Henry III's men: "I meane under a king to become equall at least with him, in creating and deposing chancelors, treasurers, and secretaries of State, to raise a strong party for himselfe; as he left both place and persons entire in their supreme jurisdictions, or magistracies under his soveraigne, as shee granted them" (p. 160). For "secretaries of State" one might read (in 1601) Secretary Robert Cecil, which might recall Lambarde's personal ties to Cecil and familiar stories of Essex-Cecil divisions.[49] But more is at stake here than personal contention, for there are institutional and cultural parameters to the division and its available articulations.

However else the contention of the Cecil and Essex factions might be articulated, Fulke-Greville represents a struggle between the values of sword and robe, chivalry and clerisy.[50] The "prosperity" of Essex's

49. The story has often been told; for one classic example, see Lytton Strachey, *Elizabeth and Essex* (New York: Harcourt Brace, 1928). Cf. Thomas Wilson's apparent references to the fate of Essex at the hands of those who "make the Queene looke through a payre of spectacles & make the fault seeme greater than it is, as hath been lately approved in the actions of some of the greatest," in *The State of England, 1600, Camden Miscellany* 16 (1936), p. 41. Lord Burghley was Lambarde's friend and patron (Read, introduction to *William Lambarde*, p. 11), and in a letter of 1591, Lambarde dedicated his *Archion* (London, 1635; STC 15143) to Robert Cecil.

50. On this contention, see James, *Society, Politics, and Culture*, pp. 429ff. As an example, Lord Burghley's advice to Robert Cecil on children: "Neither by my consent, shalt thou train them up in wars. For he that sets up his rest to live by that profession can hardly be an honest man or a good Christian." Joel Hurstfield, *The Queen's Wards: Wardship and Marriage under Elizabeth I*, 2d ed. (London: Frank Cass,

pursuit of "the standard of Mars" inevitably entails "the falling of their scales," and thus awakens the "envious and suppressing crafts of party" (p. 160). In this choice Fulke-Greville's utterance is far from alone, and, I would argue, it is precisely in an atmosphere charged by such utterances that the representation of Elizabeth's exchange with Lambarde takes shape. The chosen language of homiletic tragedy with its religiously universalized account of human nature and its inexplicable sinful propensities addresses (by precluding) other available accounts that might articulate specific conditions and tensions of profession, class, and economy. Evidence of such tensions riddles the surviving documentation. So, for example, in that letter of 1598 to Thomas Egerton, which would become notorious for refusing to identify "absolute infiniteness in heaven" with "infinite absoluteness on earth," Essex locates the clerical offices but little above abjection: "I owe her majesty the duty of an earl and lord marshal of England. I have been content to do her majesty the service of a clerk; but can never serve her as a villain or slave."[51] Bacon himself rhetorically invokes the tension between civil and military values when he advises Essex to give up the appearance of "military dependence," while disclaiming the intention "to play now the part of a gownman that would frame you best to mine own turn."[52] And Essex writes to Anthony Bacon with an analysis of professional solidarity that is meant to address the charge that he favors men of war: "Every man doth love those of his own profession. The grave judges favor the students of law; the reverend bishops the laborers in the ministry; and I, since Her Majesty yearly used my service, in her late actions, must reckon myself among her men of war."[53] Popular stories and devices repeated similar divisions of sword and robe, or, as the Duke of Stettin Pomerania puts it, of "cannon" and "writing-pen."[54]

A differing evaluation of this contention is instanced most tellingly in Secretary Cecil's remarks at the trial of Essex. Cecil attacks the values of the honor culture for un-Christian warlikeness and economic

---

1973), p. 257. More generally, see Norbert Elias, *The Court Society*, trans. Edmund Jephcott (New York: Pantheon, 1983).

51. Thomas Birch, *Memoirs of the Reign of Queen Elizabeth* (London, 1754), p. 387.

52. Walter Devereux, *Lives and Letters of the Devereux* (London: John Murray, 1853), 2:398.

53. Ibid., 2:488.

54. "Diary of the Journey of Philip Julius Duke of Stettin-Pomerania through England in the Year 1602," ed. Gottfried von Bulow, *Transactions of the Royal Historical Society*, n.s. 6 (1892): 1–67, 24–25.

self-interest. Essex would have him appear odious, Cecil says, because he always worked "for the good and quyett of my countrye," while Essex is denounced: "But with yo it hath euer bene a *Maxime* to pr'fer warr before peace, in respecte of the consequence to yo followers and dependers."[55] Cecil further articulates differences between the honor culture and civil culture in a rhetorical flourish that epitomizes the stakes over which the two contend: "My Lo. ffor witt I giue yo the p'eminence, you haue it aboundantlie. ffor birthe I give yo place. I am not noble, yet I am a gent: neither am I a sword man. You haue therefore the oddes of me. But I haue inocencye to p'tect me."[56] Not noble, neither "sword man," nor "witt," and yet a "gent"—over the definition of gentility, factions and values of robe and sword contend, at court or in the city, and, as Lambarde's anecdote might suggest, in private chambers of counsel as well.

If semantically the analogical tragedy of personal ingratitude appears to override politico-analytical categories such as estate or profession which are available in Lambarde's own phrasing, nevertheless formal elements of the whole anecdotal utterance conform it not only to royal needs but also to values of gentility as redefined by Tudor humanists.[57] Although these very formal qualities of the anecdote make it appropriate that Lambarde be described as an "antiquary," or "archivist," such designations—like the anecdote itself—fail to convey either the political and economic value of scholarship such as his to early modern

55. *The Dr. Farmer Chetham MS.*, ed. Alexander B. Grosart (Manchester: Chetham Society, 1873), p. 18.

56. Ibid., p. 15.

57. On this redefinition, see Arthur B. Ferguson, *The Chivalric Tradition in Renaissance England* (Washington, D.C.: Folger Library, 1986), esp. pp. 59–63, on Sir Thomas Elyot's *Boke Named the Gouvernour* (1531) and *A Preservative agaynste Deth* (1545). Compare the redefinition of honor in terms of "obedience and duty toward the king his Majesty, his councillors, officers, and administrators, both high and low," in *The Institucion of a Gentleman* (London, 1568), STC 14105; or Lambarde's own version of the ideal justice of the peace as "Valiant," "Learned," and "Good": "under the word *Good*, it is meant also that hee loue and feare God aright, without which hee cannot bee *Good* at all" (*Eirenarcha*, p. 33). Peter Laslett claims, "The term gentleman marked the exact point at which the traditional social system divided up the population into two extremely unequal sections," in *The World We Have Lost* (New York: Scribner's, 1965), p. 26. Sir Julius Caesar describes Lambarde in a revealing combination of terms as "a deep and learned scholar, a great common lawyer, and a religious, conscionable, and worthy gentleman," in *Acta Cancellaria*, ed. Cecil Monro (London, 1847), p. 15n, cited in Read, introduction to *William Lambarde*, p. 11.

England or the depth of Lambarde's involvement in the theory and practices of that state, and hence fail to register possible heteroglossic resonances of the anecdote itself. In speaking *as* they do, monarch and official do not speak as they *might*. In fact, the intimate yet disinterested quality of their exchange, with its combination of royal proclivity and councilor's capacity to take up and drop, apparently at random, past monarchs, old laws, ancient languages, recondite terms, and antique portraits, manages to bracket, contain, and all but displace *present* threats or concerns. That these achieve articulation only in two royal excursions into present tense ("I am Richard 2d" and "the Witt of the Foxe is every wheare on foote") embodies significant evaluative orientations and displaces others.

Terms surrounding and interpenetrating Elizabeth's two present-tense utterances certainly touch upon areas of her interlocutor's expertise which are of immediate interest to crown and council in the present of August 1601. Most strikingly, Lambarde's capacity as an authority on legal and parliamentary history to expound terms such as *Parliamenta* and *Litterae patentes* in their "originall diversities" could render their exchanges highly pertinent to present governmental concerns.[58] August 1601 was a time of preparation for the Parliament that had been anticipated since spring (the last of the treble subsidy approved in 1597–98 had been collected by then, and money was needed to counter Spanish incursion in Ireland).[59] Of special interest to the Privy Council, as correspondence from that August reveals, were patents of monopoly. At issue since the previous Parliament and obviously threatening to arouse debate again since little had been done to fulfill royal promises of reform, disputes over regulation of monopoly patents threatened territory contested among royal prerogative, parliamentary initiative, and common law.[60] Lambarde's learning in the politically charged histories of Parliament and common law might be far more interesting to Elizabeth than the title "antiquary" suggests;

---

58. For example, in the coming Parliament Cecil would invoke Parliament's institutional evolution to argue against "precedent." Simonds D'Ewes, *The Journals of All the Parliaments During the Reign of Queen Elizabeth* (1682; rpt. Shannon: Irish University Press, 1973), p.649.

59. Neale, *Elizabeth I and Her Parliaments*, 2:370.

60. For the Privy Council communications, see Johnson, *Elizabeth I*, p. 415. On the potential conflict of monopoly regulation and prerogative powers, see Lord Keeper Egerton's Parliament address of 1598 (Neale, *Elizabeth I and Her Parliaments*, 2:354–55) and the Commons debates of 1601 (2:377–86).

yet to judge by the record, neither accords such present concerns significant attention.

Nor do they appear to explore related areas of Lambarde's expertise in fiscal policy and real property, which are also objects of considerable contemporary royal concern and are obliquely touched on by *Oblata, Praestita,* and *Rediseisnes.* Instead of enjoining current disputes concerning instruments of royal revenue, the legal connivances of concealed tenure, the continuing struggles over enclosure, or emerging claims of absolute private property, the anecdote records observations on "good" Henry VII's practical economies and moral denunciations of historically "unlawfull" and open "force and armes" against "lawfull Possessions."[61] In each such choice of language the identification of Elizabeth with Richard II might be considered a factor, for her exchanges affirm values opposing those widely associated with Richard. Repudiating craft as well as violence, concerned for law and the subject's possessions, for financial practicality, and for precedent rather than innovation, Elizabeth appears the antithesis of the prodigal autocrat—and, conversely, the fitting monarch for her civil servant's allegiance.

Furthermore, the *manner* of their discussions embodies an antithesis to the sly purposefulness characterized as the "Witt of the Foxe." Instead of raising narrowly instrumental matters of strategy and policy, their intimate, wide-ranging exchange never once descends to a discussion of *uses* for Lambarde's labors. Rather than be seen as a practical instrument of statecraft, his efforts are appreciated in and for themselves as the "service" of a "Scholler," fit cause of "delectation," and occasion for freely associative conversation articulated in terms of law, religion, history, morality, and practical benevolence, not immediate issues of state. These exchanges grant Lambarde's labors and those of the professional class he represents the status of humanist learning, and in the process associate them with an *afactional* discursive mode which Lambarde elsewhere characterizes as writing "academically, and without taking any part."[62] Whatever the validity of his claim

---

61. Compare Coke on the inflammatory potential in Hayward's terms "associations" and "yearly and double subsidies" (SPD 274, item 61). For debate concerning royal prerogative in relation to letters patent and enclosure, see D'Ewes, *Journals of All the Parliaments,* p. 675. One dramatic parliamentary instance of discrepant views of property occurs when laughter greets the claim that "precedent" dictates the queen's right to all English lands and goods (p. 633).

62. Lambarde, *Perambulation,* p. 492.

to academic disinterest in other contexts, Lambarde's quarter session addresses of the years 1600–1601 are highly relevant to these evaluative orientations.

In his 1600 address to the justices assembled for the sessions at Maidstone, Lambarde defines the most pressing public enemy as a "wickedness and contempt of good laws" that "boldly lift[s] up the head and hopeth to prevail":

> For such is nowadays the bold sway of disobedience to law that it creepeth not in corners but marcheth in the open market, and is not only to be seen plainly of such as have any eyes at all but is become in manner palpable and to be felt of such as be utterly blind. Yea, such is the inundation of wickedness in this last and worst age that if speedier help and hand of justice be not applied, we are justly to fear that we shall every one be overwhelmed thereby. For albeit every man of us feeleth more or less the present evil, foreseeth future danger, feareth the end, and complaineth of the case; yet how few are there found amongst us that will use the bridle of authority which they have in their own hand and cast it upon the head of this unruly monster![63]

It is difficult to say how precisely Lambarde's "open market" is meant to be taken for a physical location rather than to stand metonymically for the popular, public nature of disobedience. The address does invoke villains from a familiar litany—"seducing papists, thieves, extortioners, usurers, engrossers, and the rest of that rabble" (p. 141)—yet here, in the year preceding the Essex uprising, is a sense of the "open" space of public gathering, in this case the market rather than Elizabeth's "streets," as a place where disobedience to "law" exercises "bold sway" and "marcheth" unchecked by "authority" vested in the commons themselves. "Marcheth" might be merely a rhetorical antithesis to the stealth of "creepeth," but in 1600 Lambarde's figure of troops marching under the "bold sway" of disobedience preemptively appropriates the potentially authoritative appearance of order which might be mustered by an aristocratically marshaled and militarily deployed rebellion, assimilating this civil nightmare to that of the monstrous mob flowing in market and street.[64] At the same time, responsible

63. Read, *William Lambarde*, pp. 140, 143; subsequent citations appear in the text.
64. Riots by Londoners impressed for Irish service occurred at the market town of Towcester in 1598; probably the worst disturbances by troops connected with the Irish campaign occurred in Chester and Bristol in 1600. Peter Clark, ed., *The European Crisis of the 1590s: Essays in Comparative History* (London: George Allen & Unwin, 1985), p. 55.

"authority" is located in the lowest individual upholders of the common law: "private men" serving in the much demeaned office of justices.[65]

The work of these "private men," moreover, is repeatedly articulated in 1600 in terms appropriated from the honor culture. The law and its most humble upholders are said to defend God, England, and the queen against "intestine enemies" (p. 144); the law-abiding, not the military, "advance the honor of her Majesty" (p. 144), protect against the "period of the English honor" (p. 144), and serve England as a wall defensive: "If laws be duly administered they be the very walls of our country and commonwealth. But what walls, though of brass itself, be not expugnable if there be not men to defend them?" (p. 142). In 1601, shortly after the Essex rebellion, however, Lambarde's address written for the Easter sessions (but apparently not delivered) subordinates this appropriated language of honor to that of religion, arguing that "as the minister of the word soundeth the inward heart, so doth the magistrate and minister of the law exact the outward sign and testimony of a well-persuaded mind," with "honor" itself now recast as a *religious* reverence not to be diverted from God or prince to fractious religions, states, or nobles:

> So as in religion it is utterly unlawful for the servants of God to erect any golden calf or other idol and to transfer unto it the honor that ought to be proper to God alone, and in policy it is not sufferable that subjects should set up any glittering calf of Rome, of Spain, of Norfolk, or of Essex and to communicate thereunto that royal, obedient, and filial love which they owe to their natural prince, the mother of our country and earthly God over us. (p. 147)

Essex, like the rebellious Norfolk, is an idol, an image of authority rather than the thing itself.

But whatever their apparent shift in semantic register, Lambarde's addresses consistently invoke a continuity between public and "private" realms that contrasts with the public aspect of chivalric honor considerations.[66] Insistently "common good" and "public benefit" are

---

65. In 1598 Elizabeth suggests (through Sir Thomas Egerton) the resemblance of justices of the peace to greedy dogs who bark at loyal subjects rather than at rebels (Neale, *Elizabeth I and Her Parliaments*, 2:366). Such opinions were denounced as "slanderous and defamatory" by Sir Francis Hastings in 1601 (2:423).

66. On public recognition and honor values, see James, *Society, Politics, and Culture*, esp. pp. 339–40.

equated with the "proper business and particular profit" of "private men" (pp. 140, 141, 142). In doing good, one could do well. So in 1600 Lambarde writes that one's "own profit is so fast conjoined with the good of other men that if he neglect theirs his own also must of necessity decay and perish therewithal" (p. 140); and in 1601 he maintains the "end" of the justices' endeavors is "the glory of God, the general welfare of your prince, the church, and commonwealth, and the particular profit of every of yourselves and yours" (p. 149). Integrating the open, public values of chivalric honor, national survival, apocalyptic Protestantism, and commonwealth with the domestic and personal value of "private" profit, Lambarde's addresses suggest an evaluative orientation for the intimate form of his exhange with Elizabeth.

Her denial of courtly mediation in asserting that Lambarde need not have sent his manuscript through the Countess of Warwick when she would "thankfully accept" such "service" from "any subject"; the refusal to permit him to kneel; the self-deprecation of her scholarly ability while she avows the value of scholarship; the combination of vulnerability and linguistic exhibitionism in her reading; the personal reliance of monarch on dependent (slightly eroticized by tucking his gift "in her Bosome"); the equation of individual gratitude and piety—in these the anecdote represents that very royal generosity and openness which would constitute Essex's behavior as impious ingratitude rather than a response to compromised status or economic desperation, to be sure. But it also represents, in an intimate setting, the congruence of the publicly acclaimed values of her reign with their "private" expression as personal thrift, piety, openness, fairness, generosity, and humanistic learning. Caught in a moment between state business and devotion, neither she nor her justice of Kent spends a word on merely factious, political, or instrumental reasoning, nor on public appearances. What they are, whether in open streets or private chambers, is what they are; neither plays for an audience.

Above all, Elizabeth's image of a tragedy played over and over again admits what people could see—Essex's so-called popularity of the streets as well as his alliances among the great "houses" of England—while revaluing those undeniable facts as instances of hypocritical *playing* before an audience that could not see the real personal and religious tragedy that such playing represented. The invocation of self-destructive "tragedy" played out between a single player and his God and/or benefactor occludes the appearance of *ressentiment* potential in Lambarde's self-proclaimed station as "common" passing judgment on the fitness of a noble to share the designation of "Gent" and as legal official commenting in lawyerly terms on a cultural subgroup of martial adherents who denounced professional jurists for pettiness and rigor. The anecdote itself represents the private world of Elizabethan officials as characterized by the same mixed values of earnest piety tempered with scholarly disinterest and practicality alloyed with generosity which are so much a part of its public presentations. Elizabeth and Lambarde, at least, should not be mistaken for playing one thing publicly while being another. Rather than calculating factional division, financial advantage, or parliamentary strategy, the two pause between business and prayer to regret one dependent's suicidal self-destruction and to appreciate the contrast provided by the steadfast values "good and honest Lambarde" represents. Their exchanges repeatedly touch on divisive issues articulated in Parliament and the open streets between 1598 and 1601 without getting closer than religion, history, scholarship, and drama: form and silence turning word against word.

The Critic, the Poor Player,
Prince Hamlet,
and the Lady in the Dark

BARBARA HODGDON

I begin by situating the pleasures and dangers of interpretation in a scene of Shakespearean reading. On May 10, 1972, at Queen's University, Belfast, F. R. Leavis is considering two passages from *Othello*. In his prefatory remarks to this lecture, "Reading Out Poetry," he recalls reading Dickens's "Uncommercial Traveller" to Ludwig Wittgenstein, who at one point curtly remarked, "Don't interpret." Noting that Wittgenstein knew that "one can't read out things neutrally," Leavis observes, "what he meant was that he didn't like my interpretation." "Interpret," he admits, is a term he himself tries to avoid: "No clear distinction being made, it means so often what the great Shakespearean actor, say Sir Laurence Olivier, does to Shakespeare."[1] What lies behind his antipathy to performance, Leavis later explains, is that "even if one can imagine [the actor] intelligent, he will, in his accomplished and trained conceit, ignore the poetry, having decided on his own interpretation. He will see only opportunities for elocutionary impressiveness" (p. 263). Instead, Leavis prefers to think of the reader

Parts of this essay circulated in James C. Bulman's 1991 Shakespeare Association of America seminar "Performance as Interpretation," and an earlier version of the last part was read at a 1991 conference, "Shakespeare: Film, Performance, Hypermedia," at MIT. I am grateful to the National Endowment for the Humanities for the support of an NEH Fellowship for College Teachers.

1. F. R. Leavis, "Reading Out Poetry," in *Valuation in Criticism and Other Essays,* ed. G. Singh (Cambridge: Cambridge University Press, 1986), p. 260; subsequent citations appear in the text.

as an ideal executant musician, one "who, knowing it rests with him
to re-create in obedience to what lies in black print on the white sheet
in front of him, devotes all his trained intelligence, sensitiveness, intu-
ition and skill to re-creating, reproducing faithfully what he divines
his composer essentially conceived" (p. 260).[2]

By opposing the self-insistent performer who imposes meanings
on a text to the subservient reader who locates meanings in the precise
letter of the text, Leavis not only collapses the distinctions between
scores and poetic drama but insists on an antitheatrical stance. Neither
the musical analogy nor the mistrust of performance would have come
as any surprise to his auditors at Queen's; his position was familiar
enough. In retrospect, however, targeting Olivier's 1964 performance
as Othello at Britain's National Theatre as the only slightly occluded
antithesis to his own (presumably) antihistrionic "reading out" gives
his lecture a curious recuperative charge. For both Olivier and John
Dexter, the production's director, had based their thinking about
Othello on Leavis's own "Diabolic Intellect and the Noble Hero: or
The Sentimentalist's Othello" (1962), extracts of which, reproduced
in the souvenir program, primed spectators to see the self-deluded
"brutal egotist" the essay describes.[3] Eight years later, Leavis's Belfast
lecture, in which he promises to illustrate how "shifting tone, inflection, distance and attack" (all terms with musical connotations)
contribute to the re-creative fidelity he admires, can be seen as a re-
speaking of Olivier's (extremely musical) Othello which reaffirms
Leavis's own critical practice. Leavis brackets his reading of "It is the
cause; it is the cause, my soul" (5.2.1–22)[4] by remarking that Othello's
"nature" (as man and tragic hero) as well as the theme or essential
situation that makes the play a tragedy occur "locally in this part of the
play, locally in the poetry." Examining the trajectory of the speech, he
links tone to the character's psychological economy and marks the

2. Aptly enough, Leavis's father was a dealer in musical instruments. See Terry
Eagleton, *Literary Theory* (Minneapolis: University of Minnesota Press, 1983), p. 30.
3. Julie Hankey summarizes the debate occasioned by the production, including
Dover Wilson's outrage at Leavis's challenge to A. C. Bradley's time-honored notion
of Othello's dignity, in *Othello, Plays in Performance* (Bristol: Bristol Classical Press,
1987), pp. 109–13. For Leavis's antitheatricality, see Christopher J. McCullough, "The
Cambridge Connection: Towards a Materialist Theatre Practice," in *The Shakespeare
Myth,* ed. Graham Holderness (Manchester: Manchester University Press, 1988), pp.
116–17.
4. References throughout are to *The Riverside Shakespeare,* ed. G. Blakemore Evans
et al. (Boston: Houghton Mifflin, 1974), except where otherwise indicated.

shifts from a "tone of holy horror at the unspeakable obscenity of Desdemona's offence" ("Let me not name it to you, you chaste stars!") to "Yet I'll not shed her blood," which comes as a "recoil . . . at the thought of irrevocable homicide" and elicits a further change to "caressing appreciation"—"Nor scar that whiter skin of hers than snow, / And smooth as monumental alabaster." Leavis's move toward Desdemona's body prompts this comment:

> Well, now, that of course is sensuality; this is an essential psychological observation. I'm not being moral, no, not in the least, at the moment. As a person with feelings and rights to be respected, Desdemona simply doesn't exist for Othello. He knows that she is worthless—this is the final *donnée* for him at the moment. . . . He is not thinking about her as a person at all. . . . It's his own feelings about her person that are in question; these he with noble resolution replaces: "Yet she must die, else she'll betray more men." And before the end of the speech he reinforces this good reason with another—justice. Immediately he dwells on the irrevocableness of what's coming and he moves into an indulgent self-pity. (p. 263)

Although Leavis's use of the present tense suggests that reader and character occupy a common space, his language also opens up a gap between himself as speaking subject (or self) and Othello as object (or other): "he knows," "he is not thinking," and so on. Evoking a scientific discourse ("this is an essential psychological observation") from which he excludes moral judgment ("I'm not being moral, no, not in the least, at the moment") enables Leavis to make Othello's "voluptuous sensuality"[5] intelligible, to confirm his diagnosis of Desdemona's worthlessness. Here, Leavis's critical gesture even overreaches Othello's "poetico-dramatic" one, which accords Desdemona *poetic* value, dissolving her "blood" and "skin" into metaphors for the whole: "light," "cunning'st pattern of excelling nature," "rose," "tree," and, finally, her "balmy breath." For both character and critic, Desdemona (as "person" or "mere body")[6] exists under erasure. And Leavis's reading out further intensifies that erasure, for no Desdemona assists him: she remains in the realm of Leavis/Othello's imaginary, expressible only as a poetic surface.

5. From F. R. Leavis, "Diabolic Intellect and the Noble Hero: or The Sentimentalist's Othello," first published in *Scrutiny* and later in *The Common Pursuit* (London: Chatto and Windus, 1952), p. 130.

6. A distinction Leavis makes in "Diabolic Intellect," p. 150.

At this point, the text of Leavis's lecture reproduces Othello's entire speech, including the editorial stage direction, "Kisses her," which Leavis may or may not have read out. To include the speech here would frame it as a representation of a representation (the published lecture) of a representation (Leavis's reading out) of a representation (a speech from Shakespeare's play, which, as printed in Leavis's text, records several so-called actor's, or in this case critic's, corruptions).[7] By calling attention to these layers of representation but omitting the speech, I want to stress the obvious: that much is withheld from a reader who cannot hear (or see)[8] Leavis's particular shifts of "tone, inflection, movement, and attack." Although reprinting the speech would invite a reader of this essay to produce her or his own reading, that could not recover Leavis "reading as one who reads not only by the ear" (perhaps as G. Wilson Knight read the "noble *Othello* music") "but by the body" (p. 268), even though that body may not be black.[9] Moreover, readers of both Leavis's published lecture and this essay would probably not reread Othello's (already familiar) text but would instead skip from Leavis's initial observations to those that follow his reading out. What commands attention in this context, after all, is the voice—and, as it turns out, the body—of Leavis the critic: "Well, it's plain enough what the nature of the inner conflict is, but Othello, the man of action, is, for all his self-ignorance and, worse, self-deception, impressive, so we can feel the conflict to be in its way tragic. But—well, the 'but' points to what makes our response almost untragically painful—we feel exasperation surely; I think that's the right word. I myself want to kick Othello and he—at the end of the play, I mean—wants to kick himself. But that doesn't, I think, improve one's valuation of him" (p. 264).

"Doing" Othello seems to have done something to Leavis, for after speaking "She wakes," it is as though Leavis himself also awakens. Quickly changing subject positions (if not bodies), he turns from text

7. Although Leavis appears to be reading from the Cambridge edition, edited by Alice Walker and John Dover Wilson (1960), he transposes two words, changing "O balmy breath, that doth almost persuade" to "O balmy breath that almost doth persuade," and substitutes "this" for "that's" in "One more, and this the last." The first is anomalous, his own; the second a familiar textual variant.

8. Cf. Harry Berger, Jr., "We sense how much is withheld from an audience that can only hear and see, how much is occulted in the text they cannot read," in *Imaginary Audition: Shakespeare on Stage and Page* (Berkeley: University of California Press, 1989), p. 149.

9. See G. Wilson Knight, "The *Othello* Music," in *The Wheel of Fire* (London: Methuen, 1949), pp. 97–119.

producer to moralizing spectator, steps away from speaking as Othello and drifts from his pseudoscientific discourse toward what "we" feel for a neo-Aristotelian Othello who suffers but never learns to know himself. Most remarkably, his "but" launches a slangy confession ("I myself want to kick Othello") which evokes the carnivalesque participation of nineteenth-century American music hall audiences Lawrence Levine describes.[10] Leavis clearly constructs Othello as an upper-middle-class, middle-aged egotist of no particular color, yet when he deflects his interventionary response into Othello's own clownlike gesture ("and he . . . wants to kick himself"), that move also conveniently displaces any covert racist burrs onto Othello, who then turns them on himself. Finally, by noting how Othello's "dangerous" habit of self-dramatization enables him to "enjoy a magnificent death in his own private theatre, which is also for the actor the only theatre" (p. 266), Leavis chastises Othello in terms similar to those he used earlier to reprove the self-aggrandizing actor. As the character now emerges in the space of theatricality, the trajectory of Leavis's reading comes full circle. Like the Shakespearean actor, Othello is merely a theatrical body and as such merits less value than the body with textual credentials (Leavis), who remains superior to both.

I begin with this double scene of reading not only to model a critical practice and to deconstruct Leavis's antitheatricality but also to appropriate his essentialized, masculinist reading of character to serve my own interest in gender and the performed and performing body. Reading in Leavis's margins reveals that however insistently he skirts *Othello*'s theatrical (and social) bodies, traces of them keep slipping—or kicking—in; like Desdemona, they give the lie to all attempts at disembodiment. To be sure, I am reading Leavis against what he claims as his own grain—preserving intact Shakespeare's "poeticodramatic felicity" (p. 263) from the actorly excesses of theatrical culture. His province is the autotelic text, transcendent of history and still bearing scars from A. C. Bradley's moralized characterology, which classifies and marks Shakespeare's bodies with the form and pressure of the critic's own time. Although that province occupies a space that recent academic criticism has vacated, it remains influential within British theatrical culture, where Bradleyan characterology and, ironically enough, Leavisite reading strategies undergird the Royal

10. See Lawrence Levine, *Highbrow/Lowbrow* (Cambridge: Harvard University Press, 1988).

Shakespeare Company's rehearsal work, a practice that combines and recombines texts and bodies to textualize character as performance, to make the body readable.[11] Significantly, however, to move from a critical reading to a theatrical performance is to move from the politics of one location to that of another—a shift that any reading practice must take into account.

Since the practice of close reading—associated with producing a self-driven, universalized text—bridges two discursive environments (study and rehearsal room), how, I want to ask, can that practice stretch to encompass both venues? And how can the resulting performance be rearticulated within a materialist matrix that operates as cultural critique? Beginning with Leavis's foundational moment of theatrical disavowal (undoing Olivier's Othello by means of the critical body), my own trajectory of reading moves in two directions to negotiate among several kinds of texts, bodies, and reading practices. First, I want to examine how close reading constructs and accommodates the performing and performed body. Here, the body (and text) in question is Ian McKellen's reading/performance of Macbeth's "Tomorrow, and tomorrow, and tomorrow" (5.4.18–27), which offers a complex, disjunctive instance of close reading doing double work. Then I turn to *Hamlet* and, locating myself more overtly as a reading subject, move from the body of Richard Burbage to that of Mel Gibson, or from "lively player" to "lethal weapon."

DOUBLE, DOUBLE, TOIL AND (SOME) TROUBLE

The context framing Leavis's "performance" at Queen's is not all that different from McKellen's close reading of Macbeth's "Tomorrow" speech followed by a film clip of his enactment, the climax of a 1979 "South Bank Show" which features RSC actors and directors explo-

11. Edward Burns sees the current vogue for books by and about actors as filling the gap where character used to be; see his *Character: Acting and Being on the Pre-Modern Stage* (New York: St. Martin's Press, 1990), pp. 221–23. The RSC directors Peter Hall, Trevor Nunn, and John Barton all name Leavis as the "father" of their textual approach. Barton's *Playing Shakespeare* (London: Methuen, 1984) offers a series of Leavisite master classes on verse speaking which reconstitute anthologies such as William Dodd's "Beauties of Shakespeare" (1752) as performed "chunklets" and which, W. B. Worthen argues, stages not performance but performance criticism. See W. B. Worthen, "Deeper Meanings and Theatrical Technique: The Rhetoric of Performance Criticism," *Shakespeare Quarterly* 40 (1989): 448–50.

ring the company's approach to verse speaking before a studio audience.[12] As exemplary Scrutineers, both performers assume that a character's intelligibility emerges from analyzing his or her speech. Indeed, McKellen might be playing Leavis. But only up to a point, for while Leavis extrudes the actor, replacing him with a reader obedient to the "composer's" conception, McKellen restores the actor's centrality. Acting Shakespeare at its best, he observes, occurs when "the actor is the playwright and the character simultaneously"—a move that draws Shakespeare, character, and actor into a space of shared intentionality. If such a fusion can be justified when the playwright is (as many conjecture Shakespeare was) the director, then, arguably, McKellen's particular politics of location—wearing the Royal Shakespeare Company's mantle—amounts to the next best thing, insofar as it authorizes the actor to see his or her craft as serving the playwright's, and the play's, intentions.

The sharpest distinction between Leavis's reading out Othello and McKellen's double reading of Macbeth, however, is one of textual form: the difference between the body in print and on video, between a specializing technology of language production in which body is a symbolic sign and one that, by recording image as well as speech, reproduces body as an indexical sign of "the real." But an equally crucial distinction affects McKellen's reading out, for the body that performs intellectual work is and is not the same as the performing body. That is, the initial video segment (McKellen's textual analysis) was recorded three years *after* his 1976 performance (in Trevor Nunn's production for Stratford's The Other Place) was filmed by Thames Television. By reconstructing these two bodies in time, the videotext fabricates the illusion of a seamless union between the critically produced text and its theatrical performance,[13] priming viewers to see the results of one in the other. If it is possible to decode McKellen's performing body by means of his prefatory analysis, then "close reading" can encompass both. Now, I am not suggesting that McKellen invents out of whole cloth an account that conforms to what he actu-

12. McKellen repeated his double reading of Macbeth in his immensely popular one-man show, *Acting Shakespeare,* which widely toured the United States during the late 1980s.

13. Cf. Gayatri Spivak, who characterizes the preface as "a pretense at writing *before* a text that one must have read *before* the preface can be written," in her introduction to Jacques Derrida's *Of Grammatology* (Baltimore: Johns Hopkins University Press, 1974), pp. ix–x.

ally did in the theater. Without question he attempts to clarify his preparation process, even if that *actual* process (at both individual and collaborative levels) remains outside this reconstitutive representation.[14] But the "South Bank Show," eager to demonstrate how the actor transforms one kind of work into another, not only forestalls reading McKellen against his own grain but privileges a relationship between text and performance that invites spectators to hear and see what they are told to expect. Such prescience, of course, figures famously in *Macbeth,* especially for Macbeth himself. Indeed, in reconstructing this history of the performed speech, McKellen acts like a weyward sister. By prophesying a future he then performs, he need not ride out to visit the witches; his close reading speaks them from within.

McKellen begins by characterizing Macbeth's speech as a "description of total blackness, total despair"—phrases that evoke Bradleyan resonances[15] and also dovetail with the New Critical notion that poetic utterance contains a core structure or essence. And even though McKellen commits the "heresy of paraphrase," he does so only in order to deny it: "It isn't enough just . . . to put that quality of despair into the voice and . . . follow the rhythms. . . . You have to . . . have analyzed [the speech] in rehearsal totally so that your imagination, being fed by the concrete metaphors [and] images . . . can then feed through into the body, into gesture, timbre of voice, into eyelids, into every part of the actor's makeup so that it seems . . . he is making it up as he goes along, although the actor of course knows that he isn't." What Leavis called "reading . . . by the body," McKellen describes as a process of *incorporation*[16] through which the text, feeding the imagination, is then absorbed and channeled into the body, where it is made visible, repatterned into elaborate physiological sequences of muscle and nerve, flesh and blood. Text, one might deduce from his statements, both disciplines and energizes the body. Paradoxically, of

14. Changing the segments' temporal order might enable viewers to make different connections between critical and performance work; VCR technology makes testing this hypothesis possible.

15. Of the first two lines, Bradley remarks: "He has no time now to feel. Only, as he thinks of the morrow when time to feel will come—if anything comes, the vanity of all hopes and forward-looking sinks deep into his soul with an infinite weariness." A. C. Bradley, *Shakespearean Tragedy* (1904; rpt. Greenwich, Conn.: Fawcett, 1967), pp. 202–3.

16. My thanks to Lorraine Helms for suggesting this term and for comments on drafts of this essay.

course, the spontaneity McKellen insists on ("making it up as he goes along") depends on automating the physiological work words do so that it becomes second nature, permitting the actor's physical performance to be (more or less precisely) replicated night after night.[17]

If, as Catherine Belsey argues, iambic pentameter "simulates a voice expressing the self 'behind' the speech," an illusion of interiority heightened by the convention of soliloquy,[18] McKellen comes closest to Macbeth's "authentic" self when, by rigorously anatomizing the soliloquy's prosody, he observes how short lines ("She should have died hereafter"), gear shifts between regular and irregular blank verse lines ("There would have been a time for such a word. / Tomorrow, and tomorrow, and tomorrow"), and the frisson of particular words within a line, especially in a terminal position ("To the last syllable of recorded *time*"), give the actor access to Macbeth's psychological economy. Guiding listeners to *sound* the psychological by means of its physical traces,[19] McKellen's reading glosses his enactment perfectly. As though mirroring the way the speech accumulates—and uses up— temporal references, McKellen-speaking-Macbeth takes his time. His voice overstays each line ending, marks midline sentence breaks, lingers over the *m* in the repeated "tomorrow," further slowing the line, ekes out the monosyllables and consonants of "*Creeps* in this *petty pace* from *day* to *day*," sounds each syllable of *syl-la-bell* in "To the last syllable of recorded time," and halts abruptly after the line, as though its thought stops speech. Throughout, his delivery seems paced to an inner metronome, gauged to expose versification as yet another artifice of time.

As he articulates the "to-be-played-ness"[20] of Macbeth's speech,

17. Cf. Joseph Roach, *The Player's Passion* (Newark: University of Delaware Press, 1985), pp. 16–17.

18. Catherine Belsey, *The Subject of Tragedy* (London: Methuen, 1985), p. 43. On soliloquy, Philip C. McGuire reminds me that the Folio gives no indication that Seyton exits after telling Macbeth, "The Queene (my Lord) is dead"; if Seyton remains on-stage, his presence calls into question a fundamental soliloquy convention: that the character giving it is alone. Although McGuire's comment points to how traditionally ascribed conventions need to be rethought in terms of material bodies, because McKellen, like most Macbeths, *plays* the speech as "soliloquy" and because such playing (even if Seyton were present) sustains the illusion of interiority, I use the term.

19. Cf. Stanislavski, "The psychological is the physical," quoted in Roach, *Player's Passion,* p. 205.

20. Cf. Laura Mulvey's "to-be-looked-at-ness," in "Visual Pleasure and Narrative Cinema" (1975), in *Feminism and Film Theory,* ed. Constance Penley (New York: Routledge, 1988), pp. 57–68.

McKellen speaks from a liminal space slightly removed from the character, looking in. At one point, however, it is as though he opens a door
to reveal a closetful of bodies waiting in the wings. Noting that the
repeated "tomorrow" becomes "a nonsense word if you say it three
. . . or twenty times," he associates such wordplay with "the lack of
meaning that Macbeth detects in his life" through the figure of "a kid
skipping"—possibly his own remembered body but nonetheless one
ironically pertinent to Macbeth, who "has no children" (4.3.216). Two
lines later, the kid, together with the idea of senselessness, reemerges,
now reembodied as the fool ("And all our yesterdays have lighted
fools / The way to dusty death"). "What," says McKellen, "is the image I must have clearly in my mind so that I can get the right emotion
of despair?" He goes on: "A fool is—what?—a village idiot?—wandering along a country lane with . . . a guttering candle. 'Fool' is a pun, of
course. Fools, like Lear's Fool, Feste in *Twelfth Night*, are professional
entertainers, and that will be relevant in a moment, and I have to contain in my mind as I say the word that it is a pun and see two sorts of
fools. That line is completed with the . . . harsh rhythm of 'Out, out,
brief candle': the fool's candle has caught a gust of wind and is blown
out and he collapses into a dusty death in the unmade road of Elizabethan England." Who is speaking here? Voicing the actor's part,
McKellen in his simplified explanation of Stanislavski's psychotech-
nique of affective memory[21] ("I have to . . . see two sorts of fools")
mystifies the actor's work while masking the presence of another
voice. For by locating both village idiot and fool in an Elizabethan-
Jacobean past, McKellen not only situates the speech as a transparent
channel to the playwright's imaginative field but also generates the
illusion that he can think (if not speak) like Shakespeare himself.

In this case, thinking like Shakespeare also means speaking as the
soliloquy's historian or as its historicizing critic. After locating the
fool's double image in social as well as theatrical bodies, McKellen's
trajectory of reading fixes on the fool's candle, which prompts him

21. "We cannot directly act on our emotion, but we can prod our creative fantasy
in a necessary path, and fantasy, as scientific psychologists have discovered, stirs up
our *affective memory*, calling up from its secret depths, beyond reach of consciousness,
elements of already experienced emotions, and regroups them to correspond with the
images which arise in us." Constantin Stanislavski, "Art of the Actor and Director,"
in *Stanislavski's Legacy: A Collection of Comments on a Variety of Aspects of an Actor's Art
and Life,* trans. Elizabeth Reynolds Hapgood (New York: Theatre Arts Books, 1958),
p. 187. Stanislavski's formulation closely approximates Eliot's famous "objective correlative."

to remark that "the last candle or light we saw in the play was Lady Macbeth's candle in the sleepwalking scene, and she's dead," and to connect her death[22] to those of the fool, the village idiot, Macbeth himself, and (waxing thematically prophetic) "everybody's death." With the body count elevated to universals, he turns to the play's theatrical venue to note that "about the time Shakespeare wrote *Macbeth*, candles were being used in indoor theaters" and to gloss "walking shadow" with "walking gentleman"—a phrase still used to denote an actor who plays walk-on parts. Of all the information McKellen supplies, these comments seem most after-the-fact, designed more to fill up analytic space than to reconstruct the logic of his performance. But once he returns to the speech, remarking that "life is not even a walking gentleman, he's a 'walking shadow,' less than even the meanest player," his digressions come into focus. For at precisely the point where Macbeth's soliloquy evokes the player's body and diminishes its power, McKellen reasserts his own, which includes naming himself: "Shakespeare is making the vasty concepts of time very concrete . . . not just to Macbeth but to the actor who is playing Macbeth, because we are now talking about players, and the audience, who know they are an audience, know that McKellen playing Macbeth is an actor, and they are beginning to be drawn in to Macbeth's dilemma as he relates it to a player, an actor." Undeniably, the soliloquy's logic makes the seam joining character to actor highly visible. As Macbeth the character melts, thaws, and resolves into the body of the "poor player," the slippage between character and actor exposes the theatrical illusion and, in a familiar paradox drawn from postromantic psychopathology, intensifies a spectator's awareness of (as McKellen puts it) "Macbeth's dilemma." Perhaps this soliloquy's most striking feature is how it exchanges social for theatrical bodies; certainly McKellen's analysis, which introduces the idiot and the fool only to "kill" them off, makes the point. Whereas Macbeth's earlier "My way of life / Is fall'n into the sere, the yellow leaf" mentions "honor, love, obedience, troops of friends" (5.2.22–25), the only social space left by the end of "Tomorrow" is that of the player, whose occupation, according to Elizabethan and Jacobean antitheatrical commentators,

---

22. Arguably, Macbeth's speech meditates on and deconstructs the Lady's "I feel now / The future in the instant" (1.5.55–56). On repetitions of "hereafter," see Stephen Booth, *"King Lear," "Macbeth," Indefinition, and Tragedy* (New Haven: Yale University Press, 1983), pp. 94–96.

was (in a curious echo of the soliloquy's own skewed chronology) a misuse of time.

But if these moments figure a radically undetermined identity for character and performer alike, McKellen's language works to validate such indeterminacy. Consider, in the passage quoted earlier, how that hegemonic "we" cuts two ways. On the one hand, the context invites reading it as an inclusive pronoun joining speaker to audience; on the other, it just as plausibly gathers up Shakespeare, Macbeth, and the actor playing Macbeth in a "cry of players" where the actor ("McKellen playing Macbeth") gets top billing. Given the direction of McKellen's analysis, one might anticipate further connections between his insistent self-dramatizing of the actor, the player "who struts and frets his hour upon the stage," and the "tale / Told by an idiot." Much like Leavis, whose comments on Othello's "dangerous" self-dramatizing set him apart from and allowed him to condemn both character and actor, McKellen also steps away, but to a rather different position— that of a Jacobean spectator who recalls "King Cambyses, Marlovian regular verse, and people who do stamp out the rhythm as they parade." Read historically, his reference to the strutting player attacks an out-of-fashion acting style characteristic of Edward Alleyn, famous for his bombastic Tamburlaine, but McKellen does not make that precise association. Instead, his move into the audience seems designed to suggest that the actor's powerful part, including the idiot's tale, can be ratified only by a spectator. Yet both his move to the spectator's position and his gloss on "idiot," for which he reaches back to the fool "walking along the country lane with the candle that went out," also evade the possibility that the strutting player, the idiot/fool, and Macbeth occupy the same space. And that evasion gathers up contradictions when McKellen's performance wrests power from powerlessness to turn "Signifying nothing" into its opposite.

In closing, McKellen disavows his critical role—and potentially those of spectators and readers—to take sole ownership of Shakespeare's "poetico-dramatic felicity," a stance opposite to but no less elitist than Leavis's: "I must have all that in my mind . . . not so that you, the audience, can understand those complexities, because I'm not giving a lecture. I think the poetry, the rhythm, and all those devices that Shakespeare uses are not for the audience's benefit; they are for the actor's, so that having absorbed them into his heart and his mind he can then express them with all the other things at his command, such as his body, his facial expression, and . . . the way the production is blocked, the way the scenery is painted, and the way the lights are lit." Mise-en-*corps*, it seems, provides a center for mise-en-scène. Although McKellen does suggest that the performing body is part of a larger sign system, any more specific mention of how one might decipher a theatrical event is subsumed within the context of a workshop devoted to verse speaking. But by insisting that performance constitutes a signifying practice that differs from close reading ("I'm not giving a lecture"), McKellen implies that a spectator "reads" through or beyond the actor's expressive body, which has absorbed and transformed "the poetry, the rhythm, and all those devices Shakespeare uses" to *theatrical* meaning. Although the "South Bank Show's" format may propose an organic relationship between analysis and performance, the ensuing film clip reveals that the performance speaks more than the close reading knows. Even at the level of prosody, where the two are least disjunctive, little McKellen has said anticipates either his chilling vocal tones or the pauses that dare listeners to stay with him as he bends the soliloquy's syntax into unfamiliar shapes.

Given this overdetermined context, one possible response is wonder: first at how McKellen read so much "in" the text, and then at how his performed Macbeth, Ariel-like, "flamed [further] amazement." But I am less concerned with such seemingly innocent responses than with negotiating an interface between literary and theatrical reading practices. Following McKellen, I would insist on a distinction, similar to that between reading and rereading, between experiencing and analyzing a performance. And because Shakespeare's text—however indeterminate that entity has recently become—precedes any theatrical enactment, the means and mechanisms (including close reading) whereby that text has been, and is, "productively activated" condition and colonize the analysis of any performance.[23] Reviews of the stage production offer a case in point.

23. For "productive activation," see Tony Bennett, "Texts, Readers, Reading Formations" (1983), reprinted in *Modern Literary Theory: A Reader,* ed. Philip Rice and Patricia Waugh (London: Routledge, 1989), pp. 206–20. Anthony B. Dawson argues for distinguishing critical from theatrical maneuvers in "The Impasse over the Stage," *English Literary Renaissance* 21 (1991): 309–27. Yet he paints himself into the "impasse" of his title by selecting and focusing his evidence in order to claim that a particular "reading effect" of *Hamlet* resists performance and that a particular "scene of viewing" in *As You Like It* remains unknowable, a phenomenon that "cannot be read or written"(see pp. 322–26). His move mystifies theater or, at the very least, turns it into a

Without exception, reviewers were alert to McKellen's expressive body: the sleeked-back hair that gave his Macbeth "a reptilian look"; his "quivering facial muscles and back-of-the-throat voice"; his "tiger-ish spareness"; his intense watchfulness of himself and others, making him seem "doubly alert."[24] Curiously enough, these phrases figure McKellen's Macbeth as an animal: by creating a phenomenological distance between the character's inhumanity and the more humane spectator, each says, "I am not like Macbeth." Insofar as such re-sponses speak to whatever physical threats a Macbeth may trigger, they could be thought of as attributable to McKellen's acting—a *the-atrical* effect. Other critics, however, focused more expressly on how his performance reproduced the ideology of the text—and the charac-ter—as conceived by the dominant literary culture. Noting Mc-Kellen's "alert and sensitive" hands, which became, toward the end, "lifeless . . . gone, with his conscience and his sensibilities, into de-cay," Robert Cushman relies (as McKellen himself had done) on a Bradleyan moral characterology. For Michael Billington, "And make our faces vizards to our hearts" was the central emblem of McKellen's performance, which revealed "the gradual tearing away of Macbeth's public mask until we reach the driven psychopath beneath."[25] Perhaps most conditioned by literary understanding, Billington (again, like McKellen) views the actor's expressive body as a direct channel to Shakespeare's language: McKellen's Macbeth succeeds because his performance not only evokes a particularly resonant line but makes it *visible*.

Might imitating McKellen's own move to import a range of social and cultural signifiers "into" the text produce a less overdetermined ideological complicity between performance and literary, or exclu-sively "Shakespearean," reading formations?[26] Gareth Lloyd Evans,

---

purely phenomenological event where "being there" is all. For all his inventiveness, the insistence on the "thisness" of performance not only resembles a New Critical move but protects the theatrical event from theoretical intervention.

24. In order, the comments are from John Barber, *Daily Telegraph*, September 10, 1976, and Gareth Lloyd Evans, "*Macbeth*: 1946–1980 at Stratford-upon-Avon," in *Fo-cus on Macbeth*, ed. John Russell Brown (London: Routledge & Kegan Paul, 1982), p. 108. Although obvious distinctions separate theatrical and cinematic events, the 1976 The Other Place production and the film shared an intense focus on the actors. See Richard David, *Shakespeare in the Theatre* (Cambridge: Cambridge University Press, 1978), p. 85.

25. Robert Cushman, *Observer*, September 12, 1976; Michael Billington, *Guardian*, September 17, 1976.

26. See Bennett, "Texts, Readers, Reading Formations."

for instance, mentions how McKellen's hairstyle and somewhat slanted eyes gave him a "Japanese look," an otherness reflected in the production's stylistics, which he describes as combining the physical ritualism and inner reflection associated with Eastern theatrical culture.[27] Although Evans does not mention it, the most obvious reference point is Akira Kurosawa's film *Throne of Blood* (1957), a highly formal rendering of Shakespeare's narrative through the conventions of the Japanese samurai film, scroll paintings, and No drama.[28] Whether or not Kurosawa's film directly influenced Nunn's production, the reception of late twentieth-century theatrical events is inescapably embedded in a wide network of visual and aural discourses. Moreover, within the present-day cultural dominant of postmodernity, the video, which circulates widely within the academic community, not only is always already contiguous with other cultural products but also generates meaning in relation to whatever signifying practices it shares with them.

Situating McKellen's performance of Macbeth's "Tomorrow" speech within such a variable matrix jostles loose its status as high culture and also suggests how review discourse, by locating the performance in relation to inherited reading habits and institutionalized categories, protects that status. To explore the relations between McKellen's Macbeth and just one intertextual field outside such cultural apparatuses, consider how the signs reviewers associated with animalism—"tigerish spareness," "sleeked-back" hair, and "reptilian" black leather—evoke the "spare, lean, temporary" cyberpunk male body; how McKellen's chilling voice can be articulated with the "wounded, fatalistic" vocal tones of ambiguous figures such as Deckard (Harrison Ford) in Ridley Scott's *Blade Runner* (1982). Activating such relations invites reading McKellen's performing body as a sign of masculinity in crisis, which in turn points to how there are always differences in the historical surfaces or bodies on which the content of a text can appear. Just as the cyberpunk male body, as theorized by Andrew Ross, figured that crisis for the 1980s, within that decade scholars such as Janet Adelman and Jonathan Goldberg identified similar contours in the psychoanalytic dimensions of Macbeth's character

27. Evans, "*Macbeth:* 1946–1980," p. 109.

28. On Kurosawa's film, see Jack Jorgens, *Shakespeare on Film* (Bloomington: Indiana University Press, 1977), pp. 153–60, and Peter S. Donaldson, *Shakespearean Films / Shakespearean Directors* (Winchester, Mass.: Unwin Hyman, 1990), pp. 69–92.

and the historical contexts of Shakespeare's play.[29] Locating the body
as the site on which this crisis *shows* and is played out is the point at
which critical and theatrical moves intersect; by aligning the two, I
argue that any performance carries a history of reading relations on
its back.

In McKellen's close reading, the fool's candle serves as a focus for
social and theatrical bodies (the village idiot, Lady Macbeth, Macbeth
himself); in the videotext, the close-up of his face, privileging his
deadened voice and empty eyes, is its analogue, the condensed sign,
as Gilles Deleuze and Félix Guattari write, of the corporeal.[30] In film
or video, of course, the close-up, which treats the face as a landscape
or screen, is the symbolic space of illusionistic interiority, the axis of
subjectification. Here, the soliloquy videotext renders the textual
move that theatricalizes the performing body with particular intensity. "Fools" brings a contemptuous snarl to McKellen's face; his
blank eyes, staring straight out, overcode the face as a map of "nothing." When he mentions the actor who "struts and frets his hour upon
the stage, / And then is heard no more," a downward glance seems to
mark the fracture from character to "poor player," an effect intensified
by the graininess of my own videoprint, which heightens the illusion
that "Macbeth" is dissolving into a theatrical (or in this case an elec-
tronic) surface; abstracted into white patches and shining black holes,
the performing body shrinks to the limit-figure of a face to register
presence as absence of meaning, the death of the subject. Ultimately,
of course, Macbeth escapes face altogether, dismantles all facializations
of power. As the "Tomorrow" soliloquy ends ("Signifying nothing"),
McKellen breaks the last word into two ("no . . . thing"), anticipating
Macbeth's eventual disembodiment in the play's last scene, where the
final sign of his character is the property head, the literal "false face"
that joins "nothing" to the signifying theatrical body. In an early scene
Duncan remarks, "There's no art / To find the mind's construction in

29. See Ian Hunter, "Reading Character," *Southern Review* 16 (1988): 228–33; Andrew Ross, "Cyberpunk in Boystown," in *Strange Weather: Culture, Science, and Technology in the Age of Limits* (London: Verso, 1991), pp. 152–53; Janet Adelman, *Suffocating
Mothers* (London: Routledge, 1992), pp. 130–64; and Jonathan Goldberg, "Specula-
tions: *Macbeth* and Source," in *Shakespeare Reproduced: The Text in History and Ideology*,
ed. Jean E. Howard and Marion F. O'Connor (London: Methuen, 1987), pp. 242–64.

30. Gilles Deleuze and Félix Guattari, "Year Zero: Faciality," in *A Thousand Plateaus: Capitalism and Schizophrenia*, trans. Brian Massumi (Minneapolis: University of
Minnesota Press, 1987), pp. 167–91.

the face" (1.4.11–12). McKellen's Macbeth gives his naïveté the lie. In fact there is an art that does just that. It is called theater.

TAKING UP THE BODIES

Among Shakespeare's plays, *Hamlet* offers the most precise instructions on what the actor's performing body *ought* to do. Indeed, Hamlet's advice to the players has often been read as giving transparent access to early modern theatrical practice. Moreover, although both *A Midsummer Night's Dream* and *Love's Labor's Lost* rehearse the pleasures and dangers of amateur theatricals, *Hamlet* is one of only two Shakespearean plays (*Taming of the Shrew* is the other) that bear witness to and include material evidence of *professional* acting troupes—the "little eyases" (Children of the Chapel) and the traveling players. Much of that evidence suggests that players were anarchic and unreliable and that the process of performance itself was especially treacherous—circumstances that *Hamlet*'s three texts reflect.[31] By according Q1 (1603) and Folio (1623) theatrical provenance and identifying Q2 (1604; 1605) as a *literary* text, the Oxford editors validate distinctions between literary and theatrical cultures which continue to play out the competition between a culture of print and a culture of performance that Lynda Boose associates with the turn of the seventeenth century and that still marks the play.[32] Fixing texts in such configurations, of course, also fixes how each writes the gendered body. Yet, as a selective history of the reading relations between *Hamlet*'s literary and theatrical bodies suggests, neither is especially stable, nor is it easy to lock each into a particular space.

Reading early modern theatrical gossip uncovers some fragmentary

31. On rethinking mimesis in *Hamlet,* see Robert Weimann, "Mimesis and *Hamlet,*" in *Shakespeare and the Question of Theory,* ed. Patricia Parker and Geoffrey Hartman (New York: Methuen, 1985), pp. 275–91. For a critique of New Historicist analyses of a powerful theater, see Paul Yachnin, "The Powerless Theatre," *English Literary Renaissance* 21 (1991): 49–74; on *Hamlet*'s play-within-the-play, see especially pp. 57–58.

32. See *William Shakespeare, A Textual Companion,* ed. Stanley Wells and Gary Taylor, with John Jowett and William Montgomery (Oxford: Clarendon Press, 1987), pp. 396–402; and Lynda E. Boose, "The 1599 Bishop's Ban and Renaissance Pornography," in *Enclosure Acts in Early Modern England,* ed. Richard Burt and John Archer (Ithaca: Cornell University Press, 1994). My thanks to Boose for sending me her work in manuscript.

traces of body—and voice—surrounding the performances of *Hamlet's* initial configurations. In the preface to Robert Greene's *Menaphon,* Thomas Nashe remarks that "English *Seneca* read by candlelight . . . will afford you whole *Hamlets*—I should say handfuls—of tragical speeches"; and Thomas Lodge, an apparent eyewitness of the so-called Ur-*Hamlet,* writes of a devil appearing "as pale as the vizard of the ghost, which cried so miserably at the Theatre, like an oyster-wife, 'Hamlet, revenge.'"[33] Despite associating *Hamlet* with what they perceive as stale conventions, Nashe and Lodge circulate some of its signifiers as satirical anecdotes, providing evidence of how quickly the play moved outside the space of theatrical discourse. As William Empson argues, such comments may have shaped Shakespeare's (probable) revision of the "old" play and, I would add, forged the reading rules for a "new" *Hamlet* more suited to changing dramatic tastes.[34] Some have thought that *The Hystorie of Hamblet* (1608), an anonymous English translation of the Belleforest tale acknowledged as one of Shakespeare's sources, reflects contemporary performances of this "new" play, largely because it incorporates phrases from Shakespeare's text and links them to physical actions. In the closet scene, for example, Polonius hides "behind the hangings" into which Hamblet thrusts his sword, cries out, "A rat, a rat!" and, later, pulls the dead body "out by the heels." If this description does indeed rely on theatrical memory, it is tempting to conjecture that *Hystorie* also records details of Gertrude's performance and reveals how its author, perhaps betraying his own (and the culture's) aversion to incest, reads her body to moralize her eloquent gesture: "Having long time fixed her eyes upon Hamblet . . . at the last [she] embrac[ed] him in her arms (with the like love that a virtuous mother may or can use to kiss and entertain her own child)."[35]

Admittedly, reconstructing what might be called an early modern reading formation from such relics resembles an attempt to legitimate

---

33. See *Works of Thomas Nashe,* ed. R. B. McKerrow (1904–10), with supplementary notes by F. P. Wilson (Oxford: Oxford University Press, 1958), 3:315–16; and Geoffrey Bullough, *Narrative and Dramatic Sources of Shakespeare* (London: Routledge and Kegan Paul, 1958–73), 7:24.

34. See William Empson, "Hamlet," in *Essays on Shakespeare* (Cambridge: Cambridge University Press, 1986), pp. 79–136. Mining much of the same evidence I rehearse, Empson focuses on the process of making an "old" play new again; like my reading, his, which imagines the cultural contexts of *Hamlet*'s first audiences, has to do with what I call a reading formation.

35. See Bullough, *Narrative and Dramatic Sources,* 7:98.

a bastard child. But in terms of resurrecting Hamlet's performing body, readers may reach toward a less cryptic or problematic territory. For one thing, Shakespeare's *Hamlet* dates from a moment when the Lord Chamberlain's Men had eliminated the exaggerated affectations associated with strutting players and achieved an aesthetic of "life-like" action (inaccurately labeled "Elizabethan naturalism") which made a "false / And acted passion" capable of drawing "true tears." This "new" style was especially associated with the company's star actor, Richard Burbage, whose contemporaries consistently praised his "lively" playing and his mastery of telling gesture: gallants, so the story goes, copied the way his Richard III sheathed and resheathed his knife. According to editorial narratives, *Hamlet* bears particular traces of Burbage's voice and body: he has been held responsible for Hamlet's habit of repeating words, the elaborative trait so peculiar to the character.[36] Some have even read Gertrude's "He's fat and scant of breath" (5.2.287) as an accurate description of the famous actor. But, although Burbage's portrait certainly represents a man of substantial girth, editors, by glossing Gertrude's "fat" as "sweaty" and her behavior as "maternal solicitude," protect his ideal body image, silently attributing its deflation to the woman's part.[37] More pertinently, Burbage's anonymous elegist singles out his playing of "young Hamlet" and "old Hieronimo"—evidence of his flexibility in portraying characters of various ages which also lashes together roles and plays linked by genre signs into a father-son revenger act. Yet the moment in Burbage's "personation" of Hamlet his elegist most admires was not Hamlet's final revenge but his leap into Ophelia's grave, "Suiting the person which he seemed to have / Of a sad lover with so true an eye, / That there, I would have sworn, he meant to die."[38] Although being able to negotiate that leap argues for Burbage's fitness, what is more to the point is that the elegist identifies his ability to convey a social stereotype and to counterfeit dying as the memorable characteristics of his Hamlet.

Tracing these vestiges of Hamlet's body opens up a gap between the early modern spectator's posthumous praise for the "sad lover's"

36. See Andrew Gurr, *The Shakespearean Stage, 1574–1642* (Cambridge: Cambridge University Press, 1980), pp. 110–11, 111–12.

37. See, respectively, *The Riverside Shakespeare* and *Hamlet,* ed. G. R. Hibbard (Oxford: Clarendon Press, 1987).

38. For the elegy, see E. K. Chambers, *The Elizabethan Stage* (Oxford: Oxford University Press, 1923), 2:309.

physical body and the late twentieth-century critical preoccupation
with Hamlet's intellectual dilemma, his subjectivity and interiority.
Yet perhaps the two are not so far apart after all. For that leap into
the grave coincides with the moment when Hamlet gives himself his
father's name, identifies his nationality, and, arguably, declares his
kingship: "This is I, / Hamlet the Dane" (5.1.247–48). It would be
convenient for my argument to assume that Burbage was also at least
partially responsible for the so-called corruptions in Q1's "To be or
not to be" soliloquy,[39] the speech that epitomizes Hamlet's self-ques-
tioning and has indeed come to stand for the play. All that can be said
with any certainty, however, is that Q1, thought to be constructed by
a reporter with the help of an actor (or actors) who played minor roles,
may record the disruptive improvisations characteristic of early modern performance. Indeed, until the 1980s, Q1 had been considered a
text not worth reading closely, one that not only lacks the "poetico-
dramatic felicity" Leavis so much admired but falls apart under
scrutiny.[40]

To pursue these disruptions and perceived lacks a bit further, I want
to consider five lines of Hamlet's "To be or not to be" soliloquy, beginning with its more familiar Folio guise:

> For who would beare the Whips and Scornes of time,
> The Oppressors wrong, the poore man's Contumely,
> The pangs of dispriz'd love, the Lawes delay,
> The insolence of Office, and the Spurnes
> That patient merit of the unworthy takes. . . .
>   (TLN 1724–28)

39. On "soliloquy" as a term, see note 18. As with Macbeth's "Tomorrow," Hamlet's "To be or not to be" is, strictly speaking, not a soliloquy, since Ophelia remains
onstage, and Claudius and Polonius overhear his words. Philip McGuire argues that
"if the 'To be' speech is a soliloquy, it is one because we—all who perform, watch, and
read *Hamlet*—have made and continue to make it one, privileging that option from
among those the play allows and marginalizing all others" (private correspondence).

40. G. R. Hibbard, the Oxford editor, concludes that the reporter "failed to reconstruct the speech because he had never properly understood it" (*The Oxford Shakespeare
Hamlet*, p. 85). Hibbard's comment is fairly typical: he seems to assume that, had he
himself been there, he would have produced a better text, one that does not incapacitate
the poetry. Recent attention to multiple-text plays has invited a reconsideration of
Q1; see especially the essays in *The Hamlet First Published (Q1, 1603): Origins, Forms,
Intertextualities*, ed. Thomas Clayton (Newark: University of Delaware Press, 1992),
including one by Hibbard, "The Chronology of the Three Substantive Texts of Shakespeare's *Hamlet*," pp. 79–89, in which, doubting the accuracy of his earlier edition, he
concludes that "it looks more likely that Q1 preceded F rather than vice versa" (p. 89).

Quite unlike Hamlet's other soliloquies in its generalizing, universal matrix of referentiality, the Folio text seems constructed to include a spectator—whether Q1's "the ignorant" or F's "groundling"—more likely to have experienced such oppressions than Prince Hamlet, who suffers none of these particular wrongs, however "out of joint" his time may be. In contrast, Q1's soliloquy patterns itself after the others (in both Q1 and F) by mentioning much more specific material conditions, as well as particular social bodies:

> Who'ld bear the scorns and flattery of the world,
> Scorned by the right rich, the rich cursed of the poor?
> The widow being oppressed, the orphan wrong'd,
> The taste of hunger, or a tyrant's reign,
> And thousand more calamities besides. . . .
>
> (sig. D4^v–E1^r)

Although accepting the strand of bibliographical invention that locates F as prior to Q1 and attributes Q1 to an actor's or reporter's faulty memory can account for changes in the more broadly inclusive references as "misreadings," it does not explain the sudden appearance of social identities—the oppressed widow, the wronged orphan—so pertinent to Hamlet and *Hamlet*. That would require imagining Q1's reporters as deconstructing or, better, psychoanalysing F to make the bodies it represses readable—in other words, behaving much like McKellen does when he brings forward the skipping kid, the village idiot, and the out-of-fashion player to flesh out his reading of "Tomorrow." And pursuing that strand of explanation, of course, circles back to resituate Q1's mention of particular bodies within a process of theatrical quotation.[41]

Characterizing Q1 as giving a "crude sense of the real thing," Harley Granville-Barker calls it the "sort of thing which, recollection failing, anybody familiar with Elizabethan theater could improvise out of the scraps and ends of plays floating in his memory."[42] Curiously

41. Since I am neither a bibliographer nor an editor, I stand outside the fluctuating opinions over textual sequence; I am interested only in reading Q1 and F in terms of how each writes the performing body. References to F and Q are from, respectively, *The Norton Facsimile: The First Folio of Shakespeare*, ed. Charlton Hinman (New York: W. W. Norton, 1968), and *Shakespeare's Plays in Quarto*, ed. Michael J. B. Allen and Kenneth Muir (Berkeley: University of California Press, 1981).

42. Harley Granville-Barker, *Preface to Hamlet* (1946; rpt. New York: Hill and Wang, 1957), p. 173.

enough, *Henry V,* which preceded *Hamlet* in the Lord Chamberlain's
Men's repertory, also lashes widows and orphans together, albeit in a
more threatening context, when Exeter, acting as Henry's ambassa-
dor, warns the King of France that the coming war will "[turn] the
widows' tears, the orphans' cries, / The dead men's blood, the 'prived
maidens' groans" on his head (2.4.105–7). Shakespeare's plays, of
course, often echo or repeat themselves, as in Lear's "Crack nature's
moulds, all germains spill at once" (3.2.8) and Macbeth's "Of nature's
[germains] tumble all together / Even till destruction sicken" (4.1.59–
60). But since any search for origins or influence can be ultimately
futile and misleading,[43] and since *Hamlet*'s actor/reporter may (as yet
another editorial narrative goes) be "bringing in stray phrases"[44] from
a non-Shakespearean play or simply improvising, I am less concerned
with thinking the relations between *Henry V* and Q1 *Hamlet* than with
problematizing those editorial accounts by turning to the relations between the social and theatrical bodies they inscribe. How might the
connection between widows and orphans rehearsed in Q1 *Hamlet,* in
Henry V, and also in Sonnets 9 and 97 trope a historical disenfranchisement acutely particular to early modern social realities?

When, in the 1991 film *The Addams Family,* Anjelica Huston's Mor-
ticia Addams murmurs, "Widows and orphans: we need more of
them," to a charity volunteer for the Widows and Orphans Society,
she could be alluding to circumstances that pervaded early seventeenth-century family life. Although the existing historical evidence
is not without contradictions, women's legal rights as widows were
limited to whatever claims were written down in the marriage contract. A widow, however, could also be barred from her dower rights,
and the medieval common-law right to a share of her husband's personal estate was effective only in parts of England, a situation that
remained unchanged until late in the seventeenth century. Yet in exer-
cising administrative control over their dead husbands' estates, many
widows had a uniquely independent status that made them the targets
of satire, especially in the early modern drama, where the anxiety

---

43. Cf. Michel Foucault, *Language, Counter-Memory, Practice,* ed. Donald F.
Bouchard, trans. Bouchard and Sherry Simon (Ithaca: Cornell University Press,
1977), p. 142, quoted in Paul Werstine, "The Textual Mystery of *Hamlet,*" *Shakespeare
Quarterly* 39 (1988): 26.

44. Harold Jenkins, the New Arden editor (London: Methuen, 1982), identifies
this as one of the effects of performance (p. 31). Ralph Richardson was notorious for
conflating speeches from one play with those of another.

arising from their potential economic power became folded into a wholesale sexual demonization, expressed by charging them with unregenerate lechery. Hamlet's concern with policing his mother's body and legislating its use marks *Hamlet* as a play that anticipates the misogyny of Jacobean dramas such as Webster's *Duchess of Malfi;* however subjective, his obsession is not entirely misplaced: widows who remarried were considered *lawful* adulteresses. Contemporary statistics on orphans are equally telling. Among the English aristocracy one in three children had lost one parent by the age of fourteen, and the proportion was even higher among the lower classes. Lawrence Stone reports that in records of first marriages in Manchester in the 1650s, over half the brides and nearly half the grooms had lost their fathers: as Claudius remarks, the condition was indeed "common." Even more pertinent to Hamlet's situation is that, by law, children belonged solely to the father; unless appointed their guardian by her husband's will, a widowed mother had no rights over them.[45]

Although it has long been a commonplace of *Hamlet* criticism to consider Gertrude an adulteress whose hasty remarriage could be thought of as posthumous cuckoldry, the strands of historical evidence documenting her widowhood as well as those positioning Hamlet as an orphan (who, as it turns out, becomes an orphan maker) have been suppressed in favor of seeing both as caught in a dysfunctional family romance. The hegemony of this Freudian narrative indicates how twentieth-century readers have (always already) activated *Hamlet* through Hamlet's eyes and have eroticized Gertrude's body to mask the consequences, for both the oppressed widow and the wronged orphan, of being disconnected from the apparently stable subject positions of husband-father and son. An expanded account of *Hamlet*'s social bodies reinflects that familiar psychoanalytic narrative but does not dismiss it.[46] F's "To be or not to be" figures a Hamlet who, unable

45. See Linda Woodbridge, *Women and the English Renaissance: Literature and the Nature of Womankind, 1540–1620* (Urbana: University of Illinois Press, 1984), pp. 20, 177–78; and Lawrence Stone, *The Family, Sex, and Marriage in England, 1500–1800* (Harmondsworth: Penguin, 1977), pp. 136–37, 48, 222.

46. Expanding that account further would include considering not only the closet scene but also the passage in Q1 (not present in either F or Q2) where Gertrude indicates to Horatio her willingness to help Hamlet "in that he goes about" (H3r). See Steven Urkowitz, "Five Women Eleven Ways," in *Images of Shakespeare: Proceedings of the Third Congress of the International Shakespeare Association, 1986*, ed. Werner Habicht, D. J. Palmer, and Roger Pringle (Newark: University of Delaware Press, 1988), pp. 292–304.

to address the most painful loss of his life, disavows it to generalize on "the human condition"; voicing his precarious social status more precisely, Q1's Hamlet speaks first of his mother's disenfranchisement and then of his own. But by expressing the vulnerability he and Gertrude share in terms of popular stereotypes, he also further confines and constrains their voices.[47] There is, it would seem, repression—no end of repression—for either of Hamlet's textual embodiments as well as for his readers.

Insofar as examining Q1 through a set of intersecting discourses maps out a slightly altered reading of *Hamlet*'s social and psychological identities, it opens up a space for a text that is not quite Shakespeare and not quite *Hamlet,* a space where the traffic between literary and popular reading formations flows in more than one direction. To move from the traces of early seventeenth-century discursive practices to those of the late twentieth century is to encounter another such *Hamlet,* one produced by an enterprising, popularizing director who, by embodying *Hamlet*'s social and theatrical identities with stars whose thoroughly modern personas recommodify the play, once again gives an "old" play new bodies and reactivates its spectatorly pleasures. And no small part of the pleasures Franco Zeffirelli's 1990 film puts on offer has to do with the body of Mel Gibson, on which and through which Hamlet gets played out.

THE RETURN OF THE REPRESSED, REDRESSED MALE BODY

First, another bit of gossip, in the form of a joke mapped out on a different playing field, or stage—that of *Field of Dreams,* the 1988 Os-

47. Arguing that conventions of character develop outside the confines of class or estate to give Shakespeare's plays a new breadth of social reference, Robert Weimann figures Hamlet as a representative humanist and as a spokesman for the politically voiceless, a subject position enhanced by Q1's even more populist guise. See Robert Weimann, *Shakespeare and the Popular Tradition in the Theatre: Studies in the Social Dimension of Dramatic Form and Function,* ed. Robert Schwartz (Baltimore: Johns Hopkins University Press, 1978), pp. 126, 130. See also Annabel Patterson, *Shakespeare and the Popular Voice* (Oxford: Blackwell, 1989), esp. pp. 95, 99, and 179 n. 21. Although both Weimann and Patterson move from essentialism toward a materialist analysis, ascribing such liberal values to Hamlet ignores the extent to which early modern texts represent "the popular" in terms of stereotypes, which serve precisely to contain voices consistently associated with the potential rebel, the masterless man, or the unruly woman. As I read *Hamlet* and Hamlet, evoking such stereotypes becomes a means to define Hamlet's princely disenfranchisement and to reinstall class distinctions, not to level them.

car candidate which recuperates, on the mythical space of a baseball diamond located in America's heartland, a familiar narrative that, as Lynda Boose argues, "perpetuates and celebrates boys' rites *of* and rights *to* passage by which sons confirm their authority through their fathers."[48] Complaining that she felt left out of this and of similar representations of white male adolescent fantasies which circulated in late 1980s blockbusters, a woman columnist who had just seen the film announced to her puzzled male companion that she was going to build a model of Australia in her back yard. "If I build it," she said dreamily, "he will come." "Who?" asked her friend. "Mel Gibson, of course."

Like all anecdotes, this one speaks more than it knows, invites asking what is being served, at the level of fantasy, by creating a space for the deep blue eyes and alert, athletically supple body of Mel Gibson. That he happens to have come, so to speak, as Hamlet certainly gives "What a piece of work is a man!" a "hot" new spin, even makes it possible to hear "What an ass *have* I!" in place of Shakespeare's more familiar line. As these swerves of misreading suggest, lashing the body of Mel Gibson, the high-energy star of action comedies, to Hamlet, classical drama's most famous deliberator, creates a disturbance within looking. That disturbance goes deeper than simply noting that Gibson's star image does not resemble Hamlet, either in his guise as thinking prince or as "the Danish chicken."[49] Nor is it as simple as rethinking Hamlet as a fabulous New Man toyboy—tough but tender, masculine but vulnerable. When I told a feminist colleague I was busy theorizing Mel Gibson's body, she laughingly said, "I think you're in trouble." What she meant, as it turned out, was, "Why bother to account for your looking? 'Just Do It.'"

Her response, however, also cuts another way. For, although a growing body of work considers how men look at women, how men look at men, and how women look at women, when one searches for work on how women look at men, one encounters a relatively undiscovered country, a realm of guilty pleasure theory has only re-

---

48. Lynda E. Boose, "Techno-Muscularity and the 'Boy Eternal': From the Quagmire to the Gulf," in *Gendering War Talk*, ed. Miriam Cooke and Angela Woollacott (Princeton: Princeton University Press, 1993). My thanks to Boose for letting me see this essay in manuscript.

49. The phrase comes from an anonymous burlesque, "Hamlet! The Ravin' Prince of Denmark!! or, The Baltic Swell!!! and the Diving Belle!!!" (1866), reprinted in *Nineteenth-Century Shakespeare Burlesques*, ed. Stanley Wells (London: Diploma Press, 1978), 4:131.

cently begun to address.[50] Highly visible as a sociocultural, historical, ideological entity whose gaze, in spite of the rapidly accumulating critique of its hegemony, still structures talk of looking relations, the male body remains curiously *invisible*—not looked at because always already there. Although women clearly *do* cast desiring looks at men's bodies—I myself have gazed at Sean Connery for years, a phenomenon I might attribute to my childhood desire to be a Hardy boy and, later, a counterspy—the best theory can do is suggest that codifying the male body via male gay discourse makes possible a female erotic gaze, a move that (once again) robs women spectators of any *direct* access to looking.[51] Visual pleasure, it would seem, not only must be arrived at secondhand but is consistently theorized along a sadomasochistic axis. Although taking pleasure in watching Gibson's Hamlet—a figure who so relentlessly moralizes and polices women's bodies, prescribes their location (in nunneries and out of inappropriate beds), and monitors their use value—undoubtedly taps into a masochistic dynamic, I want to explore a slightly different take on the kind of male trouble his Hamlet represents.

First, to situate Shakespeare in the video store. In that enticingly postmodern configuration, canonization works not by authors or even auteurs but in terms of genres—action, drama, sci-fi, musicals, classics (*Gone With the Wind, Casablanca, Imitation of Life*), and (predominantly) male stars: John Wayne, Clint Eastwood, Mickey Mouse, Sylvester Stallone. At my local video outlet, *Hamlet* is shelved (out of the usual alphabetical order) between *Hard to Kill* and *He Said, She Said*. On *Hard to Kill*'s video jacket ("The star of *Above the Law* is back," reads the caption), Kelly Le Brock caresses Steven Seagal's massively muscled neck and upper body, and Seagal holds up his cocked weapon in the familiar Rambo-ready position. Substitute a sword, point down, for Seagal's revolver, and you have *Hamlet*, where Gibson, framed by Glenn Close (Gertrude) and Helena Bonham-Carter (Ophelia), gazes intently at the consumer of what the blurb calls "the extraordinary telling of a classic tale." And on *He Said, She Said*, Kevin Bacon appears startled by Elizabeth Perkins's puckered-up

50. See, for example, Steve Neale, "Masculinity as Spectacle," *Screen* 24 (1983): 2–16; and Paul Smith, "Action Movie Hysteria, or Eastwood Bound," *differences* 1 (1989): 88–107.
51. See, for example, Suzanne Moore, "Here's Looking at You, Kid!," in *The Female Gaze: Women as Viewers of Popular Culture*, ed. Lorraine Gamman and Margaret Marshment (London: Women's Press, 1988), pp. 44–59.

mouth. In this happy conjuncture of cultural products—a kind of *Hamlet* sandwich—all three images draw on a well-established body of cultural masculinities. And in each, a woman's face or figure serves to construct masculinity along a familiar axis of dominance/submission; in each, too, the male body as spectacle functions both as a figure of identification and as desired object, allowing its replications to appeal across a wide range of gendered spectator/subject positions. To play Goldilocks in the video store: whereas Seagal's Terminator-like body is too hard and Bacon's juvenile image, his masculinity at risk from an alternative narrative, is too soft, Gibson—even with his astonishing good looks somewhat muted by Hamlet's hairstyle—seems just right. Given such a spectrum of choice, I am entirely willing to pass up masochism and marginality and buy into what, for the moment, I want to call Mel's old-fashioned masculinity.

Although I will return to the question of how, by exploiting the specular appetite for this particular brand of masculinity, Zeffirelli's Shakespeare-Italian connection sutures a woman spectator into *Hamlet,* before leaving these images I want to give *Hamlet*'s video jacket a Close-r reading. Not only is Glenn Close's face nearly the same size as Gibson's, but, given the light that falls across her, it is she, not Hamlet, who is "too much i' the sun." Moreover, her coquettish sidelong glance at Hamlet speaks desire, and if the viewer's eye follows the curve of his cloak, the two merge into one body; only the sword, as with Tristan and Isolde, separates the two, turns the forbidden toward the chaste. Hamlet's forthright gaze marks his resolution; any potentially feminized anxiety associated with the character is thrown onto Bonham-Carter's Ophelia, whose clasped hands weakly echo Hamlet's firm grip on his weapon and who is framed by Hamlet and Alan Bates's Claudius, not her own father (Ian Holm as Polonius). And behind Polonius, Paul Scofield's Ghost almost disappears into the surrounding void. Just as this image figures the coincidence of family scandal, affairs of the heart, and links with the netherworld intrinsic to *Hamlet*'s narrative, that constellation of family, desire, and the phantasmic precisely tropes the nexus lying at the core of the television apparatus itself.[52] In the hands of a director who has so consistently lashed Shakespeare to the conventions of Hollywood cinema, using star presences to commodify the patriarchal bard's commercial viabil-

52. Sandy Flitterman-Lewis makes a similar point in "Thighs and Whiskers—The Fascination of 'Magnum, P.I.,'" *Screen* 26 (March-April 1985): 42–59.

ity,[53] *Hamlet* is always already mainstream culture, the play's ultimate soap-opera road show.

But this image also hints at another, equally intriguing family romance—a kind of cross-national menage à trois, with Shakespeare as the contested figure—played out at the level of casting. Whether or not Joyce Nettles (an ex-RSC casting director) was responsible for persuading Bates, Holm, and Scofield (all of whom have played Hamlet on one of Britain's royally subsidized stages) to give Gibson's Hamlet three ghostly fathers, Zeffirelli's decision to colonize the roles of Hamlet and Gertrude with Hollywood hyperstars not only widens the film's address but invests it with additional cultural capital. Moreover, the U.S.-British casting split has further local implications. For one thing, the film supplements the play's interaction between high and low culture with distinctions between English and Australian-American sound, making audible—and "newly" historical—the relations between Hamlet and the popular voice.[54] For another, it means that the film is structured by a tension between different modes of performance as well as by different generations of actors, a situation apparent in the actors' first read-through, where Gibson and Close sat facing Scofield, Holm, Bates, and Bonham-Carter on opposite sides of a long table. Awed by working with actors who were her heroes yet clearly allying herself with Gibson, Close remembers that when they reached "To be or not to be," she thought, "Go for it, Mel."[55]

Gibson and Close, of course, carry on their backs particular images of masculinity (*Mad Max* and *Lethal Weapon* 1 and 2) and femininity (*Fatal Attraction, Dangerous Liaisons,* and *Reversal of Fortune*) which project an ideological mobility across films, a factor less pertinent to the British actors, noted primarily for character roles. But perhaps the most profound local effect of this cross-national casting is that it threatens to tip Zeffirelli's *Hamlet* into a (questionably perverse) kind

---

53. As in Zeffirelli's casting of Elizabeth Taylor and Richard Burton in *The Taming of the Shrew* (1966). On star images in general, see Richard Dyer, *Stars* (London: BFI, 1979), and *Heavenly Bodies: Film Stars and Society* (London: Macmillan, 1987).

54. The U.S.-British casting split, as well as notions of culturally specific ownership, are also reflected in review discourse. Compare, for example, Jonathan Romney's review in *Sight and Sound,* n.s. 1, no. 1 (May 1991): 48–49, which calls Zeffirelli's film "set-text cinema Shakespeare at its most inexpressive," with *Time's* Richard Corliss, who focuses almost exclusively on Gibson's suitability for Hamlet ("Wanna Be . . . or Wanna Not Be?," January 7, 1991, p. 73).

55. A clip of the read-through appears in the HBO special "Classic Mel Gibson," details of which I refer to in what follows.

of buddy film, replacing *Lethal Weapon*'s Martin Riggs (Gibson) and
Roger Murtaugh (Danny Glover) not with Hamlet and Horatio but
with Gibson and Close. Because they belong together and seem made
for each other, it is entirely possible to read Close's Gertrude less as
Hamlet's mother than as his potential partner, and the stars' similar
ages give an added edge to the pleasures and dangers of the Oedipal
scenario.

To account for the mother–son relationship, Gibson and Close invented a history for their characters loosely linked to early modern
social practices, and also perhaps extrapolated from Zeffirelli's *Romeo
and Juliet,* whose Lady Capulet sees herself trapped by her early marriage to an older man. Taking Hamlet's part, Gibson conjectured that
the encounter with the Ghost represents the first time he and his father
have talked; taking the father's, he imagined a group of "old sixteenth-
century guys" sitting around a club, smoking long cigars and musing,
"Let's get some hard bodies." Given the critical tradition—repeated
by Frank Kermode in a laudatory press-packet essay—that locates
Gertrude's all too volatile, yielding body as the tragedy's "problem,"
it is hardly surprising that Gertrude has the most to account for.[56] In
Close's view, since only fifteen years separate Gertrude from Hamlet,
she derived sensual and physical comfort from her son; after her husband's death, marrying Claudius released her youthful athleticism as
well as her sexuality. With brilliant economy, the film's opening,
grounded on Old Hamlet's body, embodies *her* initial dilemma, situates her as the object of a triangulated gaze; Close herself noted that
three men revolve around her. Although Gertrude seems deliberately
constructed to counter the femme fatale stereotypes Close brings with
her, the film thoroughly investigates her girlishly revitalized body.
Captured in tracking shots or long pans and seen consistently from
Hamlet's point of view, Close's Gertrude floats through castle corri-
dors, rides horseback, and skips down flights of stairs; mid-shots
privilege her more intimate moments with Bates's Claudius. Yet since
the film represents Claudius as the "bloat king" of Hamlet's imaginary
(an image enhanced by his heavy, enveloping robes) and, by contrast,
puts Hamlet in trim doublets (as Close remarks, "Mel looks great in
black leather"), it is hard to forget that the familiar Oedipal narrative
turns on fleshly matters, material bodies. In fact, Close and Gibson so

56. See, for example, Jacqueline Rose's discussion of T. S. Eliot's famous opinion
in "Sexuality in the Reading of Shakespeare: *Hamlet* and *Measure for Measure*," in *Alternative Shakespeares,* ed. John Drakakis (London: Methuen, 1985), pp. 95–119.

resemble a romantic couple that it is tempting to conjecture that Zeffirelli adopted Q1's outlines in order to exploit spectators' appetites for the possibility of leaving *Hamlet*'s narrative behind and bringing them together again.[57] Certainly Hamlet's clowning at the duel, where a shot/reverse shot catches his wink at Gertrude and shows her pleasure at his performance, not only marks off the characters'—and the actors'—shared experience from that of the other performers but serves as the final sign of Gibson's stylishly playful Hamlet, which evokes and often mocks his highly physical performances as Mad Max or *Lethal Weapon*'s Riggs.

Far from being "the kind of guy who leans up against a wall," Gibson's Hamlet is simply the most physically alert man in Denmark. Putting the matter succinctly, John Lahr observes that Gibson "thinks with his body."[58] That body is a highly salable commodity: after *Hamlet*, Gibson would command $8 to $9 million per film. And the very presence of Gibson's extraordinarily well formed body calls into question the critical narratives that have shaped the play almost exclusively as a contestatory site for interiority and gendered subjectivity, as a source of primarily *intellectual* pleasures.[59] For many, Gibson's ordinariness (read non–British, non–upper-class image) threatened to dismantle this reading formation. Charles Marowitz—whose own *Hamlet* collage, ironically enough, had indicted Hamlet, for valuing intellectual analysis over action, as the supreme prototype of the conscience-stricken but paralyzed liberal—had this to say: "We are always conscious of a coiled physical energy in his body, but no comparable charge in his brain."[60] As a corrective, recall that Burbage's elegist

57. Kathleen Campbell explores the consequences briefly in "Zeffirelli's *Hamlet*—Q1 in Performance," *Shakespeare on Film Newsletter* 16, no. 1 (December 1991): 7–8. Gary Taylor notes that William Poel used Q1 for his 1881 production; see his *Reinventing Shakespeare: A Cultural History from the Restoration to the Present* (New York: Weidenfeld and Nicolson, 1989), p. 267. It is not unusual for performance texts, both stage and film, to adopt vestiges of Q1; Olivier's 1947 film, for example, gives "To be or not to be" its Q1 placement.

58. John Lahr, "Mel Gibson: Hollywood's Male Man," *Cosmopolitan* 209, no. 6 (December 1990): 160.

59. Such a statement, of course, is not without contradictions. Few would label Hamlet's thinking profound; praise for what turn out to be deeply felt commonplaces is, in the final analysis, praise for "Shakespeare-the-Author," for what Leavis called "poetico-dramatic felicity."

60. Charles Marowitz, quoted in Cyndi Stivers, "Hamlet Re-Visited," *Premiere* 4, no. 6 (February 1991): 54; for his *Hamlet* collage, see *The Marowitz Shakespeare* (New York Drama Book Specialists, 1978), pp. 28–69.

remembered not the self-investigative soliloquies but the intensely "life-like" action of Hamlet's leap into Ophelia's grave. Although I do not want to push the parallel too far, Burbage did play Henry V and Richard III, the Lethal Weapons and Terminators of his day.

It was, however, certainly true that the question driving *Hamlet*'s narrative—"Can he do it?"—did transfer to its star, spawning two ancillary film projects, "Mel Gibson Goes Back to School" and an HBO special, "Classic Mel Gibson," devoted to canonizing *Lethal Weapon's* rogue cop as Hamlet. Characterizing Shakespeare as "some literary Boris Becker serving Hamlet up to Burbage and saying, 'Return that if you can, you s.o.b.,'" Gibson himself admitted, "It's a stretch." Zeffirelli, however, saw no gap at all between the suicidal Riggs, whose ineptitude in dealing with his own past makes his heroism possible, and quintessential Hamlet, where, in the "To be or not to be" soliloquy, close-ups and physical movement (two ways that film codes masculinity) evoke the turns of Hamlet's restless questioning; and mise-en-scène ("down among the dead men where it belongs," remarked Gibson) fleshes out Hamlet's agony at his own despair. Although critical narratives as well as Olivier's 1947 film stress this soliloquy's "to-be-heard-ness" (Olivier's voice-over performance literally disembodies the speech), Gibson *embodies* the scars of Hamlet's introspective life, reconstituting to-be-*looked-at*-ness as chief among *Hamlet*'s spectatorly pleasures.

This is not to claim that no disjuncture separates Gibson's distinctly old-fashioned image of masculinity from Hamlet's role.[61] That disjuncture can perhaps best be illustrated by the HBO film—a collage of comments from Gibson, his co-stars, and Zeffirelli; rehearsal footage; and snippets from the film. Praising Mel's emotional honesty, Bates remarks that he can't tell a lie; Bonham-Carter mentions how funny and attractive he is; Holm admires his "amazing confidence"; and Close fixes on his charismatic ability to be "riveting doing nothing." Somewhat appropriately for the Ghost, Scofield has nothing to say. Although these voices construct the illusion of a unified, coherent

---

61. Unlike Madonna (the crucial figure in discussions of the postmodern star image), whose persona and sexuality are constructed and reconstructed for each performance, Gibson's star image, which draws on that of the Western hero, an old-fashioned loner who works not only within but also outside the law, is remarkably stable. Particularly in the *Lethal Weapon* films, his actions as Martin Riggs suggest that fractures exist in the law (implicitly defined as the law of the father) which can be handled only by the codes of personal revenge.

subject—the persona of Mel Gibson, the actor—they pull against what the HBO film and Zeffirelli's *Hamlet* reveal elsewhere: the fragmented subjectivity of Hamlet, the character. What Terry Eagleton writes of Hamlet—that he is never identical with himself and that what it is to be a subject is a political problem—becomes for Gibson (and, I would argue, for anyone playing Hamlet) a (no less ideological) acting problem in disavowing one self for another.[62] As Peter Donaldson has observed, Olivier was so wary of Hamlet's irresolution, passivity, and sense of failure that he dyed his hair so that spectators would think, this is Hamlet, not Olivier playing Hamlet.[63] Although both Gibson's body and his star image insulate his Hamlet from those particular risks—and, more important, from their attendant connotations of femininity—he was well aware of its ghosts. He tells, in "Classic Mel Gibson," of being given the shirt Olivier wore when he played Hamlet and of waiting until he was alone in his hotel room, where he turned out all the lights before trying it on. Averting his eyes, he remarks, "It was a bit small, but it fit well enough."

Citing Gibson's modernity, vitality, and humor as traits admirably suited to Hamlet's, Zeffirelli speaks of giving young people a *Hamlet* that will belong to them. But, unlike his *Romeo and Juliet,* which became a cultural icon for late 1960s love children,[64] or Kenneth Branagh's *Henry V,* which works to install a heroic subject position hollowed out by 1980s representations of the Vietnam War, Zeffirelli's *Hamlet* never quite intersects with late twentieth-century history. To be sure, it is very much of the moment in putting on offer a misogynist vision which, insofar as it makes "woman" responsible for a crisis in the sociosexual order, speaks to the retro mindset of the early 1990s. And because Gibson's magnetic presence favors examining not femininity but masculinity as excess, it works to get women spectators to

62. Terry Eagleton, *William Shakespeare* (Oxford: Blackwell, 1986), pp. 73–75. And see, for example, Michael Pennington's account of playing Hamlet in *Players of Shakespeare 1: Essays in Shakespearean Performance by Twelve Players with the Royal Shakespeare Company,* ed. Philip Brockbank (Cambridge: Cambridge University Press, 1985), pp. 115–28.

63. Peter S. Donaldson, "Olivier, Hamlet, and Freud," *Cinema Journal* 26 (1987): 22–48.

64. See Barbara Hodgdon, "Absent Bodies, Present Voices: Performance Work and the Close of *Romeo and Juliet's* 'Golden Story,'" *Theatre Journal* 41 (1989): 341–59.

share that vision.[65] But given its release dates—it opened in New York on December 19, 1990, and nationwide by mid-January 1991, when the Gulf War began—the time was indeed out of joint. To force historical synchrony, one might argue that *Hamlet*'s ending models what many feared might happen—but just to "American boys"—in Iraq: that George Bush's drive to remasculinize himself, and the country, would destroy yet another generation in "the mother of all battles." But Bush was neither Prince Hamlet nor Fortinbras, whom Zeffirelli had, in any case, omitted. For wasn't Gibson, playing Hamlet in disguise, his own Fortinbras? And who (the perennial Fortinbras problem)[66] could have been cast as his successor? Kevin Costner? A Terminator-Robocop, the more mainstream lethal weapon? Or perhaps a Jeanne d'Arc-Fortinbras, played by Sigourney Weaver? The obvious candidate, however, is Kenneth Branagh. Since the RSC's Adrian Noble has directed Branagh as Hamlet in a production that opened at London's Barbican Theater in December 1992, it is entirely possible (depending on the box-office success of Branagh's 1993 *Much Ado About Nothing*) that a film will follow, in which Branagh, as in his *Henry V,* will again play out the role of Olivier's true successor assigned to him by critics, return the play's cultural capital to its national home, and make *Hamlet*'s U.S.-International ownership as "momentany" as the sound of Gibson's American-Aussie–accented Received Standard Pronunciation.

But I want to back away from this larger view of Zeffirelli's *Hamlet* as cultural work to locate myself more overtly as a reading subject and fix my attention on several particularly striking images from the film's closing moments. The first is the incredulous look that flashes over Gibson's face as, feeling the effects of the poison, he stumbles—it's almost a comic turn—and falls. In spite of knowing that Hamlet *must* die, I feel an extra added shock because it is Mel Gibson who seems so surprised. When, in the film's last shot, the camera booms up, isolating Hamlet and Horatio together, surrounded (at a distance) by stunned courtiers, I experience a distinctly visceral loss. For I had thought that nothing bad could happen to a body so perfectly formed,

---

65. See Rose, "Sexuality and the Reading of Shakespeare"; and Tania Modleski, *Feminism without Women: Culture and Criticism in a "Postfeminist" Age* (New York: Routledge, Chapman, and Hall, 1991), esp. pp. 135–64.

66. For a riff on the "Fortinbras problem," see Lee Blessing's play *Fortinbras* (New York: Dramatists Play Service, forthcoming).

so transparently whole. Although I know full well that *Hamlet* is merely a classical arabesque between *Lethal Weapon 2* and *Lethal Weapon 3*, one among many in the long wave of *Hamlet*s and the even longer wave of "Shakespeare," in which Gibson's body circulates only briefly (there is no *Hamlet 2*), I am obsessed enough with this loss that I want to replace that last image with one from *Lethal Weapon 2*— aptly enough, a similar image, in which Gibson's Martin Riggs, badly wounded, is urged to live by his partner, Roger Murtaugh. So refiguring *Hamlet*'s ending with one that allows Gibson to live does more than simply point to how, in the late twentieth century, "Shakespeare" gets caught up in a set of intersecting discourses which activate relations between "high culture" and "the popular." It also points to the gap between the turn of the seventeenth century and that of the twenty-first, between an age when tragedy (and tragic closure) could still "show . . . the body of the time *his* form and pressure" (my emphasis) and one where such narratives no longer figure, or even address, what many have perceived as a widespread crisis within masculinity. Given such present-day anxieties, and a cultural climate in which representations of sexuality and gender are most especially wrought with contradictions, the image of masculine perfection Gibson embodies works to reassure spectators that, although masculinity as a category may be under stress, it can nonetheless be articulated in terms of an apparently stable subject position. Even more important, especially at a historical moment when even the most ordinary daily routines can seem life threatening, Gibson's persona provides a potent, enduring icon of survival against all odds. Although the promise held out by such an icon has, I think, a ready appeal across the entire range of gendered spectator positions, it also invites my even more "excessive" response: that what I want is to be Mel Gibson's buddy.

Although that desire is clearly fraught with masochistic and retro undertones, I do not want to be close to Gibson in order to masquerade in Glenn's clothes or to draw power from Gibson's appealingly legitimate masculinity. And given what happened to Thelma and Louise, turning him into a female buddy would simply reiterate the already known: that within representation, women's bodies offer an especially unstable site for working out the gender politics of our lives. Instead, I prefer to think of my desire to be Mel Gibson's buddy as akin to that of "Star Trek's" slash fans who, adhering to the principle of Infinite Diversity in Infinite Combination (the Vulcan version of liberal values), write fantasies of transcendent gender across the bodies of Spock and Kirk.[67] Like that move, though perhaps less outrageously, mine affirms that the subject, at the level of the unconscious, is bisexual. And in voicing the desire that fundamental antagonisms between gender and sexualities need not, should not, exist, that move imagines a relationship of radical equality that one could, I think, call feminist work.[68] So here's looking at you, Mel Gibson: "Breathe in your life. You're not dead until I tell you."[69]

67. See Constance Penley, "Feminism, Psychoanalysis, and Popular Culture," in *Cultural Studies,* ed. Lawrence Grossberg, Cary Nelson, and Paula Treichler (New York: Routledge, Chapman, and Hall, 1992), pp. 479–94. One of Penley's most fascinating observations (which she does not attempt to explain) is that a large proportion of "Star Trek's" "slash" fans (those who write and read same-sex narratives about Kirk and Spock) are intensive-care nurses. It seems highly suggestive that a group of professionals who see the human body at its most vulnerable write narratives that construct relationships that transcend biological sexuality. See also Henry Jenkins, "'Star Trek' Rerun, Reread, Rewritten: Fan Writing as Textual Poaching," in *Close Encounters: Film, Feminism, and Science Fiction,* ed. Constance Penley et al. (Minneapolis: University of Minnesota Press, 1991), pp. 170–203.

68. I am indebted to Henry Jenkins for telling me of a fanzine (a publication produced by fans) called *Walkabout* devoted to Mel Gibson's film roles. Interestingly enough, the flier for the zine announces that it will not accept same-sex (slash) stories, and says it twice, a move that protects Gibson's masculinity. Jenkins, however, reports that he recalls seeing *Lethal Weapon* slash; and it is possible that gossip in the national press (March 1992) about Gibson's insistence that he is not gay just because he is an actor reflect some knowledge of slash fandom. *Lethal Weapon* 2 certainly glances at a same-sex relationship between Riggs and Murtaugh. Indeed, the film continues beyond the images I have mentioned, simultaneously revealing its homophobic anxieties and attempting to disavow them. Turning to Murtaugh, Riggs comments, "Rog, did anyone ever tell you you're really a beautiful man? [*He laughs.*] Give us a kiss before they come." To add just one more layer of referentiality, Jonathan Crewe reminds me of how Lord Nelson's dying words, "Kiss me, Hardy" (spoken to one of his officers), have caused his biographers and historians so much embarrassment.

69. Roger Murtaugh's line in *Lethal Weapon* 2.

Contributors

HARRY BERGER, JR., is Professor of English and Art History at the University of California, Santa Cruz, and the author of books on Shakespeare and Spenser. A volume of his uncollected essays, edited by Peter Erickson, has been published by Stanford University Press.

LYNDA E. BOOSE, Associate Professor of English and Women's Studies at Dartmouth College, is the coeditor, with Betty Flowers, of *Fathers and Daughters* (Johns Hopkins University Press, 1988). The essay included here, along with "Scolding Brides and Bridling Scolds" (*Shakespeare Quarterly* 2 [Summer 1991]), is part of a forthcoming study of shrews and scolds in early modern England.

STEPHEN BOOTH is Professor of English at the University of California, Berkeley, and is best known for his Yale University Press edition of *Shakespeare's Sonnets.*

BARBARA HODGDON, Ellis and Nelle Levitt Professor of English at Drake University, is the author of *The End Crowns All: Closure and Contradiction in Shakespeare's History* (Princeton University Press, 1991) and *Henry IV, Part Two* in the Manchester Shakespeare in Performance series.

RUSS MCDONALD is the author of *Shakespeare and Jonson / Jonson and Shakespeare,* as well as articles on Shakespeare, Massinger, Flannery O'Connor, and opera. He is Associate Professor of English at the University of North Carolina, Greensboro.

PATRICIA PARKER, Professor of English and Comparative Literature at Stanford University, is the author of, among other works, *Literary Fat Ladies: Rhetoric, Gender, Property,* and coeditor, with Margo Hendricks, of *Women, "Race," and Writing in the Early Modern Period* (Routledge, 1994).

JAMES R. SIEMON is Associate Professor of English at Boston University. He is the author of *Shakespearean Iconoclasm* (University of California Press, 1985) and the editor of the New Mermaid *Jew of Malta* (forthcoming). He is currently working on a book-length study of social distinction and dialogic relationships in early modern England and its drama.

HELEN VENDLER is William R. Kenan, Jr., Professor of English at Harvard University and poetry critic of *The New Yorker*. She has written books on Yeats, Stevens, Herbert, and Keats, and her essays on poetry have been collected in *Part of Nature, Part of Us* and *The Music of What Happens*. Harvard University Press will publish her *Commentary on Shakespeare's Sonnets*.

DAVID WILLBERN is Associate Professor of English and Associate Dean of Arts and Letters at SUNY Buffalo. He is also on the faculty of the Center for the Study of Psychoanalysis and Culture. Among his publications are essays on Renaissance literature, modern literature, and psychoanalysis. The contribution to this volume comes from a work in progress titled *POETIC WILL: Shakespeare and the Play of Language*.

SUSANNE L. WOFFORD is Associate Professor of English at the University of Wisconsin, Madison. In addition to articles on Shakespeare and Spenser, she has published *The Choice of Achilles: The Ideology of Figure in the Epic* (Stanford University Press, 1992). She is currently completing a book on Shakespeare called "Theatrical Power: The Politics of Representation on the Shakespearean Stage."

GEORGE T. WRIGHT, Regents' Professor of English at the University of Minnesota, is the author of *Shakespeare's Metrical Art* and of books and articles on Shakespeare and modern poetry. Each of his articles in *PMLA* ("The Lyric Present: Simple Present Verbs in English Poems" and "Hendiadys and *Hamlet*") won the Modern Language Association's William Riley Parker Prize.

Index